The Piano in Beethoven's Chamber Music

The Piano in Beethoven's Chamber Music

Misha Donat

THE BOYDELL PRESS

© Misha Donat 2025

All Rights Reserved. Except as permitted under current legislation
no part of this work may be photocopied, stored in a retrieval system,
published, performed in public, adapted, broadcast,
transmitted, recorded or reproduced in any form or by any means,
without the prior permission of the copyright owner

The right of Misha Donat to be identified as the author of this work has been
asserted in accordance with sections 77 and 78 of the
Copyright, Designs and Patents Act 1988

First published 2025
The Boydell Press, Woodbridge

ISBN 978 1 83765 218 1 (hardback); 978 1 83765 219 8 (paperback)

The Boydell Press is an imprint of Boydell & Brewer Ltd
PO Box 9, Woodbridge, Suffolk IP12 3DF, UK
and of Boydell & Brewer Inc.
668 Mt Hope Avenue, Rochester, NY 14620-2731, USA
website: www.boydellandbrewer.com

Our Authorised Representative for product safety in the EU is Easy Access System Europe
– Mustamäe tee 50, 10621 Tallinn, Estonia, *gpsr.requests@easproject.com*

A CIP catalogue record for this book is available
from the British Library

The publisher has no responsibility for the continued existence or accuracy
of URLs for external or third-party internet websites referred to in this book,
and does not guarantee that any content on such websites is,
or will remain, accurate or appropriate

*To my children
Hannah, Sophie & Joseph,
and to my grandson Kit*

Contents

List of Illustrations	ix
Foreword by Alfred Brendel	x
Preface and Acknowledgements	xi
Abbreviations	xv

1	Introduction	1
2	Prelude: Apprentice Years	21

Piano Quartets WoO 36 • Trio for flute, bassoon and piano WoO 37 • Piano Trio in E flat WoO 38 • Variations for piano and violin on 'Se vuol ballare' WoO 40

3	The Three Piano Trios Op.1	41
4	Interlude 1: The Quintet for piano and wind instruments op.16	81
5	Works for piano and cello, 1796–1801	90

Sonata in F op.5 no.1 • Sonata in G minor op.5 no.2 • Variations on 'See, the Conqu'ring Hero Comes' WoO 45 • Variations on 'Ein Mädchen oder Weibchen' op.66 • Variations on 'Bei Männern, welche Liebe fühlen' WoO 46 • Music for mandolin and piano WoO 43 and 44

6	Interlude 2: The Clarinet Trio op.11	140
7	Sonatas for piano and violin, 1798–1800	151

Sonata in D op.12 no.1 • Sonata in A op.12 no.2 • Sonata in E flat op.12 no.3 • Sonata in A minor op.23 • Sonata in F op.24 ('Spring')

8	Interlude 3: The Horn Sonata op.17	188
9	Sonatas for piano and violin, 1802–3	196

Sonata in A op.30 no.1 • Sonata in C minor op.30 no.2 • Sonata in G op.30 no.3 • Sonata in A op.47 ('Kreutzer')

10	Works of 1807–8	237

Cello Sonata in A op.69 • Piano Trio in D op.70 no.1 ('Ghost') • Piano Trio in E flat op.70 no.2

11 Works of 1810–12   293

   Piano Trio in B flat op.97 ('Archduke') • Allegretto for piano trio WoO 39 • Violin Sonata in G op.96

12 Works of 1815–16   327

   Cello Sonata in C op.102 no.1 • Cello Sonata in D op.102 no.2 • Variations on 'Ich bin der Schneider Kakadu' op.121a

13 Postlude: Beethoven and George Thomson   365

   Variations for piano and flute opp.105 and 107

Bibliography   389

Classified index of works by Beethoven   397

Index of Beethoven's works by opus number   401

General index   405

Illustrations

Illustration 1. Dittersdorf. 'Ja, ich muß mich von ihr scheiden' from *Das rote Käppchen*. (Public domain, held by British Library)   78

Illustration 2. Jean-Louis Duport, Sonata in D, op.4 no.6 (iv). Sieber, Paris, c.1795. (Public domain, held by Bayerische Staatsbibliothek)   97

The author and publisher are grateful to the institutions listed above for permission to reproduce the materials which they hold.

Foreword

Misha Donat's splendid book on Beethoven's piano chamber music ploughs a neglected field. His familiarity with this repertoire seems, at least in part, the result of many years of experience as a recording producer for the BBC and other institutions. For a performer whose concerts are being recorded there is no greater favour than to be able to rely on a producer's technical knowledge, his musical intuition, and his ear for the quality and three-dimensionality of sound, on his alertness as a critical listener as well as his appreciation of performances that spontaneously hit the right note. With Misha Donat, I invariably found myself in the safest hands.

Besides this, I have much enjoyed Misha Donat's analytical notes, which count among the finest. At a time when live recordings are no longer the exception, introductory texts take on a new significance. The question arises as to whether and how such texts can be helpful to the listener, and the player, at all. In Misha Donat's case, there are three things I particularly admire: his professionalism that goes far beyond the notes in the score; the familiarity with the material as a whole, that enables him to compare, point out, and synthesise a grasp that generates insights both formal and historical; and, last but not least, the luminous clarity of his style. Programme notes can be a respectable bread-and-butter task or, in rare cases, provide the springboard for a comprehensive framework. Misha Donat's book, representing the work of a lifetime, is an all-embracing summing up of this kind. How fortunate we are to be able to savour it in print.

Alfred Brendel
October 2024

Preface and Acknowledgements

While there has been no shortage of monographs on Beethoven's symphonies, string quartets and piano sonatas, his chamber music with piano has received relatively scant attention, particularly in the Beethoven literature in English. Yet this area of the composer's output contains some of his greatest and most famous works, among them the 'Ghost' and 'Archduke' piano trios, the 'Spring' and 'Kreutzer' violin sonatas, and the A major Cello Sonata op.69. It is true that the combination of piano and strings produces by its very nature a more heterogeneous form than the string quartet, and that Beethoven reserved some of his most profound and spiritual utterances for his late quartets in particular; but his piano trios, violin sonatas and cello sonatas together make up a larger corpus of works, and one that covers scarcely less stylistic ground – from his very first efforts at composition during the years when he was living in Bonn, to the threshold of his last period (the two cello sonatas op.102) and beyond (the two series of variations for piano and flute opp.105 and 107). No other composer, moreover, made as significant a contribution to all three principal forms of chamber music with piano. Haydn's piano trios, it is true, belong among his most remarkable and original chamber works, but the special nature of their textures assigns them a place apart in the history of the genre. Haydn, moreover, made no excursion into the field of duo sonatas; and if Mozart's violin sonatas number among them some of the finest works in the repertoire, and his piano trios contain a comparable number of masterpieces (though none, perhaps, that quite matches the grandeur and visionary quality of Beethoven's 'Archduke' and 'Ghost' trios), he never attempted to cultivate the more problematic medium of the sonata for piano and cello. Beethoven's five cello sonatas remain a unique achievement: not only did he essentially create the genre and contribute considerably more to it than any later composer of the front rank, he also raised it to a level of perfection that was never to be matched.

The present book offers a chronological study of the nearly thirty full-scale chamber works of Beethoven's maturity for piano in combination with various instruments. The music is placed in its historical context with reference to Beethoven's letters and to contemporary reviews, and is examined in some detail with the help of copious music examples. In addition, an introductory chapter examines the origins of the various genres in which Beethoven worked, while a further chapter covers his apprentice years in Bonn, and the indebtedness of the pieces he composed there to the violin sonatas of Mozart. A postlude concerns itself with a series of lesser, but fascinating, pieces that has hitherto been largely ignored: the folksong variations opp.105 and 107. These occasional pieces were treated by the composer as something of a laboratory for ideas he was to explore more fully in his late piano works – the four last sonatas , the 'Diabelli' Variations op.120 and the Bagatelles op.126 – and parallels are drawn between ideas found in the variations and those later works.

Beethoven is a composer of seemingly fathomless genius, and any attempt to cover every aspect of his art in a study of this kind would be futile. One feature of his music that must immediately strike us is the breadth and variety of its form and character: not for nothing did his contemporaries refer to him as their musical Shakespeare. More than any other great composer before him or since, Beethoven sought to reinvent himself with each successive work. This feature of his persona was recognised at a relatively early stage during his lifetime, and an 1807 review of the op.22 Piano Sonata in the *Zeitung für die elegante Welt* remarked that 'Beethoven's inexhaustible genius lends each of his works such a wholly individual character that it is not easy to compare one with the other'. Even – or perhaps especially – when it came to works of the same genre published under a common opus number, Beethoven seems to have been determined to ensure that each of them would have a wholly different nature and form. Particularly striking instances among the pieces discussed in the present volume are the two violin sonatas opp.23 and 24 (originally issued under a single opus number) and the two piano trios op.70, but Beethoven's determination to stamp his personality on his music from the very first note is apparent in every one of his works – indeed, his conscious striving after originality was a feature of his art that sometimes met with resistance from his contemporaries. This was notably true of his earlier works, though in 1805 a review of the 'Kreutzer' Sonata in the *Allgemeine musikalische Zeitung* remarked that Beethoven had for some time 'obstinately been using his immense natural gifts and his industriousness not only to do as he likes, but above all simply to be completely different from other people' (see pp.226–7); and as late as November 1818 the same journal complained that the two op.102 cello sonatas showed the composer deliberately having written the music in such a way as to make it appear as unusual as possible.

In Beethoven's day – and, indeed, throughout the nineteenth century – it was the pianist who was regarded as the senior partner in chamber music with keyboard, and the *Allgemeine musikalische Zeitung*'s reviewer of the op.102 sonatas even went so far as to describe them as piano music, without mentioning the string player at all. By then, that was no doubt an exceptional instance, but the notion of referring to Beethoven's duo chamber pieces as violin sonatas or cello sonatas would have perplexed both the composer and his contemporaries: to them, these were keyboard sonatas with violin or cello. Beethoven's early 'Figaro' Variations WoO 40 were actually published with a title page announcing them as being *Pour le Clavecin ou PianoForte avec un Violon ad lib*. That, not surprisingly, prompted a complaint from the composer, and the piece was duly reissued with an amended description of the violin's role, as *obligé* (see p.36). All the same, things were not much improved a full decade later, when the Vienna Bureau d'Arts et d'Industrie published the three sonatas op.30 as *Trois Sonates pour le Pianoforte avec l'Accompagnement d'un Violon*.

Almost as though deliberately to belie such outdated descriptions, Beethoven set no fewer than four of his chamber sonatas in motion by allowing the stringed instrument to be heard before the pianist entered, thereby establishing its elevated status from the start. The beginnings in question – those of the violin sonatas opp.47 and 96 and the cello sonatas opp.69 and 102 no.1 – are among Beethoven's most breathtakingly effective and original, though that did not prevent Robert Birchall in his London edition of the op.96 Sonata, which appeared more or less simultaneously with S.A. Steiner's Vienna publication, from issuing the work as 'A Sonata for the Piano Forte with an Accompaniment for the Violin'. More presciently, Birchall printed the music in score, with the violin part given in a smaller font above the piano part. (Steiner, as was customary at the time, published the work only with separate parts, but at least he more accurately described it as a *Sonate für Piano-Forte und Violin* [sic].) In view of their complexity, the two op.102 cello sonatas were also issued in score, but when it came to the remainder of the works discussed in this book the pianist saw only his or her own part. In the case of the op.69 Sonata, the original edition gave an indication of the cellist's solo beginning in the left-hand stave of the piano part, but with the 'Kreutzer' Sonata the keyboard player was confronted at the start with only four bars' rest, and no hint as to their content.

This study is addressed to performers and scholars, as well as to music lovers, whether listening at home or in the concert hall. Every single work Beethoven wrote in the field of chamber music with piano is examined, though comments on some of the less significant pieces have been kept to a realistic minimum. As many analytical points as possible have been illustrated with music examples, but readers may wish nevertheless to equip themselves with scores where possible.

❧ ❧ ❧

This book has been many years in the making, and I am grateful to a large number of individuals and organisations for their help in its preparation. My thanks are due to Talia Pecker-Berio, without whose advice at an early stage my writing would have been much impoverished. The late Charles Rosen kindly looked though my manuscript in one of its first manifestations, and suggested the addition of the introductory chapter on the history of chamber music with keyboard. More recently, Jonathan Del Mar read my text with his characteristic attention to detail, and saved me from several blunders. Anthony Halstead gave me invaluable advice about horn technique when it came to the chapter on the op.17 Sonata, and Steven Isserlis provided me with similar help in connection with the two op.5 cello sonatas. András Schiff's contribution to my endeavours included the generous gift of the facsimile of the 'Archduke' Trio published by Henle Verlag. My thanks are due, too, to Andrew Jones for preparing the many music examples and for his seemingly limitless patience with my exacting demands, and to Michael Middeke of Boydell & Brewer for his belief in this project and his encouragement in its realisation. My profound gratitude goes, too, to the late Alfred Bendel for having provided the book with a foreword written in his characteristically elegant style.

Several libraries on both sides of the Atlantic have been of great help in the preparation of this study. The staff of the BBC Music Library tirelessly supplied me with scores, books and periodicals at a time before internal divisions within the BBC pursued in the name of Thatcherite economics made the borrowing of such material increasingly difficult, and eventually put paid to the existence of the library itself. I owe a debt of gratitude, too, to various other libraries for allowing me access to

Beethoven's autograph scores and sketches: in particular, to the British Library, the Staatsbibliothek zu Berlin and the Beethovenhaus in Bonn. The late Jadwiga Grzybowska of the Biblioteka Jagiellońska in Cracow kindly furnished me with Beethoven's sketches for the 'Archduke' Trio on microfilm, and J. Rigbie Turner, formerly of the Morgan Library in New York, permitted me to examine the autograph of the Violin Sonata op.96 in his office at a time when the library was closed to the public.

Translations of letters and documents from German and French (and in the case of Beethoven's voluminous correspondence with George Thomson, pidgin French) are my own, and for that reason I have preferred to cite the original foreign-language texts as my primary sources in footnote references. However, for those wishing to consult the standard English edition of the composer's letters I have additionally provided references to Emily Anderson's three-volume *The Letters of Beethoven* (1961). My translations are, no doubt, less elegant than hers, but they are more literal renderings of Beethoven's originals, and they make no attempt to smooth over the roughness of their style. The correspondence included by Anderson was strictly one-sided – an omission that was rectified with the appearance in 1996 of *Letters to Beethoven & Other Correspondence*, translated and edited by Theodore Albrecht. Where relevant, footnote references to that publication have also been given.

Last, but by no means least, I must mention the life-enhancing experience of being in daily contact with the works of Beethoven themselves. To play, read and listen to this music is to marvel anew each time at the towering intellect of its creator, and at the seemingly inexhaustible wealth, variety and beauty of the ideas it contains. As the composer's own favourite motto (set by him as a canon on several occasions) has it, *Ars longa, vita brevis.*

Abbreviations

AMZ	*Allgemeine musikalische Zeitung*
AMZÖ	*Allgemeine musikalische Zeitung mit besonderer Rücksicht auf den Österreichischen Kaiserstaat*
Anderson	*The Letters of Beethoven*, trans. and ed. Emily Anderson (London, 1961)
BAMZ	*Berliner allgemeine musikalische Zeitung*
BGA	Ludwig van Beethoven, *Briefwechsel. Gesamtausgabe*, ed. Sieghard Brandenburg (Munich, 1996)
Czerny	Carl Czerny, 'Anekdoten und Notizen über Beethoven', *Über den richtigen Vortrag der sämtlichen Beethoven'schen Klavierwerke*, ed. Paul Badura-Skoda (Vienna, 1963)
Johnson/Fischhof	Douglas Porter Johnson, *Beethoven's Early Sketches in the 'Fischhof Miscellany'*, Berlin autograph 28 (Ann Arbor, 1980)
LTB	*Letters to Beethoven & Other Correspondence*, trans. and ed. Theodore Albrecht
MBA	Mozart, *Briefe und Aufzeichnungen*, ed. Wilhelm A. Bauer and Otto Erich Deutsch (Kassel, 1962–75)
Schindler	Anton Felix Schindler, *Biographie von Ludwig van Beethoven* (Münster, 1860)
TDR	Alexander Wheelock Thayer (rev. Hermann Deiters and Hugo Riemann), *Ludwig van Beethovens Leben*, 5 vols (Leipzig, 1907–23).
Thayer/Forbes	*Thayer's Life of Beethoven*, rev. and ed. Elliot Forbes (Princeton, 1977).
Wegeler/Ries	Franz Wegeler and Ferdinand Ries, *Biographische Notizen über Ludwig van Beethoven* (Koblenz, 1838)
WoO	Werke ohne Opuszahl (Works without an opus number)

Bibliographical references in footnotes are given in a shortened form throughout. Full details can be found in the Bibliography at the end of the volume.

Pitch Notation

Notes in the upper range of Beethoven's pianos are indicated by their position in whole octaves above 'middle' C, which is designated as C^1. Thus, C^4 denotes the pitch three octaves above middle C, and F^4 a further perfect fourth higher. The latter was the topmost note available to Beethoven on the keyboards of his middle and late years, and was first used by him in two works he composed in 1808: the Piano Trio op.70 no.2, and the *Choral Fantasia* op.80.

1
Introduction

The incursion of keyboard instruments into the domain of chamber music began with their participation in the continuo of the Baroque sonata. With the music's harmony firmly delineated by the harpsichord, and the bass line more often than not strengthened through the presence of a viola da gamba, the two melody instruments of the characteristic trio sonata were able to weave their contrapuntal lines with increased freedom. If the distinction of having emancipated the bass line of the continuo part so that it became an integral component of the musical discourse belongs above all to Corelli, it was Bach who carried the process a stage further by at the same time elevating the keyboard player's right-hand contribution to the status of an independent part.

Bach's six sonatas for violin and keyboard, and the three for viola da gamba, are the first significant works of their kind. They are essentially trio sonatas whose texture has been refashioned in such a way as to make it perfectly feasible for the music to be performed by only two players, the part traditionally assigned to the second melody instrument being transferred instead to the upper register of the keyboard. (Significantly, the first of the viola da gamba sonatas, BWV 1027, is a transcription of a work originally scored for two flutes and continuo.) Moreover, even in those movements – such as the opening Adagio of the E major Violin Sonata BWV 1016, or the Siciliano of the C minor Sonata BWV 1017 – where the keyboard instrument clearly assumes the role of accompanist, its part is written out in full. Only in the quick fugal movements are remnants of a figured bass notation intermittently in evidence. At the same time, the sonatas contain several movements in which the bass line acquires at times a thematic importance of its own, momentarily lending the music a third voice.

The unification of the chamber sonata's sonority was carried a stage further by Bach in his six trio sonatas for organ (BWV 525–30), which manage to encompass the entire texture of the traditional form in a single instrument. Paradoxically, it was not until near the end of his life that Bach took an interest in the traditional trio sonata scoring, and he did so with what is one of the most profound of all his chamber works. By that time, the age of the genre was to all intents and purposes over, and Bach was composing for a new type of instrument: despite its old-fashioned figured-bass notation, it is likely that the sonata for flute, violin and keyboard from the *Musical Offering* was written, like the two keyboard Ricercars of the same work, with the sound of Frederick the Great's Silbermann fortepiano in mind.

Solo sonatas and trio sonatas with continuo were composed by Bach's second son, Carl Philipp Emanuel, until the mid-1750s, and there is even an isolated sonata of his for flute and continuo (Wq.133) written as late as 1786, representing perhaps the last significant flowering of the form. The majority of the composer's earlier sonatas were written with his flute-playing employer Frederick the Great in mind, but the most unusual among the trio sonatas is an example in C minor for two violins and continuo (Wq.161.1) published in 1751 under the title of *Gespräch zwischen einem Sanguineus und Melancholicus* (Conversation between a sanguine person and a melancholic), which provides the genre with what is a very rare instance of programme music.

In the majority of his chamber sonatas with continuo C.P.E. Bach gives the players the option of allotting one of the melodic parts to the keyboard player's right hand, so that the pieces can be performed in the guise of solo violin or flute sonatas. When played in this way, they become descendants of his father's works for violin or viola da gamba and keyboard.

C.P.E. Bach composed around a dozen sonatas for violin with obbligato keyboard, and, in the 1770s, a similar number of trios, described for the most part as 'keyboard sonatas with a violin and cello as accompaniment'. In the last year of his life came a set of three quartets for piano, flute, viola and bass in which the two upper melody instruments take a much more active role, so that the music clearly cannot be performed without their participation. (In describing these works as 'quartets for piano, flute and viola', Bach did not supply a cello part. Its contribution was to be derived from the bass line of the piano part.[1])

Although a few of the chamber works with piano of Haydn, Mozart and Beethoven pay open tribute to the music of the Baroque era (Mozart's incomplete Adagio and Fugue K.402 for keyboard and violin, and the fugal finale of Beethoven's Cello Sonata op.102 no.2, for instance, or the passacaglia-like middle movement of Haydn's E major Piano Trio H.XV.28), the repertoire owes its origins not to any Baroque models, but to a genre known today as the accompanied keyboard sonata: a popular form of domestic music-making that had begun to manifest itself as early as the 1730s, with such works as the *Pièces de clavecin en sonates* op.3 by Jean-Joseph Cassanéa de Mondonville. Mondonville's music is melodically formulaic and uninspired, but the violin part is far from a mere accompaniment, especially in the slow movements, which are invariably described as an 'Aria'. The violin's contribution to the Aria of the F major Sonata op.3 no.2 is independent enough for its ornate melodic line to proceed in 6/8 time simultaneously with a harpsichord part in duple metre. A later collection by Mondonville, *Pièces de clavecin avec voix ou violon* (op.5, 1748), intermittently replaces the violin part with a vocal setting of a sacred text. The composer's preface explains: 'I felt that this plan would particularly interest those whose talent for the harpsichord is joined by that for the voice, since they will be able to perform this kind of music alone.' The skill in multi-tasking required to carry out Mondonville's intention is, however, not inconsiderable.

During his early years in London, Bach's youngest son, Johann Christian, composed a set of six keyboard sonatas with violin or flute accompaniment, op.2. The accompanying instrument plays for the most part a subsidiary role, though the

---

[1] See Schmid, *Carl Philipp Emanuel Bach und seine Kammermusik*, p.139.

pieces cannot satisfactorily be performed without its presence. The latter half of the minuet-like finale in the F major first sonata of the series, for instance, begins with two bars for the flute or violin alone; and in the opening stages of the G major second sonata the melody instrument fulfils a function almost equal in importance to that of the keyboard. The second work in a later set of six sonatas with violin, op.10, composed in 1773, has a minuet finale in which the trio section allots its melody to the stringed instrument throughout, and the violin part assumes increasing importance as the series progresses. The dynamic markings in the keyboard part indicate that the music was conceived for fortepiano, rather than harpsichord, and the pieces were published in score, with the violin part printed above the keyboard – a format that is not to be found in the original editions of Beethoven's chamber music before the two cello sonatas op.102.

Keyboard sonatas with violin accompaniment are found among Mozart's earliest compositions. The four works of the kind he completed in Paris in 1764 (K.6–9), probably under the influence of the expatriate Johann Schobert, whose music he admired, were his first pieces to appear in print. A further group of similar sonatas (K.10–15) was composed that same year in London, perhaps as a result of Mozart's friendship with Johann Christian Bach. Some copies of the first edition of this collection appeared with an additional part for cello playing in tandem with the keyboard's bass line, and a title page describing the works as *Six Sonates pour le clavecin qui peuvent se jouer avec l'accompagnement de violon, ou flaute [sic] traversière et d'un violoncelle*, a description similar to that used in Schobert's early sonata collections. As late as 1776 the first edition of a set of sonatas by C.P.E. Bach (Wq.89) was published in London by Robert Bremner with a title page that failed altogether to mention the accompanying violin and cello, the pieces instead being listed simply as 'Six Sonatas for the Harpsichord or Piano Forte'. Some two years later when the pieces appeared in Berlin and Amsterdam under the imprint of Johann Julius Hummel they were more accurately described as being *Accompagnées d'un Violon & Violoncelle*.

Remnants of the tradition of the accompanied keyboard sonata can be felt right up to the last decade of the eighteenth century in the piano trios of Haydn. These works, the large majority of them written towards the end of the composer's life, contain some of his most visionary and forward-looking keyboard writing, and it could be argued that their much-maligned textures, in which the strings – and in particular the cello – are subordinated to the piano, represent an ideal, if radical, solution to a problematic medium in which one member of the ensemble plays an instrument whose sound begins to decay as soon as its notes are struck. Rather than ignore, or attempt to smooth over, the inherent differences between the two types of instrument involved, Haydn's trios create a sonority in which each player lends support to the others. While the pieces clearly cannot be played adequately on the piano alone, it is true that the cello and the pianist's left hand pursue for the most part the same line. That line, however, springs from the very presence of the cello: there is nothing in Haydn's solo keyboard sonatas that can compare in intricacy with the left-hand part of the trios. To a certain extent, Haydn's trio textures represent a means of overcoming the limited sustaining power of the eighteenth-century piano. Consider the following passage from the closing stages of the finale 'In the German Style' of the Trio in E flat H.XV.29. At its given dynamic level the long B flat pedal note in the keyboard part will clearly have ceased to sound at all after three or four bars, even at the prescribed *Presto assai* tempo, and is sustained thereafter only by the cello.

Ex. 1.1. Haydn. Piano Trio in E flat, H.XV.29 (iii) bars 273–85.

Such passages may lead us to suspect that it was the cello part, and not the bass line of the keyboard, that took precedence in Haydn's conception of the music; and they raise the question as to whether it is not in fact the piano that is doubling the cello, rather than the other way round.[2] If Haydn supposedly paid such scant regard to the cello's presence, we might ask ourselves why it was that he showed such a singular lack of interest throughout his life in cultivating the form of the sonata for piano and violin.[3] To whatever degree the piano assumes the primary role in Haydn's trios, these works contain strikingly idiomatic chamber textures and sonorities of a kind that neither Mozart nor Beethoven attempted. The 'gypsy-style' improvisation in the slow movement of the A flat Trio H.XV.12 of 1789, with the sporadic pizzicato chords of the two stringed instruments vainly striving to impose some sense of order on the piano's wild flights of fantasy, or the *Andante cantabile* middle movement of the grandly virtuosic Trio in B flat H.XV.20, where the initial melody, played by the

---

[2] This and other textural aspects of the Haydn trios have been perceptively examined by William Dean Sutcliffe in 'Haydn's Piano Trio Textures', pp.319–32, and 'The Haydn Piano Trio: Textual Facts and Textural Principles', pp.246–90.

[3] Haydn's only work once thought to have been conceived as a duo for piano and violin was, in fact, the Piano Trio in E flat minor H.XV.31. When, in the autumn of 1803, Prince Nicolaus Esterházy II informed Haydn that the wife of General Victor Moreau wished to have a new sonata by him, the composer, who was too elderly and frail to embark on a project of that magnitude, simply suppressed the trio's cello part, and presented the work to Mme Moreau in the guise of a new composition.

pianist *solo con la mano sinistra*, gives way to a variation that has the violin doubling the piano's inner melodic line, while the cello picks out the lowest voice pizzicato – these are just two among Haydn's many indelible trio textures which would be unthinkable in any other medium. Even more original are the opening bars of the E major Trio H.XV.28, which present a curiously etiolated sound in which the strings again play pizzicato, while, in an apparent reversal of roles, the pianist's right hand sustains a smooth melodic line, and the left, playing *staccato assai*, imitates the dry sonority of the two stringed instruments. At the same time, each of the right hand's melody notes has its own appoggiatura, as though to mimic the effect of an imperfectly synchronised pizzicato ensemble. This skeletal beginning is followed in bars 5–8 by its obverse side: a smooth, richly harmonised variant of the same melody, its notes now played *tenute*, and warmly embellished with chromatic passing-notes.

Ex. 1.2. Haydn. Piano Trio in E, H.XV.28 (i) bars 1–8.

Far from being merely accompanied keyboard music, Haydn's piano trios show a profound awareness of the medium for which they are written. Nor will those hoping to find instances where Haydn allows the cello to assume a melodic role be entirely disappointed, as is shown by the slow opening movement of the A major Trio H.XV.9 of 1785, where from the very outset the violin and cello move together in mellifluous tenths, their effect enhanced from the ninth bar onwards by a piano accompaniment in rippling arpeggios.

Ex. 1.3. Haydn. Piano Trio in A, H.XV.9 (i) bars 1–16.

There is a sense in which, for all its undeniable beauty, writing of this kind might strike us as curiously old-fashioned when set beside the remaining trios of Haydn's late years. The Gluckian sweetness of the melody which unfolds on the stringed instruments from the eighth bar onwards harks back to the slow movements of Haydn's string quartets op.20, of 1772; and the use of the cello in its tenor register moving in parallel with the violin also seems a throwback to an earlier style. Cellists, were they aware of its existence, would no doubt welcome the piece with open arms, but others might find more to admire in the same trio's only other movement – a virtuoso *Vivace* which, for all that it reverts to Haydn's characteristic piano trio textures with the cellist pursuing essentially the same line as the pianist's left hand, seems to be an altogether more forward-looking piece. The third and fourth bars of its main subject throw their melodic emphasis on the notes E and F sharp, and the conjunct interval formed by those two notes is inverted at bars 4–5 to form a descending minor seventh. Finally, in bars 5–6, the same two pitches in retrograde inversion yield a falling major ninth.

Ex. 1.4. Haydn. Piano Trio in A, H.XV.9 (ii) bars 1–8.

The start of the development section expands the major ninth of Ex. 1.4 to form a series of descending tenths, broken only by a single intervening major ninth (bars 85–6), and the whole passage is capped with a rising tenth. The new-found independence of the cello in the work's opening movement appears to have rubbed off on this piece: instead of lending support to the piano's pedal C sharp in bars 82–6 the cello moves in parallel thirds with the violin.

Ex. 1.5. Haydn. Piano Trio in A, H.XV.9 (ii) bars 78–90.

Even more spectacular is the start of the recapitulation. Here, Haydn seizes on the theme's descending major ninth, in order to launch on an unbroken chain of no fewer than a half-dozen occurrences of that unusual melodic interval.

Ex. 1.6. Haydn. Piano Trio in A, H.XV.9 (ii) bars 136–52.

—(continued)

Ex. 1.6—*continued*

Writing of such wit, sophistication and intellectual rigour was not to be surpassed in the piano trio literature for nearly a quarter-century, until Beethoven's two trios op.70, though it is true that the five mature piano trios of Mozart (six, if we include the 'Kegelstatt' K.498, for piano, clarinet and viola), composed between 1786 and 1788, form a series of works of great originality and beauty. They were preceded a full decade earlier by the trio Divertimento K.254, of 1776 – a piece in which the cello assumes a rather more subsidiary function than it does in the trios of Haydn. However, the violin takes on an increasingly important role as the work progresses, stepping briefly into the limelight in the closing subject of the first Allegro, and taking the melodic lead at the start of the two remaining movements.

The first of Mozart's mature trios, K.496, was composed in the year following the Haydn A major trio discussed above. During the exposition of its opening Allegro, following the long initial rhapsodic piano solo the cello has to be content for the most part to pursue the same course as the keyboard's bass line; but with the advent of the development section it takes an active part in the contrapuntal discourse, in what is likely to be one of the earliest independent uses of the cello in this medium.

Ex. 1.7. Mozart. Piano Trio in G, K.496 (i) bars 79–94.

This, indeed, is a work that is experimental in all directions – from its opening subject (elaborated at the start of the development section quoted in Ex. 1.7 above), which gives the impression of setting off in 5/4 time, to the coda of its variation finale which takes the highly unusual step of reverting to the material of the earlier minor-mode variation, while at the same time transforming it into the major.

A more tightly knit contrapuntal discourse involving all three players is presented at the second stage of the exposition in the opening movement of Mozart's E major Trio K.542, composed in 1788. Here, following the unexpected change in tonal direction that occurs at bar 74, each member of the ensemble contributes to the melodic discourse on an equal basis.

Ex. 1.8. Mozart. Piano Trio in E, K.542 (i) bars 63–88.

Independent parts for the two stringed instruments are found in the work of lesser composers of the period, too, though generally without achieving the type of closely argued writing found in Mozart. One of the most prolific trio composers of the day was the pianist Johann Franz Xaver Sterkel, who met Beethoven in 1791. Beethoven's friend and early biographer Ferdinand Wegeler recounts that Sterkel played – apparently from memory – some of Beethoven's Variations on Righini's 'Venni Amore' (WoO 65), which had been published that year. 'Sterkel's playing', says Wegeler, 'was very light, highly pleasing, and ... somewhat ladylike.'

> Beethoven stood beside him concentrating intensely. Then he was asked to play but only complied when Sterkel intimated that he doubted whether even the composer of the variations could play them all the way through. Beethoven played not only these variations, as far as he could remember them (Sterkel could not find the music), but also a number of others no less difficult; and, to the amazement of his listeners, he played everything in precisely the same pleasant manner with which Sterkel had impressed him.[4]

4   Wegeler/Ries, p.23. Mozart was far less favourably impressed by Sterkel's playing. In a letter to his father of 26 November 1777, he complained that Sterkel had performed 'so quickly

Sterkel's easy-going performance style is reflected in his music, whose generally relaxed character enabled him to adopt a concertante manner in which violin and cello alternate, with the latter more often than not placed in the alto register. Reviewing Sterkel's three trios op.30, published by Artaria in 1789, the *Musikalische Real-Zeitung* commented: 'No series of modulations into remote keys, no awkward difficulties or wrist-breaking passages, but instead pleasantly flowing melody, well-ordered development, and – as is so seldom the case with some of today's fashionable composers – unity of tonality characterise these sonatas by Herr Sterkel.'[5]

The following is taken from the 'Romance' slow movement of the last of Sterkel's three trios op.30. The manner in which the entries of violin and cello begin gradually to overlap, until the two instruments move together in parallel, makes for a conversational style that is not without its attractions:

Ex. 1.9. Sterkel. Piano Trio in B flat, op.30 no.3 (ii) bars 69–84.

that you couldn't make it out, and not at all clearly, and not in time' (MBA no.379).

[5] *Musikalische Real-Zeitung*, no.43 (28 Oct. 1789), p.338, col.1.

Another successful composer of piano trios, and one whose music impressed the young Mozart rather more favourably than did Sterkel's, was Johann Schobert. He was among the composers who visited the Mozart family in Paris in 1764, presenting the two children with copies of their sonatas.[6] Mozart included an arrangement of the opening *Andante poco allegro* from Schobert's keyboard sonata with violin op.17 no.2 in his *pasticcio* Piano Concerto K.39, and he seems to have remembered its accompaniment in throbbing triplets when he came to write the famous slow movement of his C major Concerto K.467.

Schobert's piano trios are texturally similar to those of Haydn, though their central minuet more often than not adopts a rather different layout, assigning the

---

[6] See Leopold Mozart's letter of 1 February 1764 to his Salzburg landlady, Maria Theresia Hagenauer (MBA no.80).

melody to the violin and cello in parallel sixths, while the piano accompanies. A typical example is the minuet from the trio op.16 no.1.[7]

Ex. 1.10. Schobert. Piano Trio in B flat, op.16 no.1 (ii) bars 1–12.

Much less widely cultivated than the piano trio in the latter half of the eighteenth century was the form of the piano quartet. Among the earliest examples of the genre are Schobert's three *Sonates en quatuor* op.7 for keyboard with the accompaniment of two violins and a bass *ad libitum*, which were issued in Paris in 1767, the year of the composer's death. They are generally less adventurous than his piano trios, with the rather unidiomatic string parts often doubling the keyboard at length. (Curiously, Schobert's chamber music seems to gain in imaginative freedom the fewer the players involved. The opening *Moderato* movement of his A major sonata for keyboard and violin op.14 no.5, with its pervasive harmonic suspensions, has a grace and lyricism which lift it above the average.)

Despite his admiration for Schobert's music, Mozart is unlikely to have been influenced by his piano quartets when, in the autumn of 1785, he composed his own G minor Quartet K.478, a work whose textural perfection has perhaps never been surpassed, but one whose turbulent atmosphere seems to have gone beyond the bounds of what was considered suitable for the domestic market. According to Georg Nikolaus von Nissen, who married the composer's widow, Konstanze, in 1809, the poor sales of the work led the publisher Franz Anton Hoffmeister to

---

7 Reprinted in *Denkmäler der deutschen Tonkunst*, 39 (Leipzig, 1909), pp.55–67.

cancel his contract with Mozart for a series of three piano quartets, despite the fact that he had gone so far as to engrave all but the violin part of the second work.[8] That second quartet, K.493, although no easier to play, is more obviously a pleasing display piece, and its finale assumes at times the aspect of a piano concerto. It may have been in view of his awareness of the pitfalls of a medium which encourages the composer to divide his instrumental forces into two self-sufficient opposing groups that Beethoven composed no original piano quartet in his mature years. (His single example was a transcription of the op.16 Quintet for piano and wind.[9])

Beethoven cannot have known Mozart's piano quartets at the time he composed his own three works of the kind, WoO 36, since they actually predate the first in Mozart's pair by a matter of a few months. Nevertheless, those early quartets are based on Mozartian models: each shows the influence of one of the six violin sonatas Mozart published in 1781.[10] That same set of works by Mozart also left its mark on Beethoven's Trio for piano, flute and bassoon WoO 37, and even as late as 1800 Beethoven's lingering affection for Mozart's violin sonatas can be heard in the slow movement of the 'Spring' Sonata op.24, which lovingly recreates the atmosphere and textural layout of the Adagio from Mozart's A major Sonata K.526.

Beethoven's single chamber work with piano which clearly emulates Mozart within the same genre is the Quintet op.16. Its scoring, for piano, oboe, clarinet and horn, pays homage to Mozart's quintet in the same key of E flat, K.452, and Beethoven's alternative version of his work as a piano quartet learns a further lesson from Mozart in its striving for greater interplay between the two contrasting types of instruments involved.

With his sonatas for piano and cello Beethoven invented an entirely new genre. If the opening movement of the first of his five works of the kind, op.5 no.1, is weighted in favour of the keyboard part, both its concluding rondo and the G minor second sonata of the pair find him seeking a more evenly balanced sonority between the two players, while his working draft of the first movement of the A major Sonata op.69 shows the extent to which he refashioned his material in order to achieve greater textural clarity as well as closer integration of the two instruments.

For all the elevated status of the stringed instruments brought about in the sonatas and trios of Beethoven, the title page of every work examined in this book gave pride of place to the piano. As we have seen, Beethoven's op.30 was published as *Trois Sonates pour le Pianoforte avec l'Accompagnement d'un violon,* and as late as 1818 the op.102 cello sonatas were referred to by the reviewer of the Leipzig *Allgemeine musikalische Zeitung* simply as piano music. Beethoven himself was inconsistent about such matters: in a letter of 19 April 1817 to the English pianist and cellist Charles Neate, he described the op.102 pair as 'piano sonatas with violoncello' (*Klavier-Sonaten mit Violonschell*),[11]

---

[8] See Nissen, *Biographie W.A. Mozart's*, p.633.
[9] See pp.85–9
[10] See pp. 22ff.
[11] BGA no.1116; Anderson no.778

while in writing to Archduke Rudolph at the end of 1818 or the beginning of 1819, he referred to the same pieces as *Sonaten mit Violonschell oblig*.[12]

Such descriptions which relegated the stringed instrument to the role of an accompanist were common currency, and if they were plainly anachronistic they nevertheless contained a grain of truth: at least until Beethoven's op.69 Cello Sonata, the piano was very much *primus inter pares*. Those works of Beethoven which do marry mastery of invention with a perfect and unstrained integration of the instrumental forces involved – besides the op.69 Sonata they include the 'Ghost' and 'Archduke' trios, as well as the op.96 Violin Sonata – owe their success in part to advances in the construction of the stringed instruments themselves. The end of the eighteenth century saw a lengthening of the neck of the violin (which, at the same time, was thrown back at a slight angle), as well as an increase in the height of the bridge. The greater tension of the strings – which consequently had to be strengthened – resulted in a sound of considerably heightened power and penetration. At the same time, the improved bows produced by the Parisian makers Louis and François Tourte allowed for greater variety of articulation as well as increased sustaining power. Although Mozart had been able to write for the violin in a grand style (the slow introduction to the B flat Sonata K.454, for instance), and with considerable brilliance (as in the Sonata K.526), a work of the sustained forcefulness of Beethoven's 'Kreutzer' Sonata would have been unthinkable on the instruments of his day.

As the nineteenth century progressed, rapid advances in piano-building techniques in response to the performing style of players such as Liszt, Thalberg and Kalkbrenner made the piano's participation in chamber music increasingly problematic. Those advances were not matched by further changes in the construction of the violin or cello, and the combination of stringed instruments and piano is consequently one that has always raised difficulties of blend and balance. The problem was neatly summarised by Schoenberg, in a characteristically laconic response to a query as to why he had made his orchestral transcription of Brahms's Piano Quartet op.25.

1. I like this piece.
2. It is seldom played.
3. It is always very badly played, because the better the pianist, the louder he plays and you hear nothing from the strings. I wanted [for] once to hear everything, and this I achieved.[13]

The seemingly irreconcilable differences between the piano, whose sound begins to diminish in volume as soon as its notes are struck, and stringed instruments, with their more flexible expressive capabilities, were acknowledged by E.T.A. Hoffmann in his detailed review of Beethoven's two piano trios op.70. (Hoffmann's article, originally written for the *Allgemeine musikalische Zeitung*, was subsequently included in an abridged form in his second *Kreisleriana* collection.)

> It is surely true that the piano remains an instrument more useful for harmony than for melody. The most subtle expression of which the instrument is capable does not

---

[12] BGA no.1278; Anderson no.551.
[13] Letter of 18 March 1939 to Alfred V. Frankenstein, in Stein, *Arnold Schoenberg Letters*, p.207.

give the melody the mobile life in thousand upon thousand nuances that the bow of the violinist, the breath of the wind player, is able to call forth. The pianist wrestles in vain with the insuperable difficulty with which the mechanism, which makes the strings vibrate and sound by striking them, confronts him. On the other hand, there is (apart from the far more limited harp) certainly no instrument that can, like the piano, embrace the world of harmony in full-blooded chords, and reveal its treasures to the connoisseur in the most wonderful forms and shapes. If the composer's imagination has been stirred by a complete tone picture with rich details [*reichen Gruppen*], bright highlights and deep shadows, he can bring it to life at the piano so that it comes forth from the inner world in all its colour and splendour.[14]

※ ※ ※

Beethoven's chamber music with piano spans the entire period of his activity as a performer. The three piano trios op.1 were among the very first works with which he made himself known in Vienna in the dual capacity of pianist and composer. Some twenty years later, performances of the 'Archduke' Trio op.97 at benefit concerts for the composer given in April 1814 marked what were to all intents and purposes his final attempts to play the piano in front of an audience.[15] The *Allgemeine musikalische Zeitung* reported: 'On 11 April at midday in a room at the *Römischer Kaiser* a musical-declamatory concert was organised by Herr Schuppanzigh and the administrator of the hotel for the benefit of military purposes. The reviewer was unable to attend, but heard that Herr Lud. van Beethoven himself performed a newly composed trio by him, and that both his playing and the composition received the greatest applause.'[16] However, Ignaz Moscheles, who at the time was working, under Beethoven's supervision, on the vocal score of *Fidelio*, was present at one of the performances, and was more critical. He noted in his diary on 11 April:

> At a midday musical entertainment in the 'Römischer Kaiser', heard a new trio by Beethoven in B flat major, played by himself. With how many compositions is the tiny word 'new' misplaced! But never with Beethoven's compositions, and least of all with this one, which again is full of originality. His playing, apart from its spirit, satisfied me less, because it has no cleanness and precision; and yet I noticed many traces of the grand manner, which I had long recognised in his compositions.[17]

Already five or six years earlier, at the time of the 'Ghost' Trio op.70 no.1, Louis Spohr – never, it is true, an unreserved Beethoven admirer – had painted an altogether darker picture of the composer's playing:

---

[14] AMZ, 9 (1813), col.141.

[15] On 25 January 1815 Beethoven made a final public appearance as pianist at a concert celebrating the birthday of the Russian Empress, when he accompanied the tenor Franz Wild in a performance of his song 'Adelaide' op.46.

[16] AMZ, 16 (25 May 1814), col.355.

[17] Moscheles, *Aus Moscheles' Leben*, vol.1, pp.15–16.

Since at the time I made his acquaintance Beethoven had already stopped playing, both in public and in private gatherings, I only once had the opportunity of hearing him, when I happened on the rehearsal of a new trio (D major, 3/4 time) in his lodgings. It was not a pleasure, for in the first place the piano was badly out of tune, which worried Beethoven little, as he did not hear it; and secondly, as a result of his deafness there was almost nothing left of the virtuosity of the artist that had formerly been so greatly admired. In *forte* the poor deaf man pounded so hard that the strings jangled, and in *piano* he played so softly that whole groups of notes were left out, so that one lost the thread if one could not look at the piano part at the same time. I found myself deeply saddened at so hard a fate. If it is a great misfortune for anyone to be deaf, how shall a musician endure it without despairing? Beethoven's almost continual depression was now no longer a mystery to me.[18]

The year following the two first performances of the 'Archduke' Trio Beethoven's output of chamber music for piano and strings came to an end with the two cello sonatas op.102. During the remaining twelve years of his life his creative energies were concentrated on piano music (the five last sonatas, the 'Diabelli' Variations op.120 and the Bagatelles opp.119 and 126) and the string quartet, as well as the two largest among his non-theatrical scores – the Ninth Symphony and the *Missa solemnis*. However, the two series of folksong variations for piano and flute opp.105 and 107 form a fascinating postscript to Beethoven's career as a composer of chamber music with piano, and one whose relevance to the development of his late style has largely been overlooked. Just as Bach's interest in the traditional trio sonata, as shown in his *Musical Offering*, was awakened only once the age of the form itself was over, so Beethoven's late variations for piano and flute mark a return to the distinctly old-fashioned – if still widely popular – concept of accompanied piano music.

---

[18] Spohr, *Selbstbiographie*, p.203.

2
Prelude: Apprentice Years

At the end of 1786 the sixteen-year-old Beethoven set off from his home town of Bonn to travel, via Regensburg and Munich, to Vienna, in the hope of making contact with Mozart, and perhaps being accepted by him as a pupil. Although the plan came to nothing (Mozart was busy composing *Don Giovanni*, and Beethoven was in any case forced to return after a relatively brief period when he received a letter from his father informing him that his mother was dying), Beethoven may at least have heard Mozart play. Whether the two men actually met is much more doubtful. Otto Jahn claimed to have had a 'reliable source' for the following anecdote which he included in his biography of Mozart, and which, as he says, seems to have escaped the ever-eager attention of Beethoven's one-time secretary, and later biographer, Anton Felix Schindler.

> Beethoven, who as a youth of much promise came to Vienna in the spring of 1787, but had to return home again after a short stay, was taken to Mozart, and at his invitation played something to him, which the latter, thinking it was a memorised display-piece, praised rather coolly. Beethoven, who noticed this, then asked him for a theme for a free improvisation, and as he always used to play excellently when he was vexed, and as he was in addition fired up by the presence of the master he so revered, launched himself in such a manner on the piano that Mozart, whose attention and interest were increasing by the minute, finally went quietly to his friends seated in the next room and said to them in a lively fashion, 'Take note of him, one day he will make a mark in the world.'[1]

The claim made by Beethoven's pupil and early biographer Ferdinand Ries that Beethoven actually received some lessons from Mozart[2] has never been substantiated, but if he was in a position to show the great composer some of his own pieces they might have included a set of three piano quartets (WoO 36) which he had completed some two years earlier. His autograph score indicates that he was thirteen years old at the time – an error that arose not out of any desire to make himself appear more of a prodigy than he was (he was in fact fourteen), but out of his own mistaken belief that he had been born in 1771, rather than in December 1770.[3] The quartets remained unpublished during his lifetime, and were first issued in 1828, by Artaria & Comp. Their edition placed the E flat quartet first, followed by the D major

---

[1] Jahn, *W.A. Mozart*, vol.2, p.40.
[2] Wegeler/Ries, p.75.
[3] See Solomon, *Beethoven Essays*, pp.35–42.

and C major works, whereas Beethoven's manuscript has the order C major, E flat and D major.

Beethoven's decision to cast his earliest ambitious chamber works in the form of quartets for piano and strings is a surprising one, not least in view of the fact that in terms of their scoring, though not of their musical content, he can have had few, if any, significant models. Mozart composed the first of his two piano quartets, K.478, during the same year of 1785, and although Beethoven cannot have known it at the time he wrote his own pieces of the kind, they are heavily influenced by Mozartian models. Hermann Deiters seems to have been the first to point out that Beethoven's model for the Piano Quartet WoO 36 no.1 was clearly Mozart's G major Violin Sonata K.379[4], and the parallels between the two works were explored in greater detail by Ludwig Schiedermair.[5] However, Schiedermair's commentary did not extend to the influence on the young Beethoven of the remaining sonatas from the set of six (K.296 and 376–80) which had been published in Vienna in November 1781. The rondo finale of Beethoven's C major quartet follows closely the outline of the last movement from Mozart's sonata in the same key K.296, and in their central episode the material of the two works is remarkably similar. (Note, however, the already characteristic juxtaposition of contrasting dynamics in the Beethoven.)

Ex. 2.1.
(a) Mozart. Violin Sonata in C, K.296 (iii) bars 70–3.

(b) Beethoven. Piano Quartet in C, WoO 36 no.3 (iii) bars 75–8.

In view of its otherwise symmetrical material, it is curious to find the C major quartet beginning with a subject consisting of five bars – an asymmetry that is heightened by the irregularly placed accents within the theme itself. Further pointers towards the composer's mature style may be heard in the startling plunge into E flat major at the start of the development section, followed immediately by its echo on the dominant of F major, or the hushed moment heralding the imminent arrival of the recapitulation. The harmony of the latter moment – a diminished seventh

---

4   TDR, vol.1, p.209.
5   Schiedermair, *Der junge Beethoven*, pp.212–25.

chord above a dissonant dominant pedal – provides a momentary pre-echo of the parallel point in the C major Piano Concerto op.15.

More impressive, however, is the central section of the slow movement – an ornate aria in which the violin suddenly takes wing, to be answered a few bars later by the viola. The effect is not so far removed from that of the elaborately expressive episodes in the slow movement of the Piano Quartet op.16, Beethoven's transcription of the more familiar quintet for piano and wind. Following this episode the reprise of the initial theme is imaginatively rescored, the melodic line given this time not to the piano, but to the violin and viola in octaves. The Adagio variation from the second movement of the E flat Quartet, WoO 36 no.1, is another intricate viola solo, and the proliferation of material Beethoven allotted to the instrument may reflect the fact that he himself played it in the court orchestra at Bonn for some four years.

The unusual sequence of movements in Beethoven's E flat quartet is identical with that of Mozart's Violin Sonata in G K.379: both works begin with an Adagio, complete with a repeat of its exposition, which is too substantial to function as no more than a slow introduction, yet at the same time lacks the weight of a self-contained movement. The pieces are essentially curtailed sonata forms that break off before the recapitulation can get under way. In place of any recapitulation there follows a dramatic Allegro in the minor (in the case of the Beethoven, in the unusual key of E flat minor). The only remaining movement in each case is a set of variations.

The melodic outline of Beethoven's initial bars clearly mirrors its Mozartian model:

Ex. 2.2.
(a) Mozart. Violin Sonata in G, K.379 (i) bars 1–4.

(b) Beethoven. Piano Quartet in E flat, WoO 36 no.1 (i) bars 1–5.

Further parallels between the two pieces may be found at the start of their second group, where the left-hand piano part makes prominent use of rising arpeggios in demisemiquaver motion. (Again, however, the Beethoven stands apart through its profusion of dynamic contrasts.) While Beethoven's first subject, with its elaborate flights of fantasy for the pianist, had no more than a rudimentary accompaniment for the stringed instruments, the second subject has the strings in florid dialogue, with even the cello participating, albeit for no more than a single bar.

In common with its Mozartian model, the start of Beethoven's development section moves from the dominant towards the relative minor (C minor). Beethoven's development, with its consistent dynamic contrasts, is considerably more elaborate and restless than Mozart's. The music, which has the pianist's right hand in dialogue with the violin, modulates constantly and unfolds largely in the minor, until, in its closing bars, immediately preceding the onset of the Allegro, it clearly recalls the parallel moment in Mozart's sonata.

Ex. 2.3.
(a) Mozart. Violin Sonata in G, K.379 (i) bars 45–9.

(b) Beethoven. Piano Quartet in E flat, WoO 36 no.1 (i) bars 63–9.

Despite such patent similarities, the intricate ornateness of Beethoven's keyboard part in the Adagio's first stage is far removed from the restraint of the Mozart, and it is in their Allegro that the two works are actually closer in spirit. Mozart's Allegro conveys not the heightened expressiveness of his later G minor music, but the *Sturm und Drang* agitation of some of his pieces of the 1770s in this key, such as the Symphony K.183, or the aria 'Tiger! Wetze nur die Klauen' from the unfinished Singspiel *Zaide* K.344. Beethoven does not hesitate to emulate the subdued close of Mozart's exposition, and the manner in which he takes over the quasi-orchestral tremolos of his model was noted by Schiedermair.[6]

Ex. 2.4.
(a) Mozart. Violin Sonata in G, K.379 (i) bars 78–82.

(b) Beethoven. Piano Quartet in E flat, WoO 36 no.1 (i) bars 86–90.

However, while Mozart caps his movement with a powerful coda, Beethoven allows his to come to rest with a conclusion similar to that of the exposition, as though all energy were spent. It is symptomatic of his precociously dramatic piece, too – surely the most characteristic movement to be found among the three quartets – that its exposition remains in the minor throughout, with the second group firmly set in B flat minor. No less remarkable is the chromatic closing subject's Neapolitan harmony – an idea that was to find its way into the opening movement of the Piano

[6] Schiedermair, *Der junge Beethoven*, p.218.

Trio op.1 no.3. The Neapolitan tinges also anticipate a passage Beethoven was to admire in a later work by Mozart: the coda of the C minor Piano Concerto K.491.

Beethoven seems to have contemplated using a subject derived from the 'rocketing' main theme of his Allegro as the basis of a symphony in C minor. His outline for the orchestral work's beginning is contained in the 'Kafka' sketchbook,[7] and the neatness with which it is set out makes it likely that it postdates the piano quartet.[8]

Ex. 2.5.
(a) Beethoven. Piano Quartet in E flat, WoO 36 no.1 (i) bars 70–6.

---

[7] Beethoven, *Autograph Miscellany*, f.70 r.

[8] Gustav Nottebohm (*Zweite Beethoveniana*, p.567) thought the composer had taken over the pre-existing theme from the projected symphony into the piano quartet, but his reasoning was founded on the purely speculative basis that the same process had been applied to material from the early quartets which subsequently found its way into the op.2 piano sonatas.

Ex. 2.5.
(b) Beethoven. Symphony in C minor, sketch.

The rocketing theme echoes the opening subject of Mozart's Piano Sonata in C minor K.457, and Beethoven was to remember it when he came to write his F minor Piano Sonata op.2 no.1.

The variation finale of Beethoven's E flat Piano Quartet follows the plan of its Mozartian model closely, the first variation in both pieces featuring smooth semiquavers for the pianist's right hand, and the second transforming the theme into semiquaver triplets for the violin. As in the Mozart, there is a march-like variation in the minor, and in dotted rhythm (infinitely less affecting, however, in its superficial agitation than the gentle pathos of the Mozart), and an eventual return to the theme in its original form, followed by a coda. A significant difference between the two pieces is that Beethoven places his Adagio variation considerably earlier in his scheme than does Mozart, allowing it to form the third variation, whereas in the Mozart sonata it immediately precedes the final reprise of the theme. The intricate viola solo of Beethoven's slow variation accords with a scheme he was to adopt in several of the chamber variation sets of his early Viennese years, whereby the melodic line is given in successive variations to each player in turn.[9]

The plan of Beethoven's D major Quartet WoO 36 no.2, with its slow movement in the submediant minor, is again highly unorthodox. It is borrowed from

---

[9] Beethoven was not the only great composer to have been inspired by the finale of Mozart's K.379 Sonata: Schubert's 'Im Frühling' D.882, his only song in variation form, is patently modelled on the same piece.

Mozart's Violin Sonata in E flat K.380, and the key scheme is one that will not readily be found elsewhere in the work of either composer. The handling of the ensemble in Beethoven's opening movement, particularly in its initial bars, has new-found assurance, and the second subject, with its turn from major to minor in its answering phrase, has an elegance not altogether unworthy of Mozart. The triplets of the closing subject seem to echo the similar motion of Mozart's second subject, though without managing to capture its melodic gracefulness. Beethoven's development section is undistinguished, consisting, as it does, of an unvaryingly syncopated piano part in sequential repetition, and displaying a notable lack of melodic inventiveness. In view of the music's virtuoso character – it includes some distinctly awkward keyboard figuration – it is curious to find that, as in the E flat quartet, there is a coda that allows the music to die away, *mancando*, to a *pianissimo* conclusion.

Following the tonal scheme found in Mozart's Sonata K.380, the slow movement is in F sharp minor. Only on one occasion in his mature years did Beethoven write a movement in this key: the Adagio of the 'Hammerklavier' Sonata op.106. Mozart, too, composed only a single piece in F sharp minor – the slow movement of his A major Piano Concerto K.488.[10] In both the Mozart concerto and Beethoven's op.106 Sonata the pull towards the Neapolitan region of G major makes itself felt, enhancing the music's expressive effect: the final phrase of Mozart's melancholy opening subject is preceded by a delicate rising G major arpeggio, and in the slow movement of the 'Hammerklavier' the opening theme twice passes through the Neapolitan region. Although the slow movement of Beethoven's early piano quartet moves into the relative major key following its initial eight-bar theme, and the recapitulation omits the first subject altogether (the soaring melody that inaugurates the second group is, however, recapitulated in its entirety in the tonic), a two-bar Neapolitan intervention shortly before the piece comes to its *pianissimo* close lends the pizzicato passage that follows an intensity it did not have in the parallel moment of the exposition.

The waltz-like theme of the rondo finale in the Piano Quartet WoO 36 no.2 has a charm all of its own, though the childlike subject of the first episode is less than worthy of its composer. Given that nowhere during the course of the work has the piano paused before, it is curious to find the keyboard part petering out three bars before the end of the movement, leaving the strings to provide their own emphatic conclusion. The pianist may well have been expected to contribute to the final chords as he would in all likelihood have done had he been playing a concerto.

In terms of pure craftsmanship, Beethoven's early piano quartets cannot stand comparison with the three identically scored works Mendelssohn was to compose at a similar age. The writing for the strings is often rudimentary, and despite the fact that the piano plays a leading role Beethoven seems reluctant to provide textural variety by allowing the remaining three players to pause. (A notable exception is the rondo theme of the C major quartet, which is given out by the pianist alone before the strings make a subtle entrance in the theme's last bar.) Nevertheless, and despite

---

[10] The more intrepid Haydn, however, wrote several works having F sharp minor as their fundamental key: the 'Farewell' Symphony no.45, the String Quartet op.50 no.4, and the Piano Trio H.XV.26.

the fact that the cello has to be content for the most part with reinforcing the keyboard's bass line, this is by no means merely accompanied piano music. There are, indeed, several passages which display a chamber texture of some inventiveness: the intricate duet for violin and viola that launches the second group of the E flat quartet's opening Adagio, for instance, or, in the D major work, the closing subject of the first movement and the start of the second group in the Adagio, both of which again have the violin in close dialogue with the viola.

If the material of these early works is sometimes repetitive and discursive, the pieces nevertheless retain an attractive freshness. Beethoven himself thought highly enough of some of the ideas in the C major quartet to use them again, with little alteration, in his set of three piano sonatas op.2 which he dedicated to Haydn. (At the same time his procedure clearly shows that he did not expect this unpublished music of his youth ever to see the light of day.) The passage leading into the opening movement's second group reappears at the parallel moment in the C major Sonata op.2 no.3, and an expressive G minor melody heard shortly thereafter, to a gently agitated accompaniment from the strings, assumes a prominent role in the same movement of the sonata. The initial theme of the quartet's slow movement is reproduced at the start of the Adagio from the F minor Sonata op.2 no.1, though with the repetitive tonic/dominant harmony of its second half replaced by a more subtle answering phrase.

Among Beethoven's acquaintances in Bonn during the late 1780s was the family of Westerholt-Giesenberg. The elder daughter, Maria Anna Wilhelmine von Westerholt, became an accomplished pianist: she was Beethoven's pupil for a while, and he appears to have been strongly attracted to her. The cellist Bernhard Romberg, one of Beethoven's colleagues in the Bonn opera orchestra, later spoke to Franz Wegeler of the composer's 'Werther-like' passion for her.[11] Her father, the head stable master at the Bonn court, played the bassoon, and one of her brothers, the flute. It was in all likelihood for them that Beethoven wrote a Trio in G major (WoO 37), and also the Romance (Hess catalogue no.13) for piano, flute and bassoon, with an orchestral accompaniment of two oboes and strings.[12] Despite a rather un-Mozartian scheme which has all three movements in the same tonality, the trio again shows strong signs of the influence of Mozart's violin sonatas. This is particularly true of its finale, the most successful of the three movements, where Beethoven again adopts the broad plan of the variations from the G major Sonata K.379. This time, he borrows what to all intents and purposes is Mozart's theme itself:

---

[11] Wegeler/Ries, p.43.
[12] The piece has become known under the title of *Romance cantabile*, though the adjective is clearly no more than a performance direction.

Ex. 2.6.
(a) Mozart. Violin Sonata in G, K.379 (ii) bars 1–8.

(b) Beethoven. Trio in G, WoO 37 (iii) bars 1–8.

Both composers round off their variations with a return to the original theme, though in a quicker tempo (*Allegretto* in the Mozart, *Allegro* in the Beethoven); however, while Mozart's minor-mode fourth variation is a gentle march-like piece, Beethoven's is in 6/8 time – a distant forerunner of the G minor passage in the coda of one of his great works for piano trio, the 'Kakadu' Variations op.121a. Beethoven makes a further departure from his model in failing to include a slow variation.

Beethoven had not always intended to cast his slow movement in the tonic minor. His autograph score shows a deleted beginning which has the melody setting out in C major.

Ex. 2.7. Beethoven. Trio in G, WoO 37 (ii), sketch.

The sketched melody's most striking feature is perhaps its asymmetrical beginning, with the answer to the initial four-bar phrase curtailed to three bars. This irregularity was retained in Beethoven's final version, which – perhaps prompted by the gently pathetic G minor slow movement of Mozart's Violin Sonata K.380 – transferred the theme bodily into the tonic minor, while substituting an expressive 'sighing' idea in the piano for the more neutral sixth bar of the sketch.

Ex. 2.8. Beethoven. Trio in G, WoO 37 (ii) bars 1–7.

The piece is an abridged sonata design breaking off at the expected point of its recapitulation, where a brief transition leads instead to the concluding variations – an early instance of Beethoven's interest in telescoping the last two movements of a three-movement design into a linked pair.

The opening Allegro is as over-generous with its thematic material as were the first movements in the three early piano quartets. A little more distinctive than the garrulous opening subject is the second subject, with its eventual turn to the minor where its melody is taken over by the bassoon above a shadowy piano part in syncopation. Despite the exposition's abundance of melodic ideas, the development section, unfolding in the minor throughout, is based on new material. But of the three movements, this is surely the least interesting.

Maria Anna Wilhelmine was only twelve years old at the time Beethoven composed his trio, and even if she could have met the music's virtuoso demands elsewhere, it is hard to imagine the size of her hands allowing her to negotiate such awkward passages in the first movement as the rapid, widely spaced rocking motion in semiquavers near the close of the exposition, or the similar figuration in the latter half of the development section. Such moments seem rather to have been designed to display Beethoven's own keyboard mastery. His own title for the work, which was probably composed in 1786, was 'Trio concertant'.

The four works examined thus far show Beethoven pouring forth ideas in somewhat undisciplined profusion. A conventionally scored piano trio in E flat (WoO 38), written in all probability shortly afterwards, has considerably more refinement and stylistic coherence, and may be regarded as something of a transitional work. It was published in 1830, with a certificate of authenticity signed by Anton Diabelli, Carl Czerny and Ferdinand Ries. The autograph had at one stage belonged to Schindler, who believed that it originated from the same period as the three piano quartets. On stylistic grounds, however, there can be little doubt that the trio is later, and there is more of a ring of truth to Anton Gräffer's claim that Beethoven originally intended it for the op.1 trios, but discarded it as being too weak. Gräffer, an employee of the Viennese publishing house of Artaria, made his remark in a handwritten catalogue of Beethoven's works which no longer survives. (Following Beethoven's death, he was among the first to attempt to put together a biography of the composer. It is to his copy of the diary of 1812–18, made prior to its loss shortly after Beethoven died, that we owe the survival of that document's contents.)

If the trio's material itself is rather lacking in individuality and character, the writing has an assurance and purposefulness that are scarcely hinted at in the piano quartets. Not only does the cello gain considerably greater melodic independence, but the outer movements contain contrapuntal textures of a kind that Beethoven had not previously attempted. However, the work's plan, consisting as it does of three quick movements, all of them in the tonic major, is as curious as it is unsatisfying.

The central movement is described in the work's first edition as a scherzo, though stylistically it has little to distinguish it from a conventional minuet. Since the trio was not published until 1830, and Beethoven's autograph has not survived, doubts must be cast on the authenticity of the movement's heading. Nevertheless, this early appearance of the term led Schindler to declare that the movement 'proves to be the embryo of all the later scherzos'.[13] It is a piece of some charm, and its trio section has the pianist playing in gently running quavers throughout – an idea that was taken over into the minuet movement of the Piano Sonata op.2 no.1. More closely associated with the same sonata is a passage from the first movement's development section, whose outline reappears near the start of the later work.

Ex. 2.9.
(a) Beethoven. Piano Trio in E flat, WoO 38 (i) bars 93–7.

(b) Beethoven. Piano Sonata in F minor, op.2 no.1 (i) bars 20–4.

A further anticipation of Beethoven's early Viennese manner is found in the unexpected coda following the recapitulation's emphatic full close. (See, for instance, the first movement of the Cello Sonata op.5 no.2.) The concluding bars of the exposition, moreover, with their constant alternation between major and minor – an effect the young composer seems to have relished, since it surfaces again in the first episode of the finale – offer a foretaste of the parallel moment in the G major Piano Sonata op.31 no.1:

---

[13] Schindler, vol.1, p.10.

Ex. 2.10.
(a) Beethoven. Piano Trio in E flat, WoO 38 (i) bars 54–63.

(b) Beethoven. Piano Sonata in G, op.31 no.1 (i) bars 98–108.

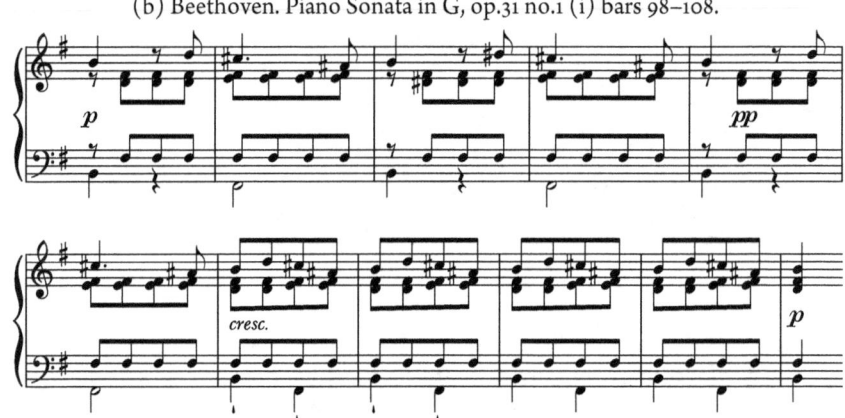

The trio's opening Allegro is largely based on the four-note descending scale figure that dominates its initial bars, with the motif appearing almost immediately in both augmented and inverted forms.

Ex. 2.11. Beethoven. Piano Trio in E flat, WoO 38 (i) bars 1–18.

The unity and coherence of the piece provide further evidence of Beethoven's increased compositional confidence, though its second-subject stage – almost all of it unfolding over an obstinately repeated dominant pedal – is melodically undistinguished. The development section, too, is largely uneventful; but the manner in which it overlaps with the start of the recapitulation, and the new syncopated version of the first subject that ensues, show signs of an emerging personality.

The theme of the rondo finale is a distant ancestor of the first Allegro subject – also in 6/8 time – of the E flat Trio op.70 no.2 (see Ex. 10.24 on p.278), and a texture heard near the close of the movement, with the two stringed instruments accompanied by quietly reiterated chords in the piano's highest register, offers a further fleeting pre-echo of Beethoven's mature style. For the rest, the work does little to explain the eruption of genius that was to occur scarcely more than two years later with the composer's first published trios, op.1.

Also mainly written during Beethoven's Bonn years is a set of variations for piano and violin on the cavatina 'Se vuol ballare' from *Le Nozze di Figaro* (WoO 40), the first of the composer's three variation works with piano on themes from Mozart operas. (The two later sets, both based on melodies from *Die Zauberflöte*, are for piano and cello.) This was not quite Beethoven's first attempt at composing for piano and violin: two fragments of an unfinished sonata in A major dating from 1790–1 have survived.[14]

---

[14] Hess no.46. See Beethoven, *Supplemente zur Gesamtausgabe*, vol.9, pp.115–18.

The first shows part of what is in all likelihood a slow movement, with the bulk of an opening section in the major in two repeated halves (the beginning of the first half is missing), followed by the initial three bars of what was presumably a middle section in the minor; while the second is little more than a sketch for a rondo, again with a central section in the minor.[15] The 3/8 triplet figuration of the first fragment perhaps owes a distant debt to Mozart's A minor Rondo for piano K.511, but neither piece betrays anything of the personality of its composer, unless it be the sudden dynamic contrasts in the 3/8 fragment's opening moments.

The 'Figaro' Variations were dedicated to Eleonore von Breuning, a close friend of Beethoven in Bonn, and the future wife of his biographer Franz Wegeler, and they provide an early record of Beethoven's prowess as an improviser. As such, it is not unlikely that the variations were initially conceived for solo piano.[16] Artaria's original edition of July 1793 bore a title page describing them as being *Pour le Clavecin ou PianoForte avec un Violon ad lib*. Beethoven's annoyance with this patent misrepresentation led him to request that any copies that had already been sold should be recalled. He wrote to one of Artaria's employees (perhaps Tranquillo Mollo or Giovanni Cappi, both of whom subsequently established publishing businesses of their own), giving a list of corrections still to be made:

> I received my variations yesterday evening. They had indeed become quite strange to me, and that pleases me, for to me this is a proof that my compositions are not entirely commonplace. But there are still a few mistakes which I must point out to you and which I beg you to have corrected immediately, since they are really very important.
>
> First of all, there is a mistake on the title page where it is stated *avec un Violino ad libitum*. Since the violin is inseparably connected with the pianoforte part and since it is not possible to play the v[ariations] without the violin, this should be worded *avec un violon obligate*, exactly as I corrected it, moreover, in one copy![17]

Artaria duly issued a second edition around December 1795, with an amended title page that contained Beethoven's requested wording in more idiomatic French. It is true that in the majority of the variations the violin part is of little consequence. Its presence may have arisen out of Beethoven's wish to evoke the guitar sound of Mozart's original cavatina: at any rate, the theme is given out in parallel octaves by the piano and pizzicato violin. Variation 2 finds the pianist's right hand playing – with no little difficulty – both an inner accompaniment and a melodic line that would more naturally have been allotted to the violin in the first place, while the violin itself actually has a superfluous accompaniment which bears the appearance of an afterthought. In the first half-dozen bars of variation 3 the violin plays in parallel with the pianist's right hand, producing a warm chain of thirds and sixths, but its role thereafter in the variation becomes that of an accompaniment. It is curious to find two successive variations in the minor (nos.6 and 7), both much the same in character, though a similar scheme is found in the variations for piano and cello on

---

[15] See Brandenburg, 'Beethoven's Opus 12 Violin Sonatas', pp.6–8.
[16] See Müller-Blatau, 'Beethoven und die Variation', pp.104–5.
[17] BGA no.10; Anderson no.5.

Mozart's 'Ein Mädchen oder Weibchen' op.66. In the first of the minor-mode pair the melodic interest lies in the violin part, while in the second it passes to the piano. Both follow exactly the same harmonic pattern, so that again the suspicion arises that the violin variation was a later insertion. Variation 10 may have been a similar addition – in compensation, perhaps, for the piano pyrotechnics of the preceding variation, in which the violin does not participate.

After his arrival in Vienna in November 1792, Beethoven appended a substantial coda to the variations, containing two highly idiosyncratic gestures: first, a brief *pianissimo* appearance of the theme in the submediant (D major) – a switch in key at a late stage of a kind to be found in several of his subsequent works of the 1790s; and second, a prolonged trill played by the fourth and fifth fingers of the pianist's right hand, while beneath it the remaining fingers of the same hand give out the theme. Beethoven was to make more fruitful use of a similar technically awkward device in the variation finales of the piano sonatas opp.109 and 111, as well as in the rondo of the 'Waldstein' op.53. In the 'Figaro' Variations he seems to have taken advantage of the violin's presence in order to mask any imperfections that may have arisen out of the extreme difficulty of the passage, though he apparently included it specifically to thwart the efforts of lesser pianists. Beethoven made no secret of his purpose in the postscript of a letter to Eleonore von Breuning, of 2 November 1793:

> The variations will be somewhat difficult to play, particularly the trills in the coda; but do not let this alarm you. It is so contrived that you need play only the trill: leave out the other notes, because they also occur in the violin part. I would never have composed anything like it; but I had often observed that here and there in Vienna there was somebody who, mostly when I had improvised of an evening, wrote down many of my individual ideas the next day, and showed off with them. As I foresaw that some of these things would soon appear in print, I resolved to forestall them. Another reason was to embarrass the local piano masters. Many of them are my deadly enemies, and I wanted to avenge myself on them in this way, because I knew in advance that here and there the variations would be placed in front of them, and those gentlemen would then make a sorry show of them.[18]

The piece was issued as Beethoven's op.1, though that status was subsequently transferred to a set of works calculated to create far more of a stir.

At the same time that he sent the 'Figaro' Variations to Eleonore von Breuning, Beethoven enclosed the charmingly unpretentious Rondo in G for piano and violin (WoO 41), which she would no doubt have been able to play without difficulty. Its theme is innocuous enough for Fritz Kreisler to have appropriated it a little more than a century later for his salon piece called 'Rondino on a Theme of Beethoven'. Beethoven's piece makes only modest demands of the two players, and the theme's gently rocking accompaniment is reminiscent of that of the second subject from a much later work written for beginners, the Allegretto WoO 39 for piano trio of 1812. At the same time, the Rondo's episode in the tonic minor seems to echo the G minor episode from the finale – also in 6/8 time – of Mozart's Piano Trio K.564:

---

[18] BGA no.11; Anderson no.9.

Ex. 2.12.
(a) Mozart. Piano Trio in G, K.564 (iii) bars 37–44.

(b) Beethoven. Rondo in G, WoO 41, bars 82–92.

When Beethoven left Bonn to commence his studies in Vienna, on 2 or 3 November 1792, Mozart had been dead for eighteen months, and so arrangements were made for him to receive tuition instead from Haydn. In the greetings album, or *Stammbuch*, the young composer took with him to the Austrian capital, Count Waldstein had written his famous prophecy:

> You are now travelling to Vienna in fulfilment of your wishes, so long frustrated. Mozart's spirit is still mourning, and lamenting the death of its ward. It found refuge but no fruition in the inexhaustible Haydn; through him it seeks to be united once again with someone. Through continual application you will receive *Mozart's spirit from Haydn's hands*.[19]

The paths of Beethoven and Haydn had already crossed on two occasions. In December 1790 Haydn travelled from Vienna to London in the company of the impresario Johann Peter Salomon, and on their way the two musicians stopped in Bonn, where, on Christmas Day, one of Haydn's Masses was performed in his presence. The conductor is likely to have been the *Hofkapellmeister*, Andrea Luchesi, and Beethoven was among the orchestral players. On his way back from London in the summer of 1792, Haydn again stayed in Bonn. According to Franz Wegeler the electoral orchestra entertained him on this occasion with a breakfast in Godesberg, near Bonn, and Beethoven took the opportunity of showing him a cantata he had composed. Beethoven, claims Wegeler, was encouraged to pursue his studies by the particular heed Haydn paid to the piece.[20]

There has been much anecdotal writing to the effect that Beethoven was dissatisfied with his lessons with Haydn. Among the purported evidence of friction and misunderstandings between the two composers is a claim, made nearly forty years after the event, by the composer Johann Baptist Schenk that he secretly supervised and corrected Beethoven's exercises in strict counterpoint at a time when Haydn was too busy composing new works in preparation for his forthcoming second visit to England to do so satisfactorily himself.[21] Already many years earlier, Ferdinand Ries reported Beethoven as having declared that although he had received some lessons from Haydn he had never learned anything from him.[22] These and several other reports of Haydn's supposedly inadequate teaching of his headstrong young pupil were convincingly debunked in an important article of 1984 by James Webster,[23] and, more recently, in a full-length study by Julia Ronge.[24] No doubt, Beethoven

---

[19] See Braubach and Ladenburger, *Die Stammbücher Beethovens und der Babette Koch*, p.19.

[20] Wegeler/Ries, pp.15–16. The cantata in question could have been either *Auf den Tod Josephs des Zweiten* WoO 87, or *Auf die Erhebung Leopolds des Zweiten zur Kaiserwürde* WoO 88.

[21] Schenk, 'Autobiographische Skizze', pp.75–85.

[22] Wegeler/Ries, p.86.

[23] Webster, 'The Falling-Out between Haydn and Beethoven'.

[24] Ronge, *Beethovens Lehrzeit. Kompositionsstudien bei Joseph Haydn, Johann Georg Albrechtsberger und Antonio Salieri*. See also Ronge's commentaries under the same title in *Beethoven Werke XIII*, vols.1–3 (Bonn, 2014), where Beethoven's exercises with Haydn in two-, three- and four-part counterpoint are reproduced in facsimile and transcription.

will have been frustrated by the fact that his long-cherished ambition to study with Mozart had come to nothing, but leaving aside the counterpoint exercises carried out under Haydn's not always scrupulous supervision, he will have had ample and valuable opportunity to become acquainted with the music of the great composer during this period. Despite the fact that so many of Beethoven's earliest compositions were modelled on specific pieces by Mozart, his mature style owes a good deal more to Haydn's example than Mozart's, and the dynamic, thrusting nature of Haydn's symphonic style and its economy of means are features of his music that clearly rubbed off on the younger composer. At the same time, it is possible that there was actually a fruitful exchange of ideas between the two men, especially when it came to the expressive possibilities opened up through new and more remote key relationships than had hitherto been exploited – a topic that will be discussed in connection with Beethoven's three piano trios op.1 (see, in particular, pp.48ff.). Beethoven paid tribute to his erstwhile teacher with his op.2 piano sonatas, whose title page bore a straightforward dedication to him, if not the wording Haydn would have liked to see (his students were apparently required to have the legend 'Pupil of Haydn' printed on their early compositions, and most of them did so[25]). Nor is there any firm evidence of ill-will between the composers. On the contrary, Beethoven played a concerto – probably an early version of his B flat Concerto op.19 – at a concert given by Haydn in the small hall of the Redoutensäle on 18 December 1795, when the programme also included the Viennese premieres of three of Haydn's 'London' symphonies;[26] and barely more than a fortnight later, at a benefit concert for the singer Maria Bolla in the same venue, the handbill informs us that not only did Haydn conduct his own music, but 'Il Sigre. Bethofen suonerà un Concerto sul Pianoforte'.[27] Moreover, as we shall see, the second in Beethoven's pair of piano trios op.70, composed in the year in which Haydn died, seems to pay affectionate tribute to his former teacher, and to his 'Drum Roll' Symphony no.103, in particular.

---

[25] See Wegeler/Ries, p.86.
[26] *Wiener Zeitung* no.100, 16 December 1795, p.3623, col.2.
[27] See Landon, *Haydn: The Years of 'The Creation'*, p.93.

3
The Three Piano Trios Op.1

The compositional history of the three op.1 piano trios has been the subject of much debate. It was Ferdinand Ries who set the cat among the pigeons, by relating that the works had been tried out in Haydn's presence at a soirée given by Prince Lichnowsky, to whom they were dedicated.

> Most artists and music lovers were invited, especially Haydn, for whose judgement everyone was eager. The trios were played and immediately made a great stir. Haydn, too, said many nice things about them, but advised Beethoven not to publish the third, in C minor. This greatly astonished Beethoven, as he regarded it as the best, just as today it is the favourite and the one that creates the greatest effect. Therefore this remark of Haydn's made a bad impression on Beethoven and left him with the idea: Haydn was envious and jealous, and bore him no good will. I must admit that when Beethoven told me this I gave it little credence. I therefore took the opportunity of asking Haydn himself about it. But his answer confirmed Beethoven's statement, inasmuch as he said he did not think that this trio would be as quickly and easily understood, and as favourably accepted by the public.[1]

For a long time, Ries's anecdote was unquestioningly accepted – not least by Alexander Wheelock Thayer, who advanced the theory that the trios had originated during the composer's Bonn years, and had been radically after Haydn had left Vienna for his second visit to London.[2] On the occasion described by Ries, explained Thayer, the trios had been heard in a preliminary form. The accuracy of Ries's testimony was, however, challenged by Gustav Nottebohm, who argued convincingly that the surviving sketches for at least the last two movements of the G major Trio op.1 no.2 must date from 1794, since they are interspersed with studies for two- and three-part fugues clearly made under the supervision of Johann Georg Albrechtsberger, who had begun to give Beethoven lessons in counterpoint in that year.[3] Haydn arrived in London on 5 February 1794, and by the time he returned to Vienna in September of the following year Beethoven's trios had already appeared in print. On the face of it, it seems impossible that Haydn could have heard the C minor trio, let alone have been in a position to advise against its publication. Serious doubts about the incident as described by Ries had already been expressed by the much less scrupulous Schindler:

---

[1] Wegeler/Ries, p.74.
[2] Thayer/Forbes, p.165.
[3] See Nottebohm, *Zweite Beethoveniana*, pp.27–8.

From the history of Haydn's life it is known that during the years 1794 and 1795 he lived almost entirely in England. His absence from Vienna accords neither with the publication date of these trios, nor with the remark attributed to him. However, if Haydn, in answer to the still very young Ries, had really explained in his remark, as the latter quotes him, that 'he did not believe this trio would be so easily understood and favourably received by the public', then this misguided interpretation can be dismissed. Perhaps, however, some hesitation over Haydn's explanation may be allowed those who know his own trios. For my part, I place this incident among the long series of misunderstandings, of which there were unfortunately too many in Beethoven's life.[4]

Since Ries's reminiscences are generally a good deal more reliable than those of Schindler, one would be loath to dismiss his report as a pure fabrication, particularly as he is so insistent about its central point. All the same, it has to be remembered that the story as it reached him was already at one stage removed, and that he did not actually set it down until more than three decades later. By the time Ries arrived in Vienna to begin his studies with Beethoven, in the autumn of 1801, eight years had elapsed since the alleged incident took place. Ries was, moreover, still only seventeen years old, so we may wonder what form his conversation with the elderly and increasingly frail Haydn can have taken. It is doubtful in any case that Haydn would have had a clear recollection of the event, even if something like it did take place, and his confirmatory remark to Ries, to the effect that he did not think the C minor trio would find as much favour as its two companion-works, has prompted more than one commentator to suggest that he could have proffered his advice to Beethoven *post facto*, and hinted to him that he would have been better advised to have withheld publication of the C minor work.[5] In view of the success all three works seem to have achieved in a remarkably short space of time, such advice would have been at best superfluous.

Haydn's high regard of Beethoven's talent is shown by a letter of 23 November 1793 to the Elector Maximilian Franz in Bonn, in which he enclosed a number of Beethoven's manuscripts as evidence of the progress his pupil was making. 'Connoisseurs and non-connoisseurs alike would have to allow from an unbiased examination of the present pieces that in time B[eethoven] will assume the position of one of the greatest composers in Europe,' Haydn declared, 'and I shall be proud to be able to call myself his teacher. My only wish is that he may stay with me for a considerable time to come.'[6]

For his pains, Haydn received a firm rebuke from the Elector, who pointed out that with the exception of a single fugue, all the pieces he received from Haydn had in fact been written and performed in Bonn before Beethoven left the city. At the same time that Haydn sent his letter, Beethoven also wrote to Maximilian Franz,

---

4 Schindler, vol.1, p.54.
5 See Johnson/Fischhof, vol.1, pp.311–12, and Landon, *Haydn: The Years of 'The Creation'*, pp.61–3. Landon goes so far as to suggest that Ries confused the op.1 trios with the piano sonatas op.2, which Beethoven did play at Prince Lichnowsky's palace in Haydn's presence shortly after the latter's return from London.
6 BGA no.13; LTB no.16.

declaring: 'I have used all my mental powers in the common pursuit of music this year in order to be in a position in the coming year to be able to send to Your Electoral Highness something which more nearly approaches your kindness to me and your nobility than that which was sent to Your Electoral Highness by Herr Heiden.'[7]

Beethoven, no doubt, was acutely aware of the fact that the pieces Haydn sent to the Elector were apprentice works (almost all of them are lost), but it is inconceivable that he would knowingly have placed his teacher in the embarrassing position of having submitted music that had already been heard in Bonn in the same form. Leaving aside the question of whether Maximilian Franz was qualified to judge the artistic value of the package he received (he was, however, a passionately keen music-lover, and since 1787 he had been receiving lessons in harmony from Beethoven's teacher in Bonn, Christian Gottlob Neefe[8]), we must assume that at the very least the pieces must have been significantly revised and improved under Haydn's tutelage. It is clear, too, from Beethoven's letter that he was already planning what he considered to be important new works: almost certainly the first of the op.1 trios, and perhaps also the op.16 Quintet for piano and wind. That the gestation period of the op.1 trios was long may be conjectured from the fact that they were evidently tried out in musical circles for quite some time before they reached their definitive form. Franz Gerhard Wegeler recounts having been present at a private performance of the G major Trio op.1 no.2 when the cellist Anton Kraft pointed out to the composer that its finale could advantageously be renotated in 2/4 time.[9] The accuracy of Wegeler's memory is borne out by Beethoven's sketches, almost all of which are in 4/4, and in note-values twice as long as their eventual form. It is true that the performance in question cannot have taken place before October 1794, since prior to that time Wegeler had been living in Bonn, but there is no reason to assume that he had witnessed the work's first airing.

It is in any case unlikely that Beethoven would have advertised for subscribers to the original edition of the trios, as he did in May 1795, without first having ensured that the works had become well known to Vienna's musical cognoscenti. As it is, the *Liste de Souscripteurs* which occupies the first two pages of the published piano part includes most of the prominent members of the Austrian aristocracy of the day. Many of the names are closely associated with Haydn: Prince Nikolaus and Countess Josephine Esterházy; Count Anton Apponyi, whose name appears on the title page of Haydn's string quartets opp.71 and 74; Count Joseph Erdödy, the dedicatee of the op.76 quartets; Prince Franz Joseph Lobkowitz, to whom the two op.77 quartets were inscribed; and Baron van Swieten, who was to provide the libretti for *The Creation* and *The Seasons*. It is doubtful that Beethoven could have amassed such an impressive list of subscribers to his official op.1 without Haydn's help.

The question of the accuracy of Ferdinand Ries's testimony regarding the op.1 trios is of much more than purely academic interest. If Haydn had been able to hear the works – or at least to see a preliminary version of them – prior to his departure

---

7   BGA no.12; Anderson no.8.
8   See Blindow, *Bernhard Romberg*, p.31.
9   Wegeler/Ries, p.32.

for London, then the possibility that there could have been an exchange of ideas between the two composers might arise. Few sketches for the first of Beethoven's trios survive, and it is reasonable to suppose that the piece is somewhat earlier in origin than its companions. It is by no means unlikely that Haydn would have been able to become acquainted with it in the summer of 1793. Its *Presto* finale contains passages of almost 'gypsy-style' exuberance which might well have appealed to the older composer. Haydn had, indeed, long been fascinated by the music of the Roma people: we have only to think of the famous 'Rondo, in the Gipsies stile' from the Piano Trio H.XV.25, the 'Menuetto alla zingarese' from the D major String Quartet op.20 no.4, or the 'Rondo all'Ungherese' of the Piano Concerto H.XVIII.11 in the same key. More remarkable, however, is the fact that Haydn's piano trio shares its unusual key-scheme with the middle work in Beethoven's op.1 series: both are in G major, and each has a serene slow movement in a radiant E major. In both cases the remoteness of the slow movement's key vis-à-vis the tonality of the work as a whole has the effect of lifting the music onto a higher expressive plane.

From the autobiographical sketches of the composer and teacher Johann Baptist Schenk we learn that Beethoven spent the latter half of 1793 with Haydn at the Esterházy palace in Eisenstadt.[10] This was the period when Haydn was composing his string quartets opp.71 and 74, as well as the first works in the latter half of the series of 'London' symphonies. The Symphony no.99 was almost certainly written in its entirety at this time, and Haydn probably also began work on its two successors. Beethoven appears to have composed little music in 1793, turning his attention instead to the revision of earlier pieces, among them the radical recasting of the Wind Octet op.103 as a string quintet (op.4). This compositional inactivity at precisely the time when Beethoven was in close contact with the greatest composer of the day is surprising, and might lead us to suspect that he must at the very least have been turning over in his mind the remaining two works in his series of piano trios. Even if sketches for the G major middle work can confidently be ascribed to the year 1794, it is clear that by no means all of Beethoven's preparatory work on the trios has survived. In the case of the C minor work we have precious few sketches, and none at all for its slow movement, which, on stylistic grounds, could well have been composed some time before the remaining movements. Moreover, such preliminary ideas for the main subjects of the finale as have come down to us are comparatively primitive, and are again likely to be of considerably earlier origin than any sustained work on the trio itself.[11]

Douglas Johnson has cited the lack of sketches for the G major trio's slow introduction as evidence that these opening pages may have been a late inspiration,[12] but the Allegro's off-tonic beginning would be inconceivable without the presence of an introduction anchored firmly in G major. It is true that two of Beethoven's

---

[10] See Schenk, 'Autobiographische Skizze', pp.75ff, and Landon, *Haydn in England*, pp.217–19. Schenk's sketches were, however, not written until 1830, and doubts have been raised as to their reliability (cf. Webster, 'The Falling-Out between Haydn and Beethoven', pp.10–14). Schenk erroneously gives the year of Beethoven's Eisenstadt visit as 1792.

[11] See Johnson/Fischhof, vol.1, pp.312–13.

[12] *Ibid.*, vol.1, p.307.

subsequent works in the tonality of G – the Cello Sonata op.5 no.2 and the Fourth Piano Concerto – contain an Allegro that sets off without any preamble as though it was to be in C major, but in each case the movement in question is the finale. Beethoven's introduction to the G major trio is the most overtly Haydnesque passage he had written up to its time, and the manner in which it foreshadows the main subject of the Allegro is an idea he could have learned from the older composer's Symphony no.90, of 1788, or the Symphony no.98, composed in 1792. And just as the initial phrase of the C major Symphony no.97, dating from the latter year, is subsequently transformed in the Allegro into a closing subject of melting beauty, so the off-tonic violin motif presented in the third and fourth bars of Beethoven's slow introduction is firmly resolved in the home key in the closing moments of the Allegro's recapitulation.

Ex. 3.1.
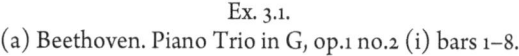
(a) Beethoven. Piano Trio in G, op.1 no.2 (i) bars 1–8.

(b) Beethoven. Piano Trio in G, op.1 no.2 (i) bars 365–8.

That Beethoven was assimilating Haydn's symphonic style in the years 1793–4 is not in doubt, and it was during the period of his study with the elder composer that he made a copy in score of his E flat String Quartet op.20 no.1. It is difficult to trace any direct influence of that particular quartet on Beethoven,[13] but he will almost certainly have studied the remaining works from Haydn's series, and the G minor Quartet op.20 no.3 offers a striking anticipation of one of the most memorable moments from Beethoven's C minor Trio op.1 no.3. Just as Haydn concludes his quartet with a composed fade-out in the major (its effect is surely weakened if the finale's second-half repeat is observed), so Beethoven allows his finale to dissolve in a chain of C major scales that fade away into the distance.

Ex. 3.2.
(a) Haydn. String Quartet in G minor, op.20 no.3 (iv) bars 98–104.

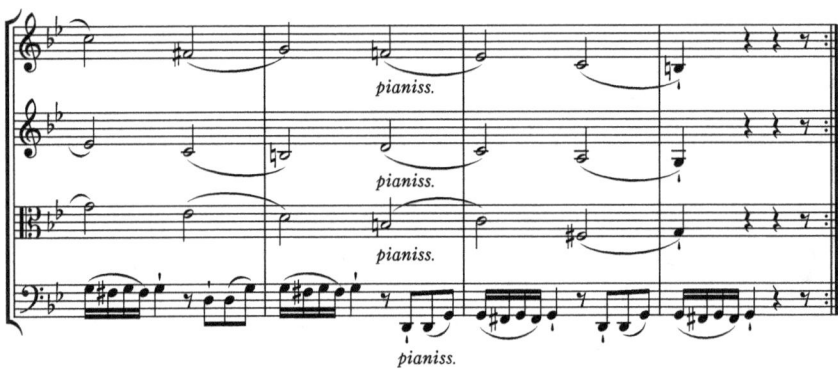

---

[13] Elaine Sisman ('The Spirit of Mozart from Haydn's Hands', pp.52–3) has, however, drawn a parallel between the theme of Haydn's last movement and that of the finale of Beethoven's string trio in the same key, op.3, a work whose overall plan is nevertheless clearly modelled on that of Mozart's string trio Divertimento K.563.

Ex. 3.2.
(b) Beethoven. Piano Trio in C minor, op.1 no.3 (iv) bars 406–20.

Two works in C minor by Mozart which Beethoven is known to have admired – the Piano Concerto K.491 and the Piano Sonata K.457 – contain a movement that dies away *pianissimo* in an atmosphere of subdued tension, though the movement in question in each case is not the finale, but the opening Allegro.[14] Moreover, the music remains in the minor until the close.[15] Beethoven was pleased enough with

---

[14] The first movement of Haydn's Quartet in C minor op.17 no.4 ends in similar fashion.

[15] While Mozart's D minor works invariably come to rest in the major (the Requiem K.626 and the Fantasy for piano K.397 would surely have followed the examples of *Don Giovanni* and the string quartets K.173 and K.421 had Mozart completed them), those in C minor almost as consistently remain in the minor until the bitter end. The notable exception to the C minor rule is the Wind Serenade K.388, whose almost manically

the evanescent ending of his C minor piano trio to invoke the effect in his next two works in the same key: the Piano Sonata op.10 no.1 and the String Trio op.9 no.3.

Of scarcely less relevance to the last of Beethoven's op.1 piano trios is Haydn's C minor Symphony no.95 – the only member of the twelve 'London' symphonies to do without a slow introduction, and a work that was first performed in Vienna just a few months after Beethoven arrived there.[16] Haydn's opening Allegro begins with a forceful jagged motif given out by the full orchestra, followed after a silence by a subdued, more conjunct idea on the strings. The effect is not dissimilar from that of the juxtaposition of opposites presented at the start of the finale in Beethoven's trio op.1 no.3.[17]

Whether the strikingly unconventional sequence of keys in the G major second work of Beethoven's op.1 series was the result of his having been able to study Haydn's music of the time, or whether Haydn had already seen a preliminary version of Beethoven's trio before his departure for London, must remain an open question.[18] It is tempting to adopt a stance midway between those of Hermann Deiters (in his revision of Thayer's Beethoven biography) and Nottebohm, and to suggest that Beethoven could indeed have done some work on the second and third trios of his series at some stage in 1793 before elaborating his ideas the following year – though, of course, the performance of the entire triptych to which Ferdinand Ries referred could not have taken place before Haydn's departure.

The long gestation period of Beethoven's op.1 trios might prompt us to look anew at the marked change that came over Haydn's music in the crucial year of 1793. Not the least significant manifestation of that change is the increasingly frequent use of mediant key relationships between successive movements from this time onwards. Previously, he had tended to venture no further than Mozart in his choice of key for the slow movement of a major-mode work: in both composers the new key would more often than not be the subdominant or the dominant.[19] Haydn, indeed, often

---

cheerful conclusion is Mozart's only concession to the function of occasional music that this otherwise austere work was ostensibly meant to fulfil.

[16] In Haydn's day the presence of a sombre introduction prefacing a minor-mode symphony, where the weight and seriousness of the opening movement were already assured through its choice of key, would have been regarded as gilding the lily. Not until Schubert's 'Tragic' and Mendelssohn's 'Scottish' symphonies did a great composer begin a minor-mode work of the kind with a slow introduction. Mendelssohn's example was followed by Schumann in his D minor Symphony; and by Brahms, whose anxiety to lend gravitas to his first essay in the genre led him to provide not just its first movement, but also its finale with a weighty slow introduction. However, Beethoven's symphonic ambitions in his early chamber works are indicated by the presence of a substantial slow introduction to the G minor Cello Sonata op.5 no.2.

[17] This and other parallels between the two works have been drawn by Douglas Johnson: '1794–1795: Decisive Years in Beethoven's Early Development', pp.18–22.

[18] Douglas Johnson, however, is firmly of the opinion that the physical evidence of the surviving sketches 'indicates beyond a reasonable doubt that Nos.2 and 3 were conceived and completely worked out, not merely revised, in 1794–95' (Johnson/Fischhof, vol.2, p.311).

[19] Haydn's A flat Trio H.XV.14, of 1790, with its slow movement in E major (not to speak of an extended B major passage at the centre of its opening Allegro) furnishes an

preferred to dispense with any change in tonality between movements, and to make do instead with a switch in mode – from major to minor, or vice versa – as a substitute means of providing contrast. Schemes of this kind were largely eschewed by Mozart,[20] though Beethoven took them up with enthusiasm: such works as the F minor Piano Sonata op.2 no.1, the two D major sonatas op.10 no.3 and op.28, or the E minor 'Razumovsky' String Quartet op.59 no.2 have all four movements in the same tonality.

Haydn's sudden fascination in 1793 with the new expressive world opened up by the use of mediant keys is indeed striking. The trio of the minuet in the C major String Quartet op.74 no.1 comes floating in to breathtaking effect in A major, and in the G minor 'Rider' Quartet from the same series the first movement, whose closing pages are in the major, is followed by a profound *Largo assai* in E major. The E flat Symphony no.99, with its slow movement in G major and the trio of its minuet in C major, finds Haydn for the first time in a work of its kind exploiting mediant keys, while among the great piano trios written between 1793 and 1795, the B flat major H.XV.20 has its slow movement in G major, as does the E flat Trio H.XV.22. We know that Beethoven was familiar with the symphony, since he copied out a passage from the development section of its finale.

Beethoven was to retain a liking for such schemes throughout his life – indeed, in his works of the 1790s mediant tonal relationships between successive movements are almost as common as more traditional key juxtapositions. The sequence of keys found in the op.1 no.2 Piano Trio is replicated in the G major String Trio op.9 no.1, while the last of the op.2 piano sonatas, in C major, again has its slow movement in E major. The op.7 Piano Sonata and the Violin Sonata op.12 no.3, both in E flat, have a slow movement in C major – while the String Quartet op.18 no.3 and the C major Piano Concerto op.15 have their slow movement in the flat submediant. (Beethoven seems at one stage even to have contemplated replacing the E flat major Adagio of the B flat Piano Concerto no.2 with a similar piece in D major.[21]) Mediant key relationships occur again in the G major violin sonatas op.30 no.3 and op.96 (both of which have a second movement in E flat), as well as in the Piano Trio op.70 no.2, and the 'Archduke' op.97.

Beethoven was eventually to carry the use of such tonal schemes further, by effectively telescoping their use within a single sonata design. With the C major String Quintet op.29 and the first of the three piano sonatas op.31, both of them composed

---

important exception. However, the keys involved, with the tonic note of the first being the enharmonic equivalent of the mediant of the second, are less radically distant from each other than is the juxtaposition found in Beethoven's op.1 no.2, where there is no such pivotal common note.

[20] Among Mozart's mature works which exceptionally use monotonal key sequences are the so-called 'Alla Turca' Sonata K.331 (where the change from major to minor quite exceptionally occurs in the finale), the F major Violin Sonata K.547 (though there must be some doubt as to whether the concluding set of variations was intended to form part of the same work at all), and two works having all their movements in E flat – the Serenade for winds K.375, and the Sinfonia concertante K.297b for oboe, clarinet, bassoon, horn and orchestra. This last work is, however, of very doubtful authenticity.

[21] See Johnson/Fischhof, vol.1, p.14.

in 1801, Beethoven began to experiment with the notion of introducing mediant keys as a substitute for the traditional dominant at the second-subject stage of the sonata-form exposition. The quintet's opening movement has its second group in the submediant (A major), and in the G major Sonata op.31 no.1 the second group sets out in B major, with the remainder of the exposition thereafter wavering continually between B major and minor. (See Ex. 2.10(b) on p.34.) And if the quintet's recapitulation places its second group in the tonic from the outset, the sonata maintains the concept of the mediant key at this late stage by allowing the second subject momentarily to be heard in E major, as a form of symmetrically related resolution of the exposition's B major, before the home key is reasserted by means of an additional statement in the tonic.

Some two years later Beethoven used a similar scheme for the chorale-like second subject in the opening movement of the the C major 'Waldstein' Sonata op.53: the subject appears in E major in the exposition, and is briefly heard in A major during the course of the recapitulation. Here, to an even greater extent than previously, the mediant key functions as a form of enhanced dominant, lending the music an expressive quality that would not otherwise have been achieved, for all the built-in contrast of sonority and articulation between the two subjects.

The use of a mediant second group was carried to an extreme in the finale of the E flat Piano Trio op.70 no.2, where the exposition's G major second group finds its parallel in the recapitulation in the sound of C major. This time, however, the recapitulation remains in that 'foreign' key, adhering closely to the pattern of the exposition right through to its close. This unprecedented procedure necessitates an expansion of enormous proportions, in which the second group is heard again in the tonic, in order to restore the tonal balance.[22] Beethoven appears to have been well aware of the radical nature of this particular piece: in his subsequent works invoking a second group in the submediant, he almost invariably stabilised the final stage of the movement by recapitulating that second group in the tonic from the outset. Such a plan is to be found in both the 'Archduke' Trio and the 'Hammerklavier' Sonata. The single significant exception among Beethoven's late works is the opening movement of the B flat String Quartet op.130, where the initial theme of the G flat major second group is recapitulated in D flat, before the remainder of the movement unfolds in the tonic. However, there is also the unique case of the Quartet in A minor op.132, whose first movement features a recapitulation in the dominant minor which allows Beethoven to maintain the same key relationship between the two main subjects as in the exposition, with the second subject placed in the submediant. A second recapitulation subsequently has both subjects appearing in the tonic.

Beethoven's innovatory use of mediant keys in place of the traditional dominant may have been an outcome of his earlier predilection for exploiting such keys in order to provide a fleeting moment of heightened expressiveness – or, perhaps more often, wayward humour – in the closing moments of some of his finales: the rondo from the C major Piano Sonata op.2 no.3, for instance, whose theme is briefly heard in A major and minor immediately prior to the work's peremptory conclusion; or

---

[22] See p.285ff.

the similarly late appearance in G major, and in an ethereally unsyncopated transformation, of the rondo theme in the B flat Piano Concerto op.19. Nor was Beethoven averse to using rather more remote tonalities in order to achieve a similar effect: the finale of the E flat Piano Sonata op.7 features an excursion into E major shortly before its close – an inspiration that echoes the more exuberant E major interpolation in the finale of the piano trio in the same key, op.1 no.1. Some of Haydn's piano trios of the mid-1790s exploit similarly distant keys with obvious relish, though they do so more often than not within the more traditionally unstable development section. The finale of the E flat Trio H.XV.22 includes an appearance of its first subject in E major, while the C major Trio H.XV.27 contains a startling plunge into B minor shortly before its close – an event that recalls the passage in that key in the coda of Beethoven's C minor Trio op.1 no.3.

Besides such unusual key relationships, another possible instance of fruitful cross-exchange between the two composers – and one that is rather more confidently identifiable as having flowed from Beethoven to Haydn – lies in the dynamic new form of the scherzo. It is true that all but the first of Haydn's six string quartets op.33, of 1781, contain a movement described as a scherzo, and the novel designation may have been one of the reasons why Haydn felt he could legitimately declare the quartets to have been written 'in a quite new special manner' (*auf eine ganz neue besondere Art*). His claim, set forth in letters addressed to potential subscribers to the first edition, has often been dismissed as little more than a piece of salesmanship; and certainly, if we seek to justify it, that justification will be found not so much in the quartets' so-called scherzos, which sometimes contain little to distinguish them from minuets (notably so in the C major and B flat quartets, nos.3 and 4), as in their establishing a form of contrapuntally enlivened, conversational texture that was to remain the basis of string quartet writing for more than a hundred years to come.

The scherzo introduced by Beethoven in the first two of his op.1 trios was essentially a new concept. Moreover, the innovation was one that expanded the traditional three-movement plan of chamber music with piano to four movements (Beethoven was to continue the four-movement design, again breaking new ground, in his piano sonatas op.2).[23] Beethoven's new scherzo form was, in turn, to leave a mark on Haydn. The first and last of Haydn's six string quartets op.76, composed in 1797, and the two quartets op.77, of 1799, contain what are to all intents and purposes genuine scherzos, each played *presto* – though Haydn, perhaps no longer feeling the need to advertise the novelty value of his style, paradoxically designated the pieces in question as minuets.

Beethoven's op.1 piano trios, then, find him attempting to match the grandeur of Haydn's symphonic style within a genre that was traditionally associated with relatively unambitious domestic music-making. The composer proudly announced their forthcoming appearance with a notice placed in the *Wiener Zeitung*:

Subscription for Ludwig van Beethoven's 3 grand trios for pianoforte, violin and bass, which will appear within 6 weeks engraved by Artaria, and which, as previously announced, will be purchasable from the composer on returning the [subscription]

---

[23] An early keyboard sonata by Haydn (H.XVI.6) has four movements, with the minuet preceding the slow movement, though the work's dimensions are otherwise small.

bill. The price of a complete copy is 1 ducat. The names of subscribers will be printed at the beginning, and they will have the advantage that this work will only be available to others two months later, and perhaps only at a higher price.[24]

Artaria listed the trios in the same newspaper on 21 and 24 October 1795, in an advertisement largely occupied with the news of the availability of three eagerly awaited new quartets by Haydn (op.71). Beethoven's trios appeared at the head of an appended list which included newly published works by Pleyel, Clementi, Süssmayr and Mozart (the vocal score of *La Clemenza di Tito*). By the following March, Beethoven's three piano sonatas op.2 were ready to be issued. The op.1 trios had achieved such success in the intervening six months that Artaria felt justified in giving pride of place in his new advertisement to Beethoven:

> Since the previous work of this composer, the three piano trios op.1 that are already in the hands of the public, has been received with so much applause, one expects the same from the present works – the more so since besides the value of the composition, one can see from them not only the strength that Herr v. Beethoven possesses as a pianist, but also the sensitivity [*Delikatesse*] with which he knows how to handle this instrument.

Even allowing for an inevitable element of publisher's hype in Artaria's advertisement, it is not hard to imagine the impression that Beethoven's trios must have made on the Viennese public of the day. All three are virtuoso works written on an unprecedentedly ambitious scale, with their outer movements having an unusually elaborate coda which in some cases is almost equal in length to the development section. Early listeners to the op.1 trios must have been struck, too, by the boldness of such strokes as the already mentioned fade-out at the end of the C minor work, the startling appearance shortly before the close in the E flat and C minor trios of the first subject in a very remote key, and the presence in the G major work of a slow movement whose breadth and serenity considerably surpass anything previously written for a piece of the kind. The violence of the dynamic contrasts used by Beethoven in these works, with *fortissimo* and *pianissimo* frequently placed in direct juxtaposition, is also of a degree seldom heard before.[25]

If we consider that the first of the trios is likely to be earlier in origin than its two successors, its assurance and fluency represent a remarkable advance over anything Beethoven had previously composed. The closely worked motivic structure, the constant changes in tone colour as thematic material is handed from one player to the next in midstream, the impudent wit of the finale – all these features herald the arrival of a composer who already at this early stage has thoroughly mastered the medium, and is ready to impose his own strong personality on it.

---

[24] *Wiener Zeitung*, 9 May 1795, pp.1343–4.

[25] What is probably the only direct confrontation of these two dynamic extremes in Mozart occurs in the development section of the opening movement in the A minor Piano Sonata K.310. Haydn has *pianissimo* followed by *fortissimo* for the famous surprise in the second movement of the Symphony no.94, and an earlier joke in the finale of Symphony no.90 has a *fortissimo* false ending followed, after a pause of four-and-a-half bars, by a *pianissimo* re-entry. A more dramatic use of the same dynamics is found at the explosion of C major light in the introduction to *The Creation*, but such juxtapositions are otherwise rare in the music of the period.

The opening bars of op.1 no.1, exerting as they do a strong pull towards the region of the subdominant, present a harmonic outline of a kind to be found on occasion at the start of a work by Mozart, though Mozart never fails to anchor the resulting unstable theme over a repeated tonic pedal. The beginnings of the A major Piano Concerto K.488, the D major String Quartet K.575, the Piano Quartet K.493 and the F major Piano Sonata K.332 provide familiar examples. Beethoven's *trouvaille* at the start of his op.1 no.1 trio lies in lending the main theme's initial rising arpeggio figure an entirely different aspect when it is repeated in identical form two bars later: as a consequence of the flattened seventh that has preceded it at the start of the third bar, the arpeggio figure is heard in a new harmonic context, and in its now transitional function it demands to be resolved. The resolution duly arrives with the subdominant harmony of the fifth bar, but it is not until bar 9 that the instability of the opening paragraph is counteracted by a tonic cadence.

Ex. 3.3. Beethoven. Piano Trio in E flat, op.1 no.1 (i) bars 1–21.

—(continued)

Ex. 3.3—continued

Although the initial subject cadences firmly into the tonic on two further occasions (bars 11 and 13), its more expansive continuation takes the music through the same harmonic progression twice more, now at last underpinned by a tonic pedal on the piano. (A model behind this continuation may perhaps be found in the opening bars of Mozart's Piano Quartet K.493, which present a similar procedure.) The subdominant leanings of Beethoven's beginning have repercussions later in the movement – not least in an extended passage of the development section set firmly in A flat major.

Having played his trump card of presenting the melodically identical rising arpeggio in its two different harmonic contexts at the beginning of the work, Beethoven does not repeat the idea in the same form in the recapitulation. Instead, he forgoes the previous ambiguity by having the second appearance of the arpeggio transferred to the violin, shadowed a third higher by the piano, so that its topmost note now falls on the flattened seventh, D flat. The recapitulation departs from the pattern of the exposition in more radical ways, too. The proportions of the first group are reduced to approximately two-thirds of their previous length, and the second group is correspondingly enlarged by means of a lengthy interpolation offering further development of both principal subjects, before the music eventually rejoins its former course at the reappearance of the closing theme, with its syncopated left-hand piano part (bar 280). The passage in question is launched with a firm root-position tonic chord – a feature that enhances the ambiguity of its function as part interpolation within the recapitulation, and part coda. There is a sense, too, in which the passage assumes the character of a cadenza, and the feeling is strengthened by the cadential trill that precedes the reprise of the closing theme. However we choose to construe it (and the long-delayed reprise of the closing theme would tend to hinder its interpretation as a straightforward coda), the moment is one that contributes significantly to the breadth of the piece as a whole.

The harmonic outline of the Allegro's first subject is echoed in the first and fifth bars of the slow movement's theme. Moreover, the Adagio's upbeat phrase is clearly borrowed from the violin figure that marks the prolongation of the opening movement's subject (see Ex. 3.3, bar 10), and further unity between the two pieces is assured by the reappearance of the repeated-note rhythm of the Allegro's second and third bars in the first full bar of the Adagio's melody.

Ex. 3.4. Beethoven. Piano Trio in E flat, op.1 no.1 (ii) bars 1–8.

Having given the cello little melodic independence in the opening movement, Beethoven makes amends by allowing it to set the first episode of the slow movement in motion. The episode shows Beethoven already at this stage weaving a piano trio texture with considerable subtlety, with the two stringed instruments in invertible counterpoint and the arpeggio-like melodic shape of the first of their two strands effortlessly absorbed into the piano's semiquaver accompaniment:

Ex. 3.5. Beethoven. Piano Trio in E flat, op.1 no.1 (ii) bars 21–9.

If the inclusion of a scherzo or minuet was the most striking structural innovation of the op.1 trios,[26] Beethoven made sure that in the first work of the series the interpolated movement would make maximum effect: its long upbeat phrase for the two string players alone gives the impression of a piece that is to be in the key of F minor. Such a prolonged off-tonic beginning would have been altogether alien to Mozart, though it is a gesture Haydn may well have appreciated. (The minuet of Haydn's F major Quartet op.50 no.5, for instance, similarly begins with a lengthy unharmonised upbeat phrase, though it is centred around the dominant, rather than

[26] The heading of the third movement in op.1 no.1 was originally *Menuetto quasi Allegro assai*, and that designation still stands in the violin part of Artaria's first edition. Beethoven must have had a change of heart while the work was already being engraved: the cello and piano parts have the familiar *Scherzo. Allegro assai*, but remnants of a title change are visible on the plates. See Del Mar, Critical Commentary to Beethoven, Trios op.1, p.138.

the supertonic.) Only with the entry of the piano in the sixth bar is the music is pulled towards the dominant, B flat, and not until bar 15 is the tonic chord of E flat sounded at all.

The entire scherzo is built out of the two thematic fragments which constitute its opening upbeat phrase: an inverted mordent figure incorporating a chirping acciaccatura, and a sinuous idea in longer notes which likewise revolves around the interval of the minor second.

Ex. 3.6. Beethoven. Piano Trio in E flat, op.1 no.1 (iii) bars 1–16.

The two strongly differentiated components of the phrase find common ground in the second half of the piece, where the violin's initial acciaccatura phrase is given out no fewer than five times by the pianist, before a series of repeated staccato piano notes traces the outline of the smooth motif of bars 2–5:

Ex. 3.7. Beethoven. Piano Trio in E flat, op.1 no.1 (iii) bars 53–65.

The trio section, played *pianissimo* and *legato* throughout, affords strong contrast to the crisp articulation of the scherzo itself, but perhaps the movement's most surprising event is its inclusion of a coda following the da capo. It is one that brings the piece to a hesitant close while at the same time serving to resolve the harmonic instability of the movement's initial bars. If the start of the scherzo's second half had provided a hint of the latent contrapuntal possibilities of those opening bars, the coda momentarily treats the same figure in a sort of triple canon. (It bears a striking similarity to the contrapuntal 'tag' exploited during the opening stage of the development section in the first movement of op.1 no.2.)

Beethoven's procedure of providing a coda to the essentially closed form of the scherzo and trio is one that is seldom, if ever, found in Haydn, though the minuet movements in several of his later string quartets and symphonies have a coda to their trio that acts as a modulatory link to the reprise of the minuet. Beethoven's model could have been the minuet from Mozart's 'Kegelstatt' Trio K.498, where, uniquely for him, there is not only a link to the da capo, but also a substantial coda. Beethoven was to write a subdued coda again for the scherzo of op.1 no.2, as well as for those of the Piano Sonata op.2 no.3 and the String Trio op.9 no.3.

The finale, as in the G major and C minor trios, is not a rondo, but a sonata design – an indication of the ambitious nature of these early works which represented Beethoven's official debut in the dual roles of composer and pianist. The reiterated leaps of its curiously hesitant main theme are notated and phrased across the bar line, though the theme itself is clearly related to the opening subject of the first movement, whose rising arpeggio it inverts. The wit of the piece arises largely from the pianist's continual overshooting of the octave: the wide ascending leaps of a tenth would lie more comfortably on the violin – which, however, answers them with a suavely conjunct melody; and the joke is carried a stage further in the coda, where the same keyboard leaps are mockingly echoed by the violin playing minor seconds, the smallest of melodic intervals.

The second subject is of deliberate banality, though it does not, perhaps, achieve the sublime tongue-in-cheek quality of some of Mozart's closing themes (those, for instance, in the finale of the 'Jupiter' Symphony and the G major String Quartet K.387, where the simplicity of the tune in question is highlighted by the contrapuntal intensity of the material that surrounds it). The basic tonic/dominant harmony of Beethoven's theme is thrown mercilessly into relief by the chromaticism of the passage that follows, where the pianist appears to be attempting to imitate violin portamentos.

An actual portamento on the two stringed instruments is what seems to be called for in the coda. Here, the pianist's leaps suffer an enharmonic change that takes the music into the remote key of E major, before the violin and cello – helped by a peremptory gesture from the pianist – slide back, *sul una corda*, towards the 'correct' key of E flat, as though to show that the entire interpolation has been some ghastly mistake. (The joke is intensified by the deliberately brash sound of the violin's open D string during the *fortissimo* of bars 358–9.)

Ex. 3.8. Beethoven. Piano Trio in E flat, op.1 no.1 (iv) bars 333–64.

—(continued)

Ex. 3.8—continued

The surprise of this splendidly witty moment is strengthened by the manner in which it fuses the movement's two main subjects, the characteristic leaping tenths being followed not, as we might have expected, by the first subject's continuation, but instead by the second subject. The amalgamation throws into relief the underlying unity of the themes, both of which contain a triadic descent from the fifth degree of the scale. The thematic coherence of the work as a whole is further ensured by the closing bars of both exposition and coda, where the four-note figure from the tail end of the opening movement's first subject and the start of the slow movement makes an emphatic return.

The E major interpolation quoted in Ex. 3.8 above provides the earliest memorable instance of Beethoven's predilection for such tonal surprises at a late stage in his finales. We shall meet with further examples in the C minor Trio op.1 no.3, the Clarinet Trio op.11 and the D major Violin Sonata op.12 no.1. Scarcely less witty is the final page, which sees a continual interplay between leaping tenths and slithering minor seconds, before all such sophisticated high jinks are brushed aside with a gesture of symphonic grandeur.

More expansive than the E flat trio is the G major middle work of the series, which has not only a substantial slow introduction, but also an exceptionally broad slow movement. Beethoven's sketches for the opening Allegro[27] show that the first subject's turn-like figure was rhythmically more impulsive, being notated in demisemiquavers followed by a crotchet rest, rather than the familiar semiquaver version with a quaver rest. The early notational form provides a further reason for feeling confident that the slow introduction was part of the composer's conception of the piece from the outset: in it, the turn figure appears more often than not in demisemiquavers, and Beethoven is likely at first to have copied its rhythmic form over into the start of the main body of the movement – possibly at a stage when its tempo was envisaged as being less quick than the *Allegro vivace* of the final version. (The sketches, one of which is given as Ex. 3.9 below, give no tempo indication.[28])

Ex. 3.9. Beethoven. Piano Trio in G, op.1 no.2 (i), sketch.

No less significant than the rhythmic shape of this draft is the much shorter form of the overall subject in comparison with its final version. What the sketch allows us to see is that following the theme's initial two phrases, Beethoven eventually inserted no fewer than 23 bars before rejoining his preliminary idea at its fifth bar. Douglas Johnson[29] has pointed out that not only does the inserted passage present the subject for the first time firmly in the tonic, at bar 51, but the cello line (doubled by the piano) at its start in bars 33–5 traces a similar outline to that of the *cantus firmus*-like opening bars of the development section (see Ex. 3.10).

Both main elements of the Allegro's theme – the dactylic repeated-note rhythm of its first bar, and the turn-like figure of its second and fourth bars – are anticipated at the start of the slow introduction, where the violin's first thematic entry presents the subject in slow motion and at the pitch at which it will be heard at the start of the Allegro. It is this off-tonic beginning that enables Beethoven to make the end of the introduction overlap with the start of the Allegro. The introduction's concluding ten bars are poised on the dominant of G, the piano giving out a series of ascending phrases each of which culminates on the note C. The C, marked *tenuto*, on which the last of these phrases comes to rest coincides with the start of the Allegro's theme, so that the listener is not able to register the change in tempo until the theme is already under way. The *tenuto* indication on the Allegro's initial note underlines its dual

---

[27] See Johnson/Fischhof, vol.2, p.5.
[28] Nottebohm, *Zweite Beethoveniana*, p.21.
[29] Ibid., vol.1, pp.306–7.

function, and players who make an agogic pause between the introduction and the Allegro merely unpick the seams so carefully sewn by the composer.

Ex. 3.10. Beethoven. Piano Trio in G, op.1 no.2 (i) bars 25–66.

As initially given out by the violin, the Allegro's jaunty second subject offers a strong contrast to the first. However, the subject is taken over by the piano at bar 113 in an ornamented form which clearly incorporates the first subject's turn-like figure, complete with acciaccatura, both in its original form and in inversion.

Ex. 3.11. Beethoven. Piano Trio in G, op.1 no.2 (i) bars 100–21.

The same figure occurs in combination with the *cantus firmus* idea at the start of the development section – a passage that may serve as a reminder that the trio was composed at the time of Beethoven's contrapuntal studies with Haydn and Albrechtsberger, though the nod in their direction, if any such there be, is perhaps given with tongue firmly in cheek. At the same time, the development transforms the main subject's dominant major ninth harmony into the minor.

Ex. 3.12. Beethoven. Piano Trio in G, op.1 no.2 (i) bars 167–78.

Since the *cantus firmus* figure is to all intents and purposes a new idea, Beethoven compensates for its late appearance with a coda presenting the same juxtaposition of material. The coda itself follows the recapitulation's firm full close in the tonic, which sounds as conclusive as could be. Beethoven clearly enjoyed this type of surprise – we have already seen an instance in the Piano Trio WoO 38 – though he was never again to use it quite so effectively as here: the violin's *pianissimo* re-entry following the two *fortissimo* chords which bring the recapitulation to a close is an effect considerably more startling – and witty – than that of the similarly unexpected coda in the opening movement of the Cello Sonata op.5 no.2, the Quintet for piano and wind op.16 or the Clarinet Trio op.11.

The slow movement of op.1 no.2 has an expansiveness and serenity that are remarkable in the work of so young a composer. This is the first of several memorable E major slow movements Beethoven was to write during his early Viennese years, and its atmosphere of profound calm is not surpassed in any of the succeeding examples – those of the C major Piano Sonata op.2 no.3, the String Trio in G op.9 no.1 and the C minor Piano Concerto. Beethoven's achievement in creating so large a structure (it includes a coda that exceeds the exposition in length) is the more remarkable given the relaxed nature of his thematic material.

In view of the absence of preliminary sketches for the piece in the 'Fischhof Miscellany', Douglas Porter Johnson suggests that this movement may have been the last portion of the trio to take shape.[30] The precious few sketches that have survived are found in the 'Kafka' sketchbook (f.69v.). They show Beethoven contemplating a simple triadic main theme in a more agitated dotted rhythm. Such a theme would clearly have lent the movement as a whole greater rhythmic impetus, but at the cost of serenity and spaciousness. It is also apparent that the exposition's tonal plan was to have included an appearance of the first subject in D major. The eventual scheme has the violin's counterstatement of the second subject giving way to a codetta in the trio's home key of G major (bars 35ff.) whose expansiveness and tonal stability allow it to be joined seamlessly to a series of echoes of the movement's opening phrase setting off in the same key. The new passage functions less as a development section than as a transition to the recapitulation occupying scarcely more than a half-dozen bars. The codetta reappears in C major in the recapitulation.

The violin's accompanimental figure in semiquavers during the latter half of the exposition's G major passage (bars 37–8) is to assume thematic importance in the long coda, where it is transferred to the piano (bars 100–1). Significantly, perhaps, that figure is not heard at the parallel point in the recapitulation, where the music takes a new tonal direction, towards A minor. Like the recapitulation itself, the coda is elaborately ornamented in order to preserve the impression of continual growth within a piece whose material is so broad. With its *fortissimo* explosions on the chord of the flat supertonic (F major), the coda provides a dramatic climax, before the music subsides in a *pianissimo* conclusion not dissimilar to that of the *Largo* in the same key from the C minor piano concerto: in each case, a fragment of the main theme is pungently harmonised by means of a diminished seventh chord over a dissonant tonic pedal.

The scherzo begins in a manner no less original than that of the corresponding movement in op.1 no.1. Here, the initial upbeat phrase is given to the cello – surely the first time in the history of the piano trio that a movement had been launched by that instrument on its own. Following as it does an extended piece in E major, the unharmonised D natural with which the scherzo begins is particularly disorientating. The start of the scherzo's second half modulates almost continually, and this no doubt explains why the reprise consists essentially of a vastly expanded affirmation of the home key of G major. Even the horn calls of the first half's conclusion, with their characteristically explosive off-beat accents, are now twice their original length, and are passed from the piano to the violin, with much use of open D and A strings.

Beethoven's first thought for the scherzo's trio was to have a syncopated theme in the tonic minor:[31]

---

[30] Johnson/Fischhof, vol.1, p.307.
[31] *Ibid.*, vol.2, p.7.

Ex. 3.13. Beethoven. Piano Trio in G, op.1 no.2, scherzo, sketch.

His ultimate choice of key for the trio section – the mediant minor (B minor) – is an unusual one, and it echoes the predominance of B minor and E minor at the start of the scherzo's second half. In view of the scherzo's emphatic ending, the presence of an inconclusive coda following the da capo comes as a surprise. Beethoven may have wanted to bring the movement to a gentle close after all in order to effect a smooth transition to the quiet opening of the following movement.

The finale has much in common with that of its E flat predecessor. It, too, is a sonata form *Presto* in 2/4 time (the quick tempo of these two finales is surpassed only by the concluding *Prestissimo* of op.1 no.3), with a second subject of almost exaggerated simplicity. Once again, the piece relies for its wit largely on the choice of a main subject that is deliberately unpianistic: its rapidly repeated notes present no problem to the two stringed instruments, but they would have been much more difficult to realise with any degree of reliability on the pianos of Beethoven's day, with their lack of an escapement mechanism. As though jocularly conceding the subject's unsuitability for the keyboard, the pianist has to be content with a quasi-trill, or, later in the movement, an octave tremolando, as a substitute for the repeated notes. Nor does Beethoven fail to capitalise on his joke in the movement's closing bars, where the theme is slowed down to a point at which it could comfortably have been managed on the keyboard instrument in its original form, only to have the player robbed of the opportunity, and forced to witness the trill-like version impudently played in leisurely fashion by the violin instead.

For all the freshness of its wit, it is hard to feel that the finale is the most successful portion of the G major trio. Its development section, in particular, is curiously relaxed and discursive; and the inclusion of two full appearances of the unadorned second subject (which, assuming the exposition repeat has been observed, is heard no fewer than five times during the course of the piece) places a considerable strain on the interpretative inventiveness of the performers. More impressive is the enharmonic pun at the end of the exposition, with the second-time bars diverting the previously heard diminished seventh chord into a wholly new tonal direction.[32] The change is achieved by reinterpreting the upper E flat of the previously heard diminished chord as D sharp, leading the music into the key of E minor for the start of the development section, and thence to E major for a further appearance of the jaunty second subject.

---

[32] The pun, of course, can be appreciated only if the exposition repeat has been taken. As we shall see, Beethoven was to invoke a similar enharmonic change between first- and second-time bars in the opening Allegro of the Cello Sonata op.5 no.1.

Once again, there is a substantial coda. Its latter half introduces a sudden element of lyricism into the proceedings, in the shape of a 'sighing' motif, marked *dolce* and given out in thirds by the piano simultaneously with its own inversion. The textural layout might suggest a kinship between the apparently new motif and the exposition's closing subject, which also features smoothly descending thirds. For the rest, the finale as a whole contains little that can prepare the listener for the dramatic impact of Beethoven's next trio.

The last of the op.1 trios, indeed, finds the composer's early style at its most intense. It is his first significant work in what was always to be his most characteristic dramatic key, and its outer movements already impart that highly charged, yet subdued, tension so typical of his C minor music. The trio's beginning, with a theme given out quietly by all three players in octaves, is not so far removed in effect from that of Beethoven's C minor Piano Concerto, and both openings recall the similarly subdued initial bars of Mozart's C minor Concerto K.491. The opening theme of Mozart's second group, with its accompaniment in constant quavers, also appears to have left its mark on the second subject of the Beethoven; and the agitated 'rocking' Neapolitan inflections of the coda to Mozart's variation finale – a moment which impressed Beethoven enough for him to recall it in the finale of the 'Appassionata' Sonata op.57 – find their echo in the closing subject.

Beethoven's quiet beginning enables the music to reach an early climax during the exposition's first stage. The effect of the *fortissimo* outburst which rounds off the first subject was one that Beethoven was to reproduce on the opening page of some of his subsequent C minor works: the String Trio op.9 no.3, the String Quartet op.18 no.4 and the Violin Sonata op.30 no.2.[33] The palpably introductory character of Beethoven's opening theme is established not only by the pause on which it comes to rest, but also by the recitative-like nature of its ninth and tenth bars. Curiously enough, the violin intervention in bars 8–10 seems to reverse the pattern of events found in the opening movement of the Fifth Symphony: whereas in the symphony Beethoven rather more effectively reserves the famous expressive oboe recitative for the recapitulation, in the trio he lays his cards on the table at the outset, while conversely allowing the recapitulation to flow unimpeded. (The violin part of the trio's original edition placed a fermata over the entire ninth bar, suggesting that the passage was to be played with considerable expressive freedom – probably as an Adagio.) The melodic outline of the piano part here, marked y in Ex. 3.14 below, foreshadows that of the more regular theme that follows immediately, and the relationship between the two is made explicit much later, in two Adagio bars contained in the coda (bars 329–30) which allow the recitative style momentarily to invade the regular theme.

---

[33] The similarity between the pieces in question, though without including the example of the string quartet, is examined by Michael C. Tusa, in 'Beethoven's "C-minor Mood"', pp.1–27.

Ex. 3.14. Beethoven. Piano Trio in C minor, op.1 no.3 (i) bars 1–18.

It is the subject's two interpolated *pianissimo* bars (figure *x* in Ex. 3.14), expanding its implied eight-bar shape to ten bars, that provide the springboard for some of the movement's most abrupt changes in tonal direction, notably at the start of the development section:

Ex. 3.15. Beethoven. Piano Trio in C minor, op.1 no.3 (i) bars 138–55.

Haydn, we feel, might have taken advantage of this enharmonic change in order to provide an extended interpolation in B major – his late piano trios contain many such large-scale tonal excursions – but the more impulsive Beethoven turns the change back on itself after only four bars, and launches instead into a dramatic and energetic passage in F minor, the key that is to dominate the development's first stage.

The exposition is brought to a close with a rapid descending scale figure which is to return in an expanded and more explosive form at the development's climax. Here, the scales burst out *fortissimo* from the predominantly subdued surrounding texture, and the tension of this moment is such that its effect is carried through into the forceful start of the recapitulation, which continues to develop the interpolated phrase from the first subject (including, significantly enough, an extended Neapolitan appearance). The notion of allowing the development's instability to spill over into the start of the recapitulation was one that Beethoven may well have learned from Haydn – the opening movement of the C minor Symphony no.95 furnishes a particularly relevant example – and it is one that was to preoccupy him throughout his life. So, too, was the idea of recapitulating *fortissimo* a theme that had originally formed a hushed beginning to the movement. Similarly altered dynamics at the start of the recapitulation are to be found in such works as the F major String Quartet op.18 no.1, the piano concertos nos.1, 3 and 4, the Violin Concerto, the Triple Concerto, and the C minor Violin Sonata op.30 no.2. That Beethoven resorted to the effect so frequently within the essentially dramatic framework of the concerto can hardly be coincidental: in this, too, Mozart's Concerto K.491, which similarly recapitulates in a forceful form what had initially been a *sotto voce* subject, is likely to have been an influence.

As he occasionally does when the opening movement has been an unusually turbulent and unruly piece, Beethoven writes his slow movement in the form of a straightforward series of variations. The Andante of the C minor piano trio may strike us as curiously unadventurous, but in the context of the work as a whole it fulfils its function as satisfactorily as does the similarly designed middle movement in the 'Appassionata' and 'Kreutzer' sonatas. This is not among Beethoven's works of the kind in which, in its early stages, the theme is given to a different instrument with each successive variation. Instead, the layout of the theme itself provides a clue to the plan of the variations that follow: each half is given first to the piano alone, while the quasi-repeats are scored for the full ensemble. The piano thereafter assumes the leading role in alternate variations, while those that intervene (i.e. nos. 2 and 4) share their thematic material equally between the two string players.

The initial eight-bar period of the theme itself offers two contrasted sonorities: the first two bars of each phrase are presented in a simple two-part texture, while the remainder is more richly harmonised. (Had he written this piece, Haydn, who retained a lifelong affection for bare two-part writing, might well have maintained the more transparent sonority throughout. The slow movement of his last completed string quartet, op.77 no.2, for instance, presents the first twelve bars of its theme in a scoring for violin and cello alone, before the inner two players enter to impart a glow of warmth to the final ten bars.) The change in texture is actually more effective in the string quintet transcription of the trio, which was substantially revised by Beethoven, though not actually made by him.[34] It gives the theme's beginning to the first violin and first viola, with their respective partners entering in the third bar.

When Beethoven made his copious corrections to the anonymous string quintet arrangement of the C minor trio, he added an inscription to the amended copyist's score describing the improved result as a 'trio arranged as a 3-part quintet by Mr Goodwill, and from the semblance of 5 parts brought into the daylight as 5 genuine parts, and also raised from extreme miserableness to some appearance of respectability, by Mr Wellwisher'. The original edition bore a title page describing

---

[34] The arrangement appeared in 1819, and soon acquired the opus number of 104. For a detailed discussion of the origins of the string quintet version, see Tyson, 'The Authors of the op.104 String Quintet', pp.158–73.

the piece as 'freely arranged and newly adapted by himself [Beethoven] from one of his finest piano trios' (*Nach einem seiner schönsten Trios fürs Piano-Forte von ihm selbst frey bearbeitet, und neu eingerichtet*). It was above all in the slow movement that the composer took the opportunity of enriching the music's texture. The rushing left-hand scales of variation 3 are given to the second violin and first viola, in warm parallel thirds; and in the fifth variation Beethoven added an entirely new viola part in dotted rhythm which considerably enhanced the music's scherzo-like transparency. The result is not so different in effect from the varied recapitulation in the second movement of the string quartet op.18 no.4. The piano's delicate chromatic scales in semiquaver sextuplets in the original trio version of this fifth variation are functional, rather than merely decorative: they plainly derive from the chromatic ascent of the original theme's fifth and sixth bars. (With the exception of the last bar in each half of the variation, the sextuplets as transferred to the violin in the quintet version are less chromatic.) The variation's final cadence is interrupted, giving way to a coda, which, with the help of much diminished seventh harmony, breathes new expressive life into the theme's concluding four bars. The close of the movement, where the semiquaver triplets return in the bass of the piano in diatonic form, bears a close resemblance to the ending of the C major Bagatelle for piano op.119 no.2, which, despite its late opus number, was probably written around the same time.

While the first two of the op.1 trios had each contained a scherzo, Beethoven is content in the C minor work to label the third movement a minuet. It is true that the heading's *quasi Allegro* qualification suggests a slightly steadier tempo than that of the corresponding movement in the first two trios, and that it lacks the off-beat accents that lend the music a characteristic scherzo-like aspect in the G major work, but the minuet is actually a more idiosyncratic piece than the parallel movement in its companions. Not that there is anything surprising about its initial four-bar phrase, other than the fact that the intermittent accompaniment from the stringed instruments falls initially on the weak second beat of the bar; but the theme's continuation is divided into two startlingly asymmetrical ideas, consisting of three and five bars, respectively. Moreover, the minuet's second half is continually developmental – so much so, indeed, that the opening theme never returns.

One of Beethoven's sketches for the trio section, in the major, bears a tangible, if distant, relationship to the shape of the theme eventually chosen, though the melody seems to have been designed for violin, rather than cello:[35]

---

[35] Beethoven, *Autograph Miscellany*, f.86.v.

Ex. 3.16.
(a) Beethoven. Piano Trio in C minor, op.1 no.3 (iii), sketch.

(b) Beethoven. Piano Trio in C minor, op.1 no.3 (iii), bars 43–54.

The delicate, fleeting piano scales which punctuate the melody's final version seem to have been a late inspiration, and their eruption in forceful octaves near the trio's close is a typically brusque gesture. (The original edition gives no indication of a change in dynamics here, though from the context in which this moment occurs it is likely that Beethoven intended an emphatic outburst. The string quintet arrangement has *crescendo* in all five parts, followed by *f* in violin 1, and *sf* on each downbeat in the remaining four parts.) On the pianos of Beethoven's day, with their slightly narrower keys and shallower action, the octaves scale would have been executed as a right-hand glissando: among more famous instances of similar glissandos in Beethoven are the lead-in to the recapitulation in the opening movement of the Piano Concerto no.1, and a passage in the coda of the 'Waldstein' Sonata op.53. (The latter instance has *pianissimo* glissandos given to the pianist's hands alternately, moving in opposite directions.) There are moments in Haydn's keyboard music, too, that must have been executed as octave glissandos – the demisemiquaver flourishes in the concluding moments of the C major Fantasia H.XVII.4, for instance, or the similar figures in semiquaver triplets in the opening Allegro of the C major Piano Trio H.XV.27.

The finale is a headlong *Prestissimo* – a tempo indication Beethoven seldom used, though it is found in the finale of his next work, the F minor Piano Sonata op.2 no.1, as well as the finale of the Sonata op.10 no.1, the middle movement of the late Sonata op.109 and the above-mentioned coda of the 'Waldstein'.[36] Once again, the piano trio's finale is a piece characterised by stark contrasts. The jagged opening bars, hurled out *fortissimo* by all three players, offer melodic and rhythmic fragmentation of a kind Mozart might have reserved for the development section – and, indeed, did in the finale of his G minor Symphony K.550 – but they are immediately followed by a smooth, subdued theme which serves as the unifying force behind the entire exposition. (Improbably enough, the latter part of the subject appears originally to have occurred to Beethoven in the guise of a slow rondo theme: it appears in the 'Kafka' sketchbook under the heading *Rondomässig – Andante*, and in the simplest of solo piano scorings.[37]) The two ideas appear on the face of it to be wholly unrelated, yet they share the same thematic outline of a chain of descending thirds, followed by a stepwise progression of three notes:

---

[36] The string quartets op.18 nos.4 and 6 both end with a *prestissimo* coda, though in each case it forms a relatively brief *envoi*.

[37] Beethoven, *Autograph Miscellany*, f.139v.

Ex. 3.17. Beethoven. Piano Trio in C minor, op.1 no.3 (iv) bars 1–22.

—(continued)

Ex. 3.17—continued

The duality of Beethoven's opening is, as we have seen, not so far removed in effect from that of the start of Haydn's C minor Symphony no.95, with its full orchestral *fortissimo* followed by a subdued violin theme.[38] The only contrasting theme heard during the course of Beethoven's exposition is the chorale-like second subject, which, although it makes no more than a brief appearance here, later provides the fundamental material for the lengthy development section. The development's first stage is surprisingly relaxed: a literal restatement in F minor of the abrupt opening bars is followed not by the conjunct melody from the first group, but by the second group's chorale theme, which is heard in its entirety in F major, and – without the refinement of any intervening modulation – D flat major. The bridge linking the two melodic appearances is a long-held violin note F, functioning at once as the concluding melody note of the F major version, and the start of the D flat restatement. The sustained violin note may be heard as Beethoven's means of preparing the listener for the much more spectacular switch of key that occurs in the movement's concluding moments.

The recapitulation bypasses the explosive opening bars altogether, though it is otherwise regular enough for the movement's chief surprises to be reserved for the coda, where the music's nervous energy subsides in an ending of striking originality. First, the smooth second limb of the main subject is heard, now shorn of its former agitated accompaniment, though even this strangely static moment cannot provide adequate warning of the startling events that unfold thereafter. As the piano's statement of the theme comes to a half-close on the dominant the violin and cello play a long-held note G, before sliding down a semitone, to F sharp – and against the latter sustained note the piano quietly gives out the same melody in the very remote key of B minor. The closing bars provide a further shock, with the music dissolving inconclusively in a chain of *pianissimo* C major runs that seem to echo, as though from afar, the C major scales of the minuet's trio. Beethoven's ending is, perhaps, not quite as original as he would have us believe: as we have seen, it is quite likely that he borrowed the idea from the similar closing gesture of Haydn's string quartet op.20 no.3.

No one listening to the last trio of Beethoven's op.1 series as the eighteenth century was drawing towards its close could have been left in any doubt about the originality and forceful personality of its creator, who was still in his mid-twenties at the

[38] Douglas Johnson ('1794–1795: Decisive Years in Beethoven's Early Development', pp.19–21) draws parallels between these two works of Beethoven and Haydn, pointing out that the slow movement in both is a set of variations in the relative major on a theme marked *Andante cantabile*, and that the trio of the minuet in each case is in the parallel major.

time he composed it. With this work the popular domestic form of the piano trio entered a new arena that was ultimately to take it away from the province of amateur musicians playing in their own home, and into the concert hall. It was a process Beethoven was to take a stage further in his next conventionally scored trios, op.70.

Connected in all likelihood with Beethoven's work on the op.1 trios, and perhaps a form of preparatory study for them, is the set of Fourteen Variations for piano trio op.44. It appeared in January 1804 under the imprint of Hoffmeister & Kühnel, who had offices in Vienna and Leipzig, though the piece is considerably earlier in origin. In the first edition of his Beethoven biography Thayer placed it in 1799, a dating that was based on a memorandum from Otto Jahn describing a sketchbook originally owned by the Austrian musicologist and bibliophile Aloys Fuchs. Besides ideas for the op.44 Variations it contained sketches for the String Quartet op.18 no.3, the fourth movement of the op.20 Septet and the piano duet variations on 'Ich denke dein' WoO 74.[39] However, already by Thayer's time the relevant leaves from the book had been removed and lost. Evidence for a rather earlier dating for the op.44 Variations was provided by Gustav Nottebohm, in the shape of sketches found alongside those for the song *Feuerfarb'* op.52 no.2, which was completed at the beginning of 1792.[40] Moreover, an idea – eventually unused – for an elaborate cadenza in the concluding variation is contained on the same sheet of the 'Fischhof Miscellany' as an isolated sketch for the closing subject from the first movement of the Trio op.1 no.1, leading to speculation that the variations had originally been intended to stand as that trio's finale.[41] Certainly, on musical grounds it would have to be conceded that at least the greater part of the variations must predate the op.1 trios: their scoring is altogether less assured, with the piano dominating to a greater extent than in op.1, and the three players tending otherwise to alternate rather than integrate. It is unlikely, moreover, that Beethoven would have contemplated using a set of variations based on a theme that was not his own for the finale of a work as ambitious as the first of the op.1 trios. The first edition gives no indication of the theme's source: the piece is simply described as *XIV Variations pour le Fortepiano, Violon et Violoncelle*,[42] and the discovery that it was taken from the aria 'Ja, ich muß mich von ihr scheiden' in the second act of *Das rothe Käppchen* by Carl Ditters von Dittersdorf was made only comparatively recently.[43] Dittersdorf's comic Singspiel was first produced at the Kärntnertor Theatre in Vienna in 1788, and Beethoven is likely to have seen it when it was staged in Bonn in 1792, shortly before his departure for Vienna. A vocal score was published by Schott & Söhne in that same year (see Illustration 1 overleaf). The aria on which the op.44 Variations are based is sung in the second act by the village mayor, Hans Christoph Nitsche, whose jealousy of his much younger wife, Hedwige, has been aroused by the attentions being paid to her by the dashing Lieutenant von Felsenberg. 'Yes, I must leave her,' declares Hans Christoph, 'it can't be borne any longer or my gall will finish me off.'

---

[39] Thayer/Forbes, p.124 n.12.
[40] Nottebohm, *Beethoveniana. Aufsätze und Mittheilungen*, p.7.
[41] See Johnson/Fischhof, vol.1, p.304, and vol.2, p.4.
[42] Similarly, the title page of the 'Kakadu' Variations op.121a gives no indication of the authorship of their theme. See Lockwood, 'Beethoven's "Kakadu" Variations, op.121a: A Study in Paradox', pp.95–6.
[43] See Weber-Bockholdt, 'Beethovens Opus 44', p.103.

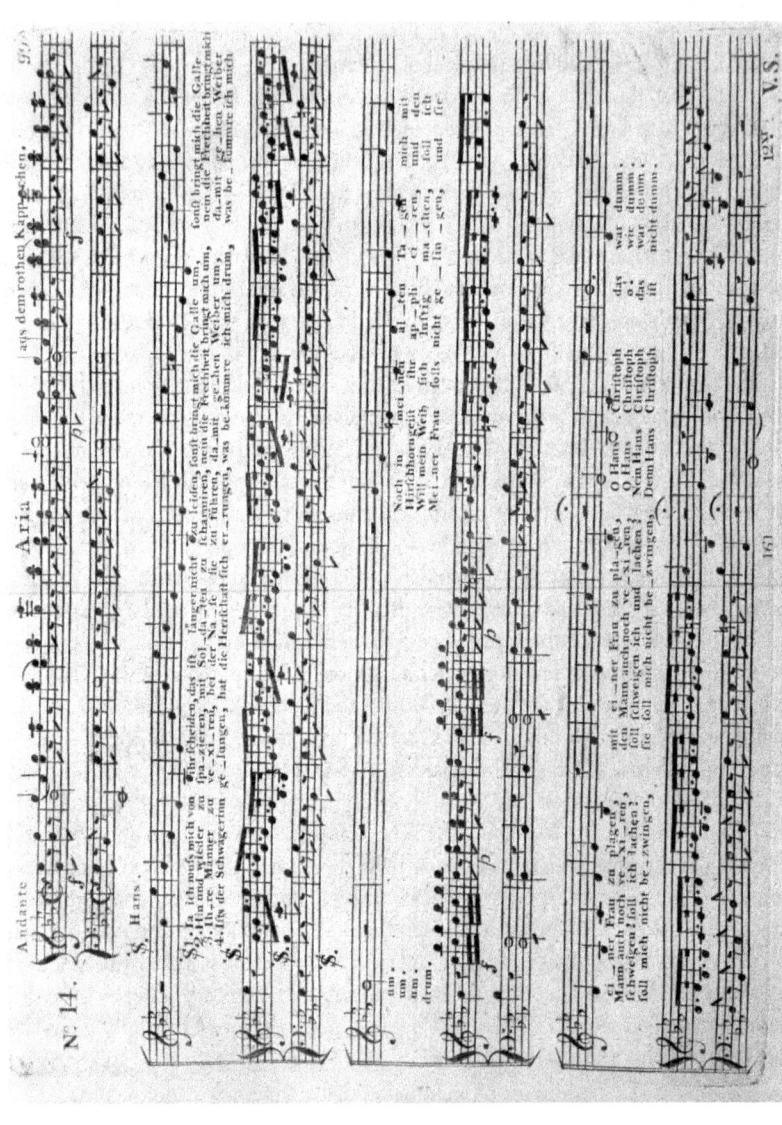

Illustration 1. Dittersdorf. 'Ja, ich muß mich von ihr scheiden' from *Das rote Käppchen*. Vocal score by Ignaz Walter (c.1794) (©British Library)

Ex. 3.18. Beethoven. Variations in E flat, op.44, bars 1–22.

Beethoven omits Dittersdorf's brief introductory flourish, as well as the four-bar orchestral outburst that separates the theme's two halves in each verse (though there is a hint of the latter in the sudden *fortissimo* explosion within Beethoven's otherwise subdued twelfth variation), but for the rest his piano trio transcription sticks closely to its source, even to the point of presenting the wryly comic tune entirely unharmonised. Only the last eight bars – again, following Dittersdorf – offer a simply harmonised codetta. The result, whose opening traces a descending and ascending E flat major arpeggio with comical monotony, has more the feel of an accompaniment than a theme, and to that extent is not dissimilar to the famous opening of Haydn's 'Lark' Quartet op.64 no.5. However, whereas Haydn's exposed accompaniment subsequently reveals itself to form the background to a soaring violin tune, Beethoven maintains the deliberate textural ambiguity throughout the opening stages of his piece. Although the solo piano second variation offers a florid melody based on the theme's harmony, it is not until the slow eighth variation that a clearly defined new theme is presented above the staccato quavers in their original form.

It has been suggested that variations 3 and 4 were subsequent additions, made in order to give greater prominence to the violin and cello, whose parts in the first half-dozen variations are otherwise more or less superfluous (they do not figure at all in variation 2), and certainly, the more dynamic fifth variation would be more logically and satisfyingly placed after the piano solo of variation 2.[44] In any case, the fifth variation is little more than a redistributed version of the third, while the cello's smooth line in constant quavers in the intervening variation merely echoes the piano melody of variation 2.

Like the 'Figaro' variations for piano and violin, the op.44 set includes two slow variations in the minor, though this time they are not placed side by side. The second of them, with some exotic chromaticism in its final bars, is followed by an extended 6/8 closing variation in 'hunting' style. The trio writing of this finale is generally more assured than that of some of the preceding variations, possibly indicating a later date of origin. In any case, Beethoven is hardly likely to have consented to the work's publication so long after its composition without allowing himself the opportunity of carrying out revisions. The coda's exuberance is interrupted by an Andante beginning in C minor, and incorporating a much shorter cadenza than is found in Beethoven's sketch for the piece.

Despite the attractiveness of much of this music, the idea of thrusting an accompaniment into the foreground is one that was to bear richer fruit in a later E flat major work in the same form – the 'Eroica' Variations op.35 for solo piano, with their introductory variations on the bass of the theme. It may have been the similarity of the two pieces in this respect – as well, perhaps, as the fact that the op.44 set bears an opus number adjacent to that of *The Creatures of Prometheus*, from which the theme of op.35 was taken – that led Hugo Riemann in his edition of the Thayer biography to assume that the trio variations were composed around the same time as the ballet.[45]

The piano trio variations were not the only piece Beethoven based on a theme from Dittersdorf's popular Singspiel: around the same time, he composed a set of variations for solo piano (WoO 66) on the first-act aria 'Es war einmal ein alter Mann', also sung by the character of Hans Christoph. A sudden full bar's rest, complete with fermata, inserted by Dittersdorf to outrageously comic effect in the middle of a phrase is maintained by Beethoven in his theme and all thirteen variations that follow.

---

[44] See Müller-Blatau, 'Beethoven und die Variation', p.106.
[45] TDR, vol.2, p.410.

4
Interlude 1: The Quintet for Piano and Wind Instruments Op.16

No chamber work of Beethoven more openly invites comparison with a masterpiece by Mozart than the Quintet op.16, scored for the same ensemble – piano, oboe, clarinet, horn and bassoon – as Mozart's Quintet K.452. Mozart's piece was composed in the wake of his piano concertos K.450 and 451, the former of them his first piece of the kind to throw the spotlight on the wind instruments of the orchestra. In the concerto's variation slow movement, their appearance is long delayed: the first half of the piece is scored exclusively for piano and strings, and when the wind instruments finally appear they make a radiant entrance against a gentle background of pizzicato strings and delicate piano tracery. Even then, Mozart manages to reserve an entirely new wind sonority for the finale, which introduces for the first time in the work the sound of a flute whose first solo entrance, hovering high above sustained strings and widely spaced piano arpeggios, comes as a breath of fresh air.

One of the striking features of Mozart's K.452 Quintet is the remarkable variety of its scoring, coupled with the manner in which each of the five instruments involved is allotted its own distinctive character. Mozart himself thought highly of the work: 'I have written two grand concertos, and then a quintet which received extraordinary applause', he proudly told his father on 10 April 1784. 'I myself regard it as the best thing I have so far written in my life.'[1]

The influence of K.452 on Beethoven's op.16 extends far beyond its instrumentation. Like Mozart, Beethoven begins with a substantial slow introduction, and his opening movement contains several details that seem to hark back to Mozart's quintet: the manner in which the start of the development section continues the new musical thought uttered in the exposition's closing bars; or the presence of a false recapitulation in the subdominant. But Beethoven's work, although very much classically conceived, with clear-cut, symmetrical themes and a general avoidance of the more revolutionary ideas found in the op.1 trios, is far from a slavish imitation. Indeed, the contrasts between it and its model are far more pronounced than any of their obvious similarities. It is almost as though, having invoked direct comparison with his great predecessor in his first movement, Beethoven thereafter deliberately sought to strike out along different paths. (It is instructive, however, to note the similarity of the 'hunting' theme of Beethoven's finale, with its repeated-note beginning, to that of another E flat major work by Mozart which makes prominent use of wind instruments: the rondo from the Piano Concerto K.482.)

---

[1] MBA no.783.

Beethoven composed his quintet in 1796, and he may at least have begun making sketches for it during his visit to Berlin in the summer of that year. It was first performed on 6 April 1797, at a concert organised by the violinist Ignaz Schuppanzigh. A meeting of the Vienna *Tonkünstler-Societät* a little more than a month later noted that 'Hr. van Beethoven produced a quintet and also distinguished himself at the same time by improvising on the pianoforte', though whether or not that improvisation occurred during the course of the quintet is not clear.[2] On at least one later occasion Beethoven did not fail to seize the opportunity to demonstrate his prowess as an improviser during the quintet's finale. Ferdinand Ries recounts that on the same evening that Beethoven conducted a rehearsal of the 'Eroica' Symphony at Prince Lobkowitz's palace (this was the occasion on which Ries very nearly had his ears boxed by the composer for suggesting that the horn player had come in too soon at the famous discordant approach to the first movement's recapitulation), he also gave a performance of the op.16 Quintet in which the celebrated oboist Friedrich Ramm took part.

> In the last Allegro there are a few pauses before the theme begins again; in one of these, Beethoven suddenly began to improvise, took the rondo as his theme and entertained himself and his listeners for some time, which however was not the case with the accompanying players. They were indignant, and Mr Ramm even very incensed. It really did look rather comical when the gentlemen, expecting to begin any moment, constantly raised their instruments to their mouths, only to take them away again quite calmly. At last Beethoven was satisfied and returned to the rondo. The whole company was enchanted.[3]

However, *quod licet Jovi non licet bovi*. On another occasion Carl Czerny played the quintet in the presence of the composer, and came to rue the liberties he took with the music. The event in question took place on 11 February 1816, and Czerny had good reason to remember it, though he mistakenly ascribed it to a much earlier date. Nearly thirty years later he recalled:

> When, for instance, once (around 1812) at one of Schuppanzigh's concerts I performed the quintet with wind instruments I allowed myself, in a spirit of youthful carelessness, some changes – making passages more difficult, using a higher octave, etc. Beethoven quite rightly took me severely to task in the presence of Schuppanzigh, [Joseph] Linke and the other accompanists. The next day I received the following letter from him, which I here copy exactly from the original I have in front of me:
>
>> 'Dear Czerny!
>> Today I cannot see you, but tomorrow I will call on you myself to talk to you. – I burst forth so yesterday that I was sorry it had happened; but you must forgive a composer who would rather have heard his work exactly as it was

---

[2] See Thayer/Forbes, p.197. The original German, given in TDR, vol.2, p.47, reads: 'Den 2ten Tag hat H. van Beethoven ein Quintett produziert, und sich dabey auf dem Pianoforte auch durchs fantasieren ausgezeichnet.'

[3] Wegeler/Ries, pp.79–80.

written, no matter how beautifully you otherwise played. But I shall soon make amends *publicly* with the cello sonata.[4]

Be assured that as an artist I have the greatest goodwill for your success and will always try to show myself

Your true friend

Beethoven.'

This letter[5] did more than anything else to cure me of my addiction to allowing myself to make any changes in performing his works, and I wish it might have the same influence on all pianists.[6]

The quintet did not appear in print until 1801, when Tranquillo Mollo issued it around the same time as his first edition of the C major Piano Concerto op.15. The concerto had been written in the year before the quintet, and Beethoven may have withheld both works in order to retain his control as exclusive performer of the music. In 1800 he produced a new manuscript score of the concerto which clearly represented a substantial revision of the now lost original; and in the case of the op.16 Quintet he must at the very least have revised the piano part prior to the work's publication, since the concerto and the quintet are his earliest compositions to contain pedal markings. Such markings are not found in any of his works featuring the piano composed in the interim – the Clarinet Trio op.11, the Horn Sonata op.17 and the piano sonatas opp.13, 14 and 22. Among previous great composers of piano music, Haydn was alone in having indicated the use of the sustaining pedal, and that on only a single occasion: the first movement of his C major Sonata H.XIV.50 contains two passages – one, in the development section, played in the bass register; the other, in the recapitulation, in the treble– which are marked 'open pedal'. The passages in question were designed to contrast with the sonority of the movement's crisply articulated main subject, and the overlapping harmonies that resulted were of a kind that clearly appealed to Beethoven, who famously made use of a similar effect in such pieces as the slow movement of his Piano Concerto no.3, the rondo of the 'Waldstein' Sonata and the recitatives in the opening movement of the 'Tempest' Sonata op.31 no.2.

Beethoven's method of specifying the use of the sustaining pedal in his first works to include such markings – besides the Piano Concerto no.1 and the op.16 Quintet, they encompass the four piano sonatas opp.26–8, composed in 1800–1 and published the following year – was to write the words *senza sordino* (or, in the case of the first pedal indication in the original edition of op.16, which occurs at the start of the opening movement's development section, the more logical *senza sordini*) to indicate the raising of the dampers by depressing the pedal, and *con sordino* to denote that the dampers were to be in place again. The notation was cumbersome, but Beethoven was nevertheless able to use it with some accuracy, not least in the finale of the 'Moonlight' Sonata op.27 no.2, where the rising arpeggios with their staccato

---

[4] Czerny was due to play one of Beethoven's sonatas op.102 with Joseph Linke the following week.

[5] BGA no.902.

[6] *Wiener allgemeine Musik-Zeitung*, no.113 (20 Sept. 1845), pp.449–50.

left-hand accompaniment are to be played *con sordino*, and the explosive chords that punctuate the music are lent greater weight by being sounded *senza sordino*.

Perhaps the most striking use of the sustaining pedal in the op.16 Quintet occurs at the approach to the last reprise of the finale's rondo theme, where a chromatic descent spanning two octaves is pedalled through, so that the theme's return emerges out of a haze of sound. For the rest, the moment at which the prescribed pedal is to be released is as often as not left to the taste and discretion of the player. The first reprise of the theme in the slow movement is similarly, if more briefly, pedalled, with a hint of a new colour introduced in the expressive *calando* that precedes the theme's return. At other times, Beethoven seems to use the pedal in an attempt to increase the music's sheer noise factor. The first movement's exposition ends with a forceful ascending staccato scale in triplets for the right hand, and the ensuing start of the development section is marked by a dramatic change of key, the same staccato scale, now in octaves, being played this time with raised dampers. The dynamic marking of *fortissimo* combined with the pedalling may be taken as Beethoven's means of implying a marking of *fff* – one that he never actually invoked in his solo piano music.[7]

The solemn fanfare in sharply dotted rhythm that begins the quintet's slow introduction is almost self-consciously written in wind-band style. Although it is given out by all five players in octaves, its dynamic level is surprisingly subdued, and it is only with the counterstatement four bars later that the latent force implied by such a sonority is allowed to make itself felt. Rather more impressive, perhaps, than the opening page is the music's continuation, first with two bars featuring the wind players in contrapuntal dialogue, and then a turn to the minor, and a piano accompaniment whose smooth, syncopated right-hand part shadows the staccato left hand, as though picking out its overtones. (Beethoven used a similar keyboard layout, albeit in a quicker tempo, in the reprise of the scherzo-like second movement of the Piano Sonata op.27 no.1.)

The main theme of the Allegro, with its yearning rising sixth followed by a stepwise descent, is a close relative of Tamino's 'Dies Bildnis ist bezaubernd schön' from Mozart's *Die Zauberflöte*.

Ex. 4.1.
(a) Beethoven. Quintet in E flat, op.16 (i) bars 22–9.

[7] The closing bars in the first movement of the 'Emperor' Concerto op.73, pedalled throughout, offer what is probably Beethoven's single instance of an *fff* indication for the piano.

Ex. 4.1.
(b) Mozart. *Die Zauberflöte* K.620.

The staccato repeated notes in the third bar of Beethoven's theme are stressed in the piano accompaniment to the wind instruments' counterstatement; and they assume importance in the development section, where, in their final appearance in the bass of the keyboard part immediately preceding the onset of the recapitulation, the pianist is encouraged to emphasise them through the instruction *queste note ben marcate*.

The first subject's prolongation – a dialogue between oboe, clarinet and bassoon, its phrases stressing the first subject's rising sixth – is not featured in the otherwise straightforward recapitulation, which, however, also severely curtails the subject itself, perhaps as a consequence of an earlier, and surprisingly substantial, false reprise in the subdominant. Instead, the return of the passage in dialogue, with its piano accompaniment in quaver triplets, is reserved for what is in effect an extended cadenza occupying the greater part of the coda. The cadenza comes to a close with a spectacular chain of horn fanfares (less acrobatic, however, than the similar examples Beethoven wrote for Giovanni Punto in the opening movement of the op.17 Sonata), followed by a chromatic scale sweeping up the keyboard over a distance of four-and-a-half octaves. The scale mirrors the similar approach to the movement's recapitulation, and the cadential trill at its apex is followed by a further echo of the same earlier moment, in the shape of a reappearance of the 'marcato' repeated notes, now played in a haze of sustaining pedal and forming a tonic anchor above which the music draws to its close.

Rather than cast his slow movement in sonata form, as Mozart had done in his K.452 Quintet, Beethoven opts for a simple rondo with episodes in the minor. The G minor first episode features the oboe and bassoon in prominent roles; while the second, in B flat minor, brings the horn to the fore. Both theme and accompaniment are increasingly ornamented on each appearance, until the counterstatement of the final return is underlain with an elaborately intricate piano part whose effect is not dissimilar from that of the ornate piano accompaniment in the reprise of the Adagio in the op.11 Clarinet Trio. The somewhat four-square theme of the rondo finale, on the other hand, remains virtually unaltered throughout. Its 6/8 'hunting' character is of a type to be found in the finale of several E flat major works by Mozart, though not, significantly enough, that of the K.452 Quintet. (Besides the already-mentioned Piano Concerto K.482, Beethoven's rondo theme bears a certain similarity to that of Mozart's Violin Sonata K.380, a work that had such a strong influence on the music he composed during his Bonn years.) The keyboard writing, too, has a distinctly Mozartian clarity and lightness that are maintained even during the substantial developmental episode that stands at the centre of the movement. The first reprise of the rondo theme is preceded by a brief piano cadenza, though one that is much less elaborate than the similar passage, scored for the full ensemble, in the finale of Mozart's quintet.

When Mollo issued Beethoven's work, he did so in two versions: in addition to its familiar quintet form it appeared in another Mozartian medium, as a quartet for piano and strings.

The latter is so much more subtly scored that it must surely be later in origin.[8] Beethoven may, indeed, have prepared it shortly before it appeared in print. In the absence of the autographs, there is no scientific evidence as to which of the two versions represents the earlier scoring, but on purely musical grounds there can be no room for doubt. Leaving aside the fact that the work was clearly intended in the first instance as a homage to Mozart's uniquely scored quintet, the piano quartet version represents both texturally and melodically such an advance over the quintet as to make it inconceivable that it could have come first.

A surviving sketch for the slow movement, labelled 'oboe', shows the start of the first episode in the following form:[9]

Ex. 4.2. Beethoven. Quintet in E flat, op.16 (ii), sketch.

At the top of the page Beethoven also jotted down – perhaps as an afterthought – a much simplified alternative which is very close to the version eventually adopted in the quintet; but the transcription for piano and string trio takes a significant step back towards the more freely rhapsodic nature of the initial sketch – as though the composer had somehow felt hampered by instrumental limitations in his original scoring:

Ex. 4.3. Beethoven. Op.16 (ii) bars 17–20.
(a) Quintet version

(b) Quartet version

The slow movement's second episode demonstrates still more strikingly how the greater flexibility of stringed instruments allowed music of an expressive intensity lacking in the quintet version. The viola's ornate improvisatory melody here is an altogether inspired variation on the original horn theme. The two are given in parallel opposite:

---

[8] Myron Schwager ('A Fresh Look at Beethoven's Arrangements') suggests that because the dynamic markings in the piano part of the two versions of op.16 are identical, it is likely that the arrangement was made shortly after the composition of the work's original form. However, the published piano part clearly remained unchanged in order to spare the expense of having to re-engrave it, and it is more likely that Beethoven made the quartet transcription at the publisher's request, in order to increase potential sales. Schwager's insightful comparison of the work's two forms concedes that the piano quartet scoring 'helps to transform a very formal and block-like dialogue (piano *versus* wind) into a more fluent conversation'.

[9] See Shedlock, 'Beethoven's Sketchbooks', p.651, col.1.

Ex. 4.4. Beethoven. Quintet/Quartet in E flat, op.16 (ii) bars 57–64.

The cello part in this passage has no bassoon parallel in the quintet scoring, and it again offers evidence of Beethoven's determination to produce more integrated textures in the quartet version. Time and again, indeed, the quartet finds him striving for a closer blending of the piano with the remainder of the ensemble than he had achieved in the quintet version. The first notable alteration occurs as early as the fourth bar of the slow introduction, where the opening fanfare-like figure had originally been followed by two bars for the piano alone. Here, the string trio makes a subtle entrance half way through the piano solo. Similarly, the Allegro's first subject is no longer allotted to the piano for the full duration of its sixteen bars: instead, the strings enter unexpectedly in the tenth bar, so that when the melody subsequently passes to the violin it is as a seamless continuation of the preceding texture, rather than incurring a complete break in sonority.

Much the same happens both in the second subject (where the accompanying players, instead of waiting for the completion of the piano's eight-bar phrase, enter in the fourth bar), and in the theme of the slow movement. Although Beethoven may well have learned this type of textural subtlety from his Mozartian model, he failed to revise the work in its quintet form in the light of this experience. The fact that, aside from their piano part, the versions are so different would seem to confirm that the provision of an alternative piano quartet scoring was a late request from the publisher, and that there may not have been time for Beethoven to revisit the wind version.

In the finale Beethoven's process of recomposition extended to a harmonic enrichment of the accompanying parts, which are also injected with new rhythmic life. In the quintet version of the following passage from the coda, the piano's phrases are punctuated by static chords from the wind players.

Ex. 4.5. Beethoven. Quintet in E flat, op.16 (iii) bars 233–42.

By introducing a simple overlapping dialogue between piano and violin in the quartet, Beethoven effectively transformed his material. (The imitation, although hardly subtle, is considerably less awkward than the canon at the start of the final reprise of the rondo theme, where the two opposing instrumental forces seem curiously out of step with each other.)

Ex. 4.6. Beethoven. Quartet in E flat, op.16 (iii) bars 233–42.

Undeniably, there are certain moments in the work that are idiomatically conceived for wind instruments: the fanfare in the very opening bars, for instance, or the horn calls during the closing stages of both outer movements. But complaints that such passages are less effective in the rescored version will not bear scrutiny: the notion of invoking the sound of one instrument on another of a wholly different nature has always been a strong weapon in the composer's armoury. Significantly, perhaps, in the quintet the horn never gets to play the finale's 'hunting' theme at all, except for one brief moment when the theme turns to the minor and is given out by the full ensemble (bars 92–8).

Beethoven's op.16 Piano Quartet is, in short, as successful a transcription as Mozart's string quintet version of his C minor Wind Serenade K.388. The work was dedicated in both forms to Prince Joseph Schwarzenberg, at whose Viennese palace Haydn's *The Creation* and *The Seasons* had first been performed.

5
Works for Piano and Cello, 1796–1801

Beethoven's cello sonatas number only half as many as his sonatas for violin, but they were composed at widely spaced intervals, and taken together they give us a clearer picture of his stylistic development. There is, indeed, a sense in which the cello sonatas more neatly define the composer's 'early', 'middle' and 'late' periods than do even his string quartets: the two op.5 sonatas were composed only a year or so after the op.1 piano trios; the A major Sonata op.69, of 1807–8, belongs to the period of the Fifth and Sixth Symphonies; while the two sonatas op.102, composed in 1815, clearly signal the emergence of Beethoven's late style.

With these five works Beethoven broke new ground. No composer since Bach had attempted to write for a stringed instrument of similar range with obbligato keyboard.[1] In the second half of the eighteenth century the prevailing method of writing cello sonatas or variations was to provide the principal part with no more than a simple accompaniment for a second stringed instrument – either another cello, or a bass. In this way the virtuoso player who held a position at court could give his aristocratic employer the satisfaction of joining in the music-making without placing an undue strain on his or her technical proficiency. This type of texture, locating the melody instrument in a high register virtually throughout, is one that was cultivated extensively by such leading players of the day as Boccherini and the Duport brothers; but such use of the cello as essentially a form of *viola pomposa* was hardly likely to be of interest to Beethoven, whose great achievement was to find instead a viable means of exploiting the distinctive lower end of the instrument's range. Even on the keyboard instruments of Beethoven's day, though to a much lesser degree than on modern pianos, the ensemble was one that posed problems of balance and blend between the two instruments, and those problems became more acute in music of a slow, sustained character, where variety of articulation and attack were at a premium. Significantly, not until his last cello sonata did Beethoven attempt to write a fully fledged slow movement. In the first four he opted instead

---

[1] An unfinished Andante for piano and cello by Mozart (K.Anh.46) breaks off after only 33 bars, many of them not written out in both parts; nor do we know if it was designed to form part of a larger work. A complete sonata of 1789 for obbligato keyboard and cello by Johann Christoph Friedrich Bach was published in 1905, in an edition which transposed it from G major into D, in order to afford the cello part greater brilliance. The sonata's slow movement is a long cantilena for the cello, with keyboard accompaniment; but its outer movements treat the two players more equally. Bach's autograph score has not survived, and so it is impossible to tell to what extent the piece was rewritten on its publication – or, indeed, if it is authentic at all. For all the novelty of its instrumentation, the music remains a quite unadventurous example of the *galant* style of the early Classical period.

for a slow introduction either to the first movement (the two op.5 sonatas) or the finale (op.69), or to both (the C major Sonata op.102 no.1). Moreover, in the last sonata, op.102 no.2, the slow movement presents an altogether dark sonority whose low-lying keyboard part allows the cello for the most part to have the upper voice.

The stimulus behind the two op.5 sonatas was Beethoven's meeting in 1796 with the famous French players Jean-Pierre Duport and his younger brother (and pupil) Jean-Louis. Beethoven's concert tour to Berlin in that year was organised by Prince Lichnowsky, who accompanied the composer at least until he reached Prague, in February. Some seven years previously Lichnowsky had arranged a similar itinerary for Mozart, and he must have felt pride in the fact that his young protégé was following directly in the footsteps of his great predecessor. Beethoven remained in Prague for some two months, where he composed, among other, smaller, pieces, the concert aria 'Ah! Perfido' op.65, before he travelled on to Berlin via Dresden and Leipzig.[2] According to Ferdinand Ries, Beethoven played at the court in Berlin several times, and also composed and performed his two sonatas op.5 there together with Duport. For his pains he received a golden casket filled with louis d'or. 'Beethoven related with self-esteem', reports Ries, 'that it was no ordinary box but one of a kind that would probably have been given to ambassadors.'[3]

It was often assumed that the Duport in question was Jean-Pierre. But Ries qualifies his mention of the player with a parenthesis describing him as the King's 'first cellist'; and by the time of Beethoven's visit that description could fit only Jean-Louis, who in the wake of the French revolution of 1789 had joined his elder brother at the court of Friedrich Wilhelm II, taking up the position of principal cellist. Ries is, however, unlikely to have been aware that both Duport brothers were active at the Prussian court, and since by all accounts it was Jean-Pierre who had the richer tone at the lower end of the instrument's range, the question of which of the two players Beethoven had in mind in composing his op.5 sonatas had perhaps better be left open. Beethoven appeared at the court more than once, so it is in any case possible that he played with both brothers. If their actual music is unlikely to have held his interest for long, he can hardly fail to have been struck by the perfection of their technique; and since both musicians have a bearing on the op.5 sonatas, it is worth considering their careers and their performing style in some detail.

Jean-Pierre Duport first rose to prominence when he appeared at the *Concert spirituel* in Paris in 1761, at the age of twenty. His security in the instrument's high register was praised by the *Mercure de France*, whose correspondent noted: 'The subtlety and precision of the violoncello's sounds astonish and delight; one is more used to hearing the violin dazzle.'[4] A subsequent series of concerts was reviewed at greater length:

> M. Duport performed new wonders on the violoncello every day, and earned new admiration. In his hands this instrument is no longer recognisable. It speaks,

---

[2] See May, 'Beethoven and Prince Karl Lichnowsky', pp.32–3, and Braubach and Ladenburger, *Die Stammbücher Beethovens und der Babette Koch*, pp.80–110.

[3] Wegeler/Ries, p.109.

[4] *Mercure de France*, 2 Jan. 1762, i, col.156.

it expresses, it renders everything beyond the charm that was thought to be an exclusive property of the violin. The agility [*prestesse*] of his playing is always accompanied by the most precise accuracy, in difficulties of which one can have no idea without knowing the instrument well. It seems universally agreed today that this young man is the most singular phenomenon to have appeared among our talents. One cannot imagine what he could add to the degree of perfection he has reached.[5]

In 1773, at the invitation of Frederick the Great, Duport established himself as principal cellist of the court orchestra in Berlin, as well as teacher to the cello-playing Prince. When the latter ascended to the throne in 1786 as Friedrich Wilhelm II, Duport was elevated to the status of Music Director – or, as the title page of his six sonatas op.4 has it, 'Sur-intendent de la musique du Roi'. When Mozart reached the Prussian court in the spring of 1789, his arrival there was announced to the King in a memorandum:

One named Motzart [*sic*] (who on entering declared himself to be a Kapellmeister from Vienna) announces here that he was brought hither in the company of Prince Lichnowsky, that he wished to lay his talents before Your Royal Majesty's feet and that he awaited the command whether he may hope that Your Royal Majesty will allow him to appear before him.[6]

The King responded by writing in the margin the words 'Directeur du Port', meaning that Mozart was to be referred to Jean-Pierre Duport. In order to ingratiate himself with the influential cellist, Mozart composed, or perhaps initially improvised, a set of keyboard variations (K.573) on the minuet finale of Duport's Sonata op.4 no.6. (That finale, itself in variation form, is a virtuoso piece *par excellence*, and characteristically includes a variation played by the first cello entirely in harmonics.) Following his visit to the Prussian court, Mozart resolved to write a series of string quartets for Friedrich Wilhelm II, as well as a set of six 'easy' piano sonatas for his daughter, Princess Friederiecke. The sonatas were never composed, but with the quartets the cash-starved Mozart set out to curry royal favour in an ambitious manner. It was one that brought with it a particular problem: how to assign a prominent melodic role to the cello without seriously compromising the integrity of his quartet style. Mozart must have been aware that Friedrich Wilhelm II's court chamber composer was Boccherini, who was not in residence but dispatched his works from Spain; and that Boccherini's quintets with two cellos as often as not treat the first cellist as a soloist, while the second provides the music's harmonic foundation. Mozart's own concession to the royal prerogative was far more radical: if the cello was to be emancipated melodically, it would have to be on equal terms with the three remaining players. While it is true that his three 'Prussian' quartets K.575, 589 and 590 occasionally echo Boccherini's high-lying cello parts (the start of the slow movement of K.589, for instance, or the trio of the minuet in K.575), such moments are invariably set within the context of a conversational quartet texture. Not by chance,

---

[5] Ibid., 1 April 1762, ii, cols.185 and 189–90.
[6] Deutsch, *Mozart. Die Dokumente seines Lebens*, p.298.

when these works were eventually published, some three weeks after Mozart's death, they were announced in an advertisement describing them as 'concertante' quartets, whereas the normal term for a string quartet in Mozart's day – and, indeed, Beethoven's – was 'violin quartet'. Ironically, Mozart seems never to have received a penny for what he described as 'this troublesome work'.[7]

Four years after Mozart, the organist, lexicographer and amateur cellist Ernst Ludwig Gerber travelled to the Berlin court, where he met Jean-Pierre Duport. Gerber recounts:

> I made his acquaintance in 1793 in his music room in Berlin as a serious, awe-inspiring but pleasant man, while I enjoyed the pleasure of accompanying him in one of his masterly solos. By the manner in which he played it, which in excellence far surpassed anything I had ever heard on the violoncello, he caused me as much admiration and astonishment as pleasure and delight. In some movements the speed with which he played them was so impetuous that faced with the impossibility of allowing my notes their due value at that speed, I found myself having to look at his stave rather than mine, simply to keep up with him. 'And my King plays this solo, too', he said, 'only not so fast.' Finally, he played me another solo, in the proper meaning of the word, in which he played the most beautiful and tasteful melody with the bow on the A and D strings, and at the same time added with the greatest possible nonchalance, a clear pizzicato bass on the lower strings, which lacked nothing.[8]

As for Jean-Louis Duport, he was only eighteen when he made his debut at the *Concert spirituel*, on 2 February 1768. The *Mercure de France* reported: 'The younger M. Duport, a pupil of his brother, played a sonata on the violoncello accompanied by M. Duport the elder. A performance that was precise, brilliant and astonishing, sounds that were rich, mellow, flattering, secure and bold playing, reveal a truly great talent, & the ensemble of the two instruments in such skilled hands was above all seen as something rare.'[9]

Jean-Louis Duport's playing was frequently compared with that of the violinist Viotti, with whom he performed on one occasion in front of Marie Antoinette. Ernst Ludwig Gerber heard him in Berlin in 1797, in a performance of a cantata by Friedrich Himmel, who had been appointed as royal Kapellmeister by Friedrich Wilhelm II two years previously, and a single aria with obbligato cello was sufficient for him to be struck by Duport's 'pure tone, and the unforced use of his bow'.[10] For a more reasoned appraisal of Jean-Louis's playing, and a valuable comparison of the two brothers, Gerber cited Johann Friedrich Reichardt: 'In perfection and precision the younger is as unsurpassable as the elder is in rich, full tone and strength and meaning in performance.' Beethoven's 'Kafka' sketchbook contains a page indicating cello fingerings and technique that were possibly entered by J.-L. Duport.[11]

---

[7] Letter of June 1790 to Michael Puchberg. MBA no.1130.
[8] Gerber, *Neues historisch-biographisches Lexikon*, Part I, cols.955–6.
[9] *Mercure de France*, Feb. 1768, p.214.
[10] Gerber, *Neues historisch-biographisches Lexikon*, col.957.
[11] Beethoven, *Autograph Miscellany*, f.109r.

For all that the musical value of the sonatas by the Duport brothers is slight, some of their characteristic cello figuration seems to have found an echo in Beethoven's op.5 sonatas. The following passagework from Jean-Pierre's C major Sonata op.3 no.2 is of a kind that appears to have left its mark on two separate moments in the rondo of Beethoven's G minor Sonata op.5 no.2.

Ex. 5.1.
(a) J.-P. Duport. Sonata in C, op.3 no.2 (i) bars 66–77.

(b) Beethoven. Cello Sonata in G minor, op.5 no.2 (ii) bars 298–304.

(c) Beethoven. Cello Sonata in G minor, op.5 no.2 (ii) bars 104–7.

The type of rapid 'across-the-strings' arpeggio figuration found in the opening movement of Jean-Pierre's Sonata in E minor op.4 no.2, from a set of six works dedicated to Friedrich Wilhelm II and probably published in the year before Beethoven paid his visit to the Berlin court, is mirrored in the same movement of the Beethoven.

(Similar figuration is also found in the development section of the first movement in Beethoven's Sonata op.69.)

Ex. 5.2.
(a) J.-P. Duport. Sonata in E minor, op.4 no.2 (i) bars 80–8.

(b) Beethoven. Cello Sonata in G minor, op.5 no.2 (ii) bars 100–3.

Arpeggiated writing of this kind is found in Jean-Louis Duport's influential *Essai sur le Doigté du Violoncelle et sur la Conduite de l'Archet*. Although his study was not published until around 1806, Duport explains in his preface that he was asked by friends, amateurs and artists more than twenty years earlier to write a treatise on cello fingering, but that he was too busy to undertake the work. He did, however, gather together the material for his essay during this time. The seventh in the famous series of 21 Studies contained in the appendix to Duport's manual deals with rapid arpeggios, and from the instructions placed above some of the shorter examples of 'Titre XI' (*Du Doigté de l'Arpégio, Et des Extensions qui s'y rencontrent*) from the *Essai* itself we can gain a clear idea of the kind of bowing Jean-Louis might have applied to the passage from the Beethoven quoted in Ex. 5.2(b) above. The following example, Duport instructs, 'se fait en tirant les deux premières notes, et en poussant les six dernières':

Ex. 5.3. J.-L. Duport, *Essai sur le Doigté du Violoncelle*, Etude VII.

In writing the word 'arpeggio' above the sustained, widely spaced cello triad in bar 30 of the slow introduction to the first of the op.5 sonatas, it is likely that Beethoven wanted the player to bow back and forth across the strings in the same rapid triplet motion as the pianist, thereby lending textural depth and dynamic strength to the introduction's climax. The moment is controversial enough to warrant a detailed examination, particularly since it is so seldom performed in a manner that reflects Beethoven's probable intention. It is obvious that if he had simply wanted the bar in question played exactly as notated, his indication would have been at best superfluous, since the cellist cannot in any case sound all the notes of the triad together:

Ex. 5.4. Beethoven. Cello Sonata in F, op.5 no.1 (i) bars 29–31.

Shorthand arpeggio notation indicating quick-fire across-the-strings motion was relatively common in the music of the earlier eighteenth century – a familiar example is found in the Allegro of Bach's A major Violin Sonata BWV 1015 – and it survived right until the time of Beethoven's visit to the Prussian court. Similar notation is found in the last of the Jean-Louis Duport's sonatas op.4, where each half of the opening Allegro ends with a series of triads in minims marked 'arpegio' [sic], while the *Allegro assai* finale contains a triple-stopped passage with the same marking, clearly to be executed in a back-and-forth triplet motion (see Illustration 2 opposite).

Illustration 2. Jean-Louis Duport, Sonata in D, op.4 no.6 (iv). Sieber, Paris, c.1795.
© Bayerische Staatsbibliothek, Munich.

Besides the op.5 no.1 sonata, Beethoven invoked an 'arpeggio' cello notation in the second movement of his Serenade op.8 for string trio. Here, the moment again coincides with the music's climax featuring the cello's open C string:

Ex. 5.5. Beethoven. Serenade in D for string trio, op.8 (ii) bars 33–5.

In this instance, the arrangement of the serenade as a 'Notturno' for piano and viola, published as Beethoven's op.42, may be of some help in gauging the type of effect the composer had in mind. It is true that the transcription was made not by him, but in all likelihood by the composer and piano teacher Franz Xaver Kleinheiz. However, in a letter of September 1803 to the Leipzig publishers Hoffmeister & Kühnel regarding the arrangements of the two serenades opp.8 and 25, Beethoven told them, 'the transcriptions are not mine, but I have looked through them and in places thoroughly corrected them.'[12]

Whether or not the pianist's left-hand tremolo in the transcription of the above-cited moment from op.8 stems directly from Beethoven, it shows an awareness that the original cello part needs to sustain its motion through the second and third beats of the bar:

[12] BGA no.157; Anderson no.82.

Ex. 5.6. Beethoven. Notturno in D, op.42 (ii) bars 33–5.

The impreciseness in notation of these two moments from the op.5 no.1 Sonata and the op.8 Serenade finds Beethoven uncharacteristically allowing the performer a considerable degree of interpretative freedom, and players might do well to respond with a gesture that is rather more fulsome than the single arpeggiated chord traditionally heard.

The Duport brothers were not the first outstanding cellists with whom Beethoven came into contact. In his early years in Vienna he became acquainted with Anton Kraft (for whom he later wrote the taxing cello part of his Triple Concerto op.56), and Kraft's son Nikolaus, who in 1801 had travelled to Berlin in order to study with Jean-Louis Duport. Nikolaus Kraft became a regular member of the well-known string quartet led by Ignaz Schuppanzigh, and he and his father were both associated with early performances of Beethoven's Sonata op.69 (see p.253). Beethoven's colleagues in the electoral orchestra at Bonn had included the cousins Andreas and Bernhard Romberg – the former a violinist, the latter destined to become perhaps the most famous cellist in the first half of the nineteenth century. Towards the end of 1796, following a two-year stay in Italy, the two cousins passed through Vienna, where, in January 1797, Beethoven played his two op.5 sonatas with Bernhard Romberg. It seems to have been he who, in the first decade of the nineteenth century, was responsible for developing one of the last modifications to the cello: a new type of grooved fingerboard which enabled the strings to lie closer together, with the C string at a greater distance from the board than the remaining three. The improved arrangement allowed the C string to be attacked with increased resonance and strength, and also facilitated cross-string passagework in the higher positions.[13]

---

[13] For a discussion of Romberg's modification, see Watkin, 'Beethoven's Sonatas for Piano and Cello', pp.89–92.

The question of resonance, or sympathetic vibrations, was one to which Jean-Louis Duport devoted considerable space in his *Essai*, providing tables of the pitches that had several perceptible resonances. According to Duport's table, the note G as played on the A string had three resonances by virtue of the sympathetic vibrations of the G and C strings (the 15th of the G string, and the 19th of the C string, as Duport specifies). It is this note, with important hairpin dynamics, that Beethoven insists upon at some length in the coda of the opening movement from the second of his op.5 sonatas:

Ex. 5.7. Beethoven. Cello Sonata in G minor, op.5 no.2 (i) bars 508–25.

The final significant modification to the cello, the addition of the end-pin, was carried out at some stage during the late nineteenth century. Before that time, the player rested the instrument on the calf of his left leg. Duport's *Essai* gives detailed instructions as to the correct method of holding the instrument in this way:

> The position of the violoncello between the legs varies greatly according to the customs and the different height of people. One can play very well holding one's instrument a little higher or a little lower. This is the most common method and the one which must be best.
>
> First of all, one must sit at the front of the chair; next place the left foot far away from oneself, and bring the right close; then position the instrument between the legs in such a way that the corner of the lower left-hand curve of the back lies in the hollow of the left knee, so that the weight of the instrument is carried by the calf of the left leg, with the left foot pointing outwards. If on the other hand the left knee itself were placed in this curve, it would prevent the bow from passing easily when using the highest string. The right leg is placed against the bottom edge [*l'éclisse d'en bas*] of the instrument, to hold it steady.[14]

No less important was the manner in which the bow was held, in order to allow variety and flexibility of expression. Duport's chapter entitled *De la Manière de tenir l'Archet* gives valuable advice in this respect:

> The thumb must lie flat against the bow-stick; the middle finger must be raised above the hair; the index finger must be placed forward on the stick at a short distance from the middle finger; it has to be mobile, because the further it moves away from the middle finger, the greater the pressure the bow has on the string.

---

[14] Duport, *Essai sur le Doigté du Violoncelle*, p.5.

This mobility, at times considerable, at times moderate or even almost imperceptible, is very necessary for expression.[15]

It was for this instrument of considerable expressive flexibility but relatively weak carrying power that Beethoven composed his two op.5 sonatas. If there are times in the opening movement of the F major first work of the pair, when the stringed instrument is in danger of being overwhelmed by the intricacy and forcefulness of the keyboard writing, to say nothing of the inflationary scope of the piece itself, Beethoven generally responds to the challenge of the new medium with remarkable inventiveness and success.

The avoidance of a fully fledged slow movement led Beethoven in the op.5 sonatas to adopt a two-movement design: a concept that may well have stemmed from some of the violin sonatas of Mozart.[16] Of the six sonatas K.301–6 published in Paris in 1778 with a dedication to the Electress Palatine Elisabeth Maria, all but the D major last work are in two movements only – while the two-movement G major Sonata K.379 of 1781, whose variation finale exerted such a strong influence on both Beethoven's early E flat piano quartet and his trio for piano, flute and bassoon, actually begins with a substantial slow introduction which is so broad as to lend it the effect of a curtailed slow movement proper. In so doing, it clearly foreshadows the shape of Beethoven's two op.5 sonatas. Mozart's slow beginning, moreover, is followed by an Allegro in the minor, so that the sonata's opening half may be regarded as a distant forerunner of the unusual scheme of Beethoven's Cello Sonata op.102 no.1, which places its first Allegro in the relative minor of the work's home key. It is true, however, that the scope of Mozart's slow introduction has a far greater influence on the proportions of the following Allegro than is the case in any of the Beethoven works cited above. Mozart's Allegro itself is highly condensed, with a development section occupying no more than a dozen bars, almost as though the movement's two opening sections were exchanging roles: such abbreviated developments are normally the province of Mozart's sonata-form slow movements.

Further two-movement works are to be found among the keyboard sonatas of Haydn. In the majority, the main weight of the argument is carried by the first movement. The D major work (H.XVI.51) from Haydn's final triptych of sonatas, for example, has a broad opening movement followed by a brief binary *Presto*; and a set of three sonatas (H.XVI.40–42) published in 1784 with a dedication to Marie Hermenegild Esterházy consists entirely of works in two movements, again with the first of the pair considerably more expansive than the finale. A similar imbalance of proportions is found in Beethoven's op.5 sonatas, though the composer seems later to have become dissatisfied with this top-heavy type of design: his middle-period works having only two movements – the piano sonatas opp.54, 78 and 90 – distribute their proportions more evenly, while his single late work of the kind, the Sonata op.111, shifts the expressive weight firmly to the finale.

---

[15] *Ibid.*, p.156.
[16] An idea for a slow movement in A flat major, marked *Moderato cantabile* and contained among Beethoven's sketches for the Sonata op.5 no.1, may possibly have been intended for that work. See Johnson/Fischhof, vol.1, p.321, and vol.2, p.18.

For all its many flashes of genius, the opening movement of the first work in Beethoven's op.5 pair is rather less successful than the parallel piece in its more intense G minor companion. Its structure is dangerously discursive, with an exposition containing no fewer than four well-defined themes, and the scope of the whole enlarged through extended excursions into the 'flatter' regions of C minor and A flat major. If Donald Francis Tovey's view of the piece may strike us as unduly harsh, it is difficult to disagree with the thrust of his argument. 'If Beethoven's early works had been mostly in the style of op.2 no.3, or of the Violoncello Sonata op.5 no.1', writes Tovey, 'and he had died before producing anything more characteristic, it would have been possible to argue that here was an ambitious composer who evidently aspired to be greater than either Mozart or Haydn, but who already showed the tendency to inflation that leads through the style of Hummel to the degenerate styles of the virtuoso pianoforte-writers.'[17]

Like the opening Allegro of the op.16 Quintet, the first movement of the F major sonata is essentially a virtuoso vehicle for the pianist, and its coda is again occupied by an elaborate cadenza. The concerto propensities of the piece are further underlined by a surprisingly conventional conclusion unabashedly written in orchestral style. Performers would nevertheless do well to remember that the tempo is no quicker than *Allegro*, in four beats to the bar – a restraint which is underlined by the contrast afforded by the scurrying concluding bars of the cadenza, where the pace quickens to *Presto* and the time signature changes to ¢.[18]

More individual, perhaps, than the Allegro is the slow introduction, with its interplay of light and shade. Particularly striking is the manner in which the warmly lyrical cello phrase following the neutral-sounding initial bars is immediately transformed by the piano into something altogether darker and more menacing:

Ex. 5.8. Beethoven. Cello Sonata in F, op.5 no.1 (i) bars 7–16.

—(*continued*)

---

[17] Tovey, *Beethoven*, p.89.

[18] Czerny, however, was of the opinion that the Allegro should be 'very lively and in the brilliant style which predominates in most of the works of his [Beethoven's] first period. A quick time is here even more necessary as the piece is of considerable length. In such cases the performer must always endeavour to maintain the interest through liveliness and brilliance of execution' (Czerny, p.80).

Ex. 5.8—continued

The remainder of the introduction, with the music more in minor than major, consists largely of an extended dominant preparation paving the way for the appearance of the Allegro's first subject. That first subject itself is one in which the instruments appear momentarily to exchange roles: the theme is given to the piano, above a repeated-note left-hand accompaniment in bare fifths and fourths that clearly imitates a cello playing 'off the string'; but as though reluctant to leave the stringed instrument suspended on an unresolved dominant seventh at the end of the introduction Beethoven allows it to share the piano's accompaniment during the initial four bars of the Allegro's theme, after which its part peters out after all on the same unresolved harmony, and the theme's extravagantly expanded second limb is left to the piano alone. The effect is one of a curiously disconcerting 'dissolve' between the introduction and the Allegro, and Beethoven does not recall it in the recapitulation, where a new cello accompaniment continues throughout the theme. The recapitulation, moreover, transposes both theme and keyboard accompaniment up an octave, and has the accompaniment more richly harmonised in a manner that no longer suggests the exposition's quasi-cello sonority.

It may have been the profusion of thematic material in the exposition's expansive second group that prompted Beethoven to launch an expedition into the more remote region of A flat in order to avoid the risk of tonal monotony over so long a stretch. Nor is the choice of key for this interpolation purely arbitrary: it seems to emerge logically out of the minor-mode tinges that colour the start of the second group (bars 73ff.), with its concentration on the note of the flat submediant (A flat), as well as the interrupted cadence that lands the music firmly on the chord of A flat at bar 98. Moreover, the chromatically descending bass line of the second group's beginning is reproduced in an expanded form in the A flat major interpolation itself (bars 131–3).

The peremptory perfect cadence that closes the exposition brings the virtuoso proceedings to a temporary halt with almost comical zeal, and the joke is intensified by the quietly understated dominant seventh chord that immediately follows, providing the simplest of bridges back to the first subject in the tonic for the exposition repeat. The function of the emphatic cadence is revealed in the second-time bars, where, by the expedient of raising the root of its initial chord from F natural to F sharp, and at the same time enharmonically renotating its flattened seventh, E flat, as D sharp, the chord is transformed into a diminished seventh which enables the music to take off in an entirely new direction for the start of the development section. Needless to say, the harmonic pun can fully be appreciated only if the exposition repeat has been observed. Haydn had invoked a similar change in tonal direction at the parallel point in the opening movement of his F major String Quartet op.74 no.2, where – as in the Beethoven – the first-time bars lead back into the tonic for the exposition repeat, and the second-time bars involve an enharmonic change that allows the music to emerge into the bright key of A major at the start of the development section. Since this was one of the works Haydn composed during the period of Beethoven's study with him, it is quite possible that the young composer took note of the passage in question.

Ex. 5.9.
(a) Beethoven. Cello Sonata in F, op.5 no.1 (i) bars 157–65.

Ex. 5.9.
(b) Haydn. String Quartet in F, op.74 no.2 (i) bars 93–105.

Beethoven was evidently fond of the sound of A major within a wider F major context: besides the above example in the op.5 no.1 Sonata, the same juxtaposition of keys is to be found at the start of the development section in the first movement of the String Quartet op.18 no.1, while the second half of the minuet's F major trio in the 'Razumovsky' Quartet op.59 no.3 is launched with a similar startling chord of A major, and the latter half of the finale in the F major Piano Sonata op.54 again begins with an unprepared – albeit less dramatic – turn to A major. In the cello sonata a similar switch in tonal direction is brought into play at the end of the recapitulation, where a further renotation of the dominant seventh harmony, this time as an augmented sixth chord resolving onto a 6/4 chord of D minor, serves to launch the preparation for the cadenza.

Ex. 5.10. Beethoven. Cello Sonata in F, op.5 no.1 (i) bars 338–47.

The prolongation following the last of the three *fortissimo* chords seems to have been an afterthought. A sketch for this moment shows that Beethoven originally intended a simple echo of the exposition's closing bars, with the second *fortissimo* chord followed by a dominant seventh – played perhaps, like the parallel chord at the two previous appearances of this moment, *piano* – leading directly to the start of the quasi-cadenza, which was to have set off in D major:[19]

---

[19] See Johnson/Fischhof, vol.2, p.17.

Ex. 5.11. Beethoven. Cello Sonata in F, op.5 no.1 (i) cadenza, sketch.

The development section, built entirely out of the first subject's initial two bars, offers a notable example of Beethoven's characteristic procedure of foreshortening, concentrating as it does on an ever diminishing fragment of the subject. The approach to the recapitulation finds the fragment transformed into the minor, and the cello's repeated statements punctuated by the piano with a subdued reminiscence of its semiquaver figuration from the earlier stage of the development section. The hushed use of the cello's open C string in this passage, until, in bar 204, no more than a single reiterated note remains, is a highly imaginative stroke. At this point the music is left suspended on the dominant of F minor, but the sidestep onto the key of D flat in the following bar seems to be the logical outcome of what has preceded it. In this key, a new chorale-like idea is introduced, before the piano tremolando that underpins it begins a long chromatic ascent that enables the music once again to reach the dominant of F, in preparation for the recapitulation. Beethoven thought highly enough of this moment to invoke a similar sudden stillness at the parallel point in the opening movement of his E flat Violin Sonata op.12 no.3, with its broad melody in C flat major unfolding above a rustling tremolando, though the later work cannot match the aura of mystery that generates the music's new-found serenity in the cello sonata. The darkness of the atmosphere here owes its effect to Beethoven's sustained exploitation of the cello's two lowest notes.

Ex. 5.12. Beethoven. Cello Sonata in F, op.5 no.1 (i) bars 194–224.

—(continued)

Ex. 5.12—continued

The emergence of the recapitulation out of this passage, following its *pianissimo calando*, with an *ffp* explosion in bar 221 on the main subject's first note, is a characteristic gesture, and one that brings the music down to earth with startling abruptness.

Given the movement's exceptionally large scope, there was clearly a need to impose a sense of unity on its various stages. To this end, the recapitulation absorbs elements of the preceding development section: in particular, the first subject itself appears in an altered form, echoing the florid shape it had assumed during the A major opening moments of the development section, and it is followed by an extended interpolation based on the development's 'rocking' keyboard figuration, now transferred to the pianist's right hand, while the left accompanies the cello's soaring melody with the first subject's arpeggio motif.

For his cadenza Beethoven had before him the elaborate example in the finale of Mozart's D major Violin Sonata K.306, but such passages in a duo sonata were rare in the eighteenth century. Beethoven's cadenza in op.5 no.1 is notable above all for the half-dozen bars of Adagio immediately preceding its helter-skelter conclusion, with the music momentarily reverting to the atmosphere of the work's slow introduction. The rising cello phrases echo the ascending motif in semiquavers given out by both players in octaves at the introduction's beginning, and in their context – and in the absence of any self-contained slow movement in the work – they carry an expressive weight out of all proportion to their brief duration.

For all the originality and effectiveness of passages such as that given in Ex. 5.12 above, from a textural point of view it would have to be conceded that the sonata's finale is rather more successful than the opening movement. The rondo is, indeed, a piece of closely knit chamber music of a kind that would not have been feasible in the opening movement, given its expansive nature and concerto propensities. The rondo's modulatory theme sounds momentarily as though it were beginning conventionally enough in the tonic. However, the piano's canonic entry immediately throws it onto the dominant of G minor, and the off-tonic effect is intensified by a strategic cross-accent in the cello part. The canonic writing is not maintained in the theme's third and fourth bars, which are contrived in such a way that the music's melodic content is inextricably interwoven between the two instruments. Nor does Beethoven pursue the counterpoint in the subject's second half. Instead, he chooses to emphasise the theme's all-important rising interval of the fourth by having it picked out at the delayed entry of the pianist's left hand. The model behind Beethoven's theme may have been the similarly two-stranded, modulatory main subject from the first movement of Haydn's 'Surprise' Symphony no.94.

Ex. 5.13.
(a) Haydn. Symphony no.94 (i) bars 17–20.

(b) Beethoven. Cello Sonata in F, op.5 no.1 (ii) bars 1–10.

The theme of the first episode is again modulatory, and underpinned by the same sequence of rising fourths in the left-hand piano part.

Ex. 5.14. Beethoven. Cello Sonata in F, op.5 no.1 (ii) bars 24–30.

The new subject itself is unusually unstable, cadencing as it does successively into G major, F major and C major; and Beethoven underlines its arrival in the last of these keys through a substantial C major expansion. His purpose, at least in part, is to intensify the return of the rondo theme, which is deflected from its expected course and occurs not in the home key, but in A flat. This obliquely approached reprise considerably strengthens the shock of the repeated note F sharp in the imitative piano entry. At the same time, the modulatory nature of the rondo theme itself is underlined through the fact that the true reprise occurs as part of a continuing harmonic sequence, and at a point where the music is poised on the dominant of F minor.

Ex. 5.15. Beethoven. Cello Sonata in F, op.5 no.1 (ii) bars 60–9.

—(continued)

Ex. 5.15—continued

The central episode, in B flat minor, is Beethoven's means of counterbalancing the asymmetrical nature of the surrounding material. Its theme is almost exaggeratedly regular, and Beethoven was to remember its layout, and its pizzicato accompaniment, in the coda of his Variations on Mozart's 'Bei Männern, welche Liebe fühlen' WoO 46.[20] In common with the parallel episode of the finale in Beethoven's first two piano concertos, its popular style provides an unusually light-hearted, almost playful, use of the minor mode.

As in the opening movement, the coda brings with it the suggestion of a cadenza; and a long rallentando leading to two Adagio bars again lifts the music onto a higher expressive plane. The entire passage is based on a transfigured version of the rondo theme's closing phrase, and it shows Beethoven, as so often in the works of his early maturity, carrying out a process of winding down shortly before the close, so that the music can gather renewed momentum for a witty final peroration.

The second of the two op.5 sonatas is Beethoven's single large-scale essay in what was for him (as opposed to Mozart!) a seldom-used key. His only other G minor work of any significance is the miniature Piano Sonata op.49 no.1, probably written – despite its late opus number – shortly after the cello sonata, whose finale is likewise in the major throughout. There is, however, also the case of the substantial introduction to the 'Kakadu' Variations op.121a.[21]

The opening movement of op.5 no.2 is again conceived on a vast scale, and its slow introduction is actually longer and more imposing than that of its F major companion. Its very presence in a dramatic piece cast in the minor is itself already an indication of the scope of Beethoven's aspirations at this early stage of his career. The introduction may be heard as a condensed sonata form, with a contrasting second subject appearing, at bar 11, in the submediant, rather than the more orthodox relative major, and an extended development section. As in Beethoven's early E flat piano quartet – and, indeed, Mozart's Violin Sonata K.379 – the Allegro begins at the point where we might have expected the recapitulation to occur.

---

[20] See p.130.

[21] A lesser work in G minor is the song collection 'Sehnsucht' WoO 134, after Goethe. Two of the late Bagatelles for piano – opp.119 no.1 and 126 no.2 – are in the same key; but the piano Fantasy op.77, often described as being in G minor, may safely be discounted, as no more than its first two bars are actually in that key.

The introduction and the Allegro are unified through their prominent use of a three-note motif moving in stepwise descent or ascent. The motif, marked *tenuto* in the second bar, continues the stepwise motion of the preceding bar in augmented form. No less important is the diminished harmony of the second bar, with its insistence on the note E flat.

Ex. 5.16. Beethoven. Cello Sonata in G minor, op.5 no.2 (i) bars 1–7.

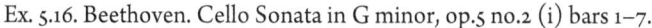

The three-note motif and the stress on the note E flat figure prominently in the introduction's final stage, which draws to a close with as startling a use of silence as to be found anywhere in Beethoven: at the music's exceptionally slow tempo the pauses separating its halting phrases are of remarkably long duration. So, too, is the final silent bar which, following on from an unresolved cadence, is all too seldom allowed its due value in performance. Although the introduction as a whole begins firmly on a downbeat, Beethoven prefers not to indicate a full bar's rest here, but to prolong the third beat by means of a fermata, and to imply that the bar is completed with cello's upbeat to the Allegro's main subject. (The upbeat also completes the exposition's final bar.) The sense of overlap between the introduction and the Allegro is underlined by the fact that the former's concluding cadence is not resolved until the end of the opening phrase of the Allegro, which sets off not in the tonic, but on the dominant of C minor. Although the Allegro's theme does cadence into G minor in its fourth bar, the resolution is weakened since the entire phrase unfolds over a tonic pedal: a firmer dominant harmony in its third bar would clearly have produced a quite different effect.

Ex. 5.17. Beethoven. Cello Sonata in G minor, op.5 no.2 (i) bars 32–52.

The C minor implications of the Allegro's beginning continue during the theme's latter half, after which the tonic is decisively established with a passionate outburst in G minor. The first subject itself is entirely based on the three-note cell which had figured so prominently in the introduction; and the Allegro's further progress is governed by the same idea (the second subject treats it in inversion), which is used towards the end of the exposition to build up an atmosphere of remarkable intensity. When the passage returns at the parallel point in the recapitulation Beethoven further tightens the screw, and interpolates an additional nine bars which have the cello intensifying the pervasive three-note figure through the addition of a winding phrase played in contrary motion to the pianist's left hand (see Ex. 5.18 below).

As in so many of Beethoven's opening Allegros conceived on an unusually broad canvas, the development section unfolds in two distinct stages. The first continues the pervasive quaver triplet motion of the exposition's latter half, while in the second, that motion gives way to much less agitated quavers, and to a new melody given out initially by the cello in the dominant minor, and answered by the piano in the tonic. The appearance of a stable new idea at this late point in the movement is surprising, though Beethoven seems occasionally to have felt the need for such melodic contrast at the mid-point of a large movement focusing with almost obsessive concentration on a single basic idea.[22]

[22] The new theme introduced at the centre of the development section in the 'Eroica' Symphony's first movement is doubtless the most famous instance of a similar procedure, though its effect is very different. Not only does the theme appear in a remote key (the flat supertonic minor), but it is more palpably related to material from the exposition: its syncopated repeated-note violin accompaniment derives from the first subject, and the pizzicato double bass interjections echo the similar pizzicatos in the initial theme of the exposition's closing group. Once again, however, Beethoven stresses the organic unity of his piece by absorbing the pizzicato figure into the start of the recapitulation. Similar, if much more brief, instances of a new thematic idea emerging at the mid-point of the development section can be found in the opening movement of the Piano Sonata op.7 and the Violin Sonata op.23.

Ex. 5.18. Beethoven. Cello Sonata in G minor, op.5 no.2 (i) bars 440–57.

Having begun his Allegro on the dominant of C minor, Beethoven is able to approach the recapitulation obliquely, allowing it to enter as part of a continuing harmonic sequence. The passage is one that concentrates on the dominant minor ninth harmony that had featured so prominently in the closing bars of the introduction, once again underlined through strategically placed *sforzandi*. Here, too, the cello part is left unresolved on the dominant (bar 307), and its re-entry at the point of the recapitulation is delayed by the piano's manifold repetitions of the three-note motif derived from the first subject. These 'empty' piano bars fulfil much the same function as did the long expectant pause between the introduction and the start of the Allegro.

Ex. 5.19. Beethoven. Cello Sonata in G minor, op.5 no.2 (i) bars 295–322.

The recapitulation comes to as decisive a close as could be imagined, with an almost orchestrally conceived passage in forceful broken octaves. The intention, it turns out, is to intensify the surprise of the coda that now follows – a surprise that is further strengthened if the movement's long second-half repeat has been observed. (Haydn, no doubt, would have made a joke out of a false ending of this kind by lengthening the gap before the music proceeds, as he did, for instance, in the finale of the String Quartet op.50 no.1 and the Symphony no.90.) The coda eventually gravitates towards the dominant of C minor, before it comes to rest not in G minor, but with an unstable cadence into the major providing a natural link to the theme of the rondo finale, which sets off as though it is to be in C major:[23]

Ex. 5.20. Beethoven. Cello Sonata in G minor, op.5 no.2 (ii) bars 1–8.

In Beethoven, such a beginning frequently serves as a means of furnishing the illusion of a wider key scheme within a large-scale work all of whose movements are in the same tonality. Perhaps the most protracted instance of a procedure of this kind occurs in the E minor 'Razumovsky' Quartet – a work in which even the scherzo's trio is in the home tonality. Here, the finale has a main theme that sets out in an unambiguous C major, and thereafter wavers continually between that key and E minor; and it is not for nothing that the theme is repeated with well-nigh obsessive frequency during the course of the movement.

An off-tonic beginning as in the finale of the sonata op.5 no.2 would have been unthinkable to Mozart, though the idea is one that Haydn exploited on occasion with obvious relish, and not only in finales. Haydn's two B minor string quartets, op.33 no.1 and op.64 no.2, both begin deceptively as though heralding a piece whose key was to be D major (a witticism anticipated by the C minor Quartet op.17 no.4, with its quasi-E flat major beginning); and several of his quartets of the 1780s contain

---

[23] Beethoven seldom ended the opening movement of a minor-mode work with a resolution in the major, and when he did so it was almost invariably in order to form a transition, whether actual or implied, to the following movement, as in the String Quartet op.131 and the Piano Sonata op.111.

movements with a similar tonally oblique beginning. The first sound heard in the D major 'Frog' Quartet op.50 no.6, for instance, is a sustained, unharmonised note E, while the finale of the A major Quartet op.55 no.1 starts with a similar move from the dominant towards the tonic.

Besides imparting the impression that the music has begun in mid-stream, a function of the off-tonic beginning as established by Haydn is to enable the initial tonal ambiguity to be exploited at a later stage, in order to disguise the moment of recapitulation. In the 'Frog' Quartet, the actual recapitulation (marked with an arrow in Ex. 5.21 below) occurs at the apex of a sequentially rising series of melodic phrases, in such a way that the listener can register this structural landmark only once it has already passed:

Ex. 5.21. Haydn. Quartet in D, op.50 no.6 (i) bars 110–17.

We have seen that the recapitulation in the opening movement of Beethoven's G minor cello sonata is similarly camouflaged, if not quite to such witty effect; and in the rondo finale Beethoven does not fail to seize upon the possibilities for deliberate deception afforded by the quasi-C major start of his theme, allowing its reprise to steal in each time unnoticed, as part of a continuing harmonic sequence. In Ex. 5.22 overleaf, the reprise begins in the latter half of the fifth bar.

Ex. 5.22. Beethoven. Cello Sonata in G minor, op.5 no.2 (ii) bars 61–7.

What is prepared on each occasion is, in other words, the return not of the home key, but of the key in which the theme sets out. Perhaps this explains why at its first appearance the rondo theme itself begins in such a spirit of gentle understatement – its first two notes unharmonised, and the predominant dynamic level *piano*. The theme's second half, however, sets off more forcefully, with the upbeat phrase now harmonised, and with each note preceded by an appoggiatura. Since the appoggiatura remains at the same pitch, the interval it affords with the successive melody note is progressively widened, with the result that the natural emphasis on the downbeat at bar 5 is strengthened (see Ex. 5.20 on p.120). At the point where the cello first enters with its accompanimental part, the piano expands its appoggiaturas still further, to become octaves.

The movement's C major undertones are accentuated by the expansive episode in that key that stands at its centre – indeed, so stable is the influence of C major at this point that Beethoven decides to approach the following return of the rondo theme obliquely, allowing a preliminary glimpse of it in the distant key of A flat. Even so, the joke is turned back on itself, as it were, in the actual reprise, which wittily attempts to force the theme – at its original pitch – into a G major straightjacket, by means of an insistent dominant pedal.

Ex. 5.23. Beethoven. Cello Sonata in G minor, op.5 no.2 (ii) bars 152–74.

The moment is one of rumbustious good humour, and it is counterbalanced by the sonata's closing bars, in which a variant of the theme played in broken octaves by the cello unfolds over an equally obstinate tonic pedal. The broken octaves iron out the theme's quirky rhythm, in a process of neutralisation that is anticipated in the final full reprise, where the melody is given out by the piano in a steady stream of demisemiquavers. The demisemiquavers subsequently pass to the cello, in a passage forcibly recalling the similar across-the-strings arpeggios of the central episode.

The G minor cello sonata is in many ways the most ambitious and remarkable chamber piece Beethoven had written up to its time. The scope and dramatic intensity of its first movement, in particular, were not to be surpassed until the opening Allegro of the C minor Violin Sonata op.30 no.2; and if Beethoven showed greater resourcefulness in terms of interplay between the two instruments with his next cello sonata, op.69, the earlier work remains a strikingly assured and inventive exploitation of what was an entirely new genre.

Thayer recounts an anecdote linking the second of the op.5 sonatas with the famous double bass virtuoso Domenico Dragonetti, who, in the spring of 1799, stayed for a few weeks in Vienna on his way back from his home town of Venice to London, where he had settled some five years previously. He met Beethoven in Vienna on several occasions, and the two musicians became firm friends. Many years later Dragonetti's solicitor, Samuel Appleby, who was a keen music lover, reported: 'Beethoven had been told that his new friend could execute violoncello music upon his huge instrument, and one morning, when Dragonetti called at his room, he expressed his desire to hear a sonata. The contrabass was sent for, and the Sonata, no.2, of op.5, was selected. Beethoven played his part, with his eyes immovably fixed upon his companion, and, in the finale, where the arpeggios occur, was so delighted and excited that at the close he sprang up and threw his arms around both player and instrument.'[24]

Also composed around the time of the op.5 sonatas, and perhaps arising out of Beethoven's same visit to Berlin in 1796, were the Variations for piano and cello on the chorus 'See, the Conqu'ring Hero Comes' from Handel's *Judas Maccabaeus* (WoO 45). Throughout his life Beethoven revered Handel as the greatest of all composers, placing him even above Mozart. Ignaz von Seyfried, who knew Beethoven, and conducted the premiere of *Leonore* in 1805, reported that the composer had hailed Handel as 'the master of all masters! Go and learn', Beethoven continued, 'how to create such a great effect with so few means.'[25] On 28 September 1823 the Englishman J.R. Schultz visited Beethoven in the company of the publisher Tobias Haslinger. The following January, Schultz wrote an account of their meeting for the London *Harmonicon*:

---

[24] Thayer/Forbes, p.208. The arpeggios in question were presumably the across-the-strings figures quoted in Ex. 5.2 above. The passage lies comfortably on the cello, but would have been far harder to execute on the double bass, with its tuning in fourths.

[25] Seyfried, *Ludwig van Beethoven's Studien im Generalbass, Contrapunkt und in der Compositions-Lehre*, appendix p.22.

> In the whole course of our table-talk there was nothing so interesting as what he [Beethoven] said about Handel. I sat close by him and heard him assert very distinctly in German, 'Handel is the greatest composer who ever lived.' I cannot describe to you with what pathos, and I am inclined to say, with what sublimity of language, he spoke of the *Messiah* of this immortal genius. Every one of us was moved when he said, 'I would uncover my head, and kneel down at his tomb!'[26]

The same sentiment was repeated the following year, when Beethoven received another visitor from London, the harp manufacturer Johann Andreas Stumpff:

> I took up the pencil again and wrote in very distinct letters: 'Whom do you consider the greatest composer that ever lived?'
> 'Handel', was his instantaneous reply; 'to him I bow the knee', and he bent one knee to the floor.
> 'Mozart', I wrote.
> 'Mozart', he continued, 'is good and admirable.'
> 'Yes', wrote I, 'who was able to glorify even Handel with his additional accompaniments to *The Messiah*.'
> 'It would have lived without them', was his answer.[27]

Beethoven's finest tribute to Handel was the overture *Die Weihe des Hauses* of 1822, which, according to Schindler, arose out of a plan to write a piece in strict Handelian style.[28] But even in 1824 Stumpff was surprised at how few of Handel's scores Beethoven had actually seen, and he resolved to send him the 40-volume edition of the composer's works edited by Samuel Arnold. That gift arrived just a few months before Beethoven's death, and his friend Gerhard von Breuning, who visited him often during his final illness, recounts how he found the composer one day in February 1827 with his precious Handel volumes stacked up on one of the two pianos in his room. 'They have given me great joy with these works', Beethoven told Breuning. 'I have wished for them for a long time; for Handel is the greatest, the ablest composer; I can still learn from him.'

> He continued saying this and similar things, in happy excitement. And now I began to hand one volume after another over to him in his bed. He leafed through one volume after another as I gave them to him, pausing from time to time at particular passages, and then put one volume after another to his right on his bed up against the wall, until they finally all lay there in a heap that remained there for hours, because I found them still piled up in the afternoon. And again he began to hold forth about Handel's greatness in lively terms of praise, and to describe him as the most classical and most thoroughgoing of all composers.[29]

By then, the cello variations on 'See, the Conqu'ring Hero Comes' must have seemed to Beethoven to belong to another era altogether. Thayer's suggestion that Handel's

---

[26] *The Harmonicon*, ii (1824), p.10. See also Thayer/Forbes, pp.870–1, where, however, Beethoven's English visitor is erroneously given as Edward Schultz.

[27] Thayer/Forbes, p.920.

[28] Schindler, vol.2, p.7.

[29] Breuning, *Aus dem Schwarzspanierhaus*, pp.94–5.

theme may have been suggested to him by Baron van Swieten is plausible enough.[30] It was van Swieten who, in his role as Prefect of the Viennese Imperial Library, and as the owner of a well-stocked music library himself, had been able to kindle Mozart's interest in Bach and Handel, and had commissioned him to make re-orchestrations of *Messiah*, *Acis and Galatea* and *Alexander's Feast*. At the time Beethoven composed his op.5 cello sonatas, van Swieten was making his own contribution to the revival of the oratorio tradition by writing the libretto for Haydn's *The Creation*. Some five years later, Beethoven inscribed his First Symphony to the Baron.

'See, the Conqu'ring Hero Comes' is one of the most famous, if not among the most subtle, of Handel's melodies. Leaving aside the question of some awkward word-setting that betrays the composer's poor grasp of English, the theme suffers from the manner in which it squats inelegantly at the end of each four-bar phrase – a deficiency that is at least partially masked in the majority of Beethoven's variations through the strategy of overlapping the figuration of its individual segments. The melody's most notable feature is the turn to the relative minor at its central point. Beethoven's search for an expressive equivalent in his two minor-mode variations (nos.4 and 8) leads him to choose the comparatively distant key of the flat submediant for this moment; and in the second of the pair the bars in question are further highlighted through the manner in which they assume the aspect of a subdued chorale-like interlude within a much more turbulent context.

Beethoven's variations are primarily a display piece for the pianist, though the cellist does a good deal more than sit idly by: the seventh of the twelve variations, in particular, demands considerable agility from the string player. Nevertheless, Beethoven establishes the piano's dominance from the outset, with an arrangement of Handel's tune that offers the cellist no more than a rudimentary accompaniment, and a first variation which dispenses with the instrument's services altogether. If the cello has a long-spun melodic line in the second variation, that line would appear to have been conceived as a secondary layer to the intricate piano writing, with its technically awkward repeated-note figuration. The third variation again relegates the cello to the background, while the pianist is let loose on a dazzling cascade of semiquavers. Perhaps it was for this reason that Beethoven deemed it wise in the following variation – the first of the minor-mode pair – to allow the cello's expressive melody to unfold above a keyboard part restricted virtually throughout to a regular pattern of quavers in bare octaves, and in a low register. Similar keyboard figuration recurs in variation 6, confined this time to the pianist's left hand, while the right plays in quasi-canon with the cello. The canon is intensified in the concluding eight bars to accommodate an illusory third part.

The virtuoso cello passagework of variation 7 would seem to have been tailor-made for the peculiar talents of the Duport brothers, though the cello's display is capped by the pianist in the stormy minor-mode variation that follows. No less characteristic are variations 9 and 10, the former with a mysteriously hushed chromatic passage at its centre followed immediately by a *fortissimo* outburst, the latter with its gruff canon between the cello and the pianist's left hand.

---

[30] Thayer/Forbes, p.196.

For the *Adagio* penultimate variation the time signature changes from ¢ to c. As a result the theme, whose 24-bar structure has hitherto been respected throughout, now occupies only twelve bars; and in order to enlarge the proportions of this expressive climax of the work, Beethoven casts it as a double variation, with each half given to the pianist alone before the theme is taken up by the cellist.

The final variation brings with it a more radical change of metre, to 3/8. The deliberate playfulness of the music here takes it as far as could be imagined from the heroic march-like style of Handel's theme, and Beethoven makes another irreverent gesture by wittily slipping, albeit briefly, into the unlikely key of C sharp minor, before winding up proceedings with a long-held trill – a distant harbinger of the culmination of some of his late variation sets – followed by two peremptory chords.

Somewhat more assured are the two variation sets for piano and cello based on themes from Mozart's *Die Zauberflöte*. The earlier of them (op.66), on the aria 'Ein Mädchen oder Weibchen', may also have been composed in 1796. Whether it was intended for Bernhard Romberg, who was staying with Beethoven in the autumn of that year, is not known. It was issued by the Viennese publisher Johann Traeg two years later, as one of several variation sets by Beethoven he brought out between 1793 and 1802.

In Mozart's Singspiel, Papageno's aria with its increasingly elaborate glockenspiel part at each recurring strophe, and its addition of wind instruments for the final stanza, is already written in the form of a miniature set of variations. It is also very much conceived in popular style – a fact that does not prevent Beethoven from simplifying the theme still further: not only does he shorten the melody, but he ignores Mozart's change in metre and tempo, from 2/4 *Andante* to 6/8 *Allegro*, for the second half of each strophe, and substitutes a compromise of a uniform *Allegretto*.[31]

As in the Handel set, Beethoven's first variation is a piano solo. The wit of its across-the-bar syncopation is as nothing compared with the lugubrious humour of the following variation, in which the theme's first half is subjected to a tortuously chromatic harmonisation (intensified by portentous *sforzando* accents) of a kind that would scarcely have invaded Papageno's worst nightmare. Having made his joke during the initial eight bars, Beethoven does not labour the point thereafter; and having given the cello the primary part here, he consigns it to an accompanimental role during the majority of the remaining variations. Only variation 4, with its double-stopped opening in imitation of a pair of horns, and the extended final variation once again bring the stringed instrument into melodic prominence.

In their contrast and individual characterisation the first eight variations represent a notable advance over the Handel set, as does the continuity between the last four variations. As far as the latter aspect is concerned, Beethoven once more takes the unusual step of writing two successive variations in the minor: the first of them an Adagio adopting the melodic outline of the preceding major-mode variation's

---

[31] Beethoven's choice of variation themes during his younger years mirrors that of the Abbé Joseph Gelinek to a remarkable degree. Gelinek, who once took part in a contest of improvisation with Beethoven, composed variations for solo piano in 1792–3 on the same theme from *Die Zauberflöte*, likewise bypassing its change in metre.

opening bars, while at the same time transforming them into a sublimated, double-dotted march rhythm; and the second having a piano part in smooth triplet quaver motion. The notion of continuity is further strengthened through a four-bar link to the final variation, which transforms Mozart's theme into a triple-time Allegro. In order to provide a more expansive conclusion, this last variation has written-out repeats in which each half of the theme is handed over from cello to piano. There is also a coda in which Beethoven indulges his fondness for introducing a distant tonality – in this case, the submediant (D major) – at a late stage. It is a moment of humour that invoked the wrath of the straight-laced *Allgemeine musikalische Zeitung* which, in its earliest mention of music by Beethoven, reviewed the variations alongside those for piano solo on the theme 'Une fièvre brulante' from Grétry's opera *Richard, Coeur de Lion* (WoO 72).

> It is well known that Herr van Beethoven is an extremely accomplished pianist, and if it were not well known it could be deduced from these variations. But whether he is an equally successful composer is a question that, to judge from the examples under discussion, would be more difficult to answer in the affirmative. The reviewer does not intend to suggest that there were not some among these variations that pleased him, and he willingly admits that with those on the theme 'Mich brennt ein heisses Fieber' Herr B. has succeeded better than Mozart, who also elaborated the same theme in his youth.[32] But Herr B. is less successful in the variations on the first theme [i.e. 'Ein Mädchen oder Weibchen'], where he has, for instance, allowed himself rough and harsh modulations that are anything but beautiful. See in particular Var. XII, where he modulates in arpeggios from F major to D major, and where, after the theme has been heard in this key, he suddenly goes back into F.
>
> However much I look at or listen to such transitions, they are and remain flat, and are and remain so only so much more, the more pretentious and noteworthy they are meant to be. Altogether – and I do not address myself only or mainly to the composer of the above pieces – such a huge amount of variations are being written and unfortunately printed nowadays, without many of their composers really seeming to know what good variations truly entail.[33]

Somewhat later in origin are the Variations for piano and cello on the duet 'Bei Männern, welche Liebe fühlen' (WoO 46), which were in all likelihood composed in 1801. During that year two new productions of Mozart's Singspiel opened in Vienna – one at the Hoftheater, the other, mounted by Emanuel Schikaneder, at the new Theater an der Wien. It seems that Beethoven may originally have intended to dedicate his variations to Countess von Fries (*née* Hohenloh), to whose husband, Count Moritz von Fries, he inscribed some rather more significant works: the op.29 String Quintet, the violin sonatas opp.23 and 24, and the Seventh Symphony. The Countess's name is given in an inscription – not in Beethoven's hand – on the title page of the autograph score, though when Tranquillo Mollo published the varia-

---

[32] K. Anh.285. The authenticity of Mozart's variations is, however, doubtful.
[33] AMZ, 23 (6 March 1799), col.366.

tions on New Year's Day 1802, they bore a dedication to Count Johann Georg von Browne. Among the other works Beethoven wrote for the Count were the three string trios op.9, the op.22 Piano Sonata and the six songs op.48 on sacred texts by Christian Fürchtegott Gellert.

While the original edition of the variations op.66 and WoO 45 described them in each case as being for piano *avec un Violoncelle obligé*, the 'Bei Männern' Variations were announced simply as being *pour le clavecin*, with no mention of the stringed instrument at all, despite the fact that this work, unlike its two predecessors, treats the two players very much as equals. (Significantly, there is this time no variation for solo piano.) Their parity is inherent in the theme itself, which is laid out in such a way that the piano takes the part of Pamina, and the cello the answering voice of Papageno; and the same disposition of voices is maintained in the majority of the succeeding variations, with the roles reversed in variations 1 and 3.

In place of Mozart's three-bar introduction Beethoven laconically writes a single E flat chord, as a sonorous call to attention, and a means of offsetting the quiet beginning of the theme itself. The following year (1802) he was to begin another E flat major variation work – the 'Eroica' set for piano op.35 – in similar fashion.

The 'Bei Männern' variations show Beethoven striving for greater clarity of texture than he had achieved in his two previous variation sets for piano and cello – or, indeed, in the op.5 sonatas. The contrapuntal first variation is written in two parts virtually throughout, its starkly linear style contrasting markedly with the richer sound of the following two variations. The minor-mode variation 4 has the cello in its lowest register, with textural transparency again being achieved by deliberately paring down the keyboard writing: the piano accompaniment here unfolds in bare octaves almost throughout. The concluding phrase of this variation involves an equal temperament notation of positively bitonal aspect:

Ex. 5.24. Beethoven. Variations on 'Bei Männern, welche Liebe fühlen' WoO 46. Variation 4, bars 9–15.

Beethoven's autograph shows that he began composing the E flat minor variation immediately after the second variation: he wrote out its first three bars, but no doubt realising that the change from major to minor came too soon in the work's scheme, he inserted the familiar variation 3.

The concluding Allegro opens straightforwardly enough, with an accelerated version of the theme. Significantly, however, Beethoven avoids the interrupted cadence that had been maintained throughout the preceding variations, whereby the theme's penultimate phrase came to an uneasy rest on the chord of C minor. His purpose is to plunge with greater effect into the coda – clearly marked thus in the score – which begins with a new, symmetrical theme in C minor. It is a passage which sounds for all the world like the episode from some rondo finale – indeed, the cello's pizzicato accompaniment is strikingly reminiscent of the central episode in the rondo from the Sonata op.5 no.1. The presence at so late a stage of a well-defined theme bearing no discernible relationship to the remainder of the work is curious, though Beethoven's desire to broaden its terms of reference with a dramatic departure from the main tonality is understandable enough. The balance is, in any case, redressed by what is in effect a further complete variation, before the work is brought to a close which plays on the horn-call implications of the theme's initial notes.

Associated with Beethoven's travels of 1796 are his four surviving pieces for mandolin and piano. One of them – the Sonatina WoO 43a – was first published in 1879, in Grove's *Dictionary of Music and Musicians*, as part of the entry on the mandolin.[34] It appeared again in 1888, together with the Adagio WoO 43b, in a new supplementary volume to the collected edition of the composer's works which had been issued more than two decades earlier by Breitkopf & Härtel. (The sonatina was prepared for publication on that occasion by Gustav Nottebohm from the autograph contained in the 'Kafka' sketchbook.[35]) It was widely believed that Beethoven had composed the two pieces in 1795 in Vienna, for his violinist friend Wenzel Krumpholz who was also an accomplished mandolin player.[36] Beethoven was affected enough by Krumpholz's death in 1817 to compose the miniature 'Gesang der Mönche' WoO 104 for male chorus in his memory. However, a study of Beethoven's sketches for the mandolin pieces reveals that, like the C major Sonatina WoO 44a and the *Andante con Variazioni* WoO 44b, they must have been written during the composer's stay in Prague, in the first half of 1796.[37] All four works seem, in fact, to have been composed for Countess Josephine von Clary-Aldringen, who in 1797 married Count Christian von Clam-Gallas (the founder, in 1811, of the Prague Conservatoire), and the autograph of the Adagio WoO 43b contains the inscription 'pour la belle J par LB'.

Besides Don Giovanni's famous serenade 'Deh vieni alla finestra', Mozart composed two songs with mandolin accompaniment: 'Die Zufriedenheit' K.349, and 'Komm, liebe Zither, komm' K.351, both dating from his visit to Munich in the winter

---

[34] Grove, *A Dictionary of Music and Musicians*, vol.2, pp.205–6.

[35] Beethoven, *Autograph Miscellany*, f.87r.

[36] See Thayer/Forbes, p.200.

[37] See Johnson, 'Music for Prague and Berlin', pp.24–40.

of 1780–1 for the premiere of *Idomeneo*. At the time of Beethoven's visit to Prague the mandolin was a fashionable instrument among the aristocracy, and the conductor of the Italian opera there, Jan Křitel Kuchař, was a celebrated virtuoso on the instrument. It was he who played the mandolin part in 'Deh vieni alla finestra' at the first performance of *Don Giovanni*, on 29 October 1787. He was also the harpsichordist on that occasion, and was the first to make keyboard reductions of *Don Giovanni* and *Le Nozze di Figaro*. The insistence of both Leporello and Don Giovanni on the excellence of their meal in the second Act finale – 'si eccellente è il vostro cuoco' – may have been intended as a pun on Kuchař's name, which in Czech means 'cook'.[38]

Josephine Clary was Kuchař's pupil, and clearly a player of some accomplishment. She was also a talented singer, and at the same time that he wrote his mandolin pieces Beethoven also composed his concert aria 'Ah! Perfido' op.65, which he may have intended for the Countess. (Drafts for several of Beethoven's mandolin pieces are found among ideas for the concert aria in a miscellany housed in the Berlin State Library.[39]) Her name appears on the title page of the only surviving manuscript copy, which bears the inscription *Recitativo e Aria composta e dedicata alla Signora Comtessa di Clari Da L. Beethoven*,[40] though the original edition published nearly ten years later has no dedication. The other Prague singer Beethoven may have had in mind was Josepha Duschek, who gave the premiere of the aria in November 1796. She performed it again in Leipzig later that month, when it was advertised as 'an Italian scene composed for Mademoiselle Duschek by Beethoven'. Since the aria had not yet been published, Duschek must have had access to a copyist's score. She had been a friend of Mozart, who had composed two concert arias for her – 'Ah, lo previdi' K.272 and 'Bella mia fiamma' K.528. The story behind the latter is that Duschek locked the composer in her summerhouse until he completed the piece; and for his part, Mozart agreed to hand it over only on condition that she could perform it at sight – a task which he deliberately made as difficult as possible. Beethoven's 'Ah! Perfido', although it certainly calls for a full dramatic range, is a good deal less awkward to sing, and for that reason, if no other, it is tempting to think that it may after all have been aimed at the more modest vocal technique of Countess Clary, rather than the seasoned professional Duschek.

Music for mandolin and keyboard is likely to have been a comparative rarity at the time Beethoven composed his pieces for Countess Clary, though there is a sonata for keyboard and obbligato mandolin or violin by the Florentine composer Vincenzo Panerai,[41] as well as the sonata in C minor op.10a by Hummel, composed around 1810. Since the mandolin was tuned in the same way as the violin and was much easier to learn, it is likely that players would have appropriated popular salon pieces originally written for the violin. Beethoven himself owned a Milanese mandolin (it disappeared in the aftermath of the Second World War, though photographs

---

[38] See Heartz, *Mozart's Operas*, p.169.
[39] See Johnson, 'Music for Prague and Berlin', p.26.
[40] See Thayer/Forbes, p.183.
[41] First movement reproduced in Tyler and Sparks, *The Early Mandolin*, pp.168–9.

of it exist), and may even have taken a lesson or two in how to play it from Wenzel Krumpholz. His pieces for the instrument show a real awareness not only of its delicate sonority, and its lack of carrying power in comparison with the violin, but also of idiomatic performing techniques. A passage such as the following from the Adagio WoO 43b is clearly conceived with a working knowledge of the use of the plectrum.

Ex. 5.25. Beethoven. Adagio in E flat, WoO 43b, bars 51–8.

The autograph of the Variations WoO 44b, together with the Sonatina WoO 44a in a copyist's hand, was rediscovered by the Czech conductor Arthur Chitz when he catalogued the archive of the Clam-Gallas family, between 1905 and 1912.[42] Chitz clearly also came across a fifth piece, because in his correspondence with the then Count Clam-Gallas he mentions that in addition to the two already published by Eusebius Mandyczewski in the Breitkopf collected edition of Beethoven's works, he had found three considerably shorter pieces in a copyist's manuscript which he was keeping 'for further research'.[43] The fifth piece, however, has since disappeared

---

[42] See Buchner, 'Beethovens Kompositionen für Mandoline', pp.38–40.
[43] Ibid., p.40.

without trace. There is evidence to suggest that Beethoven began sketching out ideas for further mandolin pieces which never came to fruition. A single-stave draft of a movement in D major found in the 'Fischhof Miscellany' may have been intended for mandolin,[44] as may a shorter draft for a piece in C minor.[45] A more substantial sketch in D major, also written on a single stave, is found in the same source.[46]

The Sonatina in C minor WoO 43a consists of no more than a sixteen-bar Adagio with a trio in the major, and short coda following the da capo.[47] The opening section in the minor seems to look back to the C minor minuet from the Piano Trio op.1 no.3, while the trio section anticipates the *Maggiore* middle section, also in C major, of the second movement from the Piano Sonata op.14 no.1. As in the piano sonata, the coda draws the threads of the two contrasting sections together.

Ex. 5.26.
(a) Beethoven. Piano Trio in C minor, op.1 no.3 (iii) bars 27–30.

(b) Beethoven. Sonatina in C minor, WoO 43a, bars 13–16.

[44] Johnson/Fischhof, vol.1, pp.419–22, and vol.2, p.193. See also Raab, Critical Commentary to *Beethoven Werke*, series V, vol.4, p.166.

[45] Johnson/Fischhof, vol.2, p.190.

[46] *Ibid.*, pp.199–200.

[47] The precise point at which the coda is to be joined to the da capo is left unclear. However, both the first half of the da capo's penultimate bar and its upbeat in the previous bar are replicated at the start of the coda, making it likely that Beethoven had this juncture in mind.

Ex. 5.26.
(c) Beethoven. Sonatina in C minor, WoO 43a, bars 17–24.

(d) Beethoven. Piano Sonata in E, op.14 no.1 (ii) bars 63–78.

More substantial, and by a considerable margin the most rewarding of these pieces, is the *Adagio ma non troppo* in E flat, WoO 43b. The existence of two quite different autograph versions of the piece led Georg Kinsky and Hans Halm in their Beethoven catalogue to assume that the composer had initially written it in Vienna for Krumpholz, and had subsequently revised it in Prague.[48] However, it is clear that not only was the earlier copy also written in Prague, but it represented a working draft that needed to be made more legible for Countess Clary. (Arthur Chitz had already reported coming across the piece in the Clam-Gallas archive in a form that corresponded, apart from a few minor details, to the version prepared in 1888 by Euseius Mandyczewski for a supplementary volume of Breitkopf & Härtel's collected Beethoven edition.[49])

[48] Kinsky, *Das Werk Beethovens. Thematisch-Bibliographisches Verzeichnis seiner sämtlichen vollendeten Kompositionen*, ed. Halm, pp.487–8.

[49] See Buchner, 'Beethovens Kompositionen für Mandoline', p.40.

Once again, we are reminded of one of Beethoven's later piano sonatas – in this case, the *Adagio con molta espressione*, also in E flat, of the Sonata op.22. Not only do the throbbing E flat chords of the mandolin piece's opening bars (Ex. 5.27) anticipate the similar beginning of op.22's slow movement, but the shift of key between bars 17 and 18, from B flat to D major (as the dominant of G minor), is echoed at bars 30–1 of the sonata, with their parallel change from B flat to the dominant of C minor. There is a similar switch in harmonic direction later in the piece, this time via an enharmonic change taking the music from B flat to the dominant of D major (Ex. 5.28). At the end, the music appears to be drawing to a gentle close over a tonic pedal; but before it can do so, an interpolation bringing into play a final mediant shift momentarily evokes the events of bars 16–18 (Ex. 5.29).

Ex. 5.27. Beethoven. Adagio in E flat, WoO 43b, bars 1–21.

—(continued)

Ex. 5.27—continued

Ex. 5.28. Beethoven. Adagio in E flat, WoO 43b, bars 39–49.

Ex. 5.29. Beethoven. Adagio in E flat, WoO 43b, bars 102–13.

Rather less of a success is the C major Sonatina WoO 44a. Indeed, in the absence of Beethoven's autograph it would be hard to believe in the authorship of the music, with its facile rondo theme, were it not for the existence of several sketches and revisions for the piece.[50] The agitated C minor second episode is marginally more individual, but hardly sufficient to lift the piece out of the ordinary. It was published for the first time by Arthur Chitz, as a supplement to his article 'Beethovens Kompositionen für Mandoline' in *Der Merker* of June 1912, and was reprinted by him in 'Une Oeuvre inconnue de Beethoven pour mandoline et piano' in the *S.I.M. Revue musicale* of December that year.[51]

---

[50] See Johnson/Fischhof, vol.2, p.127.

[51] As in the case of WoO 43a, Beethoven's intentions as to the form of the piece are unclear. At the end of the first episode, in the dominant, stands the bilingual direction *Da Capo al fine dann weiter*, but there is no indication of where the *fine* falls, and the episode cannot satisfactorily be joined to the minor-mode continuation of the piece. In publishing it for the first time, Arthur Chitz marked the 'probable' location of the *fine* as halfway through the first episode (the downbeat of bar 30); but more likely is that Beethoven intended the da capo to refer only to the reprise of the rondo theme (i.e. the first eighteen bars).

While in the remainder of Beethoven's mandolin pieces it is more often than not the stringed instrument that assumes the leading role, the D major *Andante con Variazioni* WoO 44b shares its melodic interest equally between the two players. The first variation has arpeggios for the mandolin in semiquaver triplets, to a discreet piano accompaniment, while the second features demisemiquaver passagework for the pianist (its rapid repeated notes offer a distant anticipation of the violin figuration in the second variation of the 'Kreutzer' Sonata's middle movement), with the mandolin part restricted to intermittently strummed chords. Following variation 3, which treats the two players in dialogue throughout, the piano takes up the theme in its original form, while the mandolin provides an elaborate accompaniment in rapid across-the-strings arpeggios. The minor-mode variation 5 leads to an acceleration in tempo, before a slow coda allows the music to disintegrate, and to fade away into the distance.[52]

Beethoven's mandolin pieces are, no doubt, minor chippings from the great workshop, but they have a charm all of their own, and it is clear that the composer took considerable care over them. The lack of any dynamic markings suggests that they may have been designed for performance with harpsichord, rather than piano, and the more delicate sound of the earlier instrument would have allowed for a more unified sonority in combination with the mandolin. Beethoven will almost certainly have played this music with its dedicatee during one of the regular concerts held at Count Clam-Gallas's palace which were attended by the musical elite of Prague. (In his memoirs the composer Václav Tomášek recalls having heard Beethoven at the Count's palace, where he played the rondo from the A major Sonata op.2 no.2, and also improvised on the theme 'Ah! vous dirai-je Maman'.[53])

A set of six Contredanses (WoO 42) for piano and violin written around the same time as the mandolin pieces need not detain us for long. The dances are, indeed, so unremarkable that for a long time their authenticity was questioned. Their appearance was announced on 30 July 1814 by Ludwig Maisch, of Vienna, as '6 Allemandes', and listing them among Beethoven's works of 1796 Hermann Deiters commented on the unlikelihood of a Viennese publisher of that time invoking Beethoven's name without authorisation.[54] In fact, Gustav Nottebohm had already drawn attention to Beethoven's sketches for two of the dances (nos.1 and 3) contained among ideas for 'Ah! Perfido', thus indeed allowing a precise dating of 1796 for them.[55] Each dance is in two equal halves of eight bars, though no.6 is extended through the inclusion of a trio. The violin part is rudimentary, and in almost each case the first half of the dance cadences back into the tonic. (The exceptions are no.5, and the trio of no.6, where

---

[52] There are no dynamic markings either in this piece or in the Sonatina WoO 44a, and while it would be possible to play the final cadence emphatically, such an interpretation would be incongruous in its context.

[53] See Buchner, 'Beethovens Kompositionen für Mandoline', p.48 n.32.

[54] TDR, vol.3, p.484.

[55] Nottebohm, *Zweite Beethoveniana*, p.221.

the first half moves to the dominant instead.) For the rest, Nottebohm is surely right in maintaining that these pieces reveal no trace of Beethoven's personality, although an inscription in his hand found on a copy of the dances housed in Vienna's National Library shows characteristic humour: *Deutsche für die zwei Comtessen Thun um andern Leuten danach auf dem Kopfe zu tanzen und dabey zu denken an ihren Sie verehrenden Ludwig van Beethoven, Prague, 1796* (German dances for the two Countesses Thun in order to lead others a merry dance, and in so doing to think of their admirer Ludwig van Beethoven, Prague, 1796).[56]

---

[56] See Johnson, 'Music for Prague and Berlin', p.26.

6
Interlude 2: The Clarinet Trio Op.11

On 1 and 2 April 1798 Haydn conducted two performances of the choral version of his *Seven Last Words* in Vienna. During the interval of the second concert Beethoven played his op.16 Quintet with a group of wind players that included the most celebrated clarinettist of the day, Joseph Bähr (or Beer), and it is reasonable to suppose that his unconventionally scored trio for piano, clarinet and cello op.11, composed shortly afterwards, was written for him. He was born in the same year as Beethoven, and in 1787 he entered the service of Prince Öttingen-Wallerstein of Bavaria. A fellow member of the Prince's orchestra was the cellist and composer Friedrich Witt (remembered today for having concocted the so-called 'Jena' Symphony, once attributed to Beethoven); and the two musicians, having paid a visit to the Berlin court at Potsdam in 1794, arrived in Vienna together two years later, where Bähr found employment with Prince Liechtenstein. Significantly enough, several of Beethoven's works featuring the clarinet in an important role date from the years 1796–1802. Besides the op.11 Trio, they include the slow movement of the C major Piano Concerto op.15, and that of the Septet op.20. The latter work was first performed exactly a year after the premiere of the clarinet trio, at a benefit concert for Beethoven in which Ignaz Schuppanzigh played the violin, and Bähr the clarinet. Also first performed at a Schuppanzigh concert, in April 1805, was the Sextet op.71 for two clarinets, two bassoons and two horns. The *Allgemeine musikalische Zeitung* commented that the first clarinet part had been 'absolutely perfectly played' by Bähr. 'This artist', the reviewer continued, 'has, besides extraordinary facility and security, an extremely charming and pleasant tone, and is able particularly in *piano* passages, to make it so tender and meltingly delicate that he will certainly find few equals on his instrument.'[1]

According to Czerny, Beethoven based the finale of his op.11 Trio on a popular operatic tune at the specific request of the clarinet player for whom the work was composed.[2] The tune is taken from the concluding trio in the first act of Joseph Weigl's *L'Amor marinaro*, to a libretto by Giovanni de Gamerra, which had first been produced in Vienna on 15 October 1797. Beethoven may have been the first to base a set of variations on Weigl's theme, but it very soon became popular enough for several other composers of the time to use it for the same purpose. A set of variations in E flat for piano solo by the pianist and composer Joseph Wölfl

---

[1] AMZ, 33 (15 May 1805), col.535.
[2] Czerny, p.15.

dates from around the same time as Beethoven's clarinet trio. Its last variation features a similar rhythmic transformation of Weigl's tune as found in the coda of Beethoven's variations, as well as an excursion into the distant key of E major – almost as though in parody of Beethoven's predilection for such effects. (The two musicians were well acquainted with each other, and in 1799 they took part in a celebrated piano 'duel' at the house of Wölfl's champion, Baron Wetzlar von Plankenstern.) A further set of keyboard variations was composed around 1810 by the Abbé Gelinek, and similar pieces were written in the early 1820s by the harpist and composer Nicholas Bochsa and by Frédéric Kalkenbrenner. As late as 1828 Paganini took Weigl's tune, transposed into E major, as the basis of a *Suonata con Variazioni* for violin and orchestra.

Czerny claimed that Beethoven was unhappy with the finale of his clarinet trio, and for a while contemplated writing a substitute.[3] Significantly, this was the only occasion on which Beethoven used a theme not of his own as part of a multi-movement work.

Much less credible than Czerny's statement is the story put about by the English composer Cipriani Potter, who claimed to have been told by the elder Artaria in 1797 that he had given the tune to Beethoven, at which time it must have been very new. Artaria's version of events was that he had asked Beethoven to include a set of variations on the melody in a work for piano trio, and Beethoven had discovered the provenance of the tune only after completing his variations. He was apparently angry on discovering it was by Weigl.[4] The tune, however, had very quickly become widely disseminated (its folk-like status has since given rise to the nickname of 'Gassenhauer', or street song, for Beethoven's trio), and it is worth noting that Weigl's melody is in any case clearly anticipated in the closing subject of Beethoven's first movement:

Ex. 6.1.
(a) Beethoven. Clarinet Trio in B flat, op.11 (i) bars 231–41.

—(continued)

---

[3] Czerny, p.15
[4] See Thayer/Forbes, p.214. The trio was published in 1798, not by Artaria, but by Mollo.

Ex. 6.1a—continued

Ex. 6.1.
(b) Beethoven. Clarinet Trio in B flat, op.11 (iii) bars 1–16.

Thema: Pria ch'io l'impegno

Weigl's tune was also the subject of an anecdote reported by Ferdinand Ries, involving the then fashionable pianist-composer Daniel Steibelt:

> When the greatly renowned Steibelt came from Paris to Vienna, several of Beethoven's friends were afraid he would harm Beethoven's reputation. Steibelt did not visit him; they first met one evening at the house of Count Fries, where Beethoven performed his new trio in B flat major for piano, clarinet, and cello (Opus 11) for the first time. In it, the player cannot especially display his talents. Steibelt listened to it with a certain condescension, paid Beethoven a few compliments, and felt confident of his victory. He played a quintet of his own composition, improvised, and produced a great effect with his tremolandos, which were then something quite new. Beethoven could not be persuaded to play again. A week later there was another concert at Count Fries's. Steibelt once more played a quintet with much success, but on top of this (as could be felt) he had prepared a brilliant improvisation, and had chosen the same theme on which the variations in Beethoven's trio were written. This outraged Beethoven's admirers as well as himself. He now had to go to the piano and improvise. He went in his usual, I might say unmannerly, fashion to the instrument, almost as though he had been pushed. On his way he picked up the cello part of Steibelt's quintet, put it (deliberately?) upside down on the music rack, and hammered out a theme from the first few bars with one finger. – Insulted and irritated as he was, he improvised in such a manner that Steibelt left the room before Beethoven had finished, never wanted to meet him again, and even made it a condition that Beethoven should not be invited when his own company was desired.[5]

In Weigl's opera the tune is sung by the characters of Cisolfante, Pasquale and the Captain. Cisolfante is a vainglorious composer who claims to have written more than six dozen operas. He also has a gargantuan appetite, and demands that Pasquale provide him with a boiled chicken, a stew, and a roast. But before he can finish his meal Pasquale and the Captain are anxious for him to go into the next room, and to ascertain from its appearance whether its occupant – a lady who is at present on her travels – really is a professional singer, as she claims. Cisolfante accepts: 'L'impegno prendo – ad un occhiata Cisolfante le donne musiche conosce tutte' (I accept the task: Cisolfante can identify any lady musician at a mere glance). He is, however, worried at the thought that he might go hungry: 'Pria ch'io l'impegno magistral prenda, far vuo merenda' (Before I take on the magisterial task, I want a snack).

For all the accounts of Beethoven's dissatisfaction with his finale, the challenge of creating something original and individual out of less than first-rate material was one he clearly enjoyed. The 'Kakadu' Variations op.121a do for a street song what the 'Diabelli' set manages for a simple waltz-tune: both caricature the weaknesses of their theme, and in the process create a masterpiece in which humour plays a prominent role. In the later work Diabelli's tune is decisively dismissed in the very first variation, which transforms it into an imperious march. Only the opening variation of the 'Rule, Britannia' set WoO 79, in which Thomas Arne's pompous theme immediately dissolves into ill-defined rumblings at the bottom of the keyboard, is more comical in its dismantling of its theme from the outset. Weigl's tune in the finale of the op.11 Trio likewise disappears from sight as soon as it is over, and Beethoven's

---

[5] Wegeler/Ries, pp.81–2.

impatience with its simple tonic-dominant harmony is indicated by the nature of the first variation – a piano solo consisting of a flurry of semiquavers that renders the theme's melodic outline quite unrecognisable. Not until the gruffly canonic ninth variation does it resurface. In the meantime, while respecting both its proportions and its harmonic outline, Beethoven has treated it to not just one but two lugubrious variations in the minor. The second of the pair – variation 7 – is a funeral march, and it is not without irony that nearly thirty years later Weigl was to be one of the pall-bearers at Beethoven's own funeral.

Following the piano solo of variation 1, the second variation is scored for clarinet and cello alone, and the succession of scorings is of a kind that is echoed in the early stages of the 'Kakadu' Variations. Sandwiched between the full-blooded *fortissimo* close of the piano's variation and the forceful writing of variation 3, with its merciless *sforzandi* aping the theme's dynamic markings, the transparent texture and *pianissimo* dynamic level of the second variation afford wittily exaggerated contrast. That contrast is prolonged through the inclusion of a repeat of the variation's second half – a feature it shares with variation 8, which is also set in motion by the cellist.

If the metrical transformation presented by the coda, which sees Weigl's tune given out in a syncopated 6/8 rhythm, is traditional enough, Beethoven rings the changes on his favoured procedure of invoking a sudden tonal surprise in the closing moments by instead introducing a radical change of key at the start of the Allegro, which sets off in a comparatively remote G major. (The change has been effected by means of the piano flourish that provides a link between the preceding variation and the coda.) The music soon regains both its composure and its right key; but Beethoven has a different kind of surprise up his sleeve, and following a playful echo of the theme's final phrase by the pizzicato cello, there is a last-moment swing back to the original metre. In practice, players generally treat the new crotchet as equivalent to the preceding dotted crotchet – an interpretation that entails a sudden relaxation in tempo. Such a view seems to find its confirmation in the off-beat *sforzandi* of the final bars, which echo the similar accents in Weigl's theme as given at the start of the piece. Beethoven does not, however, provide an indication that the coda's *Allegro* tempo is to revert to the theme's *Allegretto*, and so it is not impossible that a more urgent *envoi*, in which the tempo of the quaver remains constant, is called for after all.

Rather more sophisticated than Weigl's tune is the off-tonic opening subject of the trio's first movement. Its chromatic initial phrase, throwing a strong accent onto the second bar, is one that can also function as a transition, and it is heard as such as early as bars 5–6. The reappearance of the chromatic motif as a transitional phrase in bars 13–14 is accompanied by the piano with an augmented form of the same phrase, while the piano's octaves in bars 16–17 present the motif at its original pitch, its stress wittily shifted backwards, to its first note, and the entire phrase now forming the start of a cadence into the tonic:

Ex. 6.2. Beethoven. Clarinet Trio in B flat, op.11 (i) bars 1–19.

In the coda, the same elongated form of the phrase assumes the guise of an ending, with the stress this time shifted forwards by a whole bar, so that it now falls on the downbeat of the third bar.

Ex. 6.3. Beethoven. Clarinet Trio in B flat, op.11 (i) bars 247–54.

The opening Allegro is a much less prolix affair than the parallel movement in either the op.1 trios or the op.5 cello sonatas. Its unity, moreover, is assured by the rhythmic kinship of its two main subjects. (The second subject has its two halves separated by a more diatonic version of the movement's initial phrase.) But perhaps the most memorable moment of the piece is the piano's hushed D major entry following hard on the heels of the first group's full close in the dominant. The two phrases of the piano's new idea here are elegantly joined together by means of a tiny, but telling, interjection from the cello:

Ex. 6.4. Beethoven. Clarinet Trio in B flat, op.11 (i) bars 35–55.

—(continued)

Ex. 6.4—*continued*

It is a striking idea, and one that lifts the music onto a higher expressive plane. It resurfaces at the start of the development section – once again following a full-close in the dominant, but this time introducing the *pianissimo* idea in the key of the flat submediant, D flat. Wisely, perhaps, Beethoven does not attempt to draw further expressive advantage out of the idea in the recapitulation, where it does not appear.

The slow movement is akin to a sublimated minuet, and it is perhaps not by chance that Beethoven's initial sketches for its opening cello melody – the first time he had allowed that instrument to take the leading role at the start of a piece of its kind – closely resemble the minuet from the little G major Piano Sonata op.49 no.2. Beethoven was to use the minuet theme again in the Septet op.20, and his first attempts at the melody as shown in the sketches for op.11 are so similar to the minuet that Gustav Nottebohm went so far as to suggest that Beethoven may have altered the shape of his material in the trio's Adagio deliberately in order to disguise the resemblance.[6]

Ex. 6.5.
(a) Beethoven. Clarinet Trio in B flat, op.11 (ii), sketch.

(b) Beethoven. Clarinet Trio in B flat, op.11 (ii) bars 1–8.

---

[6] Nottebohm, *Zweite Beethoveniana*, p.516.

Any similarity to a minuet is, however, left far behind in the Adagio's middle section, which, beginning in the tonic minor and in an atmosphere of subdued agitation, soon arrives via an enharmonic change in the very remote key of E major. Here, the theme's second three-note phrase – still identical with the opening of the minuet from op.49 no.2 – is repeatedly given out, to a delicately elaborate piano accompaniment. The ethereal result momentarily recalls the E major slow movement of the Piano Trio op.1 no.2. So, too, does the manner in which the intricate piano writing continues during the course of the reprise. The clouded opening bars of the middle section are recalled at the start of the coda, before the piece subsides in a serene conclusion.

The scoring of Beethoven's trio, involving, as it does, instruments of three different families, is unusual,[7] and one writer has seen both the instrumentation and the choice of Weigl's theme for the finale as a bow to the Viennese taste for the Hungarian style in general, and the *verbunkos*, or recruiting dance, in particular.[8] Be that as it may, the original edition included a part for violin, as an alternative to the clarinet. While the wind instrument undeniably provides a perkiness altogether appropriate to Weigl's unrefined tune, its part lies quite comfortably on the violin. The violin part almost certainly stems from Beethoven himself, and it brings the advantage of being able to reinforce with greater strength the cello's double-stopped chords at such moments as the closing bars of the first movement's exposition and the start of its coda, as well as the forceful interjections in the finale's fifth variation.

---

[7] Among later works for the same ensemble, the best known is Brahms's Trio in A minor op.114, but there are also examples by Ferdinand Ries, Archduke Rudolph and Alexander Zemlinsky.

[8] See Pare, 'Beethoven as a Transnational Composer', pp.77–94.

7
Sonatas for Piano and Violin, 1798–1800

With the exception of the last work in the series, Beethoven's ten violin sonatas were all composed within the space of some six years, between 1798 and 1803. Of his chamber works in other forms, only the five string trios are more closely bunched together. Moreover, if that last sonata, op.96, occupies a lone position chronologically, then its predecessor – the 'Kreutzer' op.47 – stands apart stylistically: it is, as Beethoven was at pains to point out, less an intimate chamber work than a piece in concertante style. The Sonata op.30 no.1 to which its finale originally belonged is one of Beethoven's most subtly understated works, and perhaps for that reason one of the least performed of the series. But even among the remaining works, only the C minor op.30 no.2 and the 'Spring' op.24 appear with any regularity on concert programmes outside of a complete cycle of the sonatas.

There is no evidence to suggest that Beethoven himself was a string player of more than modest ability. Among his violin teachers in Bonn was Franz Georg Rovantini, a distant cousin of Beethoven on his mother's side, and a member of the Electoral orchestra.[1] However, Rovantini died of dysentry in 1781, at the age of only twenty-five, and Beethoven received further tuition from the court orchestra's director, Franz Anton Ries, the father of his future pupil Ferdinand Ries. Beethoven, who himself played the viola for a while in the Bonn opera orchestra, may have continued his violin studies during his early years in Vienna, and it is possible, though by no means certain, that he took lessons there from Ignaz Schuppanzigh. (A 1794 entry in the pocket book to which he had made sporadic contributions since the time of his first journey from Bonn to Vienna reads: 'Schupp. 3 times a week. Albrechtsberger 3 times a w.',[2] though whether or not Beethoven's visits to the Schuppanzigh household were paid in order to receive a more general education from the violinist's father, who was a professor at the Realschule, cannot be ascertained.) More likely is that Beethoven received occasional violin tuition from Wenzel Krumpholz. Ferdinand Ries remembers having played some of Beethoven's sonatas for piano and violin together with the composer shortly after his arrival in Vienna: 'In Vienna, Beethoven still took violin lessons with Krumpholz, and in the beginning (that is, when he had already experienced a loss of hearing) we occasionally played his sonatas with violin together. But it was truly dreadful music-making,

---

[1] See Schmidt-Görg, *Beethoven. Die Geschichte seiner Familie*, pp.106–7.
[2] TDR, vol.1, p.359.

because in his impassioned enthusiasm he did not hear when he attacked a passage with the wrong fingering.'[3]

Beethoven's knowledge of the violin was sufficient for him to be able to write for the instrument in a perfectly idiomatic manner, though it is perhaps not by chance that the Violin Concerto is his only work for a soloist and orchestra for which he did not provide cadenzas. Only when he transcribed the solo part for piano did he write a cadenza for the opening movement – a rich and strange piece for piano and timpani which echoes the similarly scored moment in the finale of the 'Emperor' Concerto op.73. Attempts to adapt material from the cadenza to the violin for performances of the concerto in its familiar guise have, perhaps not surprisingly, proved to be less than wholly convincing.

If Beethoven's op.5 cello sonatas sometimes showed a tendency to highlight the inherent differences between the two instruments involved, his violin sonatas generally evince more tightly knit dialogue, as well as a constant exchange of material, between the two players. In Mozart's sonatas the view of the piano as *primus inter pares* is indicated by the fact that there is scarcely a single variation theme or principal slow movement subject in which the violin is allowed to take the lead.[4] Beethoven, however, reverses the traditional roles of the two players to striking effect in the last two movements of the A major Sonata op.30 no.1. And if Mozart was capable on occasion of beginning a sonata with a cantabile violin melody (the G major Sonata K.301, or the slow introduction of the C major K.303), he never attempted to do so on quite so expansive a scale as the opening theme of Beethoven's 'Spring' Sonata op.24.

Mozart's sonatas were, of course, the great examples of the genre Beethoven had before him; and, as we have seen in connection with his early piano quartets and the Trio WoO 37, he was well acquainted with them. For all its wilful individuality, it is hardly surprising that Beethoven's first set of violin sonatas, op.12, should show palpable traces of Mozart's influence. The fanfare-like opening of the first work in the series echoes the similar beginning of Mozart's Sonata K.302[5], while the virtuoso brilliance of the opening Allegro from Mozart's Sonata K.380 seems to have left its mark on the first movement of Beethoven's op.12 no.3, in the same key of E flat. Moreover, the waltz-like subject that begins the middle sonata of Beethoven's triptych may have been inspired by the initial Allegro of Mozart's Sonata K.305, likewise in A major and in 6/8 time. K.305's middle movement, like that of op.12 no.1, is a set of variations, and it is instructive to compare Mozart's theme with Beethoven's first variation:

---

[3] Wegeler/Ries, p.119.

[4] An exception is the Adagio of the B flat Sonata K.454, specifically written to display the cantabile style of the visiting Italian player Regina Strinasacchi, while the theme of the variation finale in the Sonata K.481 is given out by the two players in octaves.

[5] See pp.155–6.

Ex. 7.1.
(a) Mozart Violin Sonata in A, K.305 (ii) bars 1–8.

(b) Beethoven Violin Sonata in D, op.12 no.1 (ii) bars 33–40.

While the piano's left-hand chord at the start of Beethoven's first bar is more fully scored than Mozart might have found ideal, his variation could in other respects almost have been written by the earlier composer. However, whereas Mozart places his *fortepiano* accents in the fifth and sixth bars firmly on the downbeat, the *sforzandi* in the corresponding bars of Beethoven's piece characteristically occur off the beat.

Paradoxically, it may have been their Mozartian undertones that caused Beethoven's contemporaries to have been so perplexed by the op.12 sonatas. The review with which the *Allgemeine musikalische Zeitung* greeted their publication in 1799 is a now famous piece of invective:

> The reviewer, who did not know the piano works of the author until now, has to admit after having with great effort worked his way through these quite peculiar sonatas overladen with strange difficulties, that the really painstaking playing of them made him feel like someone who had wanted to take a pleasurable stroll with a cordial friend through an attractive wood, and having been held up at every moment by hostile obstacles, had finally emerged tired and exhausted, without any enjoyment. It is undeniable that Herr van Beethoven goes his own way; but what a bizarre, arduous way it is! Learned, learned and constantly learned, and nothing natural, no melody! Indeed, if one looks at it closely it is only a mass of learning, with no good method; a struggle for which one feels little interest; a search for strange modulations, a revulsion for traditional relationships, a piling of difficulty upon difficulty, so that one loses all patience and enjoyment in it.[6]

The review is typical of the hostility with which the *Allgemeine musikalische Zeitung* treated Beethoven's music in the final years of the eighteenth century. Not until the publication of the opp.23 and 24 violin sonatas in 1801 did the journal express itself with wholehearted enthusiasm about the composer. Meanwhile, Beethoven had found himself constrained to write a cautionary letter to the journal's proprietors, Breitkopf & Härtel. Pointing out that the two piano concertos (nos.1 and 2) that were about to be issued in Vienna had been completed some time earlier, and should therefore not be reviewed as though they were fully representative, he took the opportunity of offering the editor of their influential publication some general advice:

> Advise those gentlemen your reviewers to exercise more caution and intelligence, particularly with regard to the works of younger composers, for many of them who might otherwise go far could be frightened off. As far as I am concerned, I am certainly far from considering myself to possess such perfection as would not bear any criticism, but the clamour your reviewers raised against me at first was so humiliating that when I began to compare myself with others, I could hardly bother myself about it. Instead, I kept quite calm, and thought, they don't understand it; and I could be all the more calm about it when I saw how men are praised to the skies who among the better ones here *in loco* count for little, and who almost disappeared here, however competent they may otherwise have been.[7]

Despite the largely negative review in the *Allgemeine musikalische Zeitung*, the op.12 sonatas seem to have enjoyed considerable success. Not only was the first Viennese edition of January 1799 reprinted no fewer than eight times within a few years, but between 1800 and 1806 further printings appeared in Bonn, Mainz, Hamburg, London and Paris.[8] Beethoven had mainly composed the sonatas in 1798,

---

[6] AMZ, 36 (5 June 1799), cols.570–1.

[7] Letter of 22 April 1801. BGA no.59; Anderson no.48. For a detailed discussion of Beethoven's changing relationship with the AMZ, see Wallace, *Beethoven's Critics*, pp.5–44.

[8] See Brandenburg, 'Beethoven's Opus 12 Violin Sonatas', p.21.

though he may have begun work on at least the D major first work of the series in the previous year. Artaria's first edition bore a dedication to Salieri, to whom Beethoven turned around 1799 for instruction in the Italian vocal style. The autograph of at least one of Beethoven's Italianate compositions of the period, the aria 'No, non turbati' WoO 92a, has corrections by Salieri, and carries a heading in Beethoven's hand of 'Esercizii'. Beethoven further ingratiated himself with the influential court Kapellmeister at this time by composing a set of piano variations (WoO 73) on the aria 'La stessa, la stessima' from his opera *Falstaff*.

The op.12 sonatas are unique among Beethoven's tripartite publications in not including a work in a minor key, and it is possible to feel that the set as a whole is less ambitious than his remaining triptychs. While the piano sonatas op.2 and op.10 both begin with a compact and dramatic minor-mode work, and reserve the largest panel of the series for last, the op.30 violin sonatas, op.31 piano sonatas and op.59 string quartets all have a work in the minor as their centrepiece. Beethoven's remaining tripartite series, the op.1 piano trios and op.9 string trios, are brought to a close in the composer's characteristically dark C minor vein. In common with the two earlier sets of piano sonatas, the op.12 group saves its most flamboyant member for last, and the slow movement of the final work – the only Adagio to be found among the three sonatas – forms the expressive high point of the series.

Perhaps it was as a symbolic gesture that Beethoven began his first violin sonata by seeming to recall the fanfare-like opening bars of Mozart's Sonata K.302. Beethoven's beginning is rhythmically more disjunct than Mozart's, and it offers a bewildering profusion of seemingly contrasting ideas within a remarkably short space of time. In its presentation of an assertive initial motif giving way immediately to a more subdued, lyrical phrase it offers a distant anticipation of two of Beethoven's later D major works – the 'Ghost' Trio op.70 no.1 and the Cello Sonata op.102 no.2.

Ex. 7.2.
(a) Mozart. Violin Sonata in E flat, K.302 (i) bars 1–8.

Ex. 7.2.
(b) Beethoven. Violin Sonata in D, op.12 no.1 (i) bars 1–21.

The quiet violin melody that begins in Beethoven's fifth bar is essentially an augmented version of the initial fanfare. Its rhythmic incisiveness contrasts with the piano's smoothly moving line; and having gone their own distinctive way in bars 5–11, the paths of the two instruments calmly meet in the twelfth bar, after which their roles are exchanged, and the piano presents a decorated version of the violin's preceding melody.

The second subject clearly grows out of the same thematic elements: the conjunct line of the piano part of bars 5–12, and the turn-like figure of bars 19–21. The violin's prolongation of the new subject (bars 59ff.) recalls the latter idea, as well as the octave leap of bar 5:

Ex. 7.3. Beethoven. Violin Sonata in D, op.12 no.1 (i) bars 43–62.

—(continued)

Ex. 7.3—continued

The unconventional key relationships about which the *Allgemeine musikalische Zeitung* complained so vehemently are exemplified by the inclusion within the second group of an extended passage set firmly in F major.[9] As so often when broad-

---

9   Another instance of a substantial F major interpolation within a broader D major context is found in the opening movement of the 'Ghost' Trio.

ening the scope of his tonal canvas in this manner, Beethoven takes a large-scale view of its implications, and here he includes not only a corresponding B flat major intervention in the recapitulation, but also a broad episode in F major in the finale.

The exposition's F major interpolation has repercussions in the development section, which begins without preamble in that key; and since the entire development is centred around F major or its relative minor (i.e. the tonic minor), Beethoven makes the appropriate change in key signature. The mysterious, highly charged approach to the recapitulation is thoroughly characteristic; and here the relationship between the initial fanfare-like motif and its conjunct continuation is made explicit through a juxtaposition of the two ideas.

Ex. 7.4. Beethoven. Violin Sonata in D, op.12 no.1 (i) bars 130–43.

—(continued)

Example 7.4—*continued*

With the exception of a twelve-bar elision that hastens the arrival of the second group, the recapitulation mirrors the pattern of the exposition with a regularity that is unusual for Beethoven. Nor is there any alteration in the distribution of material between the two instruments vis-à-vis the earlier section. The question of variety of texture and colour between exposition and recapitulation is, indeed, one that seems to have exercised Beethoven rather less than it did the mature Mozart. Mozart's B flat Sonata K.378, for instance, gives its eight-bar first subject to the piano at the outset, while in the recapitulation the violin seizes the initiative in the melody's fifth bar; and the F major Sonata from the same series, K.376, has the two instruments exchanging their previous roles throughout the recapitulation's second subject. Among Beethoven's violin sonatas, only the recapitulation of op.96 presents a wholesale redistribution of events between the two players in the parallel stages of the piece. Nor in op.12 no.1 does Beethoven indulge in the luxury of a coda: instead, the movement simply comes to a halt with the same cadence that had rounded off the exposition. Much the same had happened in the opening movement of the Piano Trio op.1 no.3, but such blunt endings are otherwise as rare in Beethoven as they are in Mozart.

The variation slow movement breathes an air similar to that of the 'Kreutzer', the only remaining slow movement in this form to be found among the violin sonatas. Although the variations of the 'Kreutzer' are conceived on a grander scale (their elaborate coda, for instance, has no parallel in the earlier work), the plan of the two pieces is broadly the same: four variations, of which the third is in the minor. The layout of Beethoven's theme in op.12 no.1, each half being given initially to the pianist before it is taken over by the violin, mirrors that of the theme of the D minor variation movement from Mozart's Sonata in F major K.377, but it is one that is otherwise rarely found in Mozart's violin sonatas, where the variation theme tends to be given to the piano throughout while the violin accompanies.

Beethoven's first two variations do little to disturb the amiable atmosphere of the theme itself, but the minor-mode third variation disrupts that atmosphere with some force. Here, the *sforzando* downbeat of the theme's second bar, which – unlike the corresponding accent in the fourth bar of the melody's second half – had not been exploited in the intervening variations, is seized upon as the springboard for a series of *fortissimo* outbursts. The variation itself is through-composed, with the roles of the two instruments more or less reversed in the quasi-repeats. The final variation, again with written-out repeats, buries the theme's contour in the syncopated inner voice of the piano part – a texture that foreshadows the variation opening movement of the op.26 Piano Sonata, composed in 1800–1. In the quasi-repeats, the left-hand piano part is enlivened through an elaborately ornamented line. However, in a striking disruption of the symmetry of the piece thus far, the repeat of the melody's second half is broken off after only four bars, leaving the music hanging in suspension, and the coda that ensues seems to recall earlier moments as though from afar: the plain rise and fall of the original theme itself, and, as though in compensation for having cut short the last stage of the final variation, the semiquaver triplet figuration from the violin's quasi-repeat of that variation's first half. The short coda, offering, as it does, the only *pianissimo* moment in the piece, allows the music to sink to a close of profound calm.

The finale's rondo theme places a strong accent on the second 6/8 quaver in its second, fourth and sixth bars, and the melody's latent simplicity is further undermined by the manner in which both its initial statement on the piano and the violin's quasi-repeat are rounded off with an almost exaggeratedly neat cadence into the tonic.[10] On its reprise following the first episode, Beethoven reduces the theme's scope by eliminating the violin's restatement, and plunging instead into the minor, to dramatic effect (bars 60ff.).

The rondo's chief element of contrast is its central episode, which presents a soaring new idea in F major – the key that had figured as a secondary tonality in the opening movement. Its theme momentarily takes wing once again towards the end, where it is transformed into a closing subject – a splendid inspiration, though one that does not occur before Beethoven has indulged in one of his favoured tonal surprises, wittily taking the rondo theme into a very distant E flat major. The music finds its way home again in a passage that plays on the theme's characteristic short-long rhythm, and the same rhythm gives rise to a moment of hesitation invoking the movement's only *pianissimo* marking, before a crescendo (Beethoven optimistically directs the pianist to begin increasing the sound level on a sustained chord) and a rush of semiquavers brings the sonata to a *fortissimo* close.

Beethoven worked on the A major second of the op.12 sonatas simultaneously with the Piano Sonata in E major op.14 no.1, and the outward form of the two works is similar: each has three movements in the same tonality, with the second,

---

[10] A similar cross-accent features in the rondo theme of the B flat Piano Concerto op.19, where the displacement is considerably more unsettling in view of the fact that it occurs at the very outset, before the underlying 6/8 rhythm has had a chance to establish itself.

in the minor, being an Allegretto. (The violin sonata's tempo marking is *Andante più tosto Allegretto*.) Beethoven had carried out a similar plan in his F major Piano Sonata op.10 no.2, where, as in op.14 no.1, the second movement carries the formal implication of a minuet and trio. The corresponding movement of the violin sonata has no such obvious background; nor does it absorb the elements of a scherzo, as does the second movement of the Violin Sonata op.23. On the other hand, it is cast in the most straightforward of sectional forms, and in its notable avoidance of any structural complexities it performs much the same function as would a minuet within a more traditional overall scheme. Its theme, each half of which is played initially by the unaccompanied piano before the melody passes to the violin, might easily have formed the basis of a set of variations, were it not for the fact that Beethoven had already cast the slow movement of the first sonata of the series in that form. Instead, the theme immediately gives way to a contrasting episode of equal simplicity in F major, featuring the two instruments in constant dialogue. Following a transition of no more than four bars, an expressively intensified reprise of the initial theme with a new contribution from the violin sets in. The mood of gentle pathos is enhanced by the closing bars of the brief coda, which recall the chromatic contours of the middle section's melody. So unassuming is the piece as a whole that Beethoven seems initially to have conceived it as an introduction to the finale: the notion of allowing it to come to rest on an imperfect cadence, and having the finale follow without a pause (with the two pieces linked through the briefest of unaccompanied piano phrases), is one that survived through several draft versions of the coda, before it was eventually rejected in favour of a more orthodox full-close.[11]

The title page of Artaria's original edition of the op.12 sonatas announced the pieces as being *Per il Clavicembalo o Forte-Piano con un violino*, and as though in mocking illustration of what was a decidedly anachronistic description, Beethoven wittily begins the A major sonata with a waltz-like accompaniment in typical keyboard style played by the violin, and an idiomatic violin tune given out by the piano. It had not always been so: one of Beethoven's sketches for the movement contained in the 'Fischhof Miscellany' shows a more conventional textural layout, with the accompanimental figure assigned to the left-hand keyboard part.[12]

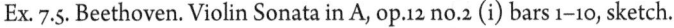

Ex. 7.5. Beethoven. Violin Sonata in A, op.12 no.2 (i) bars 1–10, sketch.

[11] See Johnson/Fischhof, vol.1, p.341, and vol.2, p.49.
[12] Johnson/Fischhof, vol.2, p.47.

Beethoven ultimately decided not only to transfer the accompaniment to the violin, but also to make use of the sighing two-note figure in both ascending and descending forms. With its tongue-in-cheek simplicity it remains a breathtakingly self-confident beginning.

Ex. 7.6. Beethoven. Violin Sonata in A, op.12 no.2 (i) bars 1–12.

The counterstatement reverses the roles of the two instruments, so that in a sense normality of instrumental characteristics is established, except that in order to avoid a mere repetition of the opening bars, Beethoven now deliberately expands the subject's compass so that each two-bar segment on the violin is answered by the piano, playing – crossed hands – what ought by rights to be a cello part beneath the continuing accompaniment figure.

If the first subject consists essentially of no more than a series of descending tonic and dominant arpeggios with lightly accented appoggiaturas, the main idea of the second group – approached via a circuitous route that takes the music through a bewildering array of keys, including F sharp minor, G major, E minor and F major (were these perhaps some of the 'hostile obstacles' that tripped up the *Allgemeine musikalische Zeitung*'s reviewer?) – is centred around an equally basic ingredient: a descending and ascending five-note scale, the descending figure embellished by quasi-mordents. Nevertheless, its canonic treatment, combined with strong syncopated accents, lends the texture a disturbingly unsynchronised aspect.

Ex. 7.7. Beethoven. Violin Sonata in A, op.12 no.2 (i) bars 44–53.

As if to counter both the second subject's out-of-phase nature and the music's general air of wittiness thus far, Beethoven introduces a mysterious chromatic passage that has the players proceeding together in sustained bare octaves (bars 68ff.), before a long crescendo leads to a four-bar focus on the minor second D sharp–E with which the first subject begins, and the exposition is brought to a close.

As in the first of the op.12 sonatas, the development section begins with a sudden shift in tonal direction – in this case, a full reappearance of the opening subject in C major, its playful straightforwardness lending the moment a deliberate sense of parody. The development is again surprisingly condensed, and it finds itself poised on the dominant of A minor after scarcely more than twenty bars. Here, the first subject's two-note phrases on one instrument are presented in conjunction with a smooth diatonic descent in echo of the second subject's shape on the other; and the passage leads seamlessly into the recapitulation, with only a solitary *fp* stress on the first beat of the bar offering an indication that this structural landmark has been reached.

The substantial coda begins, like the development section, with a sudden change of key – this time, to the subdominant (D major). At this point, Beethoven amuses himself by playing on the first subject's appoggiaturas. After repeated attempts to bring the piece to a close, the music eventually disintegrates, with the theme's two-note phrases left hanging in mid-air or, rather, deep in the bass of the piano.

In keeping with the stylistic simplicity of the sonata as a whole, the finale is again an uncomplicated piece, and its unclouded character, suggested by its tempo marking of *Allegro piacevole*, perhaps explains why Beethoven felt able to dispense with the relaxation in mood that might have resulted had he provided the sonata with a genuine slow movement. All the same, the rondo's theme incorporates a startling juxtaposition of contrasts, and the initial syncopated four-bar phrase is followed by a suave, almost chorale-like answer centred around the supertonic minor, which inverts the shape of the opening bars.

Ex. 7.8. Beethoven. Violin Sonata in A, op.12 no.2 (iii) bars 1–16.

The supertonic minor phrase of bars 5–8 is left hanging in isolation: not only is it separated from the surrounding material by the pauses that precede and follow it, but it remains harmonically unresolved. Instead, the violin's answer sets off without further ado in the subdominant – a feature that allows Beethoven at a later stage in the movement drastically to curtail the theme's return: by establishing what appears to be a false reprise in the subdominant he is able to join the theme at what is actually its mid-point, and to proceed from there to wind the movement up with a coda:

Ex. 7.9. Beethoven. Violin Sonata in A, op.12 no.2 (iii) bars 313–50.

The halting nature of the rondo theme itself, combined with a harmonic structure that has its two internal phrases set respectively in the supertonic minor and the subdominant major, throws the melody's ultimate resolution onto the tonic into strong relief. That resolution is effected by way of the simplest of cadential phrases in the last two bars of Ex. 7.8, and the same phrase appears as a recurring accompaniment figure in the movement's central episode, whose sweeping continuity stands in strong contrast to the rondo theme's fragmentary character.

The closing bars resolve the rondo theme's harmonic instability by having its initial phrase played no fewer than four times above a tonic pedal, before the work is brought to an end with a joke that has the violin bringing proceedings to a firm conclusion with an emphatic perfect cadence, only to hear the pianist continue for a further, unharmonised, bar.

That Beethoven frequently established the key of a work on which he was about to embark before formulating any of its definitive material is well known.[13] Certainly, when composing a triptych of pieces, in addition to casting one of them in the minor (a tenet which, as we have seen, was ignored only in the case of op.12), Beethoven would ensure that the major-mode works would include representatives on both the 'sharp' and 'flat' sides of the tonal spectrum. Having written the first two of the op.12 sonatas in the closely related keys of D and A major, Beethoven's first thought for the final work in the series appears to have been to set it in a key as far removed as possible from those. His surviving sketches for what we may assume to have been destined for op.12 no.3 are clearly in E flat major (with one idea for a slow movement in the tonic minor), even though they bear almost no discernible relationship to the material that eventually found its way into the piece.[14]

It is not only the enlarged scope of the E flat sonata in comparison with its two predecessors that marks it out as the culmination of the series: the inclusion of a serene slow movement of a kind that had been so palpably absent in the D major and A major works is clearly designed to provide the group as a whole with its expressive high point. The Adagio of op.12 no.3 is a piece that performs much the same function within the series as does the *Largo con espressione* from the G major piano trio among the three op.1 works, or the tragic D minor *Largo e mesto* of the last of the op.10 piano sonatas in its own wider context.

The opening movement of op.12 no.3, with its dazzling use of headlong semiquaver triplets, is a virtuoso vehicle for the pianist, and Beethoven was to remember some of its figuration when he came to write the finale of his C minor Piano Concerto no.3. The sonata's first subject finds the two instruments inextricably interwoven, with short phrases passed continually from one player to the other. Melodically more expansive and more conventionally laid out is the second subject (bars 29ff.), whose eight-bar theme is given in full first to the violin, and then to the piano. The quiet staccato closing subject that follows is to furnish the material for much of the development section.

The nervous energy generated by the sheer momentum of the keyboard writing in both the sonata's exposition and the first stage of its development section serves to set in relief the brief moment of quiet stillness that occurs in the bars preceding the onset of the recapitulation. Here, the music hangs briefly in suspension, while a broad new C flat major melody is given out by both players, above a rustling tremolando.

---

[13] See, *inter alia*, Cooper, *Beethoven and the Creative Process*, pp.120–2.
[14] See Johnson/Fischhof, vol.1, p.343, and vol.2, pp.51–5.

Ex. 7.10. Beethoven. Violin Sonata in E flat, op.12 no.3 (i) bars 96–107.

The moment is strikingly reminiscent of the approach to the recapitulation in the opening movement of the Cello Sonata op.5 no.1 (see pp.109–11), and once again the hushed atmosphere allows Beethoven to mark the arrival of the recapitulation with a peremptory gesture that characteristically brings the music down to earth at a stroke. Moreover, the arpeggios of the already intricate main subject are now accelerated, and the subject itself covers a wider compass than hitherto. (That compass is extended yet again in the coda, necessitating a further increase in the speed of the arpeggio. Beethoven carried out a similar type of progressive acceleration in his treatment of a rondo theme in the finale of the Piano Sonata op.2 no.2.)

Beethoven's choice of key for his slow movement – C major – mirrors that of the second movement of the E flat Piano Sonata op.7, and the tempo marking of the two pieces is similar: *Largo con gran espressione* in the piano sonata, *Adagio con molta espressione* in op.12 no.3. The movements are not unalike in atmosphere, though in marked contrast to the piano sonata, whose individual phrases are separated by silences that speak volumes, the violin sonata presents a single slowly evolving melody that scarcely pauses to draw breath for an instant. The theme itself conveys the effect of having its halves reversed – the first half cadencing into the tonic, and the violin's answering statement moving towards the dominant. The peculiarity is one that enables Beethoven to abridge the reprise following the middle section, so that only the first half of the theme is presented before the onset of the coda. The transferring of the short central episode's elaborate keyboard accompaniment to the violin during this condensed reprise further strengthens the music's sense of continuity.

As in the slow movement of the op.7 Piano Sonata, the most dramatic moment of the piece is an outburst on the note F sharp – the furthest point from the tonic. In the piano sonata this event is well prepared, and its presence in the final bars occurs within what is essentially a chromatically intensified reharmonisation of the main subject. In op.12 no.3 the *fortissimo* outburst of diminished seventh chords above a repeated note F sharp that occurs some dozen bars before the movement's close forms a dramatically new harmonisation of a gentle moment near the coda's beginning, and the event provides a surprise of considerable impact. The diminished seventh chords resolve in the following bar onto an implied 6/4 chord of C major, in what sounds as though it is to be the start of a cadenza. However, the cadential trill signalling the end of any such passage arrives after only two further bars, and it is, furthermore, diverted from its expected resolution by an excursion which lands the music momentarily on the chord of E flat, the sonata's home key. From this point on, the falling thirds of the movement's opening subject are expanded into a descending sequence, to form a conclusion of profound stillness.

Rather less promising than the slow movement's long-spun melody is the four-square theme of the rondo finale, whose symmetrical *sforzato* accents wittily harmonised in full-blooded style are placed firmly on the downbeat. Each of its melodically identical eight-bar halves, furthermore, cadences with almost comical abruptness into the tonic. The theme's Haydnesque repeated-note upbeat informs the material of the entire piece, including a weighty central episode in the minor which is dramatic enough to cast more than a passing shadow over the music's genial nature.

In the coda Beethoven decides – albeit briefly – to display his contrapuntal learning in a fugato based on the rondo theme, with a tiny three-note 'tag' forming a countersubject derived from an inverted form of the theme's third and fourth bars. The counterpoint itself is invertible, and it soon leads to a sustained timpani roll in the bass of the piano, and to a brief *stretto* whipping up the excitement for the final peroration. The end, when it comes, is both witty (though Haydn, we may feel, would hardly have failed to make greater humorous capital out of a theme with a similar repeated-note upbeat), and of convincing finality.

Barely more than two years separate the op.12 sonatas from Beethoven's next works of the kind, the A minor Sonata op.23 and the 'Spring' op.24. They were designed to form a strongly contrasted pair: Beethoven worked on them more or less simultaneously, and they appeared together in October 1801 under the single opus number of 23. Only a quirk of publishing led to their separation in a new edition the following year: the piano parts of the two works had been contained in a single volume, but the violin parts must have been assigned to different engravers. Through an evident failure of communication, the violin part of the A minor first sonata had been prepared in a vertical format, while that of the second was arranged horizontally. In order to spare the expense of re-engraving one of the sonatas, Mollo reissued them individually the following year with separate opus numbers. Both bore a dedication to the wealthy banker and art collector Count Moritz von Fries, who may have commissioned them. The following year the Count invoked the composer's wrath when, without authority, he handed over to Artaria the String Quintet op.29 which Beethoven had written for him. Under Beethoven's agreement, the quintet was to have been published in Leipzig by Breitkopf & Härtel – the first work of his to appear under their imprint. The Count was implicated in the lawsuit Beethoven instigated over the pirated edition, though he was conveniently absent on business at the time. All of this did not, however, prevent Beethoven from dedicating his Seventh Symphony to Fries when it appeared in print some fifteen years later.

Beethoven's first draft of the op.23 Sonata's opening bars is found among his sketches for the finale of the Piano Sonata op.22.[15] While the latter is one of the composer's graceful and relaxed rondos the op.23 Sonata is among his tersest and most austere works, and its outer movements are characterised throughout by stark, linear textures in which the piano is largely confined to bare two-part writing. In view of the dramatic forcefulness of so much of their material, it is remarkable that all three movements end *pianissimo*, as though all energy were spent.

The key of A minor is one that Beethoven, in common with Mozart, used only seldom, and Haydn almost never. Beethoven's greatest A minor work is no doubt the String Quartet op.132, but the main portion of the 'Kreutzer' Sonata's opening movement is in A minor; and in its powerful piano writing, much of it in octaves, as well as its inclusion of a sustained chorale-like theme, the finale of the op.23 Sonata contains strong pre-echoes of the later work's first movement. Even those with a thorough knowledge of the two sonatas might easily confuse the sources of passages such as the following:

---

[15] Nottebohm, *Zweite Beethoveniana*, p.380.

Ex. 7.11.
(a) Beethoven. Violin Sonata in A minor, op.23 (iii) bars 223–31.

(b) Beethoven. Violin Sonata in A, op.47 (i) bars 61–71.

The op.23 Sonata may altogether be seen as a close relative of the 'Kreutzer', but with its outer movements reversed. Certainly, the 6/8 *Presto* with which it begins is the type of piece we might sooner have expected to encounter as a finale, as in the 'Kreutzer' Sonata. At the same time, the two works do share an important feature in their opening movement: the second stage of the exposition unfolds not in the relative major, but in the dominant minor.[16] Indeed, the op.23 Sonata's first movement derives much of its intensity from the fact that it remains in the minor virtually throughout, with only a brief passage in its development section affording a glimpse of F major calm. More surprisingly, perhaps, the development also contains a stable tarantella-like theme given out by the violin in the tonic, and answered by the piano in the subdominant (bars 136ff.). Both the nature of the theme itself and the manner in which it is approached, with a winding-down and a fermata, lend this moment the aspect of a false reprise; and in order to strengthen the illusion, the true recapitulation is drastically curtailed, with the second subject following hard on the heels of the first. The recapitulation, moreover, brings into play a further deliberate structural ambiguity: the second group begins this time as though it were to be in the relative major, the key that had been so conspicuously avoided during the exposition, before the piano's counterstatement unfolds in the tonic.

The multi-functional aspect of the movement's latter half is emphasised if, like the exposition, it is played twice. Beethoven only rarely indicated a second-half repeat of this kind, and players would do well to respect his wishes.[17] The resulting delay in arriving at the coda has the additional effect of throwing greater weight onto this concluding page. Just as Mozart, when presenting new thematic material during the course of the development section, almost invariably reintroduced it during a coda (the Sonata for two pianos K.448, the G major Piano Trio K.496 and the C major Piano Sonata K.330 are among several works to carry out such a procedure), so, too, did Beethoven, and his tarantella theme duly returns to form the bulk of the coda.

---

[16] A further A minor movement having the bulk of its second group in the dominant minor is the first Allegro of the Cello Sonata op.102 no.1.

[17] Second-half repeats are found in the opening movement of several of Beethoven's earlier works: the first two of the op.2 piano sonatas, the Cello Sonata op.5 no.2, the last two string quartets of op.18, and the Piano Sonata op.10 no.2 (where in both outer movements the second repeat serves to enlarge the dimensions of an otherwise modestly proportioned piece). In the composer's later years, the second repeat fell largely into disuse. The opening movement of the E minor 'Razumovsky' String Quartet, however, indicates a second repeat not only in view of the grandly conceived coda, but also to underline the effect of the complex web of modulations characterising the movement's structural landmarks. In the 'Ghost' Trio the second repeat is included in part as a consequence of the development section's contrapuntal complexity, and partly to enhance the effect of the serene coda when it arrives, while in the piano sonatas opp.78 and 79 the repeats again enlarge the scope of a relatively small-scale work. The finale of the op.135 Quartet has, uniquely, an optional repeat of its second half, while the 'Appassionata' Sonata op.57 bypasses the traditional exposition repeat in favour of an obligatory repeat of the combined development section and recapitulation. Beethoven toyed with reusing the unusual scheme of the piano sonata's finale in the opening movement of the F major 'Razumovsky' Quartet op.59 no.1: six bars leading back to a repeat of the movement's long second half were composed, but the idea was ultimately discarded.

In common with the middle work of the op.12 triptych, op.23 has all three of its movements in the same tonality of A. Again, the second movement is not genuinely slow: its curious tempo marking of *Andante scherzoso più Allegretto* indicates its function as slow movement and scherzo rolled into one. The structural implications of the piece are once more complicated by the nature of the opening subject, whose symmetrical construction in two halves, complete with written-out repeats, brings into play the additional suggestion of a variation theme. The quasi-repeats have the theme's sighing two-note phrases played in octaves by the violin and the pianist's left hand, while at the same time filling in the pauses between those phrases with imitative echoes, in a manner that evokes – albeit in slow motion – the out-of-phase effect of the 'Spring' Sonata's famously dislocated scherzo. The variation background is eventually swept aside by the delicate fugato that follows, leading to a contrasting second subject. The fugato's staccato countersubject subsequently returns as the accompaniment to the closing subject of what turns out to be a sonata design.

The development section concerns itself with bringing to the fore the unity underlying the movement's contrasting ideas, as shown in particular by a contrapuntal combination of the fugato subject and the first subject's characteristic two-note phrases. But as though tiring of such learned procedures in what is essentially a light-hearted piece, Beethoven approaches the recapitulation by way of a passage which reduces the texture to a single melodic line that has the two instruments wittily alternating, as they had done within the first subject itself, and the violin's patient efforts to force the pianist back into the tonic at last rewarded.

Ex. 7.12. Beethoven. Violin Sonata in A minor, op.23 (ii) bars 115–27.

The violin's sustained octave at the actual moment of recapitulation is Beethoven's means of signalling this point of arrival, while the new staccato accompaniment to the first subject clearly recalls the delicate texture of the exposition's fugato. The staccato figure winds its way throughout the first stage of the recapitulation, which in other respects follows the pattern of the exposition closely, even to the point of avoiding a coda of any kind. Altogether, the piece has what would later come to be thought of as a Mendelssohnian elegance and lightness.

The similarity between the theme of the finale and that of the 'In gloria dei patris' fugue of the *Missa solemnis* was noted by the violinist Joseph Szigeti.[18]

Ex. 7.13. Beethoven. *Missa solemnis*, op.123, 'Gloria', bars 360–4.

The effect of the two pieces could, however, hardly be more different. While the fugue of the Mass is one of Beethoven's grand life-affirming conceptions, the op.23 Sonata's finale is among his most laconic utterances. It is one, moreover, that owes its curiously unsettling effect to the relentlessly unchanging nature of the rondo theme itself throughout, coupled with the deliberately fragmentary structure of the piece as a whole, juxtaposing, as it does, short passages of strongly contrasted material. Only on its final appearance is the theme modified through an inversion of the strands of its two-part texture.

The violin's contribution to the first half of the theme consists of no more than a single repeated long-held note:

Ex. 7.14. Beethoven. Violin Sonata in A minor, op.23 (iii) bars 1–8.

The theme reaches its apex in the sixth bar, whose subdominant leanings are stressed by a strong accent on the note F, and the theme's subsequent first reprise is approached via five Adagio bars which emphasise the same note, this time forming part of an implied dominant minor ninth, followed by a similar stepwise descent.

---

[18] Szigeti, *The Ten Beethoven Sonatas for Piano and Violin*, p.13.

Ex. 7.15. Beethoven. Violin Sonata in A minor, op.23 (iii) bars 49–55.

However brief, the moment provides the only genuinely slow music in the entire sonata, and in so doing it effectively transforms the character of the movement. The result is not dissimilar from that of the famous Adagio bar for solo oboe in the opening movement of the Fifth Symphony, while the idea of throwing the emphasis onto the subdominant is one that Beethoven was to explore more forcefully in the opening movement of the 'Kreutzer' Sonata.

The four long-held notes with which the violin underpins the rondo theme assume significance in the chorale-like central episode, where they are transferred to the piano.

Ex. 7.16. Beethoven. Violin Sonata in A minor, op.23 (iii) bars 114–25.

The preceding episode, in the tonic major, exploits one of Beethoven's favourite jokes: an apparent lapse of ensemble between the players. His intention may have been to provide a brief reminder of the key and scherzo-like character of the previous movement, and having served its purpose the episode is broken off almost before it has had time to establish itself. Since the ensuing return of the rondo theme is still further condensed, the F major episode quoted above is the only portion of the movement to achieve any real sense of breadth. It is, moreover, in the key that Beethoven might well have chosen for the work's middle movement had he not decided instead to cast it in the home tonality. As a result, the functions of all three movements have been split across the sonata: the first has the character of a finale, while imparting the proportions and intensity of an opening movement; the second is in a comparatively sustained tempo, but its mood is typically that of a scherzo; while the finale provides, albeit briefly, the genuine sense of repose so notably absent from the middle movement.

No greater contrast to the intensity of the A minor sonata could be imagined than the relaxation of the famous melody that begins its companion work, the so-called 'Spring' Sonata op.24. The opening subject of Clementi's Piano Sonata op.25 no.4 has been cited as the possible prototype of Beethoven's theme:[19]

Ex. 7.17. Clementi. Piano Sonata in A, op.25 no.4 (i) bars 1–4.

The parallel is striking enough (cf. Ex. 7.20 on p.179), though Clementi's rather aimlessly repetitive theme scarcely matches the poise and elegance of Beethoven's. Another possible model for Beethoven's melody was proposed by Boris Schwarz, in a valuable article on Beethoven's contact with the French school of violin playing: the Concerto no.2 composed around 1785 by Rodolphe Kreutzer, the eventual dedicatee of Beethoven's most famous violin sonata.[20]

Ex. 7.18. Kreutzer. Violin Concerto no.2 in A (i) bars 1–4.

Be that as it may, the apparent spontaneity of the 'Spring' Sonata's main theme cost Beethoven a good deal of effort, and the drafts for it contained in the 'Landsberg 7' sketchbook bear witness to the gradual way in which it evolved. In one of its earlier manifestations the theme ran as follows:[21]

---

[19] Truscott, 'The Piano Music I', p.75.
[20] Schwarz, 'Beethoven and the French Violin School', pp.431–47.
[21] Quoted in Nottebohm, *Zweite Beethoveniana*, p.232. See also Beethoven, *Ein Notierungsbuch* ('Landsberg 7'), p.17. For a detailed discussion of the sketches for the

Ex. 7.19. Beethoven. Violin Sonata in F, op.24 (i) bars 1–16, sketch.

The sudden halt in the theme's rhythmic activity from the third bar of the sketch onwards was clearly unsatisfactory, as was the threefold repetition of its initial turn-like figure in the seventh to ninth bars. However, one feature of the latter part of the draft that Beethoven did retain was the chromatic descent in the keyboard's low register followed by the A major triad, both of which feature in the sonata as we know it at the transition between exposition and development. The change in harmonic direction from F to A major seems, then, to have been an integral part of Beethoven's conception of the piece from an early stage, though the placing and role of the new key underwent a radical change between the sketch and its eventual realisation. (Beethoven's early draft for the development section shows it beginning not with the sound of A major, but with a diminished seventh chord surmounted by the note A. This was followed immediately by the first passage in triplet quavers – on the dominant of G minor – from the development's final version, suggesting that the entire first half of the section in its familiar form was a later insertion.[22])

Beethoven's definitive version of the sonata's opening melody preserves the importance of the initial turn figure from the sketch, while at the same time imparting greater rhythmic interest and variety to its third and fifth bars. Finally, the ascending octave leap of the third and fifth bars was an inspiration that enabled the melody to take wing.

---

sonata's first movement see Schachter, 'The Sketches for the Sonata for Piano and Violin op.24', pp.107–25.

[22] See Beethoven, *Ein Notierungsbuch* ('Landsberg 7'), p.18.

Ex. 7.20. Beethoven. Violin Sonata in F, op.24 (i) bars 1–10.

Expansive lyricism of this kind is found in such later works of Beethoven as the Fourth Piano Concerto, the 'Pastoral' Symphony, the 'Archduke' Trio and the op.96 Violin Sonata. At the time of the 'Spring' Sonata, however, he appears not to have been ready to write an opening movement of such large-scale serenity as in those works, and his elaborate main theme is countered by a more taut and rhythmically incisive second subject.

The choice of so seamlessly lyrical a first subject is one that confronted Beethoven with a problem if he wanted to make the theme felt during the development section. His first draft shows that he tried his hand at using it as the basis of at least a part of the development, but he eventually abandoned the idea, and only the initial four bars of the section in its final form make use of a fragment of the opening theme. The remainder of the development is entirely based on the more concise second subject, whose instability largely derives from a constant fluctuation between major and minor.

The development itself is both remarkably condensed and curiously sequential. For all the forcefulness of its material, it is as though Beethoven were deliberately keeping this portion of the movement as uneventful as possible, so that further development could be reserved for the latter stages of the piece. The development's restricted scope is emphasised by the fact that it comes to rest in the same tonal region as it had begun, with a long quasi-trill on the dominant of D minor. The resulting moment of stillness at this stage of the piece is of a kind Beethoven was to exploit with increasing frequency in the music of his last period. The trill dissolves with disarming simplicity, and without the luxury of any modulation, into the start of the recapitulation; but the first subject is already so expansive that Beethoven would hardly have been content with allowing it to be heard again in its entirety. Instead, the recapitulation is launched by the piano, with what in the exposition had been the theme's ornamented counterstatement, while the violin's answer gives way after only four bars to further development.

The beginning of the coda mirrors the start of the development section, after which the music reaches what may be heard as a form of implicit cadenza that indulges in some intricate invertible counterpoint. The cadenza propensities of the passage are heightened by the 6/4 chord resolved by a trill in bars 230–1; and since the nature of this moment had not in any formal sense been identified at its outset, Beethoven takes care to make this final cadential trill as emphatic as possible, by having it played *fortissimo* by the pianist in widely spaced octaves.[23]

Beethoven's earliest material for op.24 contained in the 'Landsberg 7' sketchbook is an isolated idea for the rondo finale's theme in the key of A major (albeit with a key signature of four sharps and a single bar of left-hand accompaniment that nevertheless suggests F sharp minor). On the following staves are notations for a passage related to the development section in the first movement of the String Quartet op.18 no.1, after which Beethoven turned his attention to the op.23 Sonata. When he resumed the threads of the 'Spring' Sonata several pages later, he jotted down ideas for its two middle movements. He seems to have worked on the Adagio at the same time as he carried out his thoroughgoing revisions to op.18 no.1, and the connection between the sonata's slow movement and the ubiquitous turn-like motif in the quartet's opening movement is clear enough:[24]

Ex. 7.21.
(a) Beethoven. String Quartet in F, op.18 no.1 (i) bars 1–4.

(b) Beethoven. Violin Sonata in F, op.24 (ii) bars 1–8, sketch.

---

[23] For a discussion of some other implicit cadenzas in Beethoven's first-movement codas, see Tovey, *Beethoven*, pp.112–13.
[24] See Mies, *Beethoven's Sketches*, pp.124–5.

Even this preliminary form of the theme of the sonata's Adagio gives primary importance to the turn-like figure in echo of the first movement's opening bars, but Beethoven's final version breathes new expressive life into the melody's second half. The ornamentation here, indeed, is of a kind that might more readily have been expected at a later stage of the piece, rather than the outset; and the impression of having begun *in medias res* is strengthened by the fact that the theme ultimately cadences so firmly into the tonic. The violin's counterstatement, moreover, replicates the piano's melody exactly.

The notion of beginning a piece with a full bar of exposed accompaniment in order to soften the subsequent thematic entry is one that is found on occasion in Mozart: the G minor Symphony K.550 and the Piano Concerto K.595 provide familiar instances. The inspiration behind Beethoven's piece, however, is much more likely to have been not these pieces, but rather the slow movement of Mozart's A major Violin Sonata K.526. The surprisingly literal counterstatement of the main theme in the Beethoven reproduces the unusually transparent texture of Mozart's opening bars, which have the pianist playing the accompaniment in bare octaves. Moreover, the initial melodic phrase of the two pieces is remarkably similar:.

Ex. 7.22.
(a) Mozart. Violin Sonata in A, K.526 (ii) bars 1–4.

(b) Beethoven. Violin Sonata in F, op.24 (ii) bars 1–11.

—(*continued*)

Ex. 7.22b—*continued*

 Both composers maintain the idea of thrusting the accompaniment into the foreground by having it intermittently sounded on its own; and in common with the development section in the Mozart, Beethoven's developmental central episode (bars 38ff.) begins with a change to the minor, and thereafter unfolds for the most part with the initial accompanimental figure still in octaves. In each case, that figure itself is of utmost simplicity – Beethoven's pattern being perhaps the more audaciously neutral of the two. No Clementi, Diabelli, Kuhlau or other contemporary purveyor of pedagogic piano sonatinas could ever have dreamed that the expedient of the 'Alberti' bass which they cultivated so assiduously could have been raised to such expressive heights. Of particular beauty is the intricately ornamented version of the theme during the first reprise – a moment where the piano's rapid repeated notes seem striving to create a vocal effect, or perhaps an approach towards recreating the type of vibrato that could be produced on the clavichord.

 When, in the opening stage of the piece, the figuration of the piano's accompaniment eventually ceases, it gives way to what sounds like no more than a simple transitional idea:

Ex. 7.23. Beethoven. Violin Sonata in F, op.24 (ii) bars 17–21.

The florid phrases in demisemiquavers are, however, to return towards the end of the movement in an inverted form, acting as a substitute for any final reprise of the principal theme; and this time there can be little doubt that Beethoven intended the listener consciously to be aware of the close relationship between the theme and the initial subject of the first movement (see Ex. 7.28 below).

Just as the op.1 piano trios had broken new ground by introducing a scherzo or minuet into the domain of chamber music with piano, so the 'Spring' Sonata is Beethoven's first work of its kind similarly to follow a four-movement plan. It is clear from his sketches that he had decided to include the additional movement even before he had formulated its character. His first thought was to cast the additional piece in the form of a staid minuet:[25]

Ex. 7.24. Beethoven. Violin Sonata in F, op.24 (iii) bars 1–8, sketch.

---

[25] See Nottebohm, *Zweite Beethoveniana*, p.235.

Realising, no doubt, that a stronger foil to the largely relaxed style of the remaining three movements was needed (indeed, it may well have been their very lack of urgency that prompted the inclusion of the additional movement in the first place), Beethoven transformed that simple idea to quite remarkable effect into a genuine scherzo – one that makes its joke out of the manner in which the violinist appears constantly to be lagging behind the pianist. This famous scherzo must be one of the shortest pieces of its kind that Beethoven ever wrote: a condensed parody, it might almost be said, of the sonata's opening movement, with which it shares the same startling chord of A major at the start of its second half.[26] So concise is the scherzo, indeed, that the trio seems to act as its extension, rather than as the start of a fresh idea. The feeling of continuity between the two sections is underlined by the fact that the trio's entire first half unfolds on the dominant: not until its final bar does the music resolve onto the tonic. At the same time, and as though to throw the scherzo's deliberate ensemble lapses into relief, the trio begins in a spirit of exaggerated togetherness, with both instruments playing in constant quavers.

In view of the strong unity displayed by the thematic material of the op.24 Sonata as a whole, it is notable that Beethoven appears to have sketched out ideas for all four of its movements at more or less the same time. A preliminary version of the rondo finale's theme begins in a form very similar to its ultimate shape, though its continuation lacks the familiar melody's concentration on the opening turn-like figure, and presents instead in its latter half a series of rising fourths.[27]

Ex. 7.25. Beethoven. Violin Sonata in F, op.24 (iv) bars 1–8, sketch.

Beethoven's final version, like the opening melody of the first movement, is so effortlessly natural in effect as to belie the amount of honing that went into it. Of particular subtlety is the manner in which the theme's chromatic inflections are absorbed into the piano accompaniment when the melody is taken over by the violin.

---

[26] A work whose scherzo is a more overt parody of the opening movement is the 'Hammerklavier' Sonata op.106.
[27] 'Landsberg 7', f.20.

Ex. 7.26. Beethoven. Violin Sonata in F, op.24 (iv) bars 1–13.

The turn-like figure which threads its way through the rondo theme clearly arises out of the same melodic impulse as the opening movement's main subject; and by now the kinship of the material of all four movements will readily be apparent:

Ex. 7.27. Beethoven. Violin Sonata in F, op.24, thematic unity.

The anapaestic repeated-note figure of the rondo theme's opening bars provides the starting point for the first episode, which sets off with a new theme in the tonic, while the new idea that appears in the dominant at bars 38–42 would seem to combine two prominent features from the first movement: the turn-like figure of its opening bars, and the constant alternation between minor and major that characterised the initial theme of its second group. Nor is this the only aspect of the opening movement that appears to have left a mark on the rondo: just as its development section had culminated in a quasi-trill on the notes A and G sharp, so the finale's D minor central episode (bars 73ff.) comes to rest on an extended oscillation between the same two notes. This time the passage prefigures not a return to the tonic, but a false reprise beginning in D major, before the music finds its way home for a full reprise whose opening bars are delicately scored with pizzicato accompaniment.

The appearance of the opp.23 and 24 sonatas marked a significant change in the critical attitude of the *Allgemeine musikalische Zeitung* to Beethoven's music. As though to make amends for its earlier conservative stance – and, no doubt, in no small measure as a direct result of the composer's intervention in the wake of its adverse review of the op.12 series – the journal greeted the new works with enthusiasm.

> If one has gone through a lot of recently published piano works, and in most of them has found the same thing over and over again, or at most occasionally a little enlivened with a fleeting new idea, it gives much pleasure at last to come across something original like these two sonatas by B. The reviewer regards them as among the best that B. has written, which really means among the best that are being written now altogether. The original, fiery and bold spirit of this composer, which even in his earlier works could not escape the

attentive listener, but which probably did not always meet with the friendliest reception because it occasionally stormed forth in an unfriendly, wild, gloomy and bleak manner, is now becoming more and more clear, is beginning more and more to reject everything superfluous, and is becoming more and more pleasant without losing anything of its character. And certainly, the more firmly an artist such as B. continues against his inclinations along this path of self-formation, the less he strives merely to impress, and controls himself, the more surely he will work for the pleasure of the cultured and at the same time for his lasting fame.

These two sonatas stand out among the others by this composer that are known to the reviewer through their strong structure, clarity and constantly true execution, as well as through the cheerful but in no way shallow scherzos that have very effectively been introduced at their centre. Finally, both, and particularly the first (Oeuvre 23, A minor), are not nearly so difficult to perform as some of Beethoven's earlier works, and are thus to be recommended to a larger public. They should only be played with character and precision, and are not hastily to be read through.[28]

---

[28] AMZ, 35 (26 May 1802), cols.569–70.

8

Interlude 3: The Horn Sonata Op.17

On the evening of 18 April 1800 Beethoven took part in a benefit concert given in Vienna's Kärntnertor Theatre by the horn player, violinist and composer Giovanni Punto. According to the theatre's poster for the occasion, the programme began with a 'new grand' symphony by Haydn, and continued with a *scena* by Ferdinando Paer (sung by the composer's wife, Francesca Riccardi), a horn concerto by Punto himself, an overture by Méhul, a clarinet concerto by Antonio Cartellieri, a further aria by Paer, and 'a brand new sonata composed and played by Herr Ludwig van Beethoven, accompanied on the horn by Herr Punto'.

Giovanni Punto was born in 1746, in the German-speaking region of Bohemia later known as the Sudetenland. His real name was Johann Wenzel (or Jan Václav) Stich, and his master, Count Thun, sent him at an early age to study first in Prague, and later in Munich and Dresden, where, from the well-known player and teacher Anton Joseph Hampel, he learned the relatively new technique of hand-stopping which allowed the production of chromatically altered pitches. Following his return, Stich found the restricted terms of his employment no longer to his taste, and together with four fellow members of Thun's private orchestra he managed to flee to Germany in the spring of 1768 – hotly pursued by the Count's henchmen, who had orders either to bring him forcibly back or to knock out his front teeth so that he could not play for anyone else.[1] Fortunately for him and posterity, Stich managed to escape both fates, but he thought it wise to change his identity. He was thenceforth known, in an Italianised form of his name, as Giovanni Punto. He died in Prague in 1803.

According to the early nineteenth-century music historian Franz Joseph Fröhlich, Punto was distinguished by 'the most magnificent performance, the gentlest portrayals, the thunder of notes and their sweetest indescribable blending of nuances with the most varied tone production, an agile tongue, nimble in all forms of articulation, single and double notes, and even chords, but most importantly, a silvery brightness in the most charming cantabile sound'.[2]

When Mozart met Punto in Paris in 1778 he declared to his father: 'Now I shall write a sinfonie [*sic*] concertante for flute Wendling, oboe Ramm, Punto horn, and

---

[1] See Morley-Pegge, *The French Horn*, p.152.
[2] *Allgemeine Encyklopädie der Wissenschaften und Künste*, ed. G. Hassel and W. Müller (Leipzig, 1834), section 2, vol.10, p.7.

Ritter, bassoon. Punto plays Magnifique.'³ Punto's later appearance in Vienna caused a sensation. Three months after he and Beethoven gave the premiere of the latter's Horn Sonata op.17, the Vienna correspondent of the *Allgemeine musikalische Zeitung* reported:

> The famous, and now probably greatest horn player in the world, Herr Punto, ... is at present residing in Vienna. A short while ago he gave a concert in which above all a sonata for fortepiano and horn composed by Beethoven, and played by him and Punto, so excelled and pleased that despite the new theatre rule, which forbids any *da capo*s and loud applauding in the Hoftheater, the virtuosi were compelled by very loud clapping once they had reached the end to start the piece again from the beginning and play it through once more.⁴

A more reasoned review appeared in the same journal some three months later:

> Herr Punto, the well-known great master on the horn, took over the theatre, and rightly astonished everyone with his art. His tone, his rapidity and above all his performance deserve to be admired. One would, however, almost like to hear more natural sounds in his beautiful Adagio. Herr Beethoven had done him the favour of writing a sonata for fortepiano with a horn, which was excellent. It did one good, too, to hear Herr Punto play a fine composition, for his own concertos have no real significance, and are even in places very bizarre.⁵

Punto and Beethoven went on to play the new sonata in Hungary; and on 30 January 1801 they performed it again at a concert given in Vienna's Redoutensaal, organised by the singer Christine Frank-Gerhardi in aid of soldiers wounded in the war against Napoleon.⁶ ('Herr v. Beethoven played on the pianoforte a sonata he had composed which was accompanied on the horn by Herr Punto. Both entirely lived up to the expectations that the public harboured of these masters of their art', commented the *Wiener Zeitung*.⁷) At the same concert, Haydn conducted two of his symphonies.

The assertion by Ferdinand Ries that Beethoven began work on his horn sonata only on the day before its scheduled first performance has been widely cited:

> Beethoven almost always postponed the composition of the majority of his works which he had to have ready by a certain date until the last moment. Thus he had promised the famous horn player Ponto [*sic*] to compose a sonata for piano and horn and to play it in Ponto's concert with him. The sonata had been announced, but it had not yet been started. Beethoven began work on it on the day before the performance, and at the concert it was ready.⁸

---

3   MBA no.440. Mozart's score has not survived in any original form, and, as previously mentioned, the published Sinfonia concertante (K.297b) is almost certainly a fabrication.
4   AMZ, 40 (2 July 1800), col.704.
5   AMZ, 3 (15 Oct. 1800), col.48.
6   See BGA no.56; Anderson no.45.
7   *Wiener Zeitung*, no.11, 7 Feb. 1801, p.398, col.1.
8   Wegeler/Ries, p.82.

Ries did not arrive in Vienna until some eighteen months after the sonata's premiere, and his anecdote is unlikely to be strictly accurate; but it is true that Beethoven was capable of composing at speed when the need arose, and he may well have played the piano part out of what was no more than a skeletal outline on paper.

The op.17 Sonata was dedicated not to Punto, but to Baroness Josephine von Braun, to whom Beethoven's two piano sonatas op.14 were inscribed. Her husband was manager of the two Viennese court theatres, the Burgtheater and the Kärntnertortheater, and he played a prominent part in organising the premiere of *Leonore*. However, his refusal to allow Beethoven the use of one of the theatres for a benefit concert subsequently aroused the composer's displeasure.[9] The greatest work on which the Baroness's name appears is not by Beethoven, but by Haydn: the F minor *Andante con Variazioni* (H.XVII.6).[10]

Beethoven's op.17 Sonata was tailor-made for the sound of Punto's horn, and for the distinctive virtuosity of his playing. Following the initial fanfare, covering a span of two octaves and ending up with the brassy sound of a bottom F, the piano's continuation of the first subject places its emphasis on its two long chromatic notes, F sharp and G sharp. The melody is subsequently taken over by the horn, which could only produce the notes in question by resorting to hand-stopping. Their novelty value, and the distinctive quality of their sound, would not have been lost on the audience of the day. That tone quality was not, however, universally admired, and the influential music historian Charles Burney, writing in 1803, complained, 'It must ... be discovered by every discriminating hearer, that the factitious half notes that are made by the hand in the mouth of the instrument, are sounds of a different quality from the natural tones of the instrument. We have often thought that Ponto, with all his dexterity, produced some of these new notes with similar difficulty, to a person ridden by the *night mare*, who tries to cry out, but cannot.'[11]

The horn concertos Mozart composed for his long-suffering friend Joseph Leutgeb contain no shortage of chromatic passages. Leutgeb was among the first to adopt the hand-stopping technique devised by Hampel, and the 'hunting' theme of the rondo finale from Mozart's Concerto K.447 is itself chromatic. (Curiously enough, when Mozart wrote a 'hunting' theme for an instrument other than the horn – as, for instance, in the finale of the E flat Piano Concerto K.482 – he generally took care to avoid any chromaticism. The apparent paradox is explained by the fact that in order to impart a clear impression of one instrument on another of a wholly different nature the material itself had of necessity to be exaggeratedly idiomatic of the instrument being evoked.)

What seems to have set Punto apart from the other players of his day, including Leutgeb, was his mastery of the horn in all its registers. (The common practice of

---

[9] See letter of 22 April 1802 from Kaspar Karl van Beethoven to Breitkopf & Härtel. BGA no.85; LTB no.38.

[10] The autograph of Haydn's work bears an inscription to Mozart's pupil Barbara ('Babette') von Ployer. The dedication to Baroness von Braun appeared when Artaria published the variations in 1799, some six years after they were composed.

[11] *The Cyclopædia; or, Universal Dictionary of Arts, Sciences and Literature*, ed. Rees (London, 1819), vol.18, p.200.

the time was for players to specialise in either the alto range or the basso, and a similar division of expertise is still widely assumed by performers today.) The remarkable agility demanded by Beethoven's op.17 sonata is shown by such moments as the dazzlingly virtuosic conclusion of the opening Allegro. A similar passage occurs towards the end of the finale, which also includes a long cadenza-like passage ending with a spectacular sustained horn trill. Nor would those present at the sonata's first performance have failed to appreciate an earlier moment from the first movement which has the pianist's hands cascading down the keyboard in toccata-like style, to land on a series of mysterious low sustained chords which, in the recapitulation, are accompanied by the horn in even longer notes, reaching right down to the bottom of the instrument's range. The horn note in the penultimate bar of this passage sounds at the same pitch as the cello's open C string, and the factitious note (i.e. foreign to the harmonic series) has to be produced by relaxing the lip – a technique known by players as 'lipping down' – with additional assistance from the right hand in the bell of the instrument, in order to assure security of pitch.

Ex. 8.1. Beethoven. Horn Sonata in F, op.17 (i) bars 157–62.

Despite its being clearly an occasional piece, the op.17 Sonata contains some strikingly individual ideas – not least, the second subject of the opening movement, which wavers continually, and almost as though in a dream state, between the keys of C major and E minor (see Ex. 8.2 below). The same two keys appear in direct juxtaposition elsewhere in Beethoven – the middle movement of the Piano Sonata op.14 no.1, for instance, or the finale of the E minor 'Razumovsky' Quartet op.59 no.2, whose theme sets off in an unambiguous C major before swinging round to the tonic – but the harmonic fluctuations of the horn sonata's theme have an exotic flavour all of their own.

Perhaps of more lasting relevance to Beethoven's future development is the overall shape of the sonata. Its middle movement is not a fully fledged slow movement (such a piece in cantabile style might well have run the danger of taxing the horn player unduly, and of relegating the piano part to the status of an accompaniment), but functions instead as an introduction to the finale. Moreover, the repeated-note figure in dotted rhythm which threads its way through it in the manner of a funeral march foreshadows the Adagio of the 'Waldstein' Sonata op.53, which is similarly designed as a preface to the concluding rondo. Beethoven was to become increasingly attracted to the notion of fusing slow movement and finale into a continuous whole: besides the 'Waldstein' and 'Les Adieux' piano sonatas, the Triple Concerto and the Fourth and Fifth Piano Concertos all have a middle movement which, if too substantial to serve as an introduction, functions essentially as an interlude in which the music appears to be holding its breath in anticipation of events to come.

The Horn Sonata's rondo, with its gavotte-like theme, bears similarities to the finale of the 'Spring' Sonata, composed around the same time. In particular, both have a central episode in the relative minor, with a running accompaniment in triplet quavers, and both come to a close with a headlong rush of triplets. Such passages in the op.17 Sonata's finale as the approach to the cadenza, with its rapid repeated quaver triplets for the horn culminating in a long-held, ringing *fortissimo*, seem to offer a hint of how much Beethoven must have enjoyed himself in writing the piece. (The passage in question is not replicated in the transcription of the sonata for piano and cello, where the cello part is – apart from the final rush of triplets – entirely different.) No less characteristic is the long rallentando near the close, followed by a sudden acceleration in tempo that brings the work to a rousing finish.

Clearly, in view of its technical difficulty, potential sales of the op.17 Sonata in its original form were limited, and when Mollo issued the work in March 1801 he did so with an alternative part for cello.[12] According to Czerny the cello arrangement stemmed from the composer himself, and certainly its skill and imagination leave little reason to doubt its authenticity. At numerous points the transcription takes advantage of the stringed instrument's greater agility in order to include a rhythmically enlivened accompaniment where there had been none before, thereby producing a more tightly knit integration between the two players. At the same time, there are strategic moments where the keyboard's sonority is newly reinforced by the intervention of the cello. The bars leading to the second subject in the opening movement provide just one of many instances where the cello lends additional support to the keyboard part, and greater vitality and animation to the music, than does the horn in the original version. The two parts are given in parallel in Ex. 8.2.

---

[12] A subsequent edition issued by Mollo between 1806 and 1808 also contained a violin arrangement of the horn part. The title page described the sonata as being *avec un Cor ou, Violoncelle*, but a line in a small type-face at the bottom of the page announced in pidgin French: *NB Il y a aussi la Parte de Violon separé.*

Ex. 8.2. Beethoven. Sonata in F, op.17 (i) bars 24–42.

—(continued)

Ex. 8.2—continued

The cello's interjections in the counterstatement of the second subject (bars 38 and 40) mirror each other – a symmetry that could not be managed for the horn, which is limited in the second of them to a single repeated pitch. On the other hand, the horn writing in the movement's closing bars – a passage which even present-day performers approach with some trepidation – has a brilliance that is not matched in the cello part.[13]

The forceful start of the development section transforms the movement's initial horn-call into the minor, giving it this time not to the horn, but to the piano. Beethoven must have been aware that Punto needed a moment's respite at this point, but there may have been another, equally pragmatic, reason for the change in tone colour. The horn would have had no difficulty in doubling the keyboard part at the upper octave, but for it to do so in the lower register would have been impracticable. Beethoven clearly wanted a dark sonority at this point, and hence left the piano to its own devices. When he came to make the transcription for cello, however, he felt no such restriction, and was able to lend the moment greater dramatic impact by having the instrument double the keyboard's bass line.

It would be hard to substantiate a claim for the op.17 Sonata as being among Beethoven's major chamber works, but the composer clearly retained an affection for it, and there is a record of his having played it as late as 1812 with the horn player of the Vienna court opera orchestra, Friedrich Starke, who gave Beethoven's

---

[13] For a detailed discussion of the differences between the two versions see Raab, 'Beethovens op.17 – Hornsonate oder Cellosonate?', pp.103–16.

nephew piano lessons. (It was for Starke's *Wiener Pianoforte Schule* that Beethoven composed the last five in his set of Bagatelles op.119.) Starke's account was given to Ludwig Nohl, who published it more than half a century later, and its accuracy is questionable (not least because it seems highly unlikely that by 1812 Beethoven's impaired hearing would still have allowed him single out *pianissimo* passages for praise), but the anecdote is worth reproducing for its curiosity value:

> Starke was often invited for lunch, after which he often had the spiritual delight of hearing Beethoven improvise. Most noteworthy and pleasant was the invitation to breakfast, which for Starke was a true breakfast for the soul. At that time, 1812, Beethoven was lodging on the Mölkerbastei. After they had partaken of breakfast, consisting of very good coffee (which Beethoven attended to himself, in a glass machine), Starke asked for an additional breakfast for the soul and heart, and Beethoven improvised in three different styles: first in the legato, secondly in the fugal, where a theme with semiquavers was developed in the most wonderful and heavenly manner, and thirdly in the chamber style, in which Beethoven could unite the greatest difficulties with his particular mood.
>
> As proof of his esteem for Beethoven, Starke had brought his horn, and offered to play the Sonata in F with horn (Op.17) with him. Beethoven accepted with pleasure, but while tuning it was found that the piano was exactly a semitone too flat. Starke said that he would tune his horn a semitone lower, but Beethoven replied with the remark that the effect would be spoiled, and he would rather transpose a semitone higher (in other words, play in F sharp instead of F). They began, and Beethoven played it in a wondrously beautiful way; the passages rolled along so clearly and beautifully that one could absolutely not believe that he was transposing. Beethoven also praised Starke because he had never heard the sonata performed with shading; he found the *pp* especially fine. The whole thing was a heavenly breakfast.[14]

---

[14] Nohl, *Beethoven. Nach den Schilderungen seiner Zeitgenossen*, pp.144–5.

9
Sonatas for Piano and Violin, 1802–3

The three violin sonatas op.30, composed in 1802, find Beethoven on the cusp of his middle-period style, which was firmly established in the following year with the 'Eroica' Symphony. The outer works of the op.30 series give, perhaps, little hint of things to come, though the contrapuntal intricacy of the A major first sonata, and the beauty and originality of its concluding variation movement, are striking enough; but the triptych's C minor centrepiece belongs among the composer's grand conceptions, foreshadowing the unprecedentedly large canvas of such middle-period masterpieces as the 'Eroica', the last two piano concertos, the Violin Concerto and at least the first two of the 'Razumovsky' string quartets op.59.

It was in the year after he embarked on the op.30 violin sonatas that Beethoven supposedly told Wenzel Krumpholz that he was dissatisfied with his previous works, and was determined henceforth to follow a new path (*Ich bin mit meinen bisherigen Arbeiten nicht zufrieden. Von nun an will ich einen neuen Weg betreten*).[1] While there may have been no sudden stylistic change in Beethoven's music once the eighteenth century gave way to the nineteenth (*pace* Wilhelm von Lenz, whose influential *Beethoven et ses trois styles* arbitrarily located the start of the composer's middle period as falling in the year 1800), there seems to be a conscious seeking after novel effects in the works he wrote around the time of the op.30 violin sonatas. As we have seen, with the opening movement of his C major String Quintet op.29, of 1801, Beethoven began to explore the idea of setting the second stage of the sonata-form exposition in a mediant key, as a form of expressively enhanced substitute for the more orthodox dominant;[2] and the second of the op.31 piano sonatas, composed in the following year, begins in unprecedented fashion with a bold juxtaposition of contrasting fragmentary ideas in opposed tempi. When, also in 1802, Beethoven announced the completion of his two variation sets for piano opp.34 and 35 to Breitkopf & Härtel, he told them that both were 'written in a quite new manner, and each in a distinct different way' (*Beide sind auf eine wirckliche ganz neue Manier bearbeitet, jedes auf eine andre verschiedene Art*).[3] His claim was entirely justified: op.34, in outright defiance of convention, has each successive variation in a different key, metre and tempo

---

[1] Czerny, p.19. See also Leitzmann, *Ludwig van Beethoven. Berichte der Zeitgenossen*, vol.1, p.33.
[2] See pp.49–50.
[3] Letter of 18 October 1802. BGA no.108; Anderson no.62.

from the last, while in op.35 – the famous 'Eroica' Variations – three variations on the theme's skeletal bass line unfold before the melody itself is heard at all.

On 22 April 1802 Beethoven's brother Karl informed Gottfried Härtel: 'At present we have 3 sonatas for piano and violin, and if these appeal to you we will send them to you.'[4] However, the sonatas are unlikely to have been completed at this stage, and their composition probably stretched on until at least the end of the following month. The last portion of the triptych to be composed was the finale of the A major opening work. Ferdinand Ries seems to have been the first to point out that Beethoven had discarded his original finale and transferred it the following year to the hastily composed 'Kreutzer' op.47.[5] Ries's assertion is borne out by the sequence of drafts for the op.30 sonatas contained in the 'Kessler' sketchbook, where ideas for what became the *Presto* finale of the 'Kreutzer' are found intermingled with sketches for the slow movement of op.30 no.1 and the opening movement of the C minor Sonata op.30 no.2.[6] Ries's claim that the original finale was too brilliant to fit in with the style of the remainder of the sonata has been widely accepted, though it is noteworthy that Beethoven did not shy away from invoking a similar contrast in character between the outer movements in his Piano Sonata op.31 no.3, on which he worked at more or less the same time, and where the finale is written in the same whirlwind 6/8 tarantella style as that of the 'Kreutzer'. Beethoven is more likely to have felt that the violin sonata's original finale was so grand in conception as to run the risk of dwarfing the preceding two movements, and of detracting from the impact of what he had planned as the largest and most dramatic panel of the op.30 triptych, its C minor centrepiece. That he took into account the fact that there was a purely practical reason for transplanting the finale from one work to the other, which was that he found himself needing to produce a new violin sonata for an important concert at short notice, is rather less likely.

Beethoven had not always intended to cast the substitute finale of op.30 no.1 as a set of variations. His amply documented drafts contained in the 'Kessler' sketchbook leave no doubt that its theme was destined for a rondo, and that there was to have been an episode in the relative minor. Significantly enough, what seems to have been Beethoven's very first idea for the finale, sketched out while he was beginning to formulate material for the opening movement – in other words, at some stage before he turned his attention to the original tarantella-style finale – was a rondo on a different subject altogether, though one that clearly shared the relaxed atmosphere of the variation theme on which he eventually settled.[7] Whether or not the finale's initial conception as a rondo remained at the back of his mind, the contrapuntal A minor penultimate variation contains an elaborate coda, in the shape of a developmental passage that might more naturally have been

---

4 BGA no.85; LTB no.38.
5 Wegeler/Ries, p.83.
6 For a discussion of the sketches for the op.30 sonatas, from which the chronology of the works is apparent, see Nottebohm, *Ein Skizzenbuch von Beethoven*, pp.19–26 and 29–32, and Reynolds, 'Ends and Means in the Second Finale to Beethoven's op.30 no.1', pp.127–45.
7 Beethoven, *Keßlersches Skizzenbuch*, f.37v.

at home in the central episode of a rondo. It is one that significantly transforms the music's character. A similar passage – albeit on a considerably reduced scale – appears at the parallel point in the variation finale of the op.96 Sonata, but it is hard to think of another conventionally laid-out set of variations by Beethoven in which such an expansion occurs at this moment, rather than during the concluding variation.

The manner in which the variation theme of op.30 no.1 is presented – the initial eight bars allotted to the violin, and the counterstatement to the piano – is unusual, and it perhaps once again reflects Beethoven's first conception of the piece as a rondo. In his remaining variation sets where the theme has written-out repeats of this kind, it is invariably the piano that leads.

One of Beethoven's early sketches shows the theme in the following form:[8]

Ex. 9.1. Beethoven. Violin Sonata in A, op.30 no.1 (iii) bars 1–16, sketch.

Although this version lacks the syncopation in the fourth and fifth bars that lends the definitive form of the theme its momentary sense of urgency, while at the same time providing added emphasis to the climactic note E in its sixth bar, two features of the sketch are of interest: first, that the 'scotch-snap' rhythm of the theme's penultimate bar which is such an essential ingredient of Beethoven's piece is already there; and second, the presence of a fermata on the note A in the preceding bar (replaced in the final version by a *sforzando*). Both have far-reaching consequences on the all-important minor-mode fifth variation of the finale as we know it. The chromatic passing-note in the bass line of the theme's sixth bar, on the other hand, does not appear in Beethoven's sketches until a late stage in its genesis. Instead, the relevant bar is harmonised diatonically, leading to the subdominant harmony on the first beat of the following bar. Ex. 9.2 shows the start of the theme in its ultimate form.

---

[8] Ibid., f.66r. See also Nottebohm, *Ein Skizzenbuch von Beethoven*, pp.31–2.

Ex. 9.2. Beethoven. Violin Sonata in A, op.30 no.1 (iii) bars 1–8.

The passing A sharp in the bass of the sixth bar reappears for the first time in variation 3, leading the music momentarily towards the region of the supertonic minor (B minor), but much stronger supertonic leanings are in evidence in the following variation, where the piano twice deflects the violin's triple-stopped A major chords firmly towards B minor. (Did Beethoven distantly remember those violin chords when he came to write the opening bars of the 'Kreutzer' Sonata?) Christopher Reynolds has suggested that Beethoven may have made the harmonic alteration to the theme's sixth bar retrospectively, once the character of variation 4 had been formulated.[9]

Ex. 9.3. Beethoven. Violin Sonata in A, op.30 no.1 (iii) bars 81–9.

[9] Reynolds, 'Ends and Means in the Second Finale to Beethoven's op.30 no.1', p.142.

Despite the change from major to minor, the contrapuntal fifth variation follows the theme's melodic outline remarkably closely. Its atmosphere of quiet mystery conceals considerable contrapuntal ingenuity, and the profusion of Beethoven's sketches for the variation shows the difficulty he experienced in composing it. It is written in invertible counterpoint throughout, and the quasi-repeat of its first half throws in the added complexity of a third, albeit false, canonic voice. Beethoven was to include a similarly subdued minor-mode contrapuntal variation in the finale of his op.96 Violin Sonata – again maintaining the contour of the theme, but ironing out its characteristic rhythm.[10]

The chief melodic alteration in the fifth variation of op.30 no.1 involves a flattening of the supertonic; and it is the chord of the flat supertonic – emphasised by a fermata that may well derive from Beethoven's very first inspiration for the theme – that is used to launch the variation's codetta, with its initial insistence on the key of B flat major. The switch from a B flat chord as the flattened supertonic of A minor to its role as a secondary tonic is carried out with disarming simplicity: all Beethoven has to do in order to effect the change in key is to suspend the music's motion, and have the flat supertonic chord sounded as a long-held fermata in Adagio tempo, before the music continues its course in the key of B flat.

In his concluding variation, for almost the last time in his career, Beethoven follows Mozartian tradition by allowing the theme to undergo a metrical transformation, to compound time (in this case, 6/8). It is a tradition that had previously found expression in such disparate works as the Clarinet Trio op.11, the op.44 Variations for piano trio, the Variations for piano and cello WoO 45, the string trio Serenade op.8, the piano variations on Wranitzky's 'Das Waldmärchen' (WoO 71), and those on Salieri's 'La Stessa, la stessima' (WoO 73). Of Beethoven's subsequent variation sets, only op.34 and a few of those from op.107 for piano and flute (nos.5, 8 and 10) involve a similar transformation – unless, that is, we accept that the entire finale of the 'Kakadu' Variations is of later origin.[11]

The A major Violin Sonata's concluding variation has its own coda, beginning with an expansion of the theme's opening three-note phrase into a broad, soaring harmonic sequence that is significantly launched with a move – via the note A sharp – towards the supertonic minor. Following this moment Beethoven prepares an enharmonic change that is on the point of taking the music into the very distant key of E flat. However, as though aware that he may have resorted to this kind of effect once too often in his career, he wittily turns the tables on himself, and moves as though by a last-minute change of heart back into A major after all, leaving the performer or listener to supply a mental image of a tonal excursion that failed to

---

[10] See p.324. Other contrapuntal variations in the minor are to be found in the 'Kakadu' Variations op.121a, and the variations for piano and flute on 'The Cottage Maid' op.105 no.1.

[11] See pp.352ff. Mention should also be made of the coda in the finale of the C minor Piano Concerto – not itself a variation movement, but so conscious does Beethoven seem to have been of his debt to Mozart's concerto in the same key, K.491, that he emulated its variation finale by invoking a similar metrical change in his closing pages. The 6/8 coda in the 'Archduke' Trio also brings into play the background of a variation form.

materialise. To cap it all, Beethoven finally introduces an ingratiating waltz-like transformation of the theme, before winding up proceedings with an emphatic close.

The opening movement of op.30 no.1 is one of Beethoven's most undemonstrative pieces, and its introverted nature may perhaps explain why the sonata is comparatively neglected by performers among his works of the kind. Its first group is unusually condensed, and the piece sounds almost as though it had begun in midstream. Beethoven's only concession as far as the latter characteristic is concerned is to place a sonorous, but subdued, chord of A major at the start of the piano's initial phrase – a chord to which the violin surprisingly contributes, before it pauses for two full bars as though the function of its early appearance were simply to establish the work's textural basis from the outset. The violin's contribution here has the further effect of making the all-important turn-like phrase in semiquavers that immediately follows stand out as though in isolation.

The brevity of the movement's opening stage clearly places additional expressive weight on the second subject. The first subject itself is, however, already so relaxed that there is little change in mood, and Beethoven feels it necessary to introduce a moment of increased tension between the two subjects, by means of a cross-rhythmic acceleration that gives the momentary illusion of a change from triple to duple metre. The climax of this passage is reached with the sustained C sharp of bars 31–2, and the apex of the second group's opening theme falls on the same note (bar 36). Beethoven was still writing for a piano of the same six-octave compass that Mozart had known, which meant that he could not mirror the latter passage in the recapitulation, since it would have taken the music up to a top F sharp – a semitone higher than the limit available to him. The ascending minor seventh of bars 36 and 40 is consequently altered in the recapitulation to a minor sixth, followed by a more chromatic descent.

Op.30 no.1's first subject is interwoven between the violin and the pianist's right hand in such a way that it is impossible to determine which of the two is melodically the more important, and the roles of the two voices are in any case exchanged during the theme's latter half. The subject is closely related to the opening theme of the second group: not only do both make prominent use of the interval of the perfect fourth (the sequence of fourths presented in a descending sequence in the first subject at bars 13–16 is counterbalanced by an ascending sequence in the second subject), but the second subject incorporates – in augmentation – the characteristic turn-like figure from the first (see bar 37 in Ex. 9.4. on pp.202–3). The second subject's latter half is, moreover, no more than a decorated version of its first half, and its shape of an ascending minor seventh followed by a stepwise descent is derived from the lower line of the first subject's two-stranded piano texture in bars 4–5:

Ex. 9.4. Beethoven. Violin Sonata in A, op.30 no.1 (i) bars 1–45.

The exposition's closing bars cadence firmly into the tonic – not only in preparation for the repeat, but also for the start of the development section, which thus follows on seamlessly. (Beethoven does, however, make one small gesture towards lessening the structural ambiguity, in the shape of an *fp* marking on the development's initial chord.) The notion of beginning this section of the movement with a fragment of the main theme in the tonic, thereby momentarily suggesting that the start of a further exposition repeat is under way, was pursued in the first and last of the op.31 piano sonatas. In all these cases, Beethoven nevertheless stipulates a full repeat of the exposition. Not until the first of the 'Razumovsky' string quartets did the implications of the idea bear full fruit, and the exposition repeat was implied without actually being carried out, by means of a literal reprise of the work's opening bars before the music proceeds in seamless fashion into the start of the development section. Beethoven invoked a similar *trompe l'oreille* in the last movement of the Eighth Symphony, and the first movement of the Ninth. The second of the op.30 violin sonatas also has the exposition played only once, without, however, introducing the idea of a feigned repeat.

The opening bars of the development section in op.30 no.1 are calm enough to include a complete appearance of the second group's opening theme in the relaxed subdominant key. Such stability at this point of the opening movement is unusual, but Beethoven's intention is to offset the closely worked fugato that follows – a passage as intense as it is short. Contrapuntal textures of this kind were clearly a major preoccupation during the composition of the op.30 series, and it is not without significance that one of the earliest sketches for the A major sonata's slow movement takes the form of a fugue-like subject in F sharp minor. Beethoven was to remember the discarded subject nearly twenty years later, as the main Allegro theme of the Piano Sonata op.111.[12]

The ascending interval of the fourth which characterises the opening movement's material is carried over into the theme of the D major slow movement (see bars 5–6 in Ex. 9.6 below). Beethoven's early drafts in the 'Kessler' sketchbook show the melody in a predominantly dotted rhythm:[13]

Ex. 9.5. Beethoven. Violin Sonata in A, op.30 no.1 (ii) bars 1–16, sketch.

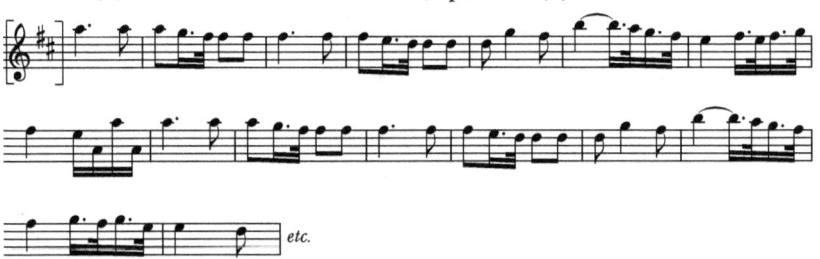

Beethoven eventually ironed out the melody (though he retained the dotted rhythm in the final bar of its first half), and at the same time, by a stroke of genius, transferred the original march-like rhythm to the accompaniment. It is the friction between the smooth theme and the military-style accompaniment that lends the piece its peculiar expressive quality, and the idea is one Beethoven was to exploit again in the slow movement of his Fourth Symphony.

The melody's definitive version owes its increased tension at least in part to its dynamic shading: the *sforzandi* on the weak fourth beat of the first and third bars; and – no less characteristic – the crescendo in bars 5 and 6, thwarted by the unexpected *piano* marking of the following bar. The deliberate absence of any natural downbeat stresses lends added weight to the climactic 6/4 harmony on the first beat of bar 15, which is followed by a firm resolution onto the tonic.

---

[12] Beethoven, *Keßlersches Skizzenbuch*, f.37v.
[13] Ibid., f.45r. See also Nottebohm, *Ein Skizzenbuch von Beethoven*, pp.21–2.

Ex. 9.6. Beethoven. Violin Sonata in A, op.30 no.1 (ii) bars 1–16.

Having maintained the same dotted rhythm throughout the first episode and the initial reprise, Beethoven presents a second episode that begins in an atmosphere of rapt stillness (bars 44ff.). (Is there, perhaps, a touch of malicious humour in the fact that having played patiently through the seven exceptionally static bars which begin this section of the piece, the pianist is suddenly confronted with an extravagantly ornate flourish of demisemiquavers offering a foretaste of the type of exaggeratedly operatic keyboard writing found in the slow movement of the first of the op.31 piano sonatas?) The episode serves not only to develop a fragment from the main theme – principally, its second bar – but also to establish the accompanying figure in flowing semiquaver triplets which is to run through the reprise.

The final reprise (bars 64ff.) has its melody accompanied by semiquaver triplets, and the avoidance of the initial march-like pattern here throws into relief the concentration on that rhythm in the coda. The coda, indeed, begins with an entire bar of repeated-note dotted rhythm for the piano, a moment martial enough to suggest the sound of a gentle drum-tap reminiscent of the closing subject in the slow movement of Beethoven's First Symphony.[14] The final bars, where the melody finally disintegrates in a series of sighing phrases followed by a dying fall with gentle pizzicato accompaniment, provide a haunting conclusion.

The grandly conceived second of the op.30 sonatas, in Beethoven's typically turbulent C minor vein, occupies much the same position within op.30 as does the D minor 'Tempest' Piano Sonata within the op.31 triptych: both have an intensely dramatic opening movement, followed by a slow movement in the submediant that forms the expressive high-point of the series.

The Sonata op.30 no.2 marks a historic stage in the history of sonata form: for the first time in the opening Allegro of an unequivocally great chamber work the exposition is not repeated, and its closing subject is instead linked seamlessly to the start of the development section. It is true that Mozart's Clarinet Trio K.498 begins with a through-composed movement, and that Haydn's String Quartet op.76 no.5 has an opening movement that does without the traditional repeat; but the Mozart is in effect a slow movement rather than a conventional sonata Allegro (it is followed only by a minuet and finale), while the Haydn is a complex fusion of rondo, variation and sonata forms. The absence of a repeat in the opening movement of Beethoven's C minor violin sonata arises in any case out of somewhat different considerations: first, a concern not to stem the music's dramatic momentum; and second, the exceptionally large scope of a piece whose coda is so substantial as to outweigh the central development section. Beethoven was to continue his experimentation with the through-composed sonata Allegro in the 'Appassionata' Sonata and the E minor Sonata op.90, while, as already mentioned, in the opening movements of the F major 'Razumovsky' Quartet op.59 no.1 and the Ninth Symphony, as well as the finale of the Eighth, he managed it have it both ways, and the close of the exposition is followed by a brief return to the work's opening bars in the tonic, as though the repeat were actually being made, before the music strikes off along new paths, and the development section gets under way.

Beethoven's model for this procedure is likely to have been the finale of Mozart's 'Haffner' Symphony K.385, which carries out a similar plan,[15] though he must surely

---

14 The 'Kessler' sketchbook f.15v. shows that Beethoven drafted an idea for a set of orchestral variations on a military-style theme at the time he was working on the op.30 sonatas.
15 In the opening movement of Mozart's Wind Serenade K.375, which was shorn of its repeats when the work's scoring was expanded from a sextet to an octet, the development again

have been acquainted, too, with the last movement of Haydn's 'Surprise' Symphony no.94. In Haydn's piece any structural distinction between sonata form and sonata rondo (already blurred where there is a return to the first subject in the tonic immediately preceding the development section) is further undermined by the nature of the opening theme, which is typically rondo-like to the extent of including a written-out repeat of its first half, and by the inclusion within the development section of a false reprise in the tonic. All the same, the theme's return following the conclusion of the second group sounds unmistakably like the start of an exposition repeat, rather than a rondo reprise. The explanation lies in the dramatic, open-ended character not only of the first subject's prolongation, but also of the material of the second group. By the same token, no one could mistake the reappearance of the off-tonic initial bars before the start of the development section in the opening movement of Beethoven's Ninth Symphony as an indication that the piece is in rondo form.

The notion of the through-composed sonata Allegro is one that owes more to the example of Mozart than has generally been acknowledged. Besides the 'Haffner' Symphony's finale,[16] such opening movements as those of the 'Paris' Symphony K.297 (a work which, when played with what is almost certainly its original slow movement, in 6/8 time, has no repeat from beginning to end), the B flat Symphony K.319 and the C major K.338 generate a cumulative energy that would have been diminished by the customary exposition repeat. Moreover, the 'Paris' Symphony, like K.338 and the 'Prague' K.504, does without a minuet, and thus presents an unbroken series of sonata-form movements.

Beethoven's C minor violin sonata shares much of the intense, yet subdued, drama of his piano trio in the same key, op.1 no.3, and both begin quietly, with a theme in bare octaves that is to make a *fortissimo* return at the start of the recapitulation. The sonata's opening movement derives much of its sense of forward propulsion from the nature of its first subject: the tension of its long-held initial note released in a group of rapid semiquavers, and its fragmentary phrases separated by expectant pauses (Ex. 9.7).

Beethoven was to achieve a similar sense of propelled tension by precisely the opposite means in his D major Cello Sonata op.102 no.2, whose initial subject reverses the rhythm and general dynamic level of the earlier work. (The initial bars of the Eighth Symphony share their melodic outline with that of the violin sonata, though in keeping with its more genial nature the symphony irons out the earlier work's tension-filled rhythm.)

The melodic collapse in the latter part of op.30 no.2's subject is noteworthy: it is left to the violin, entering for the first time in the following bar, to supply a regularly shaped counterstatement to a theme whose second half has been suppressed.

---

begins with a fleeting restatement of the initial bars in the tonic, thereby momentarily giving the impression that the repeat is being made.

[16] Mozart also struck out the repeats from the opening movement of the 'Haffner' when the work was transformed from a serenade into a symphony.

Ex. 9.7. Beethoven. Violin Sonata in C minor, op.30 no.2 (i) bars 1–15.

A more conventional form of the theme is found in one of Beethoven's preliminary sketches:[17]

---

[17] Beethoven, 'Kessler' sketchbook, f.5¹¹.

Ex. 9.8. Beethoven. Violin Sonata in C minor, op.30 no.2 (i), sketch.

The second subject is quite different in character from the relative major theme in such C minor works as the Piano Trio op.1 no.3, the String Quartet op.18 no.4, the Third Piano Concerto and the Fifth Symphony. While those pieces all have a cantabile idea whose relaxation and warmth act as a foil to the agitation of the first group, the violin sonata presents instead a clipped, military-style tune of almost nervous good humour which provides an ideal prelude to the virtuoso tone of the exposition's closing pages. The subject is given out initially by the violin, to a single-line piano accompaniment in regular staccato quavers. For the counterstatement the tune migrates to the bass of the keyboard part, while above it the running accompaniment is picked out by the violin and the pianist's right hand in bare octaves.

The smooth transition between exposition and development is effected by means of a soaring new violin tune played high above an accompaniment which has as its bass line the first subject's opening phrase. Beethoven allows the expansive new tune to be heard no fewer than three times in its entirety, taking the music from the relative major, through B major, to G major. The music's seamless continuity is underlined when the development gets under way in earnest, with the march-like second subject going through a similar descending chain of thirds, appearing first in A flat major, before moving through F minor and D flat major to B flat minor, and eventually touching on G flat major. Beethoven's decision to concentrate on the second subject at this point results in all likelihood from the fact that the first subject is itself too fragmentary to allow for further development, and the closing theme too expansive. Only in its final bars does the development make a return to the atmosphere of the first subject; and the highly charged chromatic writing of this last stage of the section has a dramatic impact and intensity that Beethoven was not to surpass until the 'Appassionata' Sonata op.57.

The soaring violin theme that had so memorably opened up the music's horizons at the end of the exposition returns during the closing stages of the recapitulation (bars 208ff.), though with a striking difference. While on its earlier appearance it had effectively straddled the boundary between exposition and development, it no longer has any such transitional function to fulfil, and as a result not only are its length and melodic compass drastically reduced, but it now revolves entirely around the tonic, in the process assuming the unambiguous guise of a closing subject.

One detail in the coda itself should be noted: the final appearance of the first subject in the violin part unfolds simultaneously with its augmentation in the piano. Although the piano ostensibly provides the role of an accompaniment here, it is a detail of which the player needs to be aware.

Ex. 9.9. Beethoven. Violin Sonata in C minor, op.30 no.2 (i) bars 236–43.

The instability and intensity of the opening movement are such as to call for symmetry and serenity in the slow movement, and the Adagio's broad cantabile melody is consequently presented as though it were to be a regular variation theme, each sixteen-bar half given out by the pianist before being restated by the stringed instrument. Several of the drafts in the 'Kessler' sketchbook indicate that Beethoven actually toyed with the idea of writing the piece in variation form. One projected variation has the theme in the style of a siciliano with a pizzicato part in chords, and it is possible that a distant echo of that early notion survives in the pizzicato triads during the closing bars of the slow movement in its familiar guise.

One of the earliest sketches for the piece, in which the theme's initial four bars appear in a form very close to their final shape, is in G major.[18] Beethoven's eventual choice of key, however, was the submediant, A flat, the key in which the slow movement of the Fifth Symphony, the Piano Sonata op.10 no.1 and the 'Pathétique' op.13 appear. The Adagio's central section, moreover, unfolds largely in A flat minor, which means that for the greater part of its length the music does not venture outside the home tonality. The tonal stability serves to offset the dramatic chain of events that is to unfold in the coda.

Following the middle section, with its delicate staccato arpeggios, the reprise brings back the initial theme virtually unchanged (though with a subtle harmonic alteration in its sixth bar), at the same time greatly elaborating its accompaniment. The elaboration is strictly functional: the piano's version of the theme is heard against a violin part that recalls the middle section's arpeggio figuration, while the violin's counterstatement is underlain with rapid piano scales of a kind that are to erupt with force in the coda.

The theme's last two bars had introduced quaver triplets, and it is their rhythm that serves as a launching-pad for the coda. The coda itself begins reassuringly enough with a gentle extension to the theme; but it is twice interrupted by surging *fortissimo* C major scales whose violence is such as to threaten to tear the music's very fabric apart. The moment is heightened by the symmetry and tonal homogeneity of the remainder of the movement, and although the interruptions are brief their impact is overwhelming. The coda thereafter is predominantly calm, and for the greater part underpinned by a repeated dominant note in regular quavers which moves progressively downwards through the texture, from the treble (violin, bars 103–4), through the tenor (the piano octaves of bars 105–6), to the bass (bars 107–9). The pedal note itself recalls the similar repeated note in the bars preceding the C major outburst, thereby underlining the interpolative nature of that passage.

Despite its conventional 3/4 time signature, the scherzo has a faintly military flavour, and a march-like background is suggested by the irregularly placed accents of its fifth and sixth bars, which have the effect of throwing the music momentarily into duple metre. The emphatic *sforzandi* of the scherzo's second half, which have the violinist playing the same pitch on the stopped A and open E strings simultaneously, represent a rare use by Beethoven of this reinforced string sonority.

---

[18] Beethoven, 'Kessler' sketchbook, f.54v.

The canonic trio is based on the scherzo's melodic outline, though with its dotted rhythm ironed out. Once again the aural impression of duple metre is created through the strategic use of cross-accents, and the effect of dislocation is strengthened by the fact that the accents occur in canon, thereby falling on alternate beats. The counterpoint itself is gruff in nature, and the canon ceases to work at all from its seventh bar onwards, from which point Beethoven is forced into artistic licence as far as the answering voice in the bass of the piano part is concerned. The same quasi-canon is invoked in the trio's closing bars, giving rise to an ending of almost comical bluntness.

Had it not been for the intervention of the scherzo, the unharmonised repeated staccato A flat in the finale's first full bar might have formed a natural means of following on from the slow movement. The A flat is eventually harmonised as the root of an augmented sixth chord that resolves onto the dominant of C minor, but the deliberate ambiguity allows Beethoven to keep surprises up his sleeve throughout the piece, and to divert the theme into a different tonal direction at each appearance:

Ex. 9.10.
(a) Beethoven. Violin Sonata in C minor, op.30 no.2 (iv) bars 1–18.

Ex. 9.10.
(b) bars 173–82.

(c) bars 264–70.

The trill-like anacrusis of the finale's beginning is used not only to herald the theme's various returns during the course of the piece, but also as a guiding thread through the contrapuntal thicket of the central episode. The movement's opening paragraph is asymmetrical, each of its halves consisting of 3 + 4 bars; and as is so often the case, Beethoven's preliminary sketches show him progressing from the conventional to the idiosyncratically individual. In a sketch which bears the heading 'L'ultimo pezzo', the trill-like upbeat figure is extended to occupy a full bar, thereby lending the theme as a whole a more regular structure. However, in beginning on the first beat of the bar, this version sacrifices the figure's upbeat character and detracts from the emphasis of the repeated A flats in the following bar.[19]

As in the last movement of the Piano Trio op.1 no.3, the rhythmically jagged opening bars give way to a conjunct C minor theme, and it is possible to feel that the finale as a whole represents something of a throwback to an earlier style, particularly in the context of the preceding movements. Not until the first episode is over does Beethoven allow his conjunct theme due breathing space, while at the same time transforming it into the major so that it can provide a moment of relaxation before the densely contrapuntal episode that follows. The double fugato itself (bars 134ff.) has as its two strands the conjunct theme, and a running passage in quavers which derives from the earlier transition between the rondo theme and the first episode. For good measure, Beethoven intermittently interjects the rondo theme's characteristic trill-like figure.

In the coda the tempo accelerates to *Presto*. For all the air of superficiality about the music's agitation here, Beethoven is careful to demonstrate that an apparently new idea introduced by the violin in bar 304 can be combined contrapuntally with the start of the rondo theme itself, and as a means of whipping up excitement in the work's final moments the passage is undeniably effective.

The last of the op.30 sonatas is one of Beethoven's wittiest chamber works, and its generally unpretentious character and dimensions have caused it to be overshadowed by its dramatic predecessor. It is a work in which motivic repetition to an almost obsessive degree plays an important role, just as it does in the opening movement of the piano sonata in the same key op.31 no.1. In view of the scherzo-like nature of the outer movements there is this time no place for an actual scherzo; nor, despite the exceptionally quick tempo of those movements, does Beethoven feel the need to provide a genuine slow movement of the kind found in the first two sonatas of the series. Instead, the middle movement is written against the background of a minuet and trio, and is similar in its lyrical relaxation to the actual minuet (also a partial substitute for any real slow movement) from the E flat Piano Sonata op.31 no.3, with which it shares its key and tempo qualification of *grazioso*.[20]

Beethoven's first sketch for the middle movement's theme in the 'Kessler' sketchbook (f.63r) shows it with an entirely different beginning, though the latter half of the melody's first paragraph is already fully formed:

---

[19] Beethoven, 'Kessler' sketchbook, f.51r.

[20] Beethoven's autograph of the violin sonata shows that the middle movement was originally headed *Andante*. This was replaced by *Tempo di Minuetto ma molto moderato*, and finally, in different ink, the words *e grazioso* were added.

Ex. 9.11. Beethoven. Violin Sonata in G, op.30 no.3 (ii), sketch.

A later sketch (f.73r.) takes a step nearer the theme's ultimate shape by introducing an ascent of a minor second between its initial two notes. Here, however, the theme's second half moves to the dominant, rather than the definitive version's more expressive relative minor:

Ex. 9.12.

In a further draft the opening bars assume their familiar wedge-shaped form, and the melody is now notated in 3/8 time.

Ex. 9.13.

Beethoven's final version avoids the unsatisfactory repetition of the theme's opening phrase in bars 5–6 of the above sketch by combining its beginning with a continuation taken from his very first idea, and the whole theme emerges transformed into an elegant minuet:[21]

---

[21] Of the eventual combination of the two earlier forms of the theme, Nottebohm (*Ein Skizzenbuch von Beethoven*, p.30) comments: 'This may indeed be called a "composition" in the strictest sense of the word.' However, the initial three bars of the second sketch quoted above are clearly no more than an ornamented form of the corresponding portion of the first one.

Ex. 9.14. Beethoven. Violin Sonata in G, op.30 no.3 (ii) bars 1–8.

The quasi-trio section, with its accents in the piano part characteristically placed on the second beat of the bar, is also in E flat, though with an abbreviated second half in the minor; and since the entire piece thus unfolds in, or at least revolves around, the tonic, it is sufficiently relaxed to offer the requisite feeling of repose between the dizzyingly fast outer movements. Beethoven's autograph – written with what was for him unusual neatness – reveals a last-minute alteration in this section where the melody is taken over by the piano (bars 67–74 and 157–62). At first, the violin was to have continued the triplet motion of the piano's accompaniment heard in the preceding bars; but in order to avoid a sense of rhythmic monotony Beethoven substituted sustained double-stops at this stage, and in so doing created an enhanced feeling of breadth and calm.

In keeping with the almost exaggeratedly straightforward minuet form of the piece, there is very little alteration to the opening theme in the reprise: a trill in place of what had been a bar of repeated quavers, and a new syncopation in the violin accompaniment of the closing bars are the only significant changes. The straightforward repetition of material – compounded by the return of the quasi-trio's first half before the start of the coda, as though the piece were to be in the expanded minuet or scherzo form typical of Beethoven's middle period, with a double appearance of the trio between three statements of the minuet – is one that confronts players with a considerable interpretative challenge.

If the middle movement is harmonically as uneventful as could be imagined, the 6/8 opening movement derives its nervous energy from an unusual degree of harmonic instability. The exposition's fragmentary style is exemplified by the curiously laconic first subject itself, with its abrupt dynamic contrasts strikingly varied between antecedent and consequent. Beethoven seems to have had some last-minute changes of heart as far as the dynamic markings were concerned. He clearly went to some lengths to avoid excessive symmetry between the theme's two halves, and his autograph score reveals three distinct stages. In the first, the violin was marked *forte* from the outset. This must have been deleted with little or no hesitation, as there is no corresponding marking in the piano part. In the second stage Beethoven struck out the *forte*, and inserted *piano* in both parts, with a crescendo in the second half of the first bar, leading to *forte* already in bar 2. Finally, the *crescendo* and *forte* markings were delayed until bars 3 and 4, respectively. The markings in bars 5–8, on the other hand, underwent no change, and in view of the fact that the recapitulation uses the dynamics of these bars for both halves of the theme (i.e. *forte* in the first bar, followed by *piano* and *forte* in the third and fourth bars, respectively), it is perhaps surprising that Beethoven did not retrace his steps and make one final alteration to the sonata's beginning.

In addition to the changes in dynamics, the opening subject underwent a further significant alteration. The violin's first note in the fourth bar was originally a dotted crotchet, after which the theme's second half would have begun cleanly, on the first beat of the following bar. However, Beethoven transformed the note in question into a dotted quaver, and the three-note anacrusis to the fifth bar was added in both parts.[22] The recapitulation shows no sign of any such alteration; but whether the exposition was changed in the light of an inspiration which struck Beethoven at the later stage of the movement, or whether the ultimate form of the opening bars evolved as they were being written, is something that cannot be determined. In either event, the change is one that enlivens the discourse to a remarkable degree.

Ex. 9.15. Beethoven. Violin Sonata in G, op.30 no.3 (i) bars 1–8.

The movement's elliptical harmonic style is typified by the approach to the exposition's second group, where Beethoven reveals that the opening subject's initial phrase can also function as a transition. Having arrived at a firm close on the dominant of D followed by a pause, as though to herald the appearance of a contrasting

---

[22] See Alan Tyson's introduction to the facsimile edition of op.30 no.3, p.vi.

subject in the dominant, the music passes instead through the more remote regions of B minor and E minor – not, however, without humorous interjections of a fragment of the first subject obstinately set in the dominant and tonic. Once again, Beethoven made a telling alteration at a late stage: the interjected reminiscences of the first subject in the last six bars of Ex. 9.16 were to have been played by both violin and piano in octaves, but the eventual change in scoring, with the piano acting alone as mediator, adds considerably to the music's wit.

Ex. 9.16. Beethoven. Violin Sonata in G, op.30 no.3 (i) bars 29–42.

The harmonic instability of this moment does not prevent Beethoven, once the tonality of D is reached again, from launching without further ado into a dramatic theme in the minor. Small wonder he feels it necessary to underpin the closing subject (bars 67ff.) with a dominant pedal – though even here the strong cross-accents in the violin part are sufficient to rob the music of any real feeling of equilibrium.

It may have been the already unstable nature of the exposition that prompted Beethoven to reduce the dimensions of the development section, which occupies a mere twenty-five bars, all of them in the minor and taking their cue from the exposition's agitated closing moments. The concision of this portion of the movement is, however, as nothing when compared with the extreme aphorism of the coda, where four bars capped by two quiet chords bring the music's momentum to an abrupt halt.

The finale displays the seeds of what was to become one of Beethoven's favourite middle-period compositional challenges: the creation of a piece in constant semiquaver motion. The process was applied with greater rigour, and to very different effect, in the finale of the Piano Sonata op.31 no.2, and again in the finale of the F major Sonata op.54, and that of the 'Appassionata' op.57.

Op.30 no.3's finale might best be described as a monothematic rondo, especially since the one episode to present any melodic contrast occurs in the tonic immediately following the rondo theme, and thereafter never reappears. The rondo subject itself is based on a textural ambiguity that deliberately blurs the borders between what is thematic, and what accompanimental. The piano's opening four-bar solo would seem at first to be no more than an exposed accompaniment; but the idea superimposed above it by the violin in the following four bars is itself scarcely more distinctive from a melodic point of view, despite the fact that it provides the basis for a very brief later episode in the relative minor (bars 56–64). The adverb *leggiermente* must have been added to the opening bars as an afterthought, since it appears in the autograph in a different ink, and in the piano's stave above the initial semiquavers. In order to lighten the texture still further Beethoven altered the articulation of the semiquavers in bars 24–8 and all further appearances of the same material: instead of having each group of four semiquavers phrased together, he restricted the phrasing to the first pair of notes in each case, adding staccato markings to the latter pair.

The textural ambiguity of the finale's beginning is compounded when the two instruments round off the opening stage of the movement by playing the initial quasi-accompaniment in parallel octaves. Such is the well-nigh obsessive degree to which this figure recurs that it is present in no fewer than sixteen of the first twenty bars. Moreover, those same twenty bars are to reappear in their entirety no fewer than three times during the course of the piece, with only the start of their last appearance involving a small change in sonority.

Despite the presence of a central episode that develops both strands of the movement's initial texture simultaneously, the brevity of the remaining episodes is such as to create an overall scheme of quite unusual repetitiveness. It is one that has parallels with the last movement of the op.23 Violin Sonata, where, again, the unvarying nature of the rondo theme is relieved by a change in sonority – albeit considerably more radical – on its last appearance. In op.30 no.3 the regularity of the plan serves to throw into relief the wittiest moment of the piece: a startling plunge into the flat submediant. This, no doubt, is a deliberate reminder of the key of the middle movement, but also perhaps a self-caricature of Beethoven's fondness for having his rondo or variation theme appear in a remote tonality at a late stage. At this point, the pianist unceremoniously plays what is in effect an accompaniment to the accompaniment with which the movement had begun. The new accompaniment is as basic as could be imagined – no more than a series of strummed chords – and in their context these 'empty' E flat major bars provide one of Beethoven's most outrageously comical moments.

The three op.30 sonatas were dedicated to Tsar Alexander I, who, however, appears to have overlooked the matter of offering the composer any form of reward in return. Not until 1814 was the omission made good, when Beethoven took advantage of the visit of the Tsarina Elisabeth Alexievna to the Congress of Vienna to dedicate to her the rapidly thrown-together piano Polonaise op.89. The piano piece was written at the suggestion of the composer's doctor and friend Andreas Bertolini, and Beethoven apparently improvised several themes before asking Bertolini to choose one. When the completed polonaise was presented to Elisabeth Alexievna, she gave Beethoven 50 ducats and asked if he had ever received anything for the three violin sonatas he had dedicated to her husband. On being informed in the negative, she threw in a further 100 ducats.[23]

On 24 May 1803 Beethoven took part in the first performance of a new and rapidly written violin sonata. His partner, whom he had met shortly before, was a violinist who rejoiced in the name of George Augustus Polgreen Bridgetower.[24] The circumstances surrounding his early life are somewhat obscure, but he appears to have been born in Biala, Poland, in 1779, and he made his debut at the *Concert spirituel* in Paris, on 11 April 1789, in a concerto by Giovanni Giornovichi. His playing on that occasion was greeted with enthusiasm by the *Mercure de France*, in a notice whose sentiments still resonate today:

> A strange debut, which caused considerable interest, was that of M. Bridge-Tower, a young Negro from the Colonies, who played several violin concertos with a cleanness, facility, an execution and even a sensitivity that it is rare indeed to meet in so tender an age (he is not ten years old). His talent, as genuine as it is precocious, is one of the best answers that one can give to those philosophers who want to deprive those of his nation and of his colour of the right to distinguish themselves in the arts.[25]

Later that year Bridgetower made his way to England, where he acquired the nickname of 'The African Prince'. He played before George III at Windsor Castle, and then travelled on to Bath, where *The Morning Post* of 8 December 1789 reported:

> The young African Prince, whose musical talents have been so much celebrated, had a more crowded and splendid concert on Saturday morning than has ever

---

[23] See Thayer/Forbes, p.603.

[24] Betty Matthews, who opts for the spelling Bridgtower found in some contemporary sources, suggested the name may derive from Bridgetown, in Barbados. See her 'George Augustus Polgreen Bridgtower', p.22. For a detailed account of Bridgetower's life see F.G. Edwards, 'George P. Bridgetower and the Kreutzer Sonata', and Josephine R.B. Wright, 'George Polgreen Bridgetower: An African Prodigy in England 1789–99'.

[25] *Mercure de France*, 2 May 1789, p.41.

been known in this place. There were upwards of five hundred and fifty persons present, and they were gratified by such skill on the violin as created general astonishment, as well as pleasure.

Rauzzini[26] was enraptured, and declared that he had never heard such execution before, even from his friend La Motte, who was, he thought, much inferior to this wonderful boy. The father was in the gallery, and so affected by the applause bestowed on his son, that tears of pleasure and gratitude flowed in profusion. The profits were estimated at two hundred guineas, many persons having given five guineas for each ticket.[27]

According to the diary of Joseph Carl Rosenbaum, an administrator of the estate of Prince Nicolaus Esterházy II, Bridgetower's father had been a footman to Prince Nicolaus I.[28] If this is true, it may have been at Esterháza that the young violinist received tuition from Haydn. His appearance at Windsor Castle is chronicled by Charlotte Papendieck:

> About this time [October 1789] an adventurer of the name of Bridgetower, a black, came to Windsor, with a view of introducing his son, a most prepossessing lad of ten or twelve years old, and a fine violin player. He was commanded by their Majesties to perform at the Lodge, when he played a concerto of Viotti's and a quartet of Haydn's, whose pupil he called himself. Both father and son pleased greatly. The one for his talent and modest bearing, the other for his fascinating manner, elegance, expertness in all languages, beauty of person, and taste in dress.[29]

Two years later, Bridgetower was to be found in London as a member of the orchestra at the Salomon concerts, where Haydn conducted his new 'London' symphonies. On 15 April 1791 he played a concerto in one of Salomon's Hanover Square concerts at which Haydn presided over a performance of his 'Oxford' Symphony no.92; and on 28 May 1792, at a benefit concert for the composer and violinist François-Hippolyte Barthélémon, who had been his teacher, Bridgetower played a Viotti concerto at the King's Theatre in the Haymarket, again with Haydn directing from the keyboard.

In the spring of 1803 Bridgetower travelled to Germany and Austria, playing a concert in Dresden on 18 March before arriving in Vienna around the middle of April. His playing in Dresden earned him letters of introduction to some of the prominent members of the Viennese aristocracy, and it was Beethoven's friend Count Moritz von Dietrichstein who was instrumental in arranging the meeting between Bridgetower and the great composer. In a note he sent to the violinist, the Count urged him: 'Allez demain à huit heures precises chez le Prince Lichnofsky. Vous dejeunerez chez lui et il vous conduira lui-même chez Beethoven pour l'engager

---

[26] The Italian singer and composer Venanzio Rauzzini (1746–1810) settled in London in 1774, and performed regularly at the King's Theatre in the Haymarket. In 1777 he moved to Bath, where – together with the violinist Franz Lamotte, who died some four years later – he managed the concerts given in the New Assembly Rooms. Haydn stayed in Rauzzini's house when he travelled to Bath on 2 August 1794, and described him in his notebook as 'a Musicus who is very famous, and who in his time was one of the greatest singers'.

[27] Five guineas in 1789 was equivalent to nearly £1,000 in today's currency.

[28] See Landon, *Haydn in England*, p.66.

[29] Broughton, *Court and Private Life in the Time of Queen Charlotte*, vol.2, p.134.

à remplier [sic] vos voeux' (Punctually at eight o'clock tomorrow, go to Prince Lichnowsky's. You will dine with him, and he will take you himself to Beethoven to urge him to fulfil your wishes).[30] In turn, Beethoven wrote an introductory letter to the prominent Viennese musical patron Baron Wetzlar von Plankenstern, describing Bridgetower (or 'Brischdower', as he called him on this occasion) as 'a very capable virtuoso and an absolute master of his instrument'.[31]

Among those who attended the concert given by Beethoven and Bridgetower on 24 May were Prince Nicolaus Esterházy, Prince Lobkowitz, Count Razumovsky, and Princess Josephine von Liechtenstein, to whom Beethoven had two years earlier dedicated his Piano Sonata op.27 no.1.[32] As we have seen, Beethoven already had the finale of his new violin sonata in his bottom drawer, having originally intended it for the A major Sonata op.30 no.1, and it seems that the two new movements were ready only just in time for the concert. According to Ferdinand Ries:

> The famous sonata in A minor with concertante violin (Opus 47), dedicated to Rudolph Kreuzer [sic] in Paris, was originally written by Beethoven for Bridgetower, an English artist. Things did not go much better in this case, either,[33] even though a large part of the first Allegro was ready early. Bridgetower put a great deal of pressure on him [Beethoven], since his concert was already arranged and he wanted to practise his part.
>
> One morning Beethoven had me called at half past four, and said: 'Write out this violin part of the first Allegro for me quickly.' – (His usual copyist was already busy.) The piano part was notated only intermittently. Bridgetower had to play the particularly beautiful theme with variations in F major from Beethoven's own manuscript at his concert in the Augarten at eight in the morning, because there was no time to copy it. On the other hand, the violin and piano parts of the last 6/8 Allegro in A major were very beautifully copied out because it originally belonged to the first sonata with violin (Opus 30) in A major, dedicated to the Emperor Alexander. As it was too brilliant for that sonata, Beethoven later replaced it with the variations that are now found in it.[34]

Ferdinand Ries's assertion that the op.47 Sonata was composed very rapidly is borne out by the position of the sketches for the work found in the 'Wielhorsky' sketchbook. They follow those for the oratorio *Christus am Ölberge* op.85, which was first performed at the Theater an der Wien on 5 April 1803. (The op.37 Piano Concerto received its premiere at the same concert.) The oratorio was also very much written at the last moment: Beethoven told Breitkopf & Härtel in 1804 that it had occupied him for a few weeks, though many years later he claimed that he and the librettist, Franz Xaver Huber, had put the work together 'in a period of 14 days'.[35] The main work on the op.47 Sonata must, then, have been carried out at some time in the seven-week period

---

[30] Cited in TDR, vol.2, p.392.
[31] Letter of 18 May 1803. BGA no.137; Anderson no.73.
[32] See Edwards, 'George P. Bridgetower and the Kreutzer Sonata', p.306.
[33] Ries is referring to the haste with which the op.17 Horn Sonata had been written.
[34] Wegeler/Ries, pp.82–3.
[35] Letter of 13 Jan 1814, to Raphael Georg Kiesewetter. BGA no.1773; Anderson no.1260.

between 6 April and 24 May. Ries's testimony to the effect that a portion of the Allegro (by which we must understand him to mean the opening Presto) was completed in good time may explain why the surviving autograph of this movement contains only its exposition. Czerny's claim that the first movement was composed in four days, and that two movements intended for another work were added to it, cannot be taken any more seriously than his story that he had been informed by a French composer that the Allegro's closing theme was based on a piece by Kreutzer.[36]

The inscription Beethoven wrote on the autograph score of the op.47 Sonata refers to Bridgetower in humorous terms that were, no doubt, in acceptable usage in his day: 'Sonata mulattica Composta per il Mulatto Brischdauer, gran pazzo e compositore mulattico.' The florid C major arpeggios with which the piano decorates bar 36 of the opening movement are not present in the autograph score, and were almost certainly improvised by Beethoven while the work was being prepared for performance.[37] When Bridgetower heard the embellishment he took it upon himself to emulate it. On his copy of the sonata he noted: 'When I accompanied him [Beethoven] in this sonata-concertante[38] at Wien at the repetition [i.e. rehearsal] of the first part of the Presto, I imitated the flight at the 18th bar of the pianoforte part of this movement, thus:

He jumped up, embraced me, saying, "Noch einmal, mein lieber Bursch". Then he held the open pedal during the flight, the chord of 6 [recte 5] as at the ninth bar.'[39]

However, the two men subsequently fell out – Bridgetower maintained their quarrel was over a woman – and the first edition of the sonata only appeared two years later, with a dedication to Rodolphe Kreutzer. The decision to inscribe the work to the famous French violinist and composer may have been prompted by a plan Beethoven seems to have harboured at the time to move to Paris.[40] Certainly, the delay in the sonata's publication caused him some annoyance. On 4 October 1804 he wrote to the publisher, Nikolaus Simrock:

> I have already been waiting with longing for the sonata which I gave you – but in vain – kindly write to me what is the state of things concerning it – whether you took it from me merely to give the moths something to eat, or do you wish to obtain a special Imperial privilege in connection with it? – Well, I thought that could have happened long ago. Where is this slow devil hiding who is to bring the sonata out?

---

[36] Czerny, p.21.
[37] See Brandenburg, 'Zur Textgeschichte von Beethovens Violinsonate op.47', p.115.
[38] Bridgetower's description of the op.47 Sonata echoes Beethoven's – see p.231.
[39] Thayer/Forbes, p.333.
[40] See Dahlhaus, *Ludwig van Beethoven: Approaches to his Music*, p.22.

You are generally the quick devil, are known as Faust once was for being in league with the Dark One, and are thus just as loved by your comrades as before. Where is your devil hiding, or what kind of a devil is it that is sitting on my sonata and with whom you have not come to an agreement? Hurry, then, and let me know when I shall see the s[onata] brought out to the light of day – When you have told me the date I will at once send you a little note to Kreutzer, which you will please be good enough to enclose when you send him a copy (as you will in any event send your copies to Paris or even have them printed there) – This Kreutzer is a dear, good fellow who during his stay here[41] gave me much pleasure. I prefer his undemanding nature and unaffectedness to all the *extérieur* without *intérieur* of most virtuosi – As the sonata is written for a competent violinist, the dedication to him is all the more appropriate – Although we correspond with each other (i.e. a letter from me once a year) – I hope he will not have learned anything about it yet.[42]

There is some irony in the fact that Beethoven's most famous violin sonata is one of his few works to have become known after its dedicatee. In that respect it joins the 'Waldstein' Piano Sonata, the 'Archduke' Trio and the 'Razumovsky' string quartets – though the little piano piece inscribed 'Für Elise' would also have to be included in the list, despite the ongoing controversy as to her identity. Not only was the violin sonata intended in the first place for another performer altogether, but it seems that Kreutzer singularly failed to appreciate it. According to Berlioz's heavily sarcastic account in his *Voyage musical en Allemagne et Italie*, Kreutzer's attitude was symptomatic of the general hostility towards Beethoven's music in France around the time of the composer's death:

> Sixteen or seventeen years ago, works by Beethoven, then completely unknown in France, were tried out at the *concerts spirituels* of the Opéra. The reprobation with which this admirable music was immediately greeted by the majority of performers would not be believed today. It was bizarre, incoherent, diffuse, bristling with harsh modulations, primitive harmonies, devoid of melody, exaggerated in expression, too noisy, and of horrendous difficulty. To satisfy the men of taste who were then teaching at the Royal Academy of Music, M. Habeneck[43] was compelled to make monstrous cuts of a kind one would rather permit oneself in a ballet by Gallenberg[44] or an opera by Gaveaux,[45] in the very symphonies that he

---

[41] Beethoven had met Kreutzer in 1798, when the violinist came to Vienna in the company of the French Ambassador, Jean Baptiste Bernadotte (later King Karl XIV of Sweden).

[42] BGA no.193; Anderson no.99.

[43] François-Antoine Habeneck (1781–1849) was a violinist and conductor, as well as director of the Académie de Musique. In 1828 he founded the *Société des Concerts du Conservatoire*, which he conducted for twenty years. It was at these concerts that Beethoven's symphonies were first heard in France, and that the premiere of Berlioz's *Symphonie fantastique* was given in 1830.

[44] Count Wenzel Robert von Gallenberg (1783–1839), musical director at the court theatre in Vienna. He was later employed as a ballet composer in Naples, and was the husband of Giulietta Guicciardi, who had been a piano pupil of Beethoven. It was to the Countess, with whom he seems to have been romantically involved, that Beethoven dedicated his 'Moonlight' Sonata op.27 no.2.

[45] Among the twenty-six operas by Pierre Gavaux (1761–1825) is *Léonore ou l'amour conjugal*, based on the same subject Beethoven later adapted for *Fidelio*.

puts on with so much care at the Conservatoire every year. Without these *corrections* Beethoven would not have been granted the honour of appearing, between a bassoon solo and a flute concerto, on the programme of the *Concerts spirituels*.

At the first performance of the passages marked in red pencil, Kreutzer fled, blocking his ears; and he needed all his courage to bring himself to listen to *what was left* of the Symphony in D at the remaining rehearsals. It was to this very man (whose talent, by the way, is not at all in doubt) that Beethoven had just dedicated one of his most sublime sonatas for piano and violin. It must be admitted that the homage was well directed: the famous violinist could never bring himself to play this *outrageously unintelligible* composition. Let us not forget that M. Kreutzer's opinion of Beethoven was shared by ninety-nine per cent of the musicians in Paris at this period, and that without the repeated efforts of the invisible fraction that held the opposite opinion the greatest composer of modern times would still perhaps scarcely be known to us.[46]

Kreutzer's neglect of Beethoven's sonata did not prevent the great composer from approaching him in the friendliest of terms again as late as 1825, when he provided the flautist Johann Sedlaczek with two copies of a letter of recommendation – one addressed to the French violinist, the other to Cherubini. The letter survives only in a draft version written by Karl van Beethoven in one of the composer's conversation books:

Monsieur!

C'est dans l'espérance que vous vous souvenez encore de votre ancien ami, que j'ose vous recommander le porteur de cette lettre, Monsieur Sedlazek, un des artistes les plus distingués; en vous priant de non point lui refuser vos conseils, ni votre appui. Je profite de cette occasion pour vous témoigner ma considération et mon amitié perpétuelle.[47]

(It is in the hope that you still remember your old friend that I venture to recommend to you the bearer of this letter, Monsieur Sedlaczek, one of our most distinguished artists, and ask you not to refuse him your advice or your support. I am taking advantage of this opportunity to assure you of my esteem and my undying friendship.)

The 'Kreutzer' is hardly typical of Beethoven's violin sonatas as a whole. It is a work very much intended for the concert hall, rather than the drawing room – or, as the composer himself put it on the title page of the original edition, one that is written 'in a very concertante style, almost like that of a concerto' (*in un stilo molto concertante, quasi come d'un concerto*). Beethoven's description probably refers not to any quasi-orchestral aspect of the writing, but to its brilliance and power. This was certainly the view taken by Czerny, who noted: 'Only this colossal sonata which has become exceptionally famous could surpass the previous ones in greatness, since it

---

[46] Berlioz, *Voyage musical en Allemagne et Italie*, vol.1, p.263.
[47] Letter of c.6 November 1825. BGA no.2087.

is extremely brilliant for both instruments, is notably difficult, and written in a *concerto*-like and highly effective style.'[48]

The *Méthode de violon* by Pierre Baillot, Pierre Rode and Rodolphe Kreutzer, published in 1803, and aimed at students of the Paris Conservatoire, makes a clear distinction between the styles of a sonata and a concerto. Its patronising attitude towards chamber music, and its decidedly outmoded view of the genre, may go some way to explaining why it was that Beethoven suffered so much at the hands of French violinists. Under the heading of 'Genius in Execution', aspiring performers are given the following advice:

> A SONATA, a sort of concerto divested of its accompaniments, gives it [genius of execution] the means of allowing its power to shine, of developing part of its resources, of allowing itself to be heard alone, without pomp, without rest, without support other than a bass accompaniment. Entirely left to itself, it draws its nuances and contrasts from its own depths, and through the variety of its resources supplies the effects which may be lacking in this type of music …
>
> It is otherwise in a CONCERTO, where the violin must develop the whole of its power. Born to dominate, it is here that it rules in sovereignty, and speaks as a master. Designed to attract a larger number of listeners and to produce bigger effects, it chooses a larger theatre and demands more space … In everything it does it aims to elevate the soul, rather than to appease it; it uses by turns majesty, strength, pathos, and its most powerful means of affecting the crowd.[49]

The 'Kreutzer' Sonata's subtitle was taken as the starting-point of a not altogether favourable review by the critic of the *Allgemeine musikalische Zeitung*:

> The additional remark on the title page – *scritta*. … *concerto* – seems curious, arrogant and ostentatious; but it tells the truth, serves instead of a preface, and defines *that* public rather well for whom this strange work can be intended. This *strange* work, I say, for it is strange indeed; and taken at face value we have nothing in this style – or rather, nothing that would extend the boundaries of this style so far, and would then really fill them. How? That is another question. The reviewer thinks after closer acquaintance with this composition that one must have restricted one's love of art to a certain circle of mundaneness, or to be very prejudiced against Beethoven, if one does not recognise this broadly and vastly executed work as new proof of the artist's great genius, his lively, often glowing imagination, and his extensive knowledge of the profoundest art of harmony; but one also has to be affected by a kind of aesthetic or artistic terrorism, or to be won over by Beethoven to the extent of being dazzled by him, if one does not find in this work new, obvious proof that this artist for some time has obstinately been using his immense natural gifts and his industriousness not only to do as he likes, but above all simply to be completely different from other people; and that in so doing not only does he drive his great abilities powerfully out into the blue yonder – which could bring forth monsters, albeit increasingly wonderful ones – but at the same time

---

[48] Czerny, p.77. In a footnote to his comment, Czerny adds that the 'North American' Bridgetower for whom the work was written was renowned for the boldness and extravagance of his playing. For a long time, explains Czerny, the sonata was known in Vienna as the 'pritschtaurische' [*sic*!].

[49] Baillot, Rode and Kreutzer, *Méthode de violon*, pp.163–4.

has before him an earthly aim, whether clear or not, from which neither his works can gain, nor the world, nor he himself.[50]

The 'Kreutzer' is alone among Beethoven's violin sonatas in beginning with a slow introduction, and its opening is among the composer's most strikingly original conceptions: four majestic bars for the violin alone, played in double, triple, or even, at its very beginning, quadruple stops. Beethoven was to have recourse to an unaccompanied opening for the stringed instrument again in the op.69 and op.102 no.1 Cello Sonatas and – in a much briefer form – the op.96 Violin Sonata, but the boldly dramatic nature of the 'Kreutzer' Sonata's beginning is unique. We may picture the surprise of purchasers of the original edition who, on opening their copy, found a piano part commencing simply with four bars' rest. (As was customary at the time, the music was not printed in score, and each player saw only his or her own part.) Moreover, when the piano did enter, it was to play the continuation of an introduction in which the only tonic chord occurred at the start of its first bar.

With the exception of the reappearance of the short chorale-like second subject during the course of the recapitulation, the violin's opening bars actually provide the only A major music in the entire movement. The remainder of the introduction is harmonically unstable, with the piano's very first answering phrase passing through the cloud of the subdominant minor (the chord on which the first subject of the Presto is to begin), while the main body of the movement is in the minor throughout.

We have seen from some of the early chamber music he composed in Bonn that Beethoven must have been acquainted with Mozart's Violin Sonata K.379, in which the first Allegro is in the minor. The G major Adagio with which that work begins is, however, far too substantial to function as no more than an introduction, and we would have no hesitation in describing the work as a whole as being in the major. Beethoven's tonal plan in the 'Kreutzer' is more ambiguous, and to designate the work as being in A major in view of its opening bars is misleading: not only does the major mode give way to the minor almost immediately at the start of the introduction, but the choice of the key of F major for the sonata's slow movement is one that would fall more naturally within the context of a work in A minor. At the same time, however, the A major implications of the introduction's beginning are kept alive by the avoidance of the relative major in the second group of the Presto, which begins instead in the dominant major. The second group, in other words, is in the key that would have been the obvious choice had the main body of the movement been in A major after all.[51]

The 'Kreutzer' Sonata's first movement owes its driving energy largely to elemental repetition – much as was to be the case in the 'Eroica' Symphony, on which Beethoven began work immediately after the sonata. Typical is the approach to the chorale-like opening subject of the second group – a vast expansion created by the

---

[50] AMZ, 48 (28 Aug. 1805), cols.769–72.

[51] In common with Ferdinand Ries, Beethoven seems to have referred to the sonata as being in A minor. His mention of a 'sonata in A minor with piano and violin that was published separately' when requesting a short-term loan of various of his works in a letter of c.28 June 1812 (BGA no.580; Anderson no.371) addressed to Archduke Rudolph's librarian, Ignaz von Baumeister, is more likely to denote op.47 than op.23, which was originally issued in tandem with the 'Spring' Sonata op.24.

manifold reiteration of a single phrase which has no other function than to generate excitement, and to throw into relief the moment of calm that follows. (Is this passage an instance of the 'aesthetic or artistic terrorism' about which the *Allgemeine musikalische Zeitung* complained so vehemently?)

The first movement's material is largely dominated by the interval of the minor second. It is this interval that is explored in the slow introduction, as it moves towards the key of D minor in preparation for the off-tonic beginning to the main subject of the Presto. Beethoven's autograph score shows that the repeated minor seconds on the notes E and F in bars 16–17 were an afterthought, and that the introduction was to have been joined to the Presto two bars earlier.

Ex. 9.17. Beethoven. Violin Sonata in A, op.47 (i) bars 13–27.

The opening subject of the Presto's second group begins with the same interval. Both in its chorale-like nature and its function of offering a glimpse of serenity within turbulent surroundings, it affords a foretaste of the parallel moment in the opening movement of the 'Waldstein' Piano Sonata. As for the forceful and unstable minor-mode closing subject, its first half concentrates with particular intensity on the minor second:

Ex. 9.18. Beethoven. Violin Sonata in A, op.47 (i) bars 144–56.

The huge development section – at a full 150 bars, probably the longest Beethoven had written up to this time – concerns itself almost exclusively with the closing theme, pitting its characteristic minor second against the driving quaver motion that propels so much of the movement. The section begins calmly in F major – the key of the slow movement to come – but thereafter explores the much more unstable tonal areas of G minor, F minor and B flat minor. Eventually, with a ritardando and a pause, the music comes to rest on the dominant of A minor, clearly signalling that the recapitulation is about to begin. But since the main subject starts away from the tonic, Beethoven has in effect paved the way for the arrival of the wrong key, and cannot easily set the reprise in motion at this point. Instead, he inserts a passage that culminates on the dominant of D minor, so that the start of the recapitulation, with its expected D minor chord, would fall naturally into place. Even then, however, he chooses to launch into a false reprise that is actually in D minor (i.e. with the subject beginning on the chord of G minor). The intention, it turns out, is to approach the recapitulation itself with a momentary reminiscence – albeit differently harmonised – of the transition between the slow introduction and the start of the Presto.

The off-beat *sforzando* accents in bars 342–3 serve to add emphasis to the actual moment of recapitulation in the following bar, with its strong first-beat stress.

Ex. 9.19. Beethoven. Violin Sonata in A, op.47 (i) bars 320–53.

The revisiting of an earlier structural transition at the moment of reprise like this is a hallmark of Beethoven's middle-period style. The *locus classicus* occurs in the finale of the Fifth Symphony, which actually reverts to the tempo and material of the preceding scherzo at the parallel point, but further instances are provided by the finale of the 'Emperor' Concerto, where the famous hushed passage joining the slow movement to the finale is recalled at roughly the mid-point of the rondo; and the 'Razumovsky' Quartet op.59 no.1, in which the violin's cadenza-like passage linking the last two movements together returns in a renotated form and a richer scoring at the close of the finale's exposition, serving again to renew the join between slow movement and finale.

The coda of the 'Kreutzer' Sonata's first movement concentrates on the all-pervading minor second with a ferocity that had not been equalled even in the development section; and perhaps in view of the fact that the development had dealt so exhaustively with the closing subject, Beethoven bases the coda largely on the first subject, before he makes as though to prepare a *pianissimo* close over a 'rocking' tremolando figure – a type of ending characteristic of his agitated minor-mode opening movements of the period. (The 'Appassionata' Sonata op.57 offers a close parallel.) Surprisingly, however, the music gathers momentum for one last time, to bring the piece to a powerful conclusion after all. It is a moment that shows an almost self-conscious determination on Beethoven's part to match the forceful style of the pre-existing finale.

If the elegantly ornate style of the variation middle movement can seem disappointingly conventional in comparison with the energetic outer movements, it fulfils much the same function as does the slow movement, also in the flat submediant and in variation form, of the 'Appassionata' Sonata: both serve to provide an oasis of order and symmetry between two explosively violent movements. Certainly, it is a far more intimate and well-ordered affair than the first movement. The background shape of its variation theme is that of a regular sixteen-bar melody, of the type found in all of Beethoven's remaining variation movements for piano and violin. However, the theme's second half is expanded by means of an interpolation (bars 24–6) which stresses the dominant key with unusual insistence. The initial four bars unfold over a dominant pedal, too, and this, combined with the fact that each of its two halves cadences almost obstinately into the tonic, creates the impression that we are joining the piece in midstream.

The variations themselves mirror the theme's pattern with complete fidelity, and with the exception of the minor-mode third variation they follow the traditional procedure of showing a progressive increase in rhythmic intricacy. Perhaps the most personal sonority Beethoven achieves here is the fourth variation, whose delicately decorated piano part and pizzicato violin accompaniment offer a distant foretaste of his late variation manner.

The symmetry of the variations serves to throw into relief the only significant modulation of the movement, which occurs at the start of the coda: a short-lived move into the supertonic minor, in a phrase whose bathos sits somewhat uncomfortably within the sweetly expressive character of the movement as a whole. More convincing is the new idea which unfolds largely over a tonic pedal in bars 205–13. It is Beethoven's means of counteracting the variation theme's leanings towards the dominant, and the passage, like much of the coda, is bathed in pedal (of the remainder of the movement, only two single bars in the minor-mode third variation have pedal markings), and, as we shall see, it may have been conceived as a means of anticipating a moment in the previously composed finale. (See Ex. 9.23 on p.235–6.)

The tarantella-like finale is a piece which exerted a considerable influence on Schubert, who seems to have been inspired by it (more, in all likelihood, than by the 6/8 *Presto con fuoco* finale of the Piano Sonata op.31 no.3) to write the rhythmically similar last movement in his G major and D minor string quartets, and the C minor Piano Sonata D.958. Particularly striking is the kinship of rhythmic momentum in Beethoven's piece and the finale of Schubert's 'Death and the Maiden' Quartet.

The full-blooded chord of A major which heralds Beethoven's finale was an afterthought, added on the composer's instructions by Ferdinand Ries to the copyist's manuscript from which the first edition of the sonata was engraved.[52] Clearly, the chord would not have been needed in the finale's original context as the concluding movement of the Sonata op.30 no.1, since the slow movement of that work had been in A minor, as opposed to the F major of the 'Kreutzer' Sonata's Andante. The chord is, however, something of a red herring: it peremptorily re-establishes the sonata's home tonality, but at the same time it heralds a first subject that begins momentarily away from the tonic. The subject is presented as though it were to be the start of a passage in fugato style, and its initial statement on the violin cadences into the supertonic minor (B minor). The piano's overlapping answer begins on the same key, and as a result – despite the initial A major call to attention – the fugato may be perceived in retrospect as having set off not firmly in the tonic, but with a strong suggestion of the relative minor (F sharp minor). The theme's tendency towards the latter key is thrown into further relief much later in the movement, at the start of the recapitulation. The development section's end is signalled by a long dominant preparation that leads us to expect a return not in A major, but in A minor. However, to launch the first subject with the sound of A minor in the air would have implied an immediate move towards C major, in parallel with the F sharp minor/A major duality of the original subject, and so in the development section's final bars Beethoven switches instead to the dominant of F sharp minor, and the recapitulation sets off unambiguously in that minor key. The conundrum is not so different from the consideration which led Beethoven to approach the recapitulation in similar oblique fashion in the opening movement.

Ex. 9.20. Beethoven. Violin Sonata in A, op.47 (iii) bars 284–301.

[52] See Brandenburg, *Zur Textgeschichte von Beethovens Violinsonate, op.47*, pp.111–24.

As if this were not enough, the coda explores the implications of the theme's F sharp minor undertones in still greater depth, slowing down the tempo at the precise point where the sound of that key is maintained with some insistence. Once again the expected cadence into the tonic is thwarted, in favour of yet another move towards the relative minor.

Ex. 9.21. Beethoven. Violin Sonata in A, op.47 (iii) bars 489–9.

The first subject's immediate ascent towards the sharper dominant is counteracted by a second subject (bars 62ff.) whose latter half sets off in the flatter region of D major; and the restlessness of the exposition as a whole is intensified by a closing subject – the only real thematic contrast – which brings with it an abrupt change of metre, from the prevailing 6/8 to 2/4. The passage in question (bars 127–47) recurs towards the end of the recapitulation (bars 404–24), and its two halves are separated each time by a dramatic interjection: two emphatic chords in 6/8 time, offering an abrupt reminiscence – albeit in retrograde motion – of the bar immediately preceding the initial change in metre. The metrical switch does not imply a change in the music's pulse, and Czerny was surely correct in maintaining that the tempo was to remain constant: 'The later passage in 2/4 time in the same tempo as everything else, so that there a crotchet lasts as long as a dotted crotchet elsewhere.'[53]

Ex. 9.22. Beethoven. Violin Sonata in A, op.47 (iii) bars 124–45.

---

[53] Czerny, p.78.

Certainly, in other pieces of Beethoven featuring a sudden disruption of the prevailing metre the underlying tempo almost always remains constant: the semibreve in the four *Alla breve* bars in the reprise of the 'Eroica' Symphony's scherzo has exactly the same metronome marking as the dotted minim elsewhere in the piece; and the similar rhythmic change in the closing moments of the quasi-trio in the minuet-like second movement of the String Quartet op.132 are clearly marked 'l'istesso tempo'. Only in the scherzo of the Quartet op.127 do the 2/4 interjections bear a slower tempo indication than the remainder of the piece (*Allegro*, as opposed to the *Vivace* of the remainder).

Almost as startling in the 'Kreutzer Sonata's finale as the change in mood afforded by the 2/4 interjections are the opening bars of the development section, where, following *fortissimo* rumblings in the bass of the piano, the music moves suddenly from A minor into a gentle C major, for an appearance of the second subject whose cheerfully straightforward nature sounds in its context almost tongue-in-cheek. It heralds the start of an extended harmonic sequence that eventually arrives in a firm F major (bars 214ff.), for a passage unfolding throughout over an oscillating pedal note of F. This elaborate F major interpolation may well have influenced Beethoven's choice of key for the subsequently composed slow movement, and its kinship to the new idea introduced towards the end of the slow movement is notable. It is almost as though Beethoven had consciously written the slow movement's coda with a view to minimising the disunity of this curious but fascinating hybrid work.

Ex. 9.23
(a) Beethoven. Violin Sonata in A, op.47 (ii) bars 205–13.

Ex. 9.23.
(b) Beethoven. Violin Sonata in A, op.47 (iii) bars 213–30.

10

Works of 1807–8

The A major Cello Sonata op.69 and the two piano trios op.70 belong to one of the most fruitful creative periods in Beethoven's life. The main work on the sonata was carried out in 1807 and 1808, following the completion of the Mass in C op.86, and at a time when Beethoven was also devoting his energies to his Fifth Symphony. By the time the piano trios were ready, in the following year, not only had the symphony been completed, but also its successor, the 'Pastoral' op.68. The five instrumental works are astonishingly different in character and outward form. Indeed, the cello sonata and the first of the trios – both of them among Beethoven's most original and perfectly achieved chamber works with piano – are in a sense complete opposites: while the sonata lacks a self-contained slow movement, and has a scherzo as its centrepiece, the trio's exceptionally quick and dynamic outer movements obviate the need for a scherzo, while at the same time necessitating the presence of a broad slow movement at the heart of the work. The success of the op.69 Sonata's plan is due not only to the largely relaxed nature of its opening movement,[1] but also to the short Adagio preceding the finale – not so much an introduction, as a drastically abridged slow movement proper.

While the op.5 cello sonatas had often been weighted in favour of the piano, op.69 is the first work of its kind to find a successful solution to the problems of balancing and blending the two instruments with an equitable distribution of material between them. Beethoven's compositional draft of the first movement reveals the extent to which he refashioned the music's texture in order to achieve a satisfactorily balanced sound. With its manifold deletions and revisions revealing various stages in the compositional process, it is a document of primary importance for the study of Beethoven's working methods.[2]

---

[1] Beethoven's detailed compositional draft significantly gives a time signature of c, rather than the ¢ that appears in several later editions. The original edition is not even consistent within itself: the c time signature appears in the piano part, and ¢ in the cello; and the same discrepancy, but with the time signatures of the two parts reversed, occurs in the finale. The detailed list of errors the composer sent to Breitkopf & Härtel in July 1809 (BGA no.393; Anderson no.221) prior to the sonata's second printing does not touch on this question. However, the copyist's score prepared by Joseph Klumpar, and containing numerous corrections in Beethoven's hand, bears an unambiguous time signature of c. See Brandenburg, 'Über die Bedeutung der Änderungen von Taktschriften', p.46, and Jonathan Del Mar's Critical Commentary to the Bärenreiter edition of the cello sonatas, p.38.

[2] The draft is reproduced and discussed in detail by Lewis Lockwood, in 'The Autograph of the First Movement of Beethoven's Sonata for Violoncello and Pianoforte, Opus

Two extreme examples will have to suffice as illustrations of the degree to which Beethoven refined the sonority of the opening movement as he worked on the piece. The passage at bars 65–70 signals the start of an important subsidiary theme within the exposition's second group. The first, heavily deleted, layer of Beethoven's draft shows that this was to have had a cello accompaniment in triplets, while the bass line of the piano part was confined to a much leaner support in octaves, occurring on the points of harmonic change. By subsequently exchanging the roles of the two parts, and by the inspired idea of having the cello play the supporting part pizzicato, Beethoven not only obtained a far more transparent texture, he also immeasurably enhanced the subsequent entry of the cello in a leading role at bar 71.[3]

Ex. 10.1.
(a) Beethoven. Cello Sonata in A, op.69 (i) bars 65–9, draft version.

69', pp.1–109; reprinted with minor alterations in Lockwood, *Beethoven: Studies in the Creative Process*, pp.17–94 and 235–47. The latest facsimile edition (*Ludwig van Beethoven. Sonata for Violoncello and Piano op.69, 1. Movement*) was issued by the Beethoven-Haus in Bonn in 2015. It contains extended commentaries by Jens Dufner and Lewis Lockwood, the former exploring the manner in which the various layers of the manuscript show Beethoven interchanging material between the cello and piano in such passages as bars 25ff., and the recasting of the right-hand piano part in bars 123ff. which exists only in the handwriting of Joseph Klumpar, and must have been taken from a now lost further stage in the compositional process of the sonata. Lockwood's commentary focuses on the complicated genesis of the movement's development section.

[3] See Lockwood, *Beethoven: Studies in the Creative Process*, pp.41–50.

Ex. 10.1.
(b) Beethoven. Cello Sonata in A, op.69 (i) bars 65–71.

A second remarkable instance of Beethoven's reworking occurs at the development section's central climax (bars 115–26). Here, his initial thought was to confine the cello's across-the-strings semiquaver arpeggios to just two bars, before transferring the figuration to the upper stave of the piano part. The *fortissimo* version of the first subject was then to have been given out in dialogue between the pianist's left hand in octaves (as in the final version), and the cello. This clearly lacked sufficient intensity, and Beethoven's eventual solution was to carry the cello's semiquaver motion right through until the end of the passage, while giving its original part to the pianist's right hand, in broken octaves. The heightened agitation resulting from the proliferation of semiquaver figuration provides the ideal foil to the two plangent versions of the first subject that frame this section. Moreover, the broken octaves of the piano part clearly recall the similar writing during the counterstatement of the first subject at the movement's beginning (bars 18–23).

The sonata's famous opening bars, for the unaccompanied cello playing largely in its low register, provide the germ of all that follows, and their open-ended character is essential to the atmosphere of quiet suspense maintained during the first page of music. As can be seen from Ex. 10.2(b), the last note of the cello's opening melody becomes a dominant pedal which is held throughout the piano's answering phrase. The manner in which the fermata at the end of this phrase is filled out is unusual: a conventional treatment would have had a more restricted compass, along the lines of the cello's answer in its corresponding *ad libitum* decoration that rounds off the sonata's opening stage. Clearly, it was of primary concern to Beethoven that the piano's descent should come to rest on the same sonorous low E that has just been relinquished by the cello. In an early sketch for the opening bars the descending scale is simply indicated graphically, by means of an irregular pen stroke;[4] but Beethoven's final version of the fermata goes to the trouble of taking the piano up to E^3 before it begins its descent. The result encompasses the range of registers through which the same note passes in the preceding bars, where the piano, stealing in as though in mid-thought, gives out the identical phrase twice, the second time an octave higher than the first. That phrase, moreover, culminates on a long-held note E.

Beethoven's compositional draft shows that he had intended the cello to play in parallel with the piano throughout the theme's counterstatement in bars 13–18. By giving the opening phrase of the counterstatement instead to the solo piano he established a clear pattern for the sonata's beginning, in which the theme's first limb is played initially by the cello, with the piano providing the answering phrase, and the roles of the two instruments are then reversed for the restatement. However, in order to avoid too predictable a symmetry, the cello enters prematurely in the last bar of the theme's first half, and the right-hand tremolando with which the pianist accompanies the cello's continuation is again focused on the note E rising twice by octaves, and thus offering a form of registral crescendo. No less notable is the manner in which the keyboard part is laid out in the restatement of the theme's beginning, with the melody given out in double octaves, but at the dynamic level of *piano*.[5] Beethoven, it seems, is willing to sacrifice true legato for the sake of achieving a sonority that will rival the warmth and richness of the cello's G and C strings in the opening bars. Not until the coda is the *fortissimo* implied by the double-octave layout unleashed (bars 253–8).

An unharmonised beginning of the kind presented in the sonata's opening bars almost invariably implies an unexpected form of harmonisation at a later stage, as we find on occasion in Mozart. It is not unlikely, indeed, that Beethoven had at the back of his mind the rhythmically similar beginning, in bare octaves, of Mozart's String Quartet K.428:

Ex. 10.2.
(a) Mozart. String Quartet in E flat, K.428 (i) bars 1–4.

---

[4] Bibliothèque nationale, Paris, MS 45.
[5] Beethoven's compositional draft even has an additional, unplayable, high A on the first note of the phrase.

Ex. 10.2.
(b) Beethoven. Cello Sonata in A, op.69 (i) bars 1–12.

Far from following Mozart's example of immediately providing a harmonised statement of his theme, Beethoven leaves the melody in its original form conspicuously unharmonised throughout, with only the start of the recapitulation offering a fleeting, skeletal harmonisation in shadowy outline, as though the richer sonority implicit in so broad a melody were deliberately being withheld. The unusual harmonic instability of the moment of recapitulation is enhanced by the diminished seventh triads implied by the third and fourth bars of its piano part; and if the *fp* stress on the theme's initial note, underlined by the octave A in the piano, provides a momentary tonic anchor, it also undermines the natural apex of the melody – the F sharp of its second bar, which is at once its highest and longest note. (Heinrich Schenker's harmonic analysis of the theme's initial three bars, as forming the sequence I-VI#3-II, was presumably influenced by its appearance at this moment[6].)

---

[6] Schenker, 'Neue musikalische Theorien und Phantasien' (iii), *Der freie Satz*, Fig. 109e (2).

Ex. 10.3. Beethoven. Cello Sonata in A, op.69 (i) bars 151–7.

The melody's background is as simple as could be: an ascent of a perfect fifth, followed by a stepwise return to the tonic from the submediant. The outline shape is presented unadorned during the development section's closing bars, in a curiously 'abstract' form which treats the ascending fifth canonically:

Ex. 10.4. Beethoven. Cello Sonata in A, op.69 (i) bars 140–7.

The same outline, if in a rhythmically more enlivened form, occurs at two crucial stages of the exposition: first, in the minor-mode outburst that follows hard on the heels of the first subject, dramatically shattering the calm and poise of the sonata's beginning; and second, the exposition's closing bars, where the all-important trill from the tail end of the opening subject is absorbed into an echo of its initial rising fifth. These are by any reckoning extraordinary examples of thematic transformation: the one intense and dramatic, the other – through a process of rhythmic change – even more serene than the version of the theme presented in the sonata's opening bars.

Ex. 10.5.
(a) Beethoven. Cello Sonata in A, op.69 (i) bars 25–30.

(b) Beethoven. Cello Sonata in A, op.69 (i) bars 85–95.

At a relatively late stage in the genesis of the movement Beethoven also clearly intended to integrate the opening subject of the second group (bars 38ff.) into his scheme of unification. Lewis Lockwood has drawn attention to the fact that in the composer's draft the keyboard part here was simply written in parallel octaves, lending it a rhythmic kinship with the first subject that was more readily apparent than in the final, contrapuntally enlivened, version.[7] No doubt, Beethoven felt the passage lacked sufficient interest as it stood, and he eventually had the right hand echoing the falling minor thirds of the left in imitative counterpoint. The rhythmic reminiscence of the sonata's opening still survives, however, in the left-hand piano part of bars 38–40.

Ex. 10.6. Beethoven. Cello Sonata in A, op.69 (i) bars 35–45.

An early sketch for the transition between the exposition's first and second groups is contained among Beethoven's ideas for the Fifth Symphony and the Overture *Leonore* no.1.[8] Its location led Gustav Nottebohm to deduce that the composer had begun to turn his attention to the overture when the symphony was

---

[7] Lockwood, *Beethoven: Studies in the Creative Process*, pp.39–41.
[8] Gesellschaft der Musikfreunde, Vienna, A 59 f.8v.

nearing completion; and that by the time the symphony was completely drafted he had already started work on the cello sonata.⁹ The sketch for op.69, written on a single staff, is in the form of a working draft, taking the music from the point at which it turns to the tonic minor (bar 25 in the finished version), right through to the midpoint of the second group (bar 76). Although already at this stage the second group's opening subject appears well developed, the preceding bars bear little resemblance to the material that eventually replaced them. What Beethoven did retain from the sketch, however, was the music's harmonic outline: not just the twofold statement of an idea in the tonic minor, but also the turn to the dominant minor which followed. (Compare the sketch below with Ex. 10.5(a) on p.243.)

Ex. 10.7. Beethoven. Cello Sonata in A, op.69 (i) bars 25–36, sketch.

The development section is based largely on the first subject's third and fourth bars, now transformed into a spacious melody soaring high above a left-hand piano accompaniment written in imitation of a cello playing across its strings. The resulting widely spaced texture offers a remarkable anticipation of the type of keyboard sonority cultivated in some of the nocturnes of Chopin, and the keyboard layout in the left hand was unusual enough for Beethoven to provide a simplified, but less attractive, alternative in which the more restricted range of the accompaniment lay comfortably under the pianist's hand.

The similarity between the theme in this highly expressive form, and the aria 'Es ist vollbracht' from Bach's *St John Passion* was noted by August Halm,¹⁰ and the parallel is heightened by the fact that Bach's aria uses an obbligato viola da gamba. Whether Beethoven was acquainted with the as yet unpublished work of Bach is open to question, though that did not prevent at least one writer from drawing significance from the coincidence between the word 'Trauernacht' in the aria, and the inscription *Inter Lacrimas et Luctum* (Amid tears and grief) which Beethoven was once thought to have written on a now lost copy of the sonata he presented to its dedicatee, Baron Ignaz von Gleichenstein.¹¹ The apocryphal story arose out of a mis-

---

⁹ Nottebohm, *Zweite Beethoveniana*, pp.68–9.
¹⁰ Halm, *Von zwei Kulturen der Musik*, p.194.
¹¹ See Tellenbach, *Beethoven und seine 'unsterbliche Geliebte' Josephine Brunswick*, pp.212–16.

print in the catalogue of Beethoven's works compiled in 1865 by Thayer,[12] who, in connection with the op.69 Sonata, quoted a passage from the biography by Ernst Münch of Gleichenstein's friend the historian and dramatist Julius Schneller: 'In his life he [Beethoven] was lively and witty, upright and straightforward, but often tinged with that elevated warm-hearted sorrow of poetic souls. In this spirit he also wrote the sonata which he dedicated to his friend Baron von Gleichenstein: *Inter Lacrimas et Luctum.*'[13]. However, Münch's 'schrieb er auch die Sonate' (he also wrote the sonata) was wrongly transcribed by Thayer as 'schrieb er auf die Sonate' (he wrote on the sonata). All the same, it is worth noting that the plangent minor-mode form of the third and fourth bars of the op.69 Sonata's opening theme as found in the development section of its first movement was echoed nearly fifteen years later in the *Klagender Gesang*, or 'Arioso dolente', of Beethoven's Piano Sonata op.110.

The recapitulation in op.69 follows the pattern of the exposition closely, with only the length and nature of the first subject significantly changed. A twofold appearance of the theme as at the sonata's beginning would at this stage have been *de trop*, and so Beethoven telescopes his opening page into a single thematic statement, giving the melody to the cello throughout. Its first half now acquires the fleeting single-line piano accompaniment whose shadowy nature and harmonic ambiguity, as already noted, invest the melody with a new-found sense of mystery. The expressive improvisatory flourish with which the cello fills out the culminating fermata seems to offer an amalgam of the two corresponding moments from the exposition – the piano's plain scale-wise descent, and the cello's more expressive response in the theme's counterstatement.

The mysterious beginning of the coda (bars 232ff.) takes up the sinuous phrase from the opening subject's third and fourth bars, and at the same time imbues them with expressive trills. In this, and in its hushed atmosphere, it offers a striking anticipation of the opening bars of the Violin Sonata op.96, and perhaps it is not by chance that a sketch dating from 1807–8 gives the variation theme of the violin sonata's finale in an early form, and notated in the key of A major.[14] The same page of sketches clearly shows the right-hand piano part of bars 58–61 from the cello sonata's finale, and so it seems possible that the variation theme was at one stage destined for use in op.69. (See p.310.)

Beethoven's decision to cast the scherzo in the tonic minor is perhaps surprising, though a similar choice of key is found in the op.96 Violin Sonata, as well as in a few of his other major-mode works where the scherzo occupies a central position, usurping the place that would normally have been occupied by a slow movement. Perhaps the closest relative of the op.69 Sonata in this respect is the Piano Sonata op.110, though its scherzo is in the relative minor, rather than the tonic minor. Further parallels are offered by the piano sonatas op.10 no.2 and op.14 no.2, albeit with a central movement in a more moderate tempo, and op.109 with its *Prestissimo* second movement.

---

[12] Thayer, *Chronologisches Verzeichnis der Werke Ludwig van Beethoven's*, p.79.
[13] Münch, *Julius Schnellers Lebensumriß und vertraute Briefe*, vol.1, p.62. See Jonathan Del Mar's Critical Commentary to the Bärenreiter edition of the cello sonatas, pp.35–6.
[14] Gesellschaft der Musikfreunde, Vienna, A 41 f.1r.

The middle movement of op.69 is in the expanded scherzo form Beethoven had begun to cultivate in the previous year, with the 'Razumovsky' Quartet op.59 no.2 and the Fourth Symphony. The design is one that has the trio played twice, between three appearances of the scherzo itself. It was the enlarged canvas of Beethoven's music at this time that necessitated a corresponding broadening of what had traditionally been the shortest of symphonic movements. Similarly expanded and seamless scherzo (or minuet) forms occur in several of Beethoven's other middle-period works – notably, the Sixth and Seventh Symphonies and the piano trios op.70 no.2 and op.97.

The op.69 Sonata's scherzo is a curiously obsessive piece, with a trio in the major entirely based on the two-note figure with which the scherzo itself comes to an end. The interval of the major second formed by the two notes is present throughout the trio as a form of rocking ostinato, either in its original rhythm, or as a quasi-trill. The scherzo's theme, from whose tail end that figure derives, is unsettlingly syncopated, and the pianist is instructed – as he was to be in the recitative and the second 'arioso' of the op.110 Piano Sonata, as well as the climax of the 'Hammerklavier' Sonata's slow movement – to change fingers on the tied notes, as though striving after a swelling of sound that is all but impossible to execute. Czerny maintained that in the op.69 Sonata the second in each pair of tied notes should be sounded: 'the first note (with the 4th finger) very *tenuto* and the other (with the 3rd finger) sharply detached and less marked ... The 4th finger must therefore glide aside and make way for the third.'[15] It is possible that the somewhat shallower action of the Viennese pianos of Beethoven's day would have allowed this effect to be reproduced with relative ease, though the quick tempo of the piece would seem to render such an execution more problematical here than in the similarly indicated passages of the two late piano sonatas. Nevertheless, Beethoven's carefully and consistently marked fingering is likely to have resulted from more than a desire to ensure that the pianist's left-hand entries during the syncopated subject were kept rhythmically in check.[16] In an article on tied notes in Beethoven, Jonathan Del Mar remarks: 'Looking at this opening theme of the scherzo of op.69, it is not difficult to see why Beethoven might have concocted this particular stratagem [i.e. of indicating a change of finger on the tied notes]. Without it, the *ker-flump* effect of the right-hand upbeat followed by left-hand downbeat – especially in his revised *ff* dynamic – would be merely perfunctory, and it is essential that the right hand does something more than merely hold the note; an altogether more meaningful approach is needed, and honour is satisfied if the note is subtly resounded in the way that Czerny says.'[17]

In the introduction to his edition of Beethoven's 'Pastoral' Sonata op.28, Donald Francis Tovey drew attention to a nineteenth-century edition by the English composer and pianist Cipriani Potter in which he indicated that the tied notes in the first movement's closing subject were to be repeated. 'The effect', says Tovey, 'which

---

[15] Czerny, p.82.

[16] In an inspired piece of intervention, Heinrich Schenker's performing edition of the Beethoven piano sonatas indicates a change of finger on the first tied note of the G major Sonata op.31 no.1, where the left hand is similarly delayed.

[17] Del Mar, 'Once Again: Reflections on Beethoven's Tied-Note Notation', pp.7–25.

occurs elsewhere, e.g. in the Scherzo of the Violoncello Sonata op.69, can be produced here by the fingering Beethoven himself indicates in op.69. It has been identified with the *Bebung* on the clavichord, but is really peculiar to the pianoforte, consisting of catching the key a second time before it has finished rising.'[18]

Czerny's advice regarding the interpretation of the tied notes in op.69 should be taken seriously, not least because he is known to have played the sonata in Beethoven's presence together with Joseph Linke, on 18 February 1816. Moreover, that performance took place just a week after Czerny had been reprimanded by the composer for having taken liberties with his op.16 Quintet.[19] Czerny's study on the interpretation of Beethoven's piano works was, however, written nearly thirty years after the event, and it is possible that he was giving advice on how he felt the passage should be played on the mechanically more sophisticated pianos of that later time.

Still more controversial than the manner in which the scherzo's syncopated theme should be played is the question of the dynamic markings at the very beginning of the piece. In July 1809 Beethoven sent a detailed list of misprints in the sonata's first edition to Breitkopf & Härtel, which, however, the publishers failed to act upon. Included among them was the instruction that the *fortissimo* at the start of the scherzo, and in all parallel passages, was to be removed (*Gleich im ersten Takt muss das ff weggestrichen werden*).[20] However, no sooner had Beethoven sent his letter than he dispatched another:

> Laugh at my authorial anxiety. Imagine, I find yesterday that in correcting the mistakes in the violoncello sonata I myself made new mistakes again. Thus in the scherzo allegro molto this *ff** right at the beginning stands as it was indicated, and also the other times. Only in the ninth bar must *piano* be placed before the first note, and similarly both the other times, at the ninth bar, where the ♯♯ resolve into ♮♮. This is how it is. You may see from this that I am really in a situation where one might say, 'Lord, into thy hands I deliver my soul!'[21]
>
> *That is, the way it stood in the first place is correct.

The subsequent confusion over this crucial matter arose because Breitkopf – following the copyist's manuscript of the sonata that was supplied to them – had printed *piano* beneath the scherzo's very first note, and *fortissimo* at the upbeat to bar 2.[22] Beethoven's previous list of corrections, dated 1 August 1809, acknowledges the existence of the *piano* marking, since it merely indicates that the subsequent *fortissimo* is to be removed. Whether his follow-up letter implies that the *fortissimo* is to replace the *piano*, or whether the wording of the footnote – 'Nämlich wie es anfangs gestanden hat, so ist es recht' (That is, as it originally stood is correct) – is meant to indicate that the two markings should still stand side by side as they were

---

[18] Tovey, Beethoven, *Sonatas for Pianoforte*, ed. Craxton, vol.2, p.68.

[19] See pp.82–3.

[20] BGA no.393; Anderson no.221.

[21] Letter of 3 August 1809. BGA no.394; Anderson no.223.

[22] This wholly improbable reading was even followed by the editor of the relevant volume in the new collected edition of Beethoven's works (Munich, 1971).

in the first edition, is less clear. Editors of the sonata have been wrestling with these contradictory markings ever since, without apparently taking due note of the phraseology in the latter half of Beethoven's vital sentence, which leaves less room for misinterpretation: 'Nur muss im neunten Takt vor die erste Note *piano* gesetzt werden und ebenfalls die beiden anderen Male' (Only in the ninth bar must *piano* be placed before the first note, and the same both the other times). Through his instruction that the only *piano* marking was to occur at bar 9, Beethoven clearly implies that the previous eight bars are to be played *fortissimo* throughout; and however much we may wish that he had never penned his second letter, and that the *piano* marking had been allowed to stand for the first eight bars, this seems to have been his final intention.[23] (In quoting the opening bars in order to illustrate his point about the piano's articulation, however, Czerny gives the dynamic marking as *piano*, albeit not without allowing himself a hairpin crescendo and decrescendo at bars 6–7.)

Given the symmetrical nature of the scherzo's material, it is highly unlikely that Beethoven would have contemplated a violent dynamic contrast within the piano's opening theme if it were not to be mirrored when the theme passes to the cello in the ninth bar. The markings at the scherzo's beginning in Breitkopf's original edition are, indeed, so bizarre and unlikely that when they published a collected edition of Beethoven's works in the 1860s they printed a dynamic of *piano*, but inserted a *sforzando* on the theme's second note. This unauthenticated reading may be preferable from a musical point of view, but it raises as many questions as it answers: once again, if there is to be an accent of this kind here, where is its counterpart in the cello's restatement?

The confused situation with regard to this passage is aggravated by the large number of misprints and textual inconsistencies in the scherzo which Beethoven failed to notice. He was, as he told Breitkopf in his letter of 26th July 1809, in a restless state of mind on account of the siege of Vienna by Napoleon's troops; and in the same letter he also confessed:

> Since I never in my life bother about things that I have already written, [the misprints] were brought to my attention by a friend ... This confirms my previous experience that my things are most accurately engraved when following my own handwriting. Presumably there are also some mistakes in the copy you have; but in looking over it, the composer actually overlooks the mistakes.[24]

Among the inconsistencies in the scherzo that Beethoven may have overlooked in Breitkopf's edition is the absence of an acciaccatura in the piano part at bar 8, despite the fact that the cello has one in the parallel passage at bar 16. The penultimate bar of the piano's version of the theme sounds curiously bare as it stands; and since in other respects the cello's counterstatement mirrors the piano's opening exactly (leaving aside the vexed question of the dynamics), it is likely that Beethoven intended the earlier grace note to be present. In addition, bar 64 gives the piano's first beat as a 6/4 chord of A minor, with an E as the bass note, whereas symmetry

---

[23] For a detailed discussion of this question, see Jonathan Del Mar's Critical Commentary to the cello sonatas, pp.42–4.

[24] BGA no.392; Anderson no.220.

with the ongoing harmonic sequence at this point would suggest a simple root position A minor triad.

One of Beethoven's concerns during the period when the op.69 Sonata was composed was the creation of a type of scherzo or minuet movement that formed a continuous musical whole. The second movement of the F major 'Razumovsky' Quartet is, in the ambiguity and complexity of its design, an extreme example; but there is also the case of the 'Pastoral' Symphony, whose scherzo is so seamless that it is not easy to define the point at which the trio actually begins. In the middle movement of the op.69 Sonata the transitions between the scherzo and its quasi-trio are equally smooth (they would have been more so, it must be said, if Beethoven had stuck to his earlier decision to have the scherzo's opening bars played *piano*); and continuity is aided by the fact that the trio takes over the scherzo's concluding two-note phrase.

While the scherzo subject hovers unsettlingly between tonic and relative major, the quasi-trio remains obstinately anchored in the tonic for most of its length. The effect, particularly when added to the repetitive character of the musical material itself, is curiously claustrophobic, and the short-breathed nature of the piece as a whole would seem to leave ample scope for an expansive slow movement to come. Beethoven appears at first willing to provide just such a piece, but doubts about the scope of the following Adagio begin to creep in already during its second bar, where the cello, rather than wait to make its mark until it can provide its own full counterstatement, enters with an accompaniment to the piano's theme; and although the start of the expected counterstatement does materialise, it is diverted from its expected course after only five bars, to give way to the briefest of transitions to the finale. The chromatic enhancement of the melody in the Adagio's fourth bar influences not only the further course of what has by now become essentially an introduction to the finale, but also the ensuing Allegro's main subject. The seventh and eighth bars of the Adagio present an augmented form of the same chromatic phrase, which appears again in diminution in the piano part within the second beat of bar 8, while the third and fourth bars of the Allegro's theme revolve around the same three chromatic notes.

As can be seen in Ex. 10.8 opposite, the first and fifth bars of the Allegro theme are given out above a tonic pedal – a harmonic feature that colours the start of the transition to the second group (bars 34–8), as well as the opening and closing stages of the intensely argued development section.[25] The static harmony lends the piece as a whole a sense of barely suppressed excitement. The flurry of semiquavers in bar 26 linking the cello's theme with the piano's counterstatement is no mere decoration, but a quasi-inversion of the pairs of thirds that constitute the theme's initial bar; and the same motif, expanded into a sinuous chromatic phrase (though retaining the repeated-note rhythm of its original accompaniment), forms the mainstay of the development section.

---

[25] Cellists faced with the risky and cruelly exposed initial theme of the second group will take little comfort from the fact that Beethoven rejected a sketch (British Library, Stefan Zweig MS 6) for this moment which clearly shows the roles of cello and piano reversed.

Ex. 10.8. Beethoven. Cello Sonata in A, op.69 (ii) bars 1–28.

—(continued)

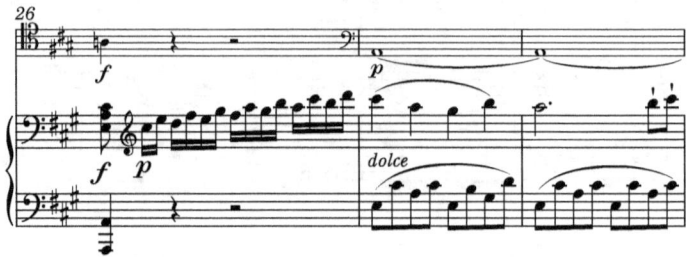

Ex. 10.8—continued

The development progresses from a mysteriously veiled A minor to a passionate C major outburst, transferring the rushing scale figures of the exposition's closing moments to the bass line of the keyboard part, before the music returns to the atmosphere and substance of its beginning.

The recapitulation is approached via a mysteriously chromatic version of the first subject's initial phrase, against which the cello gives out the repeated-note figuration of the piano's original accompaniment. The moment of recapitulation itself at bar 112 is preceded by a ritardando whose resolution coincides with the reprise of the subject, in such a way that the theme actually begins dissonantly, on 6/4 harmony which is not resolved until the following bar:

Ex. 10.9. Beethoven. Cello Sonata in A, op.69 (ii) bars 104–15.

Having explored the theme's repeated-note accompaniment at length during the development section, Beethoven substitutes new figuration in semiquavers during the recapitulation, while the coda, in a moment of ecstasy, allows the music to take wing in the keyboard's topmost register above an accompaniment in regular quavers that soon double in pace to semiquavers, increasing the excitement as the right-hand melody reaches its apex. The final bars unfold to obstinately unchanging tonic harmony, and even at the very close Beethoven refuses to indulge in the luxury of a perfect cadence, preferring instead to restrict himself to an increasingly emphatic series of reiterated A major chords in echo of the repeated tonic pedal notes over which the Allegro's first subject had been given out at the movement's beginning.

Around the time Beethoven composed the op.69 Sonata he had been receiving secretarial assistance from the work's dedicatee, Baron Ignaz von Gleichenstein. On 20 April 1807, Gleichenstein acted as witness to the contractual agreement between Beethoven and Clementi, whereby the latter obtained publishing rights in England to several of the composer's works, including the Fourth Symphony, the 'Razumovsky' string quartets, the Fourth Piano Concerto, and the arrangement for piano and orchestra – *avec des notes additionelles* – of the Violin Concerto, which Beethoven undertook at Clementi's specific request.

Gleichenstein was an amateur cellist, though it is doubtful that he would have been equal to the op.69 Sonata's challenging technical demands. From the diaries of Count Johann Nepomuk Chotek we learn that the new sonata was performed on 21 January 1809 at one of the limited-audience subscription concerts organised by the cellist Anton Kraft, where, following string quartets by Bernhard Romberg and Beethoven, 'wurde von Beethowen eine neue Sonate auf dem F.P. mit Vllo gespielt die sehr schön ist' (Beethoven played a new sonata on the fortepiano with violoncello which is very fine).[26] The inclusion of op.69 in Kraft's concert appears to have caused his cellist son Nikolaus some embarrassment. At any rate, the following month Beethoven suggested to his friend Zmeskall von Domanovecz – another keen cellist – that for a benefit concert due to be given by Nikolaus Kraft on 5 March, the pianist should be Baroness Ertmann. The sonata, Beethoven told Zmeskall, had yet to be heard adequately performed in front of a large audience. Ertmann, to whom Beethoven was to dedicate his op.101 Piano Sonata, was one of his close friends, and she was among the outstanding pianists of the day. Johann Friedrich Reichardt had recently heard her at a private gathering, where Ignaz Schuppanzigh also performed. His comments on Ertmann's playing contain revealing details about the type of instrument Beethoven preferred:

> After a difficult Beethoven quartet had been well played, we had the good fortune to hear a grand Beethoven Fantasy played by Baroness Ertmann with a strength, spirit and perfection that delighted us all. It would not be possible to hear anything more perfect on so perfect an instrument. It was a fine Streicher fortepiano, which nowadays has the soul of a whole orchestra. Streicher has abandoned the soft, too easily yielding rebounding action of the other Viennese instruments, and on Beethoven's advice and wishes has given his instruments more resistance

---

[26] See Steblin, *Beethoven in the Diaries of Johann Nepomuk Chotek*, pp.83–5.

and resilience, so that a virtuoso who plays with strength and meaning has more control over the instrument's sustaining- and carrying-power, its delicateness of touch and diminuendos [*Abzügen*]. In this way he has lent his instruments greater and more varied character, so that – more than any other instrument – they must satisfy those virtuosos who are not merely seeking superficiality in their way of playing. His whole workmanship is also of rare quality and lasting worth.[27]

Hard on the heels of the op.69 Sonata came the two piano trios op.70. Beethoven offered all three works to Breitkopf & Härtel in the summer of 1808, together with the C major Mass op.86 and the Fifth and Sixth Symphonies. He was lodging at the house of Countess Erdödy in Heiligenstadt at the time, and the trios were dedicated to her – though not without a last-minute attempt on the composer's part to transfer his loyalty once again to Archduke Rudolph. Beethoven and the Countess quarrelled over some unspecified matter in the spring of 1809, and on 20 April of that year, at a time when the threat of an imminent further invasion of Vienna by Napoleon's approaching troops was all too real, Beethoven wrote to Breitkopf & Härtel:

> The fatal moment approaching us allows me only hurriedly to write you a few lines. The uncertainty of the post does not allow me to send you anything for the moment – this is merely what occurs to me regarding the trios. First, if the title page is not yet ready I should like you to make the dedication simply to Archduke Rudolph, for which you can take his title from the concerto in G which was engraved here [Vienna] by the Bureau d'Arts et d'Industrie; I have sometimes noticed that when I dedicate something to another person, and he likes this work, a slight sadness comes over him. He has become very fond of these trios, and it would therefore no doubt cause him pain again if the inscription is to someone else. But if it has already happened, there is nothing to be done about it.[28]

Whatever its cause, Beethoven's quarrel with Countess Erdödy was soon patched up, and their continued friendship is shown by the dedication of his two cello sonatas op.102 to her in 1817,[29] as well as the greetings canon (WoO 176) written for her on New Year's Eve of 1819.

The two op.70 trios afford a striking instance of the stimulus Beethoven always found in working in close succession, if not actually simultaneously, on compositions of wholly opposite character and form within the same genre. That the two trios arose out of a single impulse is proved by the existence of a sketch which reveals that Beethoven seems even to have interchanged ideas between them, in much the same way as he did in some of his late string quartets. The sketch, in E flat major and

---

[27] Reichardt, *Vertraute Briefe*, pp.385–6. (Letter of 7 February 1809.)
[28] BGA no.380; Anderson no.218.
[29] Concerning the dedication of op.102, see pp.349–50.

in 2/4 time, is marked 'letztes Stück', and it shows an early form of what eventually became the tail end of the first subject in the finale of the 'Ghost' Trio op.70 no.1.[30]

The op.70 trios form, in fact, a pair as strongly contrasted as the A minor Violin Sonata op.23 and the 'Spring' op.24, or the Fifth and Sixth Symphonies. Of the two trios, the first has three movements, all in the tonality of D. While its outer movements are exceptionally quick – the tempo markings are *Allegro vivace e con brio* and *Presto*, respectively – the middle movement carries the unusually slow indication of *Largo assai e espressivo*. The E flat Trio op.70 no.2, on the other hand, has four movements, the middle two of which are both in a moderate tempo. Moreover, neither of those inner movements is in the home tonality – a peculiarity the trio shares among Beethoven's four-movement works only with the 'Harp' Quartet op.74, also in E flat. The resulting key scheme in the trio, with the tonalities of the successive movements forming a descending sequence of thirds, is one we might more readily associate with the symphonies of Brahms. The 'Ghost', with its uniquely atmospheric Largo, has always been the more widely performed of the pair; but according to the violinist Karl Holz, who befriended Beethoven in his last years, the composer expressed a preference for the E flat work.[31]

The key of D major was one that Beethoven clearly regarded as holding quite specific qualities. His D major works may not form so clearly an archetypal group as those in C minor, but a common thread running through them may nevertheless be discerned. Similarities between the 'Ghost' Trio and the Piano Sonata op.10 no.3 were noted by Alan Tyson,[32] but the two works also share features with the Cello Sonata op.102 no.2. All three begin with an energetic theme given out in bare octaves, and each has a dark-hued slow movement in the tonic minor. In both the cello sonata and the trio the emphatic opening subject is one whose second limb is an expressive idea that carries the marking of *dolce*, while in the trio, as in the piano sonata, the first movement has an unusually wide-ranging key scheme which may be said to compensate for the lack of tonal variety between the movements of the overall work. In addition, the shape of the rondo theme in the finale of op.10 no.3 is remarkably similar to that of the 'Ghost' Trio's last movement.

No less striking, however, are the characteristics shared by the outer movements of the 'Ghost' Trio itself. In particular, the main theme in each case is calculatedly fragmented, with an initial phrase culminating on a long-held note that takes the music in an unexpected tonal direction. Moreover, both pieces contain an excursion into the key of the flat mediant (F major) during the course of their exposition, and the moment is mirrored by a parallel stress on the flat submediant – B flat – in the recapitulation. The tail end of the first movement's B flat passage is unmistakably echoed at the corresponding point in the finale:

---

[30] See Cahn, 'Zu Beethovens Klaviertrio in Es-Dur op.70 Nr.2', pp.133–4. The sketch is found in Landsberg 10, f.108, lines 14–16.

[31] TDR, vol.3, p.108. The composer's remark, as reported by Karl Holz to Otto Jahn, does not appear in Thayer/Forbes.

[32] Tyson, 'Stages in the Composition of Beethoven's Piano Trio op.70, no.1', pp.4–5.

Ex. 10.10.
(a) Beethoven. Piano Trio in D, op.70 no.1 (i), bars 183–9.

(b) Beethoven. Piano Trio in D, op.70 no.1 (iii), bars 103–13.

Beethoven's sketches show that at one stage he planned a further similarity between the work's outer movements, and that he discarded a version of the finale's closing bars in which a fragment of the first subject was followed by a peremptory perfect cadence – in all essentials the same procedure as found at the conclusion of the opening movement[33]:

Ex. 10.11. Beethoven. Piano Trio in D, op.70 no.1 (iii), sketch.

On the same page of the sketchbook Beethoven's second attempt at a conclusion takes a step nearer to his ultimate solution, in approaching the final cadence via a threefold statement of an insistently repeated phrase from the closing stage of the exposition:

Ex. 10.12.

The definitive version retains the repeated phrase from the latter half of the second of those rejected conclusions, expanding it on a scale that will allow the final cadence to be unleashed with sufficient force. At the same time, the phrase is anchored over a repeated dominant pedal that recalls the similar pedal in the development section's closing bars, while the long chromatic ascent on the piano seems to mirror the sweeping descent with which the slow movement had shuddered to a close. As we shall see, the finale was not the only movement for which Beethoven seems to have found difficulty in hitting on an appropriate conclusion.

Ex. 10.13. Beethoven. Piano Trio in D, op.70 no.1 (iii) bars 398–411.

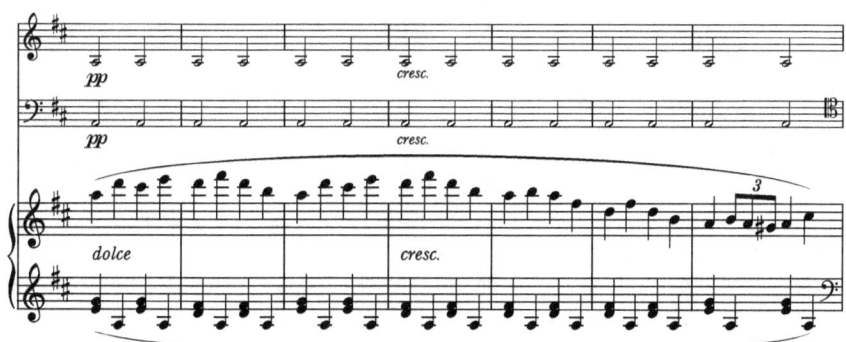

—(continued)

[33] Beethoven, *Ein Skizzenbuch zur Pastoralsymphonie op.68 und zu den Trios op.70, 1 und 2*, f.58r.

Ex. 10.13—continued

The trio's first movement begins impetuously, hurling its main theme out *fortissimo* in parallel octaves that cover an unusually wide sound spectrum. The unprepared F natural which appears in the fifth bar is an inspired surprise, its shock value intensified not only by the interruption in the preceding bar of the regular rhythmic pattern established at the outset, but also by the reversal in direction of the descending phrases that have made up the movement's opening paragraph. The subject itself falls into a sequential series of four-note descending scales, and since all but the first of them unfold in regular quavers they establish a tangible feeling of duple meter. Bars 2 and 3, in particular, give the aural impression of being made up of three bars of 2/4 time, thus creating the illusion of an accelerated pulse. With the arrival of the F natural and its aftermath, the listener experiences a double shock: an apparent change in metre, combined with an opening subject that reaches its apex on a note which appears suddenly, after such an assertive beginning, to throw the music onto the tonic minor. Nor is the subdued, warmly expressive nature of the subject's latter half any less startling. It is, in all conscience, an astonishing juxtaposition of opposites to present in so short a space of time, and one whose breathless effect is strengthened by the undermining of any semblance of symmetry resulting from the expansion of that latter half beginning at bar 11, at just the point where the listener might have expected the initial *fortissimo* subject to make a return. It is true that Beethoven fulfils that expectation at the start of the recapitulation, but only with the intention of setting up a fresh surprise.

The F natural so abruptly introduced in the fifth bar has far-reaching consequences on the harmonic design of the movement as a whole. Its influence on the subsequent course of events is, indeed, similar to that of the *fortissimo* C sharp which so brutally interrupts the opening subject in the finale of the Eighth Symphony. At first, the symphony's C sharp is greeted by a *fortissimo* restatement of the first subject still in the tonic, as though to dismiss out of hand what has been no more than a rude interruption. It is not until the start of what is perhaps the most gargantuan coda Beethoven ever wrote that the C sharp at last succeeds in making its mark. Here, the note is hammered out over and over again, with the insistence of the Stone Guest knocking on the door in *Don Giovanni*, and this time it cannot be ignored: to hair-raising effect, the orchestra plunges into F sharp minor, and the home key is not established again without a good deal more hammering. In much the same way, though to very different effect, the character of the triadic first subject in the 'Eroica' Symphony's opening Allegro is radically altered by the shadow of the 'foreign' C sharp introduced at the end of its first phrase. At this stage the note resolves quite naturally upwards, without more than momentarily ruffling the music's E flat major surface. The reappearance of the same note in the recapitulation, however, has much more significant consequences. Here, it is enharmonically altered to D flat, and resolves downwards, onto the dominant of F, in which key there ensues an expansive interpolation.

The fleeting suggestion of D minor created in the 'Ghost' Trio's fifth bar is immediately countered by the sound of the flat submediant introduced in the following bar. In having the B flat played in octaves in the bass of the piano Beethoven does more than just create a transition between the main subject's strongly contrasting halves by maintaining the sonority of the opening bars: the bare fifth which results in conjunction with the cello's sustained F natural serves to enhance the warmth of the change to the 6/4 chord of D major that ensues.

Ex. 10.14. Beethoven. Piano Trio in D, op.70 no.1 (i) bars 1–20.

—(continued)

Ex. 10.14—continued

Beethoven's sketches for the opening movement show that he experienced some difficulty in arriving at the most effective means of capitalising on the harmonic surprise of the opening bars. From an early draft for what was clearly the start of the recapitulation we can see that he considered turning the surprise back on itself, and replacing the now awaited F natural at the apex of the opening phrase with the F sharp that might have been expected in the first place, and then moving further sharpwards, towards the dominant.[34]

Ex. 10.15. Beethoven. Piano Trio in D, op.70 no.1 (i) bars 157–82, sketch.

[34] See *Ein Skizzenbuch zur Pastoralsymphonie op.68 und zu den Trios op.70, 1 und 2*, f.51r, line 15, 51v, line 1.

From this sketch it is clear that Beethoven contemplated introducing a switch to the flat submediant before the interpolated minor-mode version of the first subject had run its course. This, however, gave the game away too soon, and his eventual plan for the start of the recapitulation is at once simpler and more surprising. The exposition's initial ten bars are retained intact, but now Beethoven's D minor interpolation enables him to redefine the function of the cello's long-held F natural: instead of forming part of an implied augmented sixth chord in the tonic, it becomes the dominant of B flat major itself:

Ex. 10.16. Beethoven. Piano Trio in D, op.70 no.1 (i) bars 157–78.

—(continued)

Ex. 10.16—continued

Further consequences of the F natural introduced so early on in the piece may be heard in the exposition's inclusion of an F major interpolation in which the sinuous phrase of the first subject's latter half is passed back and forth between cello and violin, and in the F sharp/F natural conflict of the tremolos in the right-hand piano part of the exposition's closing bars.[35]

Ex. 10.17. Beethoven. Piano Trio in D, op.70 no.1 (i) bars 58–73.

[35] It is tempting to suggest that Beethoven may inadvertently have failed to indicate an F natural in the right-hand part of bar 66. If so, the omission was a stroke of genius: there can be no doubt about the augmented-second oscillation of B flat/C sharp at the parallel moment in the recapitulation (bar 242) since both notes require an accidental, and by withholding this expressive detail from the exposition its effect at the later moment is enhanced.

The quiet ending of the exposition, with its final four bars invoking one of Beethoven's rare *ppp* markings, is carried over into the start of the development, whose *pianissimo* beginning is rudely shattered by the forceful return of the first subject in the tonic, but veering already in its second bar towards G minor. The development's first stage thereafter unfolds for the main part over subdued tremolando figuration; and it is not beyond the realms of possibility that it was the texture of this moment that sparked off in Beethoven's mind the sonority of the work's slow movement.

The textural simplicity of this passage serves to offset the forceful contrapuntal writing of the development's second stage, where Beethoven at last binds together the first subject's seemingly disparate halves. The underlying unity of their contrasting ideas is revealed through a briefly canonic statement of the subject's latter half, over which is superimposed a fragmentary version of its initial phrase, both in its original form and in inversion (bars 120ff.). The counterpoint is actually less involved than it looks on paper, and the first of its two elements is abandoned after only eight bars: had the texture been more intricate, the *fortissimo* marking might well have endangered the music's clarity. It is nevertheless perhaps not so much the contrapuntal nature of this section that invokes a rare second-half repeat at this stage of Beethoven's career, as the fact that the recapitulation departs so radically from the pattern of the exposition. The changes affect not only the music's design, but also its sonority. The thematic material of the first subject's relaxed latter half, for instance, previously shared between cello and violin, is divided in the recapitulation between cello and piano; and the figure in double-dotted rhythm that characterises the second subject is no longer confined to the piano, but is given out instead by the piano and violin, with the running scale-like accompaniment in octaves – formerly the province of the two stringed instruments – transferred to the cello and the left-hand piano part.

More significant than the recapitulation's textural alterations are two large-scale interpolations which radically alter its tonal pattern. The first, diverting the first subject into B flat major, has already been noted; but in addition Beethoven now expands the subject's tail end into a substantial and delicate improvisatory passage for the piano, in a long flight of fantasy underpinned by a chromatically rising bass line which eventually reaches its goal of A major in preparation for the reprise of the second subject in the tonic at bar 207. (The start of this passage is quoted in Ex. 10.10(a), p.256.) The manner in which Beethoven chooses to present the second subject at this point is, however, curious, with what is its most distinctive melodic feature – a four-note motif in double-dotted rhythm – at first conspicuously absent. Not until there is a further interpolation, taking the music into the region of the subdominant, does the motif appear. Altogether, the recapitulation finds Beethoven expanding the scope of the exposition to a remarkable degree, and the piece, particularly if we take into account the indicated second-half repeat, offers a striking instance of his concern at this stage of his career to shift the weight of the sonata-form design to its latter stages. It is a process he carried a degree further in the finale of op.70 no.2, where the recapitulation is very nearly twice the length of the exposition.

The subdominant leanings of the interpolated passage in the recapitulation's second subject anticipate the start of the coda – the most relaxed moment of the piece, and one that has the pianist presenting the first subject's latter half in long arching phrases, played *pianissimo*, before a crescendo echoing the piano's earlier improvisatory passages winds up proceedings with an ending that is abrupt, but of convincing finality.

The famous slow movement, whose 'flickering' piano figuration has given rise to the work's nickname, is surely one of the most theatrical among Beethoven's purely instrumental pieces, and the temptation to seek some literary inspiration behind its conception is easily understood. Such a temptation was nevertheless resisted by E.T.A. Hoffmann, whose own tales are so famous for evoking the unearthly. For Hoffmann, who regarded the op.70 trios as embodying the essence of Beethoven's romantic spirit, the D minor *Largo assai e espressivo* of the first in the pair was not a vision of spectral terrors, but a depiction of 'gentle melancholy that comforts the soul'. His description of the piano's delicate tremolandos provides a vivid picture of the sonority produced by this strikingly original piece of writing when played on a piano of the time:

> With the main theme, when it is played by the violin and cello,[36] the piano for the most part has a figure in 64th-note sextuplets which need to be played *pp* and *leggiermente*. It is almost the only manner in which even the *sound* of a good piano can be made to contribute in a surprising, effective way. If these sextuplets are played with raised dampers [i.e. with the sustaining pedal] and the moderator,[37] with a skilled, light touch, there arises a rustling that suggests an Aeolian harp or glass harmonica, and, combined with the bowed sounds of the remaining instruments, is of quite wonderful effect. To the moderator and the raised dampers the reviewer also added the so-called *Harmonikazug*, which as is well known shifts the keyboard so that the hammers strike only one string; and out of the beautiful Streicher piano came floating sounds that embraced the soul like shadowy dream figures, and enticed it into the magical sphere of strange presentiments.[38]

---

[36] Hoffmann means the restatement of the main subject beginning at bar 18.

[37] The moderator, or *Pianozug*, was a stop which interposed a strip of cloth between the hammers and the strings, in order to produce a softened sound.

[38] AMZ, 9 (3 March 1813), col.147. Lawrence Kramer ('Saving the Ordinary', p.57) draws a parallel between the other-worldly nature of Beethoven's piece and the eerie atmosphere

An association between the Largo and Beethoven's collaboration with the dramatist Heinrich Collin on a *Macbeth* opera was first made by Gustav Nottebohm. (It was for Collin's tragedy *Coriolan* that Beethoven composed his overture op.62, in 1807.) Noting that sketches for the trio's slow movement followed immediately after ideas for the opera – probably for the opening witches' scene – and that they shared the same key of D minor, Nottebohm questioned whether the sombre mood of op.70 no.1 had been inspired by a reading of Collin's libretto, or whether the reverse was true.[39] However, there is no discernible relationship between the *Macbeth* sketches and the piano trio, and attempts to relate the course of events in Beethoven's piece to other scenes from Shakespeare's play (notably the apparitions of Act IV) have proved less than convincing.[40] It is instructive in any case to note that Czerny advised performers to think not of Banquo's ghost, but of the first appearance of the ghost in *Hamlet*. The piece, Czerny said, is 'ghostly and terrifying, like an apparition from the underworld'.[41] Whether Czerny was responsible for the trio's nickname, or whether he was responding to an already established title, is not known. Certainly, E.T.A. Hoffmann was unaware of it at the time he wrote his detailed *Allgemeine musikalische Zeitung* review. The key of the 'Ghost' Trio's slow movement is, however, one that appears to have been associated in Beethoven's mind with Shakespeare: the slow movement of the String Quartet op.18 no.1, inspired by the scene in the vault from *Romeo and Juliet*, is in D minor, as is the Piano Sonata op.31 no.2, which, according to Schindler's admittedly unreliable testimony, was linked in the composer's mind with *The Tempest*.

The sombre mood in which Beethoven's tragic D minor slow movements begin is created at least in part by the low register of the music. This is particularly striking in the *Adagio con molto sentimento d'affetto* of the Cello Sonata op.102 no.2, and the *Largo e mesto* of the Piano Sonata op.10 no.3, where the weight of the left-hand chords additionally serves to create a sense of oppression. But however slowly these pieces – and, indeed, the D minor *Adagio affettuoso ed appassionato* of the Quartet op.18 no.1 – are played, the music's pulse is firmly established from the very first bar. The start of the slow movement in op.70 no.1, on the other hand, is so broad that the music seems to float in suspended time until the entry of the piano in the second bar, with its left-hand chords in regular semiquavers. The piano's right-hand part clearly mirrors, in diminution, the triadic shape of the stringed instruments' opening phrase; and its turn-like figure provides the source of the movement's only contrasting thematic idea – the cantabile motif given out by the cello in the ninth bar:

---

of Hoffmann's tale 'The Mines of Falun', in which the main protagonist has a terrifying dream of the underground world.

[39] Nottebohm, *Zweite Beethoveniana*, p.226. Collin, however, seems never to have completed his libretto.

[40] See Kunze, 'Beethovens "Besonnenheit" und das Poetische', pp.146–7.

[41] Czerny, p.91.

Ex. 10.18. Beethoven. Piano Trio in D, op.70 no.1 (ii) bars 1–17.

The gothic atmosphere is enhanced by the sparing, but telling, use of diminished seventh harmony. Unlike the diminished chords at the two remaining possible pitches which occur during the course of the piece, the chord in the fourth bar is left unresolved. Only in the coda, where it is piquantly underpinned by a discordant dominant pedal, does it reach both a climax and a resolution that allows the music to collapse with a final shudder. The sense of resolution is nevertheless weakened, and the feeling of disintegration correspondingly increased, by the fact that the tonic arrives prematurely, on the final beat of bar 90.

Ex. 10.19. Beethoven. Piano Trio in D, op.70 no.1 (ii) bars 88–96.

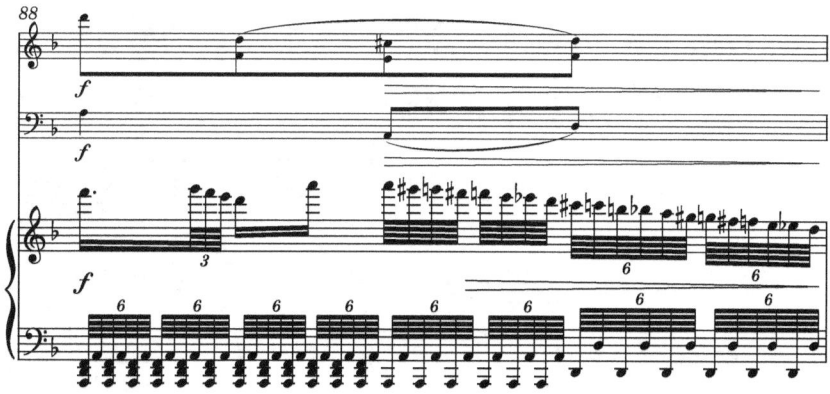

—(continued)

Ex. 10.19—continued

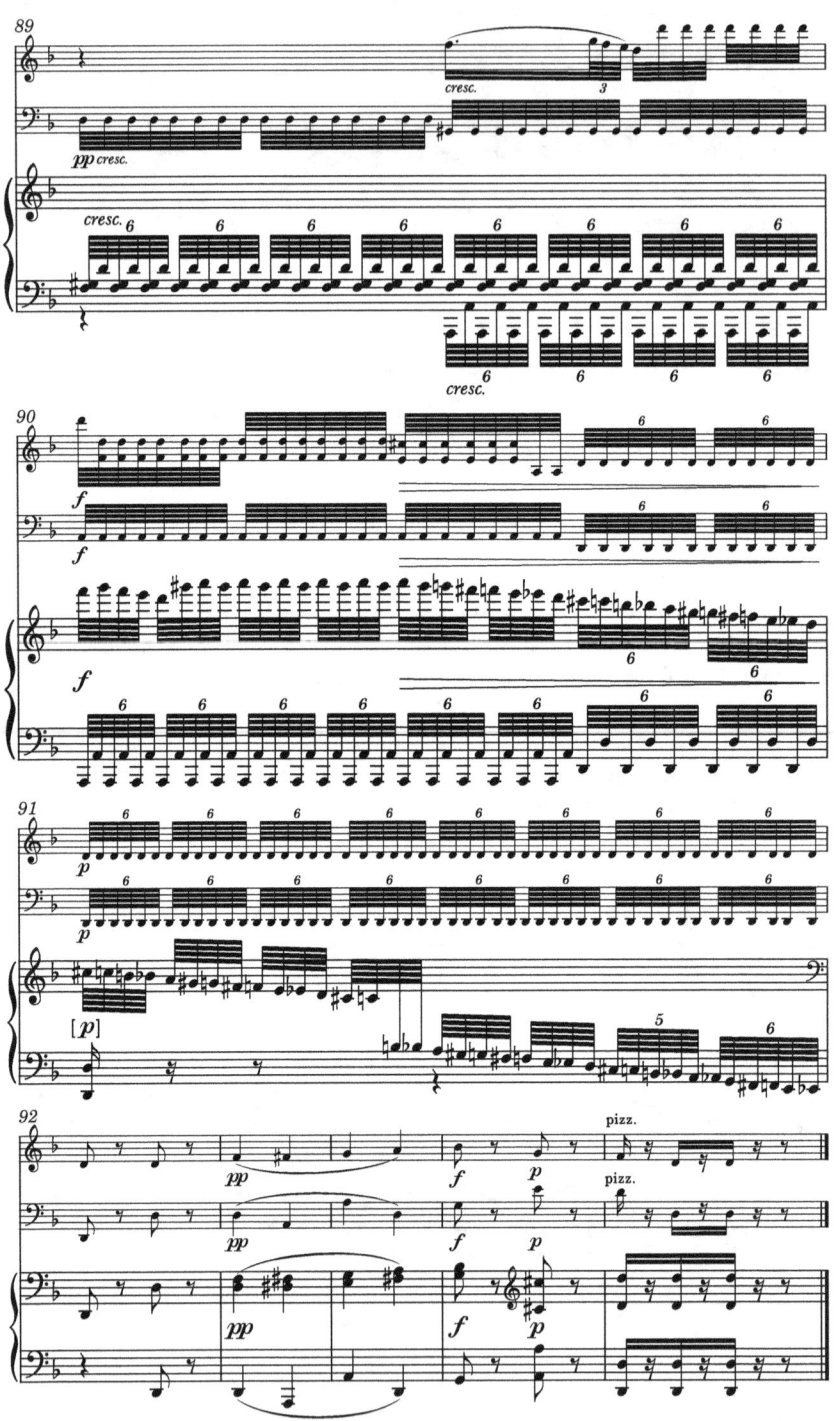

For all its tangible air of theatricality, the Largo is no mere piece of mood-painting, but a rigorously monothematic sonata structure whose secondary tonal area is not the relative major, but its dominant, C major. Donald Francis Tovey seems to have been the first to point out that the unorthodox key scheme is shared by another of Beethoven's D minor movements in sonata form – the scherzo of the Ninth Symphony.[42] Beethoven's choice of subsidiary key in the trio's slow movement may have been prompted by the fact that C major offered him a more luminous contrast to the lugubrious sound of the movement's tonic key than did F major. All the same, the pace of events in the Largo is so slow that it is difficult to speak of a second group at all: the modulation from the tonic towards C major is itself so expansive that by the time the new key has become firmly established there is room only for the briefest of closing subjects before the eight bars of development that separate the exposition from the radically recast first stage of the recapitulation.

As with the finale, Beethoven experienced considerable difficulty in finding a suitable ending for the slow movement. His sketches include no fewer than four rejected drafts of the Largo's closing bars, two of which additionally contain more than one layer,[43] and even Beethoven's heavily corrected final autograph contains a deleted forceful ending to the movement. Two of the sketches have a final paragraph of six bars, rather than the four of the definitive version. The expansion carries the slowly rising legato phrase of bars 93–5 (see Ex. 10.19 above) to an apex which takes in the notes B flat and E flat, in echo of the similar Neapolitan tinge that had occurred near the start of the movement (bar 7), though in so doing it robs this crucial moment of its essential sense of mystery. The first – deleted – layer of the earlier of the two rejected versions brings the music to a close with the hint of a turn towards the major in the penultimate bar (the last bar, as in Beethoven's final version, is a bare octave D), perhaps in an attempt to form a natural bridge to the finale. The close Beethoven eventually adopted is the plainest and starkest of the five he contemplated, and there can be no doubt that it forms the most effective means of rounding off this remarkable vision of darkness.

Perhaps in view of the striking originality of its slow movement, the trio's finale has often been underestimated.[44] It is one of Beethoven's wittiest and most high-spirited pieces, and its sweep and organic unity reflect the single burst of creative inspiration which apparently gave rise to it. It begins fitfully, with a main subject whose flow is twice halted by a fermata within the space of eight bars. The subject's two halves grow out of the same seed, the second being in essence a retrograde form of the first. Moreover, the lower line of the keyboard part in bars 5–8 reproduces the inner accompaniment of the theme's first half, with the all-important A sharp of the fourth bar replaced by an emphatic A natural dropping through an octave. The A natural and its octave drop recur as a punctuating gesture in bars 10–14:

---

[42] Tovey, *Beethoven*, p.26.

[43] The discarded endings are reproduced, together with detailed commentary, in Lockwood, 'Beethoven and the Problem of Closure'; reprinted in Lockwood, *Beethoven: Studies in the Creative Process*.

[44] The piece was, however, sympathetically examined by Joseph Kerman in 'Tändelnde Lazzi', pp.109–22.

Ex. 10.20. Beethoven. Piano Trio in D, op.70 no.1 (iii) bars 1–31.

Beethoven initially scored the theme's first four bars in a similar manner to its continuation in bars 5–6, with parallel thirds divided between the violin and the pianist's left hand, before he decided instead to give the thirds to the piano alone, and to postpone the entry of the stringed instruments until the upbeat to the fourth bar. In this way, he enhanced the surprise of the sudden change in harmonic direction at the first fermata through an equally unexpected change in sonority. An examination of the autograph score shows that Beethoven contemplated delaying the entry of the strings still further, until the upbeat to bar 9, and that the use of thirds in the left-hand piano part was to have continued through the theme's second half. The eventual placing of the entrance of the violin and cello makes for a dramatic gesture, and the three further appearances of the same harmonic twist during the course of the movement are each further intensified: the first by the addition of octaves in the left-hand line of the piano part at the crucial moment (bars 30–1); the second by an acrobatic octave plunge to a more sonorous register of the keyboard (bars 213–14); and the last by a fleshing out of the harmony in the piano writing, with its bass line doubling the cello at the octave below (bars 240–1).

In addition to the stop-go effect of the fermatas themselves, two factors contribute to the disjointed nature of the finale's beginning: the irregular placing of the stresses within the theme itself, falling as they do on the downbeat of the second and fourth bars, rather than the first and third, in its opening half, and on the second beat of the third bar in its latter half; and the fact that neither of the two fermatas is harmonically resolved. The first fermata, on an F sharp major triad, would lead naturally onto the chord of B minor, but Beethoven immediately contradicts any such suggestion with a move instead towards the subdominant. In so doing he creates not one, but two false relations: between A sharp and A natural on the one hand, and C sharp and C natural on the other. The expected resolution of the second fermata, on the home dominant, is again thwarted – this time with a momentary move towards the supertonic minor. Although the tonic is firmly established ten bars later, it is not until bars 32–5 that the fermata is swept aside, and the same melodic phrase is allowed to cadence into the tonic.

Like the F natural introduced so suddenly in the fifth bar of the opening movement, the F sharp major chord of bar 4 has long-range implications for the remainder of the piece. The exposition's second group again reaches a fermata on the chord of F sharp major (this time with an added seventh) at bar 87, whereupon the B minor resolution that might have been expected at the start of the movement actually, albeit fleetingly, occurs:

Ex. 10.21. Beethoven. Piano Trio in D, op.70 no.1 (iii) bars 81–95.

A further consequence of the F sharp major triad is revealed in the coda. Having thus far been treated throughout as an implied dominant of B minor, it is now transformed through an enharmonic change into an augmented sixth chord in the key of B flat minor, before being reinterpreted as a dominant minor ninth of the home key. It is a breathtakingly original and brilliantly humorous moment, exquisitely scored with pizzicato strings:

Ex. 10.22. Beethoven. Piano Trio in D, op.70 no.1 (iii) bars 366–96.

—(continued)

Ex. 10.22—continued

The piece of latter-day hocket from bar 388 onwards, which has the short components of a phrase from the first subject's latter half thrown continually back and forth between violin and cello in echo of the similar procedure during the second group (bars 69ff.), is characteristic of Beethoven's wit in this movement. The melodic fragmentation is reminiscent of his late string quartet writing – the 'Alla danza tedesca' of op.130, the distribution among the players of the individual notes of the *cantus firmus*-like idea in semibreves in the opening movement of op.132, or the isolated pizzicatos hurled from one instrument to the other in the *Presto* fifth movement of op.131 provide just three among many striking examples; and the procedure offers an instance of what might best be described as the finale's modular thematic structure. There is, indeed, scarcely a single melodic segment that does not reappear with a significantly altered function during the course of the piece. Woven in to the second subject, for instance, is the opening subject's initial phrase, now introduced as an inner voice by the violin (see bars 5–7 of Ex. 10.23 opposite),[45] while the gentle descending phrase that unfolds on the piano in the following bar later undergoes an astonishing transformation into a forceful staccato idea thrown out in octaves by strings and piano in overlapping phrases. (Compare the last two bars of Ex. 10.23 with the start of Ex. 10.21 on p.272.)

[45] The shadowy presence of this fragment from the first subject at this moment was noted by Kerman, 'Tändelnde Lazzi', pp.116–17.

Ex. 10.23. Beethoven. Piano Trio in D, op.70 no.1 (iii) bars 55–62.

The second group also contains the rhapsodic excursion in B flat, marked *delicatamente*, from which a fragment has already been quoted in Ex. 10.10(b). 'This passage', says Czerny, 'must be played so lightly and evenly that it seems to be like a free improvisation; but at the same time so strictly in tempo that the accompanists can come in exactly at the right moment.'[46] The passage moves to F major, in which key, and in a spirit of exaggerated continuity, the phrase from the opening subject's second half which on previous appearances had been abruptly halted by a fermata undergoes a pattern of continual repetition. From here, a process of intensive foreshortening enables the music to arrive at the dominant.

Perhaps as a consequence of the exposition's wide-ranging tonal scheme, Beethoven introduces an unusual degree of harmonic stability into the development section, whose final stage unfolds over an insistently repeated dominant pedal (bars 193ff.). At this point he presents a version of the first subject that is curiously shorn of its characteristic rhythm, with the piano at first lending an accompaniment in hurdy-gurdy style. Joseph Kerman's suggestion that the *tranquillo* episode in the finale of Brahms's Second Symphony, where the main subject is similarly simplified into smooth triplets, may have been influenced by this

---

[46] Czerny, p.92.

moment is convincing.⁴⁷ Another parallel between the two composers is offered by the opening movement of Brahms's D minor Violin Sonata op.108, whose development section is underpinned throughout by a dominant pedal. (The effect is, however, altogether darker and more serious than Beethoven's deliberate slide into country dance naivety.) Brahms counterbalances this moment by introducing a similar pedal on the tonic during the coda, and Beethoven likewise recalls his pedal-note passage in the coda, though it remains on the dominant. His treatment of the pedal note itself in the two passages is, however, markedly different. In the development section it rises in a form of textural crescendo, beginning in the bass of the piano before it is reinforced an octave higher by the cello, and finally passes to the two stringed instruments alone, each playing in octaves. The resulting increase in intensity allows Beethoven to unleash the start of the recapitulation *fortissimo*. In the coda, on the other hand, the repeated pedal note is transferred from the strings to the piano, in the process dropping through an octave, and, like an insistent drum-beat, is used in octaves to anchor the piano's final, dizzying chromatic ascent.

The second of the op.70 trios is Beethoven's homage to Haydn, who had been honoured earlier in the year the pieces were written with a gala performance of *The Creation* conducted by Salieri at the Aula of Vienna University. Beethoven was among the select company that greeted the elderly composer on his arrival at the hall. Haydn died just a few weeks before Beethoven's new trios appeared in print in the summer of 1809. Had he lived to see them, he might have been struck by the similarities between the second work of the pair and his own 'Drum Roll' Symphony no.103, in the same key of E flat. Like Haydn, Beethoven begins with a slow introduction leading to an Allegro in 6/8 time; and in both cases the theme of the introduction anticipates not the Allegro's first subject, but the passage leading to the exposition's second stage. (Haydn actually goes further than Beethoven in unifying his movement, by combining the accelerated material of the introduction with the main subject of the Allegro at the start of the development section, much as Bartók was later to do in his Sonata for Two Pianos and Percussion.⁴⁸) Furthermore, like Haydn – and, indeed, Mozart before him, in his D major String Quintet K.593 – Beethoven brings back his introduction at its original slow tempo shortly before the close.

Beethoven's second movement mirrors its model still more closely. It is in the same key as the corresponding movement of the Haydn, and cast in the same double variation form (though Beethoven reverses Haydn's modal scheme, and presents the first theme in C major and the second in C minor). The tempo of the two pieces, moreover, is similar: *Andante più tosto allegretto* in the Haydn, plain *Allegretto* in the Beethoven. In the opening moments of his piece, Beethoven even fleetingly recalls the typically Haydnesque piano trio texture that has the cello and

---

⁴⁷ Kerman, 'Tändelnde Lazzi', p.116.

⁴⁸ Curiously enough, Bartók's piece, like Haydn's, begins with a solo drum roll.

the bass line of the piano moving together in parallel. Beethoven's third movement is a minuet in all but name (it is labelled as such in his sketches, though not in the final score); and if its quasi-trio sections cast more than a passing glance sideways to Schubert, rather than backwards to Haydn, the piece is nostalgic enough to leave the impression that this hauntingly beautiful work as a whole represents – after the First Symphony, whose outer movements clearly reflect the shadow of Haydn's C major Symphony no.97 – Beethoven's most overt acknowledgement of the influence of his erstwhile teacher.[49] Not for nothing did Tovey single out op.70 no.2 above all as the work in which Beethoven 'discovers new meanings for Mozart's phrases and Haydn's formulas'.[50]

Despite the presence of a finale in Beethoven's most dynamic style (and with a structure as radically new as that of the last movement of the Eighth Symphony), the E flat trio is a less spectacular work than its D major companion, and, at least in the second half of the nineteenth century, it was one of the more neglected among the composer's great chamber works. Even so perceptive a critic as Adolf Bernhard Marx complained that it seemed to offer nothing more than 'stimulating and entertaining music',[51] while Wilhelm von Lenz went so far as to pay it the backhanded compliment of being, with the exception of its finale, 'deepened Hummel' (*ein vertiefter Hummel*).[52] Nor, in more recent times – and perhaps also in view of the relatively small number of surviving sketches for it – has the E flat trio received nearly so much scholarly attention as the 'Ghost'.

The kinship between Beethoven's second movement and the double variation form of some of Haydn's symphonic slow movements was noted by E.T.A. Hoffmann; but for the rest, Hoffmann found the work nearer to the world of Mozart. In the opening Allegro's main subject he detected a valedictory (*adelich*) character that reminded him of Mozart's E flat Symphony no.39.[53] But Beethoven's theme seems to look back not so much to his great predecessors, as to the music of his own youth, and it bears more than a passing resemblance to the rondo theme of the E flat Trio WoO 38:

---

[49] Elaine Sisman, in 'The Spirit of Haydn from Mozart's Hands', p.58, sees a melodic parallel between the third movement of op.70 no.2 and the Largo from Haydn's Symphony no.88, though the similarity between Haydn's theme and the relevant phrase in the Beethoven (bars 26–7) is likely to be no more than coincidental. Paradoxically, a rather Beethovenian *sforzando* placed on the third beat of the 3/4 bar in the Haydn does not feature in Beethoven's phrase.

[50] Tovey, *Beethoven*, p.88.

[51] Marx, *Ludwig van Beethoven*, vol.2, p.134.

[52] Lenz, *Beethoven, eine Kunststudie*, part 3, p.130.

[53] AMZ, 9 (3 March 1813), col.149.

Ex. 10.24.
(a) Beethoven. Piano Trio in E flat, WoO 38 (iii) bars 1–8.

(b) Beethoven. Piano Trio in E flat, op.70 no.2 (i) bars 20–7.

A peculiarity of op.70 no.2 is that its two middle movements are both in Allegretto tempo. This is by no means alone among Beethoven's four-movement works in doing without a slow movement, but with the exception of the Seventh Symphony the third movement in the remaining instances is not a scherzo, but a graceful minuet whose relaxed, lyrical nature compensates for the absence of a genuinely slow piece elsewhere. In the Piano Sonata op.31 no.3 and the Eighth Symphony the second movement in any case assumes the character, if not the form, of a scherzo, thereby rendering the inclusion of an actual scherzo redundant. Each of the middle movements thus absorbs elements of the other, in a characteristically Beethovenian conundrum. If the Allegretto of op.70 no.2 lacks similar scherzo-like undertones, the overlapping functions of its middle movements remain a fundamental aspect of the work as a whole.

In its quiet, understated manner, the opening of op.70 no.2 is no less striking than the more assertive beginning of the 'Ghost' Trio: indeed, the calm initial phrase for the cello alone heard at the outset forms what is perhaps the most original of all Beethoven's piano trio beginnings. Its effect is not so far removed from that of the similar start to the C major Cello Sonata op.102 no.1, except that the modulatory nature of the canon presented in the trio's opening bars lends it the aspect of a piece that has begun in midstream, with the answer to an unheard statement. Already in the second bar, the violin's entrance occurs on the supertonic minor, while the piano answers on the dominant. Since the larger part of the introduction thereafter unfolds over a dominant pedal, it is not until four bars before the onset of the Allegro that the tonic key is firmly established at all. At this point there is a clear pre-echo of the Allegro's opening theme. Beethoven marks the relevant passage *espressivo* – perhaps to indicate that the players should feel free to elongate the upbeat (notated here as a semiquaver) so that it is roughly equivalent to the quaver upbeat of the Allegro's theme. A tangible, if not necessarily precise, tempo relationship between the two sections plays a role in the organic unity of the movement as a whole: not only does such a relationship enable the rhythmically transformed reminiscences of the introduction's material within the main body of the Allegro to appear at a similar tempo, it also lends a seamless continuity to the later return of the introduction at its original speed. Significantly, both Beethoven's sketches for the piece and his autograph score give the tempo for the introduction and its return in the coda as *Adagio*, with a time signature of ¢,[54] and the same indications are found in a letter to Breitkopf & Härtel of 28 March 1809, in which Beethoven quoted the incipits of all seven movements of the op.70 trios.[55] The original edition, on the other hand, finds the introduction's tempo marking changed to *Poco sostenuto*, and its time signature to c. The difference in tempo resulting from the autograph score's marking in a slow two beats to the bar and the first edition's more flowing four beats may be small, but the alteration in the music's character implied by the change in headings is considerable.

The progressively widening melodic intervals of the introduction's last four bars pave the way for the ascending octave leap that launches the Allegro's first subject.

---

[54] See Brandenburg, 'Über die Bedeutung der Änderungen von Taktvorschriften', p.47.
[55] BGA no.370; Anderson no.204.

The subject itself is presented in the form of a rising harmonic sequence whose main stress falls on the 6/4 harmony at the start of its second bar. It is the unstable, sequential nature of the theme that later enables Beethoven to begin the recapitulation in remarkably developmental fashion. Not until the Allegro has been under way for a full twenty bars does he provide a firm tonic cadence; and when at last he does so, he launches into a new cello theme which takes as its springboard the tiny chromatic figure that had been used as an accompanimental idea during the prolongation of the Allegro's first subject (bars 28ff.). The presence of a second tonic theme acts as a stabilising influence not only here, but – more importantly – during the latter half of the movement, following the uniquely disconcerting start of the recapitulation.

A further consequence of the inclusion of a second theme in the tonic within what is a highly concentrated exposition is that Beethoven is prompted to expand the music's tonal scope through an unprepared change to the flat mediant (G flat) at the approach to the second group, for the return of the rhythmically transformed initial motif from the introduction. For E.T.A.Hoffmann, never one reluctant to invoke supernatural similes, this moment was like the unexpected appearance of a chorale, 'suddenly breaking into the artistic fabric, and rousing one's spirit like a strange, wonderful apparition'.[56]

The rising shape of the first subject's beginning is elaborated upon during the exposition's closing bars, which approach the repeat by way of a broad ascending sequential arc played by the two stringed instruments above a piano accompaniment in rapid arpeggios. Following the exposition repeat, the pattern of arpeggios is expanded in the second-time bars which lead seamlessly forwards into the development section. Here, the sweep of the music, the progressive thematic foreshortening, and the gradual crescendo towards the only *fortissimo* marking in the piece lead to a climax on the dominant of F minor at the end of what must be one of Beethoven's longest harmonic sequences. From this point onwards, the development concerns itself largely with the smoothly flowing second subject, presenting it in A flat, C flat (with the violin part notated in an enharmonic B major) and E major, before the trill and rising fourth familiar from the first subject make a return at the top of the keyboard. Despite the distance from home, Beethoven neatly takes a sidestep onto the dominant of E flat, as if to usher in the recapitulation. Instead, however, he prefers to continue his harmonic sequence downwards, and to approach the recapitulation from below, in much the same way as he had paved the way for the exposition's second group via a reminiscence of the introduction in G flat major. The cello tries to assert its authority by launching the first subject in D flat, but this plainly will not do, and it is rapidly corrected by the piano. The recapitulation, then, effectively sets in at the upbeat to bar 129, as part of a continuing rising sequence of the kind already presented at the close of the exposition. It is as though Beethoven were attempting retrospectively to lend his theme the guise of a subject with an off-tonic beginning, and the moment, described by Tovey as 'perhaps the most unexpected return in all music',[57] is rendered the more

---

[56] Hoffmann, AMZ, 9 (3 March 1813), col.149.
[57] Tovey, *Beethoven*, p.101.

disconcerting not only by the overlapping thematic entries, but also by the cello's E natural on the downbeat of bar 129, diverting the start of the actual recapitulation towards the supertonic before the tonic has had a chance to establish itself.

Ex. 10.25. Beethoven. Piano Trio in E flat, op.70 no.2 (i) bars 124–33.

There are other E flat major works by Beethoven in which the recapitulation is approached from a 'flat' direction, not least the piano sonatas op.31 no.3 and op.81a. In those cases, however, the main Allegro subject sets off on the subdominant, and the end of the development section is marked by a moment of stasis in which a repeated sounding of the subdominant allows the reprise to get under way in the manner of a seamless dissolve.[58] The unstable harmonic sequence presented at the moment of recapitulation in op.70 no.2, with the melodic reprise anticipating the harmonic resolution, is surely unique in Beethoven.

One consequence of the unusual instability of the recapitulation's first stage is that Beethoven feels the need to redress the balance with a coda so substantial as to exceed the development section in length. It begins in a manner similar to that of the development, presenting a harmonic sequence that gradually rises, first via a foreshortened version of the first subject, and then through a correspondingly expanded form of the closing subject, until it winds down to join the return of the introduction at its original tempo – albeit newly scored, with the initial phrase now given to the piano. Following this reprise, the quicker tempo returns with a reiteration of the rising minor third with which the reminiscence of the introduction comes to a close. Beethoven may have adopted the articulation of these two-note phrases from the accompaniment to the second of his two tonic themes, and the figure itself unmistakably anticipates the upbeat to the second movement's initial theme. It is notable, too, that when the strings rejoin the piano they emphasise the rising third with what are the only two instances in the piece of a *sforzando* accent on the first note of the pair (bars 234–5). These closing bars at last present a fragment of the first subject in a descending sequence, thereby counterbalancing the profusion of rising sequences heard thus far, and allowing the piece to sink to a subdued close.

According to Czerny, both the C major theme of the second movement and the 'middle section (G major) of the finale' were written in imitation of Croatian folk songs, though what led him to this conclusion is not known.[59] The second movement's material is unusually short-breathed, as though Beethoven were deliberately holding any sense of melodic expansiveness in check, lest it detract from the expressive breadth of the movement that is to follow. The initial C major theme, with its 'scotch-snap' upbeat, consists of nothing more than two four-bar phrases, with varied repeats in which Beethoven takes full advantage of the music's invertible counterpoint, transferring the two countermelodies from the middle of the texture to the top. The more sonorous second theme in the minor gives the impression of still greater compression. The quasi-repeat of its first four-bar half is already a variation in itself, and the repeated-note figuration continues directly into the melody's second half. Moreover, the section is further curtailed by a return of the 'scotch-snap' rhythm, forming a smooth transition to the reprise of the major-mode theme.

To avoid the monotony of a strictly symmetrical scheme based on such sectional material, Beethoven continually varies the music's proportions during the course of the piece. The return to C major brings with it not one variation, but two – the first of them again taking the piano into its uppermost register, in a translucent sonority of the kind the composer was to exploit in some of his late piano variations, and notably those of the C minor Sonata op.111; and the second dividing the theme into

---

[58] Much the same happens in the String Quartet op.127, though there the recapitulation momentarily imparts the impression of having begun not on the subdominant, but on its relative minor.

[59] Czerny, p.18. The section of the finale Czerny had in mind was presumably the closing subject of bars 83ff., with its sustained open-string drones.

still shorter segments, passing its two-bar phrases back and forth between violin and cello. But this expansion is followed by a corresponding contraction, and a shift of the music's emphasis in a manner that could hardly have been anticipated at the start of the piece: the second minor-mode passage is followed only by the briefest of glimpses of the initial theme, now bereft of its quasi- repeats, before the music turns once again to the minor. The concluding minor-mode section is, however, no straightforward variation, but a synthesis of the two contrasting themes. It is a curious passage, in which the music's exaggerated symmetry and the almost obsessive manner in which it continually cadences into the tonic lend it a disconcertingly constricted feel. At first, the full-blooded tonic cadences occur periodically at the end of each four-bar paragraph, but their influence is progressively increased in a codetta that has the same cadence reiterated in every single bar. The music itself appears to have ground to a halt, and the primary function of this moment is to present a form of textural and dynamic decrescendo. It is as though the village band, having overwhelmed us with its sound, is now receding into the distance; and in the end, one last tiny glimpse of the first theme – major turning almost at once to minor – is angrily brushed aside with yet another full-blooded perfect cadence into the tonic minor. This, then, is a rare instance in the music of its period of a piece which begins in the major, only to end in the turbulence and instability of the minor. The opening movement of the 'Kreutzer' Sonata will hardly serve as a precedent, since the major-mode slow introduction is effectively a separate entity, and we would have to look instead to Schubert's E flat Impromptu D.899 no.2, or his 'Moment musical' D.780 no.6, to find parallels. It could well have been the first of those Schubert pieces that influenced the similar procedure in Brahms's E flat Rhapsody op.119 no.4, while his B major Piano Trio op.8 likewise comes to a turbulent close in the minor. Such instances are, however, exceptional even in the late nineteenth century.[60]

The third movement of op.70 no.2 fulfils much the same function within the work as a whole as does the similarly relaxed, expressively warm minuet of the Piano Sonata op.31 no.3. This was the piece that so impressed Johann Friedrich Reichardt when he heard the op.70 trios at a private performance given in Countess Erdödy's house in December 1808:

> Beethoven played in a quite masterful and inspired fashion new trios which he has just completed, in which a perfectly heavenly cantabile movement occurred (in 3/4 time and in A flat major), of a kind I have never heard from him before. It lifts and melts my soul whenever I think of it.[61]

Precious few of Beethoven's sketches for this movement have come down to us. One that has, headed 'Min[uet]',[62] shows its melody at an advanced stage, though still lacking the inspiration that lends it its feeling of floating serenity. The second

---

[60] Chopin's op.38 Ballade, beginning in F major and ending in A minor, is a special case, since within the design of the piece as a whole its F major opening section may retrospectively be heard as an extensive off-tonic beginning – so much so that Brahms used to refer to the piece as being in A minor.

[61] Reichardt, *Vertraute Briefe*, vol.1, p.285. (Letter of 31 December 1808.)

[62] Beethoven, *Ein Skizzenbuch zur Pastoralsymphonie op.68 und zu den Trios op.70, 1 und 2*, f.58v.

half of the theme takes over the rising minor seventh from the first, but in so doing robs the melody of its seemingly effortless continuity, and by the fourth bar of the second half it appears about to grind to a halt on the tonic.

Ex. 10.26. Beethoven. Piano Trio in E flat, op.70 no.2 (iii) bars 1–15, sketch.

In its final form, the start of the second half expands the minor seventh to an octave, allowing the melody to take wing. The ascending octave is featured with some insistence during the reprise in the last sixteen bars of this section, where the melody is transferred to the piano while the violin has an accompaniment consisting almost exclusively of rising octaves.

Ex. 10.27. Beethoven. Piano Trio in E flat, op.70 no.2 (iii) bars 1–16.

By conspicuously avoiding the expected resolution into the tonic at the melody's end Beethoven is able to introduce a new idea in the dominant. This secondary idea, initiated by the piano in a register of the keyboard that has not previously been heard in the piece (the piano's accompaniment to the violin melody in the first 24 bars is entirely located in the bass), culminates in an instant of heightened expressiveness – a winding unaccompanied phrase whose underlying skeleton of a descending dominant seventh arpeggio is so richly embroidered with appoggiaturas as to anticipate the intensely chromatic style that Chopin raised to such a high art form in some of his mazurkas.

Ex. 10.28. Beethoven. Piano Trio in E flat, op.70 no.2 (iii) bars 37–44.

A similar moment of infinite yearning occurs in the quasi-trio, whose symmetrical beginning – a succession of four-bar phrases alternating between strings and piano – is counterbalanced by one of Beethoven's most breathtaking piano trio sonorities. The constant alternation between major and minor, the triplet keyboard figuration, the magical enharmonic change – all these conspire to make this a moment so thoroughly Schubertian that anyone hearing it out of context could be forgiven for mistaking it as the work of the younger composer. Schubert, indeed, was to raise this type of delicate triplet decoration to equally great heights in the first movement of his own E flat Trio D.929.

This is one of Beethoven's enlarged scherzo or minuet designs, with the trio played twice, between three statements of the opening section, and a note among his sketches indicates that it was to have ended, as do so many of his pieces of the kind, with a reminiscence of its trio.[63] Instead, however, the final bars amalgamate the initial theme with the yearning passage from the trio, allowing the music to wind down to a close of profound calm based on the movement's opening phrase.

If the successive tonalities of the trio's first three movements form a descending chain of thirds – E flat – C major/minor – A flat– the use of third-related keys continues within the finale itself, where the second-subject stage occurs in the submediant. We have seen that Beethoven had begun to use mediant keys as an expressively enhanced substitute for the traditional dominant with the opening movement in the C major String Quintet op.29, the G major Piano Sonata op.31 no.1, and the 'Waldstein' op.53; and he was to explore the idea further in such works as the 'Archduke' Trio and the 'Hammerklavier' Sonata. In all these cases the submediant key is maintained right through to the closing bars of the exposition, where a modulatory transition leads either back to the start for the repeat, or forwards into the development section. In the 'Archduke' and the 'Hammerklavier', as well as in the op.29 Quintet, the recapitulation brings back the second group in the tonic from the outset; but the two earlier among the piano sonatas keep the notion of the third-related key alive in the recapitulation through a brief appearance of the second subject in the mediant, before the tonal balance is redressed by means of a tonic restatement. (The two secondary keys clearly bear the same relationship to each other as do the dominant and tonic of the home tonality.) The finale of the Trio op.70 no.2, however, carries the influence of mediant keys to an extreme, and perhaps it is significant that Beethoven's treatment of such keys thereafter became notably more cautious. The opening movement of the Eighth Symphony, for instance, actually retraces its steps within the confines of the exposition: the second group sets off in the submediant, but its theme turns back on itself, and is immediately given out again in the more orthodox dominant after all.

In the finale of op.70 no.2 the exposition's second group contains two well-defined themes, both of them more emphatic in character than the impetuous first subject. As a result, the main weight of the tonal argument is thrown firmly onto the key of that second group – G major. In the recapitulation, the secondary mediant key of C major makes its presence felt even more strongly, since it follows a first

---

[63] See *ibid.*, f.58v.

subject played this time *pianissimo* throughout. (This may be a unique instance of Beethoven's reversal of his favoured procedure, whereby what had initially been a subdued main subject is recapitulated *fortissimo*.) So affirmative is the second subject material here that Beethoven takes the remarkable step of allowing the music to remain in this comparatively distant key until the entire second group has run its course.

Like the opening movement of its companion trio, this is one of Beethoven's middle-period works that show him concerned with enlarging the scope of the sonata form's latter half. In the finale of the 'Appassionata' Sonata the shift in emphasis is effected by the simplest possible means: the exposition is not repeated, and instead the pianist is instructed to play the combined development section and recapitulation twice before a coda in a quicker tempo rounds the piece off. The finale of the Eighth Symphony has what could be thought of as a written-out second-half repeat, since it features two different recapitulations interspersed with two distinct development sections. It is true that the expanded latter half in the finale of op.70 no.2 can be interpreted as containing a twofold recapitulation of its second group, the first in C major and the second in E flat; but such an analysis fails to take into account the ambiguous nature of the design, in which the C major music mirrors the pattern of the exposition's parallel stage so fully and so closely that the recapitulation appears to come to a complete close in the secondary key, and the brief passage that follows imparts the impression of forming the start of a coda. All the same, the tonal imbalance caused by the recapitulation's 'wrong-key' latter half clearly needs to be redressed, and there duly ensues a further, notably varied, reprise of the second group, this time in the tonic (bars 312 ff.), and an actual coda (bars 356ff.).

Perhaps in view of the thematic imbalance created by the twofold recapitulation of the second subject, Beethoven bases virtually the whole of the powerful development section on the first subject. Despite the fact that it unfolds over an obstinate tonic pedal the music is strangely unsettling, and its stability is undermined both by the stabbing chords on the stringed instruments which are to provide such a rich source of inspiration in the development section's central portion, and by the hesitant manner in which the music gets under way at the start of the development.

The first subject is generated by a continual process of augmentation. Its latter half, from the seventh bar onwards, freely augments the semiquaver figure of the preceding bars; and the prolongation which begins on the violin at the upbeat to bar 15 is based on the same figure, while beneath it the bass line of the piano part carries the augmentation a stage further.

Ex. 10.29. Beethoven. Piano Trio in E flat, op.70 no.2 (iv) bars 1–24.

—(continued)

Ex. 10.29—*continued*

The second group is approached by way of a series of seemingly improvisatory flourishes for each player in turn, punctuated by fragments of the first subject in juxtapositions of violent dynamic contrasts. The first of the flourishes (bars 33–7) is played by the pianist, but in a style that is curiously violinistic; and the sense of instrumental exchange continues in bars 38–9, where the piano's right-hand part clearly borrows the violin's open D and A strings. It is a moment of remarkable thematic disintegration for so early a stage in the movement, and one that throws into relief the confidence of the assertive, march-like second group that is to follow:

Ex. 10.30. Beethoven. Piano Trio in E flat, op.70 no.2 (iv) bars 31–45.

This may have been the passage Beethoven had in mind when he became concerned that the music's forward momentum should not be impeded during the course of the piece. At any rate, in the same letter to Breitkopf in which he attempted to have Archduke Rudolph's name substituted for that of the Countess Erdödy on the title page of the op.70 trios, he instructed them: 'If there is anywhere a ritardando in several passages in the same movement [i.e. the finale of op.70 no.2] then remove this too wherever you find it; there should be no ritardando in that whole movement.' In this letter of 26 May 1809 Beethoven supplied Breitkopf with fingerings for the tricky passage in the development section where the piano has the first subject's running semiquaver figure in the left hand, while the right adds its stabbing chordal interjections. It is a splendidly intense moment in which the subject's two main elements appear to tumble over each other in their haste:

Ex. 10.31. Beethoven. Piano Trio in E flat, op.70 no.2 (iv) bars 142–71.

—(continued)

Ex. 10.31—*continued*

A consequence of the audacious plan carried out in the recapitulation is that its first half has to be expanded, in order to re-establish the tonic firmly before the radical departure from home territory embodied in the reprise of the second group. Beethoven duly provides what is in effect a double reprise of the first subject, its latter half eventually moving up on its second appearance into the supertonic minor. Perhaps in view of the unorthodox key in which his second group unfolds, Beethoven mirrors the parallel part of the exposition closely in terms of instrumentation; and no doubt because neither of its two distinct themes is allotted to the cello, it is the cello that has the lion's share of the material at the point where the second group is at last presented in the home key.

This is a piece which finds Beethoven exploiting the sound of the keyboard's upper reaches as never before. The piano's decorated restatement of the second group's military-style opening subject, for instance, reaches up to E^4, while the final appearance of the parallel passage in the tonic during the movement's closing stages finds Beethoven for the first time extending that range by a further semitone. This topmost F was the highest note available to him, and it was a full octave above the range he had been able to use before the 'Waldstein' Sonata, of 1803–4.[64] (That sonata, however, finds Beethoven rather tentative in his first exploration of the extended keyboard, requiring nothing further than A^3 – a note Haydn had been able to write nearly a decade earlier, in the finale of his Sonata in C, H.XVI.50, composed for the larger Broadwood pianos he encountered in London.) The same topmost F is found in the 'Choral Fantasy' and the 'Emperor' Concerto, both composed shortly after Beethoven had completed the op.70 trios. In op.70 no.2 it is the glittering sonority of the piano's high register, not only as evinced in the finale, but also in such moments as the coda of the first movement, which finds Beethoven hammering away so insistently at the note C^4, or the delicate, rippling triplets of the third movement's trio section, that lends the music so much of its individual character.

In the finale's coda Beethoven makes a return to the *pianissimo* closing moments of the development section and the equally subdued start of the recapitulation,

---

[64] Beethoven's Piano Sonata in E op.14 no.1 contains a single instance of the note $F\sharp^3$ (first movement, bar 41), as does Mozart's Sonata for two pianos K.448 (finale, bar 98). Since no piano manufacturer would have produced an instrument with a 'black' topmost note, the pieces in question must have been written with a keyboard range reaching up to G^3 in mind.

recalling both passages closely, as though to suggest that he might be about to embark on a more orthodox form of recapitulation. The circular aspect acquired by the music as a result is ultimately brushed aside by a scale sweeping down over a span of four-and-a-half octaves, to bring the curtain abruptly down on what is a comparatively neglected work among Beethoven's chamber masterpieces.

11
Works of 1810–12

According to Czerny, the composition of the 'Archduke' Trio op.97, the grandest and most famous of Beethoven's works of the kind, stretched over a long period of time, and in view of the gap between its composition in the spring of 1811 and its appearance in print at the end of 1816 many commentators have assumed that Beethoven must have revised the work in the interim. 'As early as 1807', Czerny claimed, 'there was talk among his [Beethoven's] friends of a grand trio in B flat major which he was working on at the time.'[1] In fact, Beethoven did not begin sketching out his ideas for the trio until the latter half of 1810, while the actual process of composition seems to have occupied him for scarcely more than three weeks, from 3rd to 26th March 1811. Those, at any rate, are the dates that appear at the beginning and end of Beethoven's autograph score. (The last page carries a note to say that it was finished on 26 March 1811, the month having been altered from April.) While he was still working on the trio, and at a time when the lessons he reluctantly found himself having to give to Archduke Rudolph were temporarily interrupted by an injury or infection affecting one of Rudolph's fingers, Beethoven informed him: 'During the festivities on account of the Princess of Baden and because of Your Imperial Highness's painful finger I began to work rather diligently, among the fruits of which is a new trio for piano.'[2]

Shortly after he had completed the trio Beethoven sent it to Rudolph together with a note explaining: 'Since in spite of all efforts I could not find a copyist who could write it out for me at home, I am sending you my manuscript. You need only, if you would be so good, send to Schlemmer for a suitable copyist, who, however, must do the copying in your palace, as otherwise one is never safe from thievery.'[3] By the summer, the Archduke's hand must have healed, and he took part in the first performance of the new trio at an outdoor concert at Prince Lobkowitz's palace, on 2 June.

Beethoven offered the new trio to Breitkopf & Härtel through the intermediary of his friend and unofficial secretary Franz Oliva. The composer assured the firm on 12 April 1811 that Oliva 'has my full authorisation to discuss the matter from

---

[1] Czerny, p.15.
[2] Letter of 12 March 1811. BGA no.489; Anderson no.300. Princess Catherina Amalia Christina of Baden stayed in Vienna from 3–12 March 1811.
[3] BGA no.491; Anderson no.301. Wenzel Schlemmer was Beethoven's most reliable copyist, and he had others in his employ. In the end, however, it was Schlemmer who carried out the copying of op.97 himself.

all its aspects and to conclude an agreement with you'.[4] However, the publishers were unwilling to meet Beethoven's asking price, and with the exception of a few isolated tirades against their incompetence there was a gap of more than five years until Beethoven's correspondence with Breitkopf resumed, when he finally responded to a request for some new compositions. In a letter to Gottfried Härtel of 19 July 1816, Beethoven asked for 130 gold ducats for a group of compositions including the Piano Sonata op.101 and the 'Kakadu' Variations op.121a, reinforcing his claim to such a fee by stating: 'I remember that you refused to give me 100 gulden for a grand pianoforte trio. And yet I get 50 or even 60 gold ducats for that kind of composition.'[5] Meanwhile, Beethoven had offered the op.97 Trio to the firm of S.A. Steiner & Co., together with the Seventh and Eighth Symphonies as well as *Wellingtons Sieg* op.91, the String Quartet op.95, the Violin Sonata op.96 and the song cycle *An die ferne Geliebte* op.98. A note in the hand of Steiner's then business associate Tobias Haslinger appears at the end of Beethoven's autograph score of the op.97 Trio, indicating *Im Druck erschienen am 16. Juli 1816* (Appeared in print on 16 July 1816), but the declaration was premature. Steiner's advertisement promising the forthcoming publication of 'a completely new trio (in B flat major) for pianoforte, violin and violoncello, and 6 new songs with piano accompaniment [op.98]' was inserted in the *Wiener Zeitung* on 29 July, but even then their appearance, and that of all the other works Beethoven had sold to Steiner, was further delayed by several months. Not until 21 December did the newspaper announce them (minus the Eighth Symphony, which did not see the light of day until the following year) as being newly published. Beethoven must have received an advance copy of at least the title page of the trio, because at some time in the previous month he informed Archduke Rudolph: 'I am sending herewith the dedication of the trio to Y.I.H. It is stated on this work; but indeed all the works on which your name is not stated and which are of any value whatsoever are intended for Y.I.H.'[6].

Rudolph, the youngest son of the Emperor Leopold II, seems to have begun taking lessons from Beethoven in the winter of 1803–4,[7] and the long succession of works the composer inscribed to him began some four years later with the publication of the Fourth Piano Concerto, in 1808. When, at the beginning of May 1809, Rudolph and other members of the Imperial family withdrew from Vienna to avoid a confrontation with Napoleon's invading troops, Beethoven was moved to write his only programmatic piano sonata, *Lebewohl, Abwesenheit und Wiedersehn* op.81a, depicting his friend and pupil's departure, absence and return. His sketches for the work contain a projected title for its opening movement: *Der Abschied – am 4ten Mai – gewidmet und aus dem Herzen geschrieben S.K.H.* (The Farewell, on 4 May, dedicated and written from the heart to H[is] I[mperial] H[ighness]).[8] The inscription foreshadows the famous words written at the head of the autograph of the *Missa*

---

[4] BGA no.492; Anderson no.304.

[5] BGA no.950; Anderson no.642. 50 ducats would have been equivalent to approximately 225 gulden.

[6] BGA no.1000; Anderson no.671.

[7] See Kagan, *Archduke Rudolph, Beethoven's Patron, Pupil, and Friend*, pp.13–14.

[8] *Ibid.*, p.15.

solemnis, intended to mark the Archduke's installation as Archbishop of Olmütz on 4 June 1819: *Von Herzen – Möge es wieder – zu Herzen gehn!* (From the heart, may it in turn go to the heart!) Earlier in 1809 Rudolph had been instrumental in setting up a contract together with the Princes Kinsky and Lobkowitz whereby Beethoven was guaranteed the annual sum of 4000 florins on condition that he continue to live and work in the Austrian domains. (The composer had let it be known that he was tempted to take up an offer from Napoleon's youngest brother, Jérome, the self-styled 'King of Westphalia', to act as his Kapellmeister at a salary of 600 gold florins – equivalent to around 2,700 silver florins – plus travelling expenses. His total annual income would have amounted to approximately 3,400 florins.) In the years that followed, Beethoven dedicated to Archduke Rudolph the Piano Concerto no.5, the piano sonatas opp.106 and 111, the piano reduction (made by Ignaz Moscheles) of *Fidelio*, the Violin Sonata op.96, the *Grande Fugue* for string quartet op.133 (together with Beethoven's own piano duet transcription of the piece, op.134), and the *Missa solemnis*. In addition, the two trios op.70 were, as we have seen, intended for Rudolph, but Beethoven's instructions to Breitkopf came too late for the title page to be altered; and a similar fate befell the incidental music to Goethe's *Egmont*.

The Archduke was an accomplished pianist, and besides the op.97 Trio he took part in an early performance of Beethoven's Fifth Piano Concerto, as well as the premiere of the op.96 Violin Sonata. Schubert's lifelong friend Joseph von Spaun recounted that his school orchestra had been invited to play to the Archduke at Schönbrunn, on an occasion when Beethoven was also present. After an 'uninteresting' symphony by the Viennese court Kapellmeister Anton Teyber, who was Rudolph's former composition teacher, the orchestra performed a symphony in E flat by Haydn, which apparently went well.

> The Archduke, who was very pleased, announced that he would also like to play something for us and that if we would undertake the difficult orchestral part he would play us a Mozart concerto in B flat major. We expressed our readiness at once, and the Archduke played excellently; only since this concerto makes particular demands of the wind instruments, which were our weak point, and in addition to this the considerable heat of the day had a deleterious effect on the tuning of the wind instruments, our accompaniment was probably imperfect. Only the Archduke was satisfied. After we had taken tea, consisting of ice-cream and a large number of pastries, we were dismissed in friendly fashion.[9]

Johann Friedrich Reichardt heard Archduke Rudolph perform at several musical evenings given in Prince Lobkowitz's palace in 1809. One such occasion in January of that year prompted him to comment:

> At a grand concert given at Prince Lobkowitz's, we once again admired the outstanding talent, so rare in a prince, of Archduke Rudolph. The Archduke played the hardest concertos by Beethoven and sonatas by Prince Louis Ferdinand with the greatest level-headedness, calm and precision.[10]

---

[9] Deutsch, *Franz Schubert: die Erinnerungen seiner Freunde*, pp.406–7.
[10] Reichardt, *Vertraute Briefe*, vol.1, p.294.

A few weeks later, at another of Prince Lobkowitz's concerts, Reichardt witnessed the violinist Ferdinand August Seidler accompanying the Archduke in 'the most difficult trios by Beethoven and Louis Ferdinand', by the former of which he is likely to have meant one, or both, of the op.70 pair.[11]

Archduke Rudolph's lessons with Beethoven probably came to an end in 1824.[12] The previous year he sent the composer a set of variations he had written (almost certainly the variations for piano and clarinet on the cavatina 'Sorte! Secondami' from Rossini's *Zelmira*, the autograph of which contains corrections in Beethoven's hand[13]), and received some advice in return:

> Y.I.H. should continue particularly to practise hastily writing down your ideas briefly at the piano. For this purpose you should have a small table beside the pianoforte. In this way not only is the imagination strengthened but one also learns to pin down immediately the most remote ideas. It is also necessary to compose without a piano; and sometimes to work out a simple melody, or a chorale with simple and again with different harmonies according to the laws of counterpoint and even to develop them beyond this. This will certainly not give Y.I.H. a headache; but rather, when one finds oneself wrapped up in great art, great pleasure.[14]

The Archduke's correspondence course in composition continued in December 1823, when Beethoven told him:

> I have noticed the progress in Y.I.H.'s exercises, but also unfortunately that misunderstandings exist in them. The best thing is to extract in advance figured basses in four parts by good composers, and sometimes to compose a four-part song. Until I have the good fortune to be near Y.I.H. again, also write in four parts for piano: that can produce good results, although it is more difficult in that one cannot accomplish the rise and fall of the voices as naturally as with a song or with four stringed instruments.[15]

The 'Archduke' Trio and the G major Violin Sonata op.96 mark a new phase of melodic expansiveness in Beethoven's music. It is true that their feeling of breadth and relaxation is one that is largely shared by the Violin Concerto of 1806, and by the 'Pastoral' Symphony composed some three years before the trio, but the two chamber works have a deliberate avoidance of drama and tension that is rare in Beethoven. Certainly, in its review of the violin sonata, the *Allgemeine musikalische Zeitung* breathed a barely concealed sigh of relief:

> It almost seems as though in his latest works this great master were returning to the melodious, and (on the whole) the more or less cheerful. This would probably be very much to the wishes and the satisfaction of all his friends and admirers – first of all because it is precisely artists of *his* kind, as has always

---

[11] Ibid., p.377.
[12] See Kagan, *Archduke Rudolph*, p.32.
[13] Ibid., pp.152ff.
[14] BGA no.1686; Anderson no.1203.
[15] BGA no.1756.

been the case, who express their innermost feelings in their works, and one would therefore deduce that the admirable Beethoven is himself now content, friendly and cheerful; secondly, on account of the refreshing effect of the works themselves on the spirit; and last, for the sake of those who have taken him as an ideal, and since then.... have so often been plunged by his works into a gloomy, melancholy, or wild and even painful mood, and would now surely find their way with him to more cheerful climes.[16]

If posterity has linked the Archduke's name with op.97, rather than with any of Beethoven's other works dedicated to him, it may be on account of the grandeur of its conception, and the breadth and nobility of its opening theme:

Ex. 11.1. Beethoven. Piano Trio in B flat, op.97 (i) bars 1–40.

—(continued)

[16] AMZ, 13 (26 March 1817), cols.228–9.

Ex. 11.1—*continued*

The subtle entrance of the stringed instruments at the end of the sixth bar, their outline echoing the shape of the piano's phrase that has immediately preceded it, not only lends weight to the crescendo culminating on the forceful dominant chords that round off the theme's initial statement, it also binds the texture together in preparation for the interpolated phrases for cello and violin with which Beethoven separates the first half of the theme from its counterstatement beginning in bar 14. But the most startling event of the opening page is perhaps the sudden *pianissimo*, accompanied by diminished seventh harmony, that occurs in bar 21. Beethoven's autograph shows that he initially based the first bar of the left-hand piano part here around the chord of F minor, thinking, perhaps, that he would reserve the diminished seventh harmony for the entry of the right hand in the following bar. The premature appearance of diminished harmony in the familiar version is of magical effect, and it announces a passage of hushed mystery which effectively destroys any semblance of regularity that has been established thus far, while at the same time necessitating a subsequent emphatic reaffirmation of the tonic which leaves the listener in no doubt of the broad canvas on which the design is to unfold. Beethoven has a further reason for the threefold cadences into the tonic, each more emphatic than the last, which occur between bars 30 and 33: their insistence enhances the surprise of the sudden change in tonal direction two bars later – the start of the preparation for a second group which is to unfold in the mediant (G major).

Such an affirmation of the tonic at the parallel point in the recapitulation would have been superfluous, since the second group occurs in B flat major from the outset. Nevertheless, Beethoven fleetingly passes through the shadow of the subdominant minor in bar 208, just as he had done in bars 23–4 (the conflict between subdominant major and minor is to be renewed in the coda), while, by a wonderful inspiration, the lyrical dialogue for violin and cello which had earlier separated the theme from its counterstatement is transformed in the recapitulation into a series of sweeping arpeggios which are prolonged to form an accompaniment to the counterstatement itself.

In its repeated-note pattern and its stress on the chord of the supertonic, the second subject is a distant cousin of the main subject in the opening movement of Beethoven's Fourth Piano Concerto, while the cello's prolongation of the melody at bar 60, with its stepwise ascent through the interval of a fourth, clearly echoes the shape of the first subject's third and fourth bars.

Following a continuation of the rocking figure in triplets that brings the exposition to a close, the development section is entirely built out of the two elements that form the first subject's initial four bars: the sinuous opening phrase, and its rising scale-like continuation. The two ideas are explored in turn, and both the breadth of Beethoven's brushstrokes and the unusually calm atmosphere of the music at this stage of the piece may be seen if we compare the following passage based on the theme's initial bar with part of the coda from the 'Ghost' Trio's opening Allegro. For all the marked difference in their function within the plan of the movement as a whole, the two passages are remarkably similar. The 'Ghost' Trio's coda, however, acts as a calm resolution of a piece whose development section, in particular, has been both tense and tautly sprung, while in the similar passage as it appears in the development section of the 'Archduke' only the music's off-beat accents combined with the comparative brevity of its canonic phrase-lengths provide a hint of its position within the large-scale design:

Ex. 11.2.
(a) Beethoven. Piano Trio in B flat, op.97 (i) bars 115–25.

Ex. 11.2.
(b) Beethoven. Piano Trio in D, op.70 no.1 (i) bars 254–61.

The seamless dissolve between the 'Archduke' Trio's development section and recapitulation is symptomatic of the unusual relaxation of the development as a whole. Certainly, the moment is far removed from the type of dramatic gesture with which Beethoven so often liked to mark the arrival of this moment, though the opening movement of the 'Spring' Sonata op.24 provides a precedent, and one in which the join is similarly effected through the use of a trill or tremolando.[17]

The long build-up towards the recapitulation finds the music poised on the dominant of C minor (bars 146ff.). This hushed moment, with the pizzicato stringed instruments playing the first subject's rising scale figure while the piano interjects trills derived from its penultimate bar, belongs among Beethoven's profound inspirations, and it provides one of his most memorable uses of pizzicato since the opening movement of the 'Harp' String Quartet op.74. Following the pizzicato passage, the melodic outline of the first subject's opening bar returns, its intervals progressively contracting until they form a static trill. This is one of the many moments from the piece (they include the first subject itself) which Schubert seems to have remembered when he came to write the opening movement of his late B flat Sonata D.960. Schubert even echoes Beethoven's use of the flattened sixth degree of the scale – G flat – though in his case the shadow of that note had been there from the

[17] See pp.179–80.

outset, in the shape of a distantly menacing trill punctuating the two halves of his chorale-like main theme.

For the only time in one of his four-movement chamber works with piano, Beethoven places the scherzo before the slow movement. The sequence arises not only out of the purely practical consideration that the slow movement is to be joined to the finale, but also as a result of the unusually relaxed nature of the opening movement. Even so, the scherzo has the simplest and most unclouded of opening sections, and it reserves its symphonic tension for the position where we might least have expected it – in the alternating trio section, which presents a chromatic and mysterious fugato. Not for nothing did Beethoven copy out passages from Bach's 'Chromatic Fantasy and Fugue' BWV 903 while he was sketching his ideas for the op.97 Trio.[18]

This is one of Beethoven's enlarged scherzo designs, with the trio section played twice, between three statements of the scherzo itself. The composer's intentions in this respect were made absolutely clear in his instructions to his copyist Wenzel Schlemmer, and were respected in Steiner's first edition of 1816, which printed all 729 bars of the movement in full. That Beethoven's five-part scherzo designs were regarded by this time as quite normal is shown by a review of the op.97 Trio which appeared in April 1817, in the Austrian edition of the *Allgemeine musikalische Zeitung*: 'After the now usual written-out repeat of both movements [i.e. both sections of the scherzo], the composer ends with a humorous coda written in the spirit of the scherzo, which contributes not a little to re-establishing the cheerfulness that had been to a certain extent suspended in the lugubrious trio.'[19] However, the scherzo as given in Breitkopf's first collected edition of Beethoven's works issued in the early 1860s appeared with the large-scale repeat indicated but not written out, and all subsequent printings before the Bärenreiter edition of 2022 edited by Jonathan Del Mar have followed suit. The repeat indications make it all too easy for players to abridge Beethoven's large-scale design, whose observance is essential for maintaining the balanced proportions of the work as a whole.

In the last of his six string quartets op.76, Haydn based the trio of his minuet movement on no more than a series of ascending and descending scales. Beethoven does not attempt to emulate the *tour de force* of harmonic inventiveness with which Haydn rings the changes on his straightforward textbook material, but his scherzo theme consists of little other than a similar ascending scale – invested, it is true, with rather more rhythmic interest. With striking originality, Beethoven scores the entire first statement of the scherzo's opening half for the two stringed instruments alone, before the quasi-repeat transfers the theme to the piano, with a pizzicato accompaniment that continues through the start of what may be regarded as the scherzo's second half. The sprung rhythm of the movement's solo cello beginning may remind us of the similarly scored opening, on one note, of the second movement of the 'Razumovsky' Quartet op.59 no.1; but here it is the contrast between the carefree rising scale of its beginning and the tortuous chromatic ascent, necessarily more

---

[18] See Nottebohm, *Zweite Beethoveniana*, p.286, and Ong, 'Beethoven's "Archduke" Trio', pp.142–3.

[19] AMZÖ, 1, no.16 (17 April 1817), cols.127–8.

confined, of its trio section that lies at the heart of the piece. Only in the scherzo's last two bars does Beethoven wittily invest his ascending scale with a hint of the chromaticism that is immediately to follow.

The trio section's chromatic fugato is heard in its full form only on its first appearance, where the thematic entries occur at intervals of eight bars. On its much abbreviated first return, the fugato is heard in inversion, with the entries at two-bar intervals, while the fleeting final reprise has overlapping entries no more than a single bar apart. The appearances of the fugato are punctuated by three explosive outbursts featuring a waltz-like idea played *fortissimo* by the pianist, its fourth and fifth bars even more fully scored than the corresponding first two bars. ('Like night after day the cheerful scherzo is followed by a dark *alternativo* in B flat minor which is also laid out fugally, and in which the striking modulations … stand out like a dazzling Northern light, sharp and strident' was the description in the Austrian *Allgemeine musikalische Zeitung*.[20]) On its first occurrence the waltz idea is heard in D flat major, while on its second it appears, via an enharmonic change, in E major – the most remote point from the tonic. The prolonged excursion into that key anticipates the appearance of E major in the coda of the slow movement, and may even make a gesture towards preparing the listener, however subliminally, for the sudden plunge into A major at the start of the finale's coda. After such an intervention, it takes a sustained crescendo over a dominant pedal to prepare the ground for the final return of the waltz theme in B flat major, and thence for the reprise of the scherzo.

The coda is based almost entirely on the oscillating B flat/C flat of the quasi-trio's beginning, prolonged into an almost obsessively repeated Neapolitan cadence. Its function is to resolve the tension generated by the trio, but it nevertheless maintains a brooding atmosphere almost until the end, where the mood is lifted with a *pianissimo* reprise of the scherzo's initial four bars. Their phrases, now wittily alternating between cello and violin, are followed by an ascending scale pecked out in a rhythmically neutral form by the piano, until the final two bars form a peremptory *fortissimo* reinforced by double octaves from the pianist.

The D major slow movement is one of Beethoven's profound sets of variations, and one that seems to peer forwards across the decades to the variation movements found in his late piano sonatas and string quartets. The broad, hymn-like theme breathes a serenity that foreshadows the atmosphere of those later pieces; and in view of the fact that its stress seems to fall on the second beat of the 3/4 bar, it has often been pointed out that the melody has the character of a sarabande.[21] In this respect it anticipates the variation theme of the Piano Sonata op.109. The melody is of utmost simplicity and symmetry, and like so many of Beethoven's inspirations in his later years it is entirely made up of phrases that move by stepwise progression. The isolated figure in dotted rhythm with which it culminates (bar 23) traces a motif that is to be expounded upon at length in the movement's coda. Moreover, while the theme's first half has a full varied repeat which amplifies its sonority, the quasi-repeat

---

[20] *Ibid.*, col.127.

[21] See *inter alia* Schering, *Beethoven und die Dichtung*, p.438; Bockholdt, 'Zum Andante cantabile des Trios op.97 und seiner Stellung im Werkganzen', p.189; Kinderman, *Beethoven*, p.174.

of the second half is restricted to its last four bars. The immediate restatement of its concluding phrase that results from this compression effectively undermines the theme's symmetry, giving the impression that its second half has merely been expanded from eight bars to twelve. At the same time, the emphasis is thrown onto both the subdominant chord that forms the apex of the theme's second half, and the all-important dotted rhythm that follows it.

One striking aspect of the variations is their continuity. Gone are the sharply differentiated, individually numbered variations of the kind Beethoven had used until as recently as the finale of the 'Harp' Quartet op.74, of 1809, and in their place is a more open-ended form in which each variation leads seamlessly into the next. The notion is one that Beethoven was to explore further in the finale of the op.96 Violin Sonata – indeed, of his later variation sets forming a movement within a larger design, only the finale of the Sonata op.109 reverts to a more sectionalised form, with individually numbered variations. In the 'Archduke', the sighing phrase with which the stringed instruments make their first entrance not only joins the theme to the more sonorous written-out repeat of its first section, it also returns to form a postlude to each of the melody's halves, and thereby provides a natural link between the theme and the first variation.

The variations themselves show a progressive diminution in note-values – from quaver triplets, through semiquavers, to semiquaver triplets – until, in the fourth variation, the arrival of demisemiquavers necessitates a broadening of the tempo. In a characteristic paradox, this last and most intricate variation is at the same time the most serene, with the rippling left-hand piano part forming an accompaniment to a floating, syncopated melody in the right hand. Of the intervening variations, the first maintains the notion of texturally enriched repeats: the harmonic skeleton of the theme's first half is traced by the widely spaced piano part that has the player's hands moving in contrary motion, while the cello, *sotto voce*, interjects the dotted rhythm from the theme's penultimate bar; and the sonority of both keyboard and strings is amplified in the quasi-repeat (the cello now joined by the violin at the octave above). Variation 2 consists effectively of three variations rolled into one: a dialogue between the two stringed instruments with a chordal accompaniment from the piano gives way to a quasi-repeat which unfurls a delicate single line in which the alternating violin and cello are doubled at the octave below by the piano, while the theme's second half is represented by a smoother, expressive idea, again in dialogue between cello and violin. The throbbing repeated chords of the third variation introduce an element of disquietude which serves to enhance the effect of the slower variation that follows.

The ornate fourth variation is followed by a return to the original tempo, and to a literal echo of the theme's opening phrase. The shift in tonal direction that now follows is a surprise of overwhelming effect, the more so since there has been no intervening variation in the minor.[22] The change appears momentarily to be no more than a switch from major to minor, but the melody's second phrase cadences onto the dominant of F, and its latter half, with its halting phrases and its groping towards more distant tonal areas, opens up new vistas. Eventually, the music reaches the

---

[22] The effect is not dissimilar from that of the change to C major in the closing stages of the A major variation movement of the String Quartet op.131, where, again, there has been no preceding variation in the tonic minor.

realms of E major, without ever quite settling there, and a splendid expansion of the dotted-rhythm idea from the theme's penultimate bar ensues. It is a moment in which the music appears to be holding its breath, as the pulsating piano accompaniment to the strings' long-drawn phrases takes it through the regions of B minor and E minor, before a vastly expanded dominant preparation allows it at last to alight on the home key of D major. At this point, Beethoven introduces a soaring new melody (bars 172ff.) derived from the theme's initial phrase, first in dialogue between the two stringed instruments, and then in a repeated-note triplet figuration on the piano. Beethoven's autograph shows him even at this late stage making a significant alteration to the music's shape and proportions. A three-bar extension to the strings' melody was deleted, allowing the piano to enter immediately with its decorated version in triplets of the same melody. At the same time, the scope of the triplets was expanded, from a somewhat blunt four bars to six bars, following which, at bar 184, a series of panting two-note phrases – also a new inspiration – introduces a moment of choked emotion before the violin enters with a rising melody that seems designed to draw the piece to a profoundly calm conclusion. However, and for all its profound sense of inevitability in its context, the closing phrase turns out to be an anticipation in slow motion of the genial theme of the rondo finale, which follows without a pause. The link is effected not only melodically, but also harmonically: as the slow movement sinks to a close, Beethoven adds a quiet dominant seventh chord in the key of E flat, the chord on which the rondo theme sets off, not in the tonic, but in the subdominant – or, more accurately, on the dominant of the subdominant. (The transition is similar to the join between slow movement and scherzo in the op.96 Violin Sonata, which is carried out by means of a similar flattened seventh chord.) The rondo's E flat major leanings are intensified by a central episode that begins firmly in that key (bars 110ff.), and – more strikingly – by a full reprise of the first episode's syncopated material in E flat at bar 206.

The fact that the slow movement and finale are joined together has a bearing on the design of the rondo – as though elements of the Andante's variation form were lingering on. Already, each half of the rondo theme is divided into statement and ornate variation, with the elaboration of the theme's second half extended from eight bars to nine to allow room for a crescendo that launches the first episode. Both the extension and the crescendo are vastly amplified at the tail end of the first reprise of the rondo theme, in order to prepare the ground for the *fortissimo* start of the E flat central episode.

The coda (bars 254ff.) brings with it not only an increase in tempo and a metrical change from 2/4 time to 6/8, but also two fully-fledged variations of the theme, the first of them in a very distant A major – if not the actual key of the slow movement, then at least its close relative. A change in metre of this kind is a common characteristic of late eighteenth- and early nineteenth-century variation form, and one that had been invoked on occasion by Mozart in a non-variation context in order to create a similar ambiguity of structure: the finale of the Piano Concerto K.449 is a case in point. At the same time, following the second of his 6/8 variations, Beethoven manages to combine his metrically altered version of the rondo theme with the darker harmony of the first episode (bars 324–31); and since he had earlier brought triplet motion into play in the elaborations of his rondo theme, the coda is able to quote them more or less intact, and at what is in effect much the same speed.

Ex. 11.3.
(a) Beethoven. Piano Trio in B flat, op.97 (iv) bars 30–5.

(b) Bars 372–81.

A touching postscript to the 'Archduke' Trio is formed by a little Allegretto for piano trio in the same key of B flat (WoO 39) which Beethoven composed in June 1812, shortly before he left Vienna for the Bohemian spa town of Teplitz. It was in Teplitz barely more than a week later that he penned his famous letter to his 'Immortal Beloved', and a possible candidate for its intended recipient (the letter was never sent, and was found among Beethoven's papers after his death) is Antonie Brentano, to whom Beethoven was later to inscribe his 'Diabelli' Variations op.120. It was for Antonie's daughter Maximiliane that he wrote his miniature trio movement, and the dedication reads: 'To my little friend Maxe Brentano, to encourage her in pianoforte playing.' Maximiliane was ten years old at the time, and Beethoven helpfully wrote in the fingerings of the piano part for her. His encouragement seems to have paid off: eight years later he inscribed his Sonata op.109 to her, presumably in the hope that she would be able to play it. At one stage Beethoven had intended to dedicate his last two sonatas to Antonie Brentano. On 18 February 1823 he wrote to the Paris publisher Maurice Schlesinger, telling him that she was to be the dedicatee of op.111.[23] At more or less the same time he instructed Ferdinand Ries, who was by then living in London, to ensure that the English edition, published shortly afterwards by Clementi, should carry the same dedication. Clementi's edition duly appeared as Beethoven requested, but the composer seems to have forgotten that some six months earlier he had told Schlesinger the sonata was to be inscribed to Archduke Rudolph.[24] Whether or not Schlesinger, thinking, perhaps, that an Imperial dedication would be more advantageous to his publishing house, deliberately overlooked Beethoven's change of heart, his edition bore the Archduke's name. In the same letter Beethoven declared that the A flat Sonata op.110 was to be dedicated to one of his friends. This may well have been Antonie Brentano, but he did not make his intentions clear, and the sonata was issued without a dedication. Perhaps it was in compensation for his failure to ensure that Brentano's name appeared on the original edition of either op.110 or op.111 that Beethoven subsequently dedicated his 'Diabelli' Variations op.120 to her. The 'Arietta' variation theme of op.111's valedictory second movement is like some transcendental echo of Diabelli's waltz-tune (Beethoven had composed a substantial portion of the 'Diabelli' Variations before he turned his attention to the sonata); and when, in the last of Beethoven's thirty-three variations, that tune is transformed into a sublimated minuet, complete with delicate tracery at the top of the keyboard, we seem to hear a nostalgic recollection of the sonata Antonie Brentano failed so narrowly to acquire.

The Allegretto of 1812 is a piece of ingenuous charm, and beautifully scored for piano trio. The rising and falling opening piano theme, with its gently throbbing left-hand chordal accompaniment, is lent added resonance by the sustained sound of simple tonic and dominant triads from the strings, while the miniature exposition's second subject traces a similar shape, albeit in a more transparent

---

[23] BGA no.1572; Anderson no.1140.
[24] Letter of 31 August 1822. BGA no.1491; Anderson no.1095.

texture. Rather than continue his experiments with mediant keys within the exposition itself, Beethoven postpones the idea, and allows the development section to unfold for the greater part of its length in D major instead, and makes the appropriate change in key signature. Following a recapitulation of enriched sonority, he adds a lingering coda that actually exceeds the recapitulation in length. It comes to an end in a haze of nostalgia, with the main theme unfolding against a chain of rising chromatic scales from the piano. The piece belongs to the select rank of masterpieces written for beginners, and as such, in the piano trio literature, is a worthy companion to Mozart's G major Trio K.564, with its conspicuously simple finale.

The true companion to the 'Archduke' is, however, not the B flat Allegretto for piano trio, but the G major Violin Sonata op.96. The stimulus behind this last of Beethoven's sonatas for piano and violin was the visit to Vienna in December 1812 of the celebrated French player Pierre Rode. Beethoven appears to have composed the sonata in a short space of time prior to its scheduled first performance, by Rode and Archduke Rudolph, on 29 December. The almost complete lack of sketches for the opening movement has led to speculation that this portion of the work may be somewhat earlier in origin than the remainder; but the surviving material in the 'Petter' sketchbook for the last three movements is itself scanty, and it is likely that several leaves of the book have been lost.[25] What is certain is that Beethoven hesitated for some while before hitting on an appropriate style for the sonata's finale. A few days before the premiere at Prince Lobkowitz's palace, he told Archduke Rudolph:

> The copyist will be able to begin on the last movement tomorrow very early in the morning. As I am myself in the meantime writing several other works,[26] I did not hurry over the last movement merely for the sake of punctuality, the more so as I had to write it with more consideration in respect of the playing of Rode. In our finales we like to have more resounding [*rauschendere*] passages, but this does not mean anything to R., and it did hinder me somewhat.[27]

Gustav Nottebohm was the first to point out the relationship between the variation theme of Beethoven's finale and a tune from Johann Adam Hiller's operetta *Der lustige Schuster, oder Der Teufel ist los*, of 1766.[28] The first phrase, it is true, is similar, but for all the folk-like simplicity of Beethoven's theme the differences between the two are of greater significance than any superficial resemblance they may bear. All the same, Beethoven was clearly short of time when it came to

---

[25] See Johnson, Tyson and Winter, *The Beethoven Sketchbooks*, pp.45 and 207–19. Also, Nottebohm, *Beethoveniana*, pp.26–30.

[26] The Seventh and Eighth Symphonies were completed around the same time.

[27] BGA no.606; Anderson no.392.

[28] Nottebohm, *Beethoveniana*, p.30. The song is quoted in full in Obelkevich, 'The Growth of a Musical Idea, p.92.

writing the sonata's finale, and, as already mentioned in connection with the op.69 Cello Sonata, he did have recourse to a pre-existing idea. A sketch leaf dating from late 1807 and early 1808 containing material for the 'Choral Fantasy' op.80 and the setting of Goethe's 'Kennst du das Land?' op.75 no.1 has an accurate rendition of what was to become the upper line of the piano part in bars 58–61 of op.69's finale. Immediately following this is an idea for a theme in A major with cello accompaniment, suggesting that Beethoven may initially have thought of bringing the op.69 Sonata to a close with a set of variations. The theme clearly looks forward to the finale of op.96:[29]

Ex. 11.4. Beethoven. Violin Sonata in G, op.96. Finale theme (sketch).

Beethoven's mention of Rode's aversion to 'more resounding' passages may have been prompted by the fact that the violinist was renowned for the intimacy of his performance style, but there is no shortage of virtuoso flamboyance in the finales of his own concertos. Beethoven could have had in mind the *pianissimo calando* conclusion of what was one of Rode's best-known pieces, the 'Air varié' in G major, op.10. One of the few forceful passages Beethoven did allow himself in his finale occurs at the start of the Allegro coda. It is a moment that bears a distant kinship to the final variation in Rode's set. (Rode's original is for violin with string trio, but the piece circulated from an early date in an arrangement for violin and piano.)

---

[29] The theme is reproduced in Obelkevich, p.91, though without drawing attention to its probable connection with the op.69 Sonata. See Johnson, Tyson and Winter, *The Beethoven Sketchbooks*, p.164, and Brandenburg, 'Bemerkungen zu Beethovens op.96', pp.22–3. The example, quoted in Ex.11.4, is also given in Brandenburg's 'Die Skizzen zu Beethovens Cellosonate op.69', p.210.

Ex. 11.5.
(a) Rode. Air varié, op.10.

(b) Beethoven. Violin Sonata in G, op.96 (iv) bars 181–8.

Whatever the source of Beethoven's assumptions about Rode's musical taste, by the time of the premiere of the op.96 Sonata the French violinist's career was clearly in decline, and his performance of the new work seems to have caused general disappointment. Louis Spohr was present at Rode's concerto appearance just a week later, and testified:

> On the strength of his European fame he had chosen Vienna's largest concert hall, the big Redoutensaal, and found it quite full. I waited in almost feverish excitement for the start of Rode's playing, which ten years earlier had served me as the highest model. But already after the first solo it seemed to me that Rode at this period had regressed. I now found his playing cold and mannered, missed his former boldness in overcoming great difficulties, and felt particularly dissatisfied with the execution of cantabile .... In the performance of the E major Variations, which I had already heard Rode play ten years earlier, I was utterly convinced that he had lost his technical security; for not only had he simplified several of the most difficult sections, he played even those passages he had made easier hesitantly and unsurely. The audience seemed unsatisfied, too; at least, he did not seem able to generate any enthusiasm.[30]

On 7 January 1813, Rode and Archduke Rudolph gave a repeat performance of Beethoven's new sonata. Rudolph had asked Beethoven to supervise a further rehearsal in advance of the performance. 'If Rhode [*sic*] perhaps wants the violin part to play through', Rudolph suggested, 'let me know, so that I can send it to him; also, if and when you can come to me tomorrow.'[31] The request provoked a sarcastic reply from Beethoven:

> Concerning Rode, if Y.I.H. will only be so gracious as to send me the part by the bearer of this letter, then I will send it on to him immediately with a *billet doux* from myself. He will certainly not take it amiss that I send him the part, alas! Most certainly not! Would to God that there were reasons to beg his pardon for doing so; for in that case, things would indeed be in a better state.[32]

Whether or not Beethoven made alterations to the violin part prior to the sonata's second performance is something that cannot be ascertained, but his surviving autograph of the work, dating in all likelihood from 1815, almost certainly represents a revision. Even at that late stage Beethoven was making changes, in particular to the development section of the opening movement, and the Adagio variation of the finale. (The latter contains numerous corrections that offer evidence of the trouble Beethoven experienced in arriving at a definitive version.) When the sonata was published by S.A. Steiner in July 1816, it significantly bore a dedication not to Rode, but to Archduke Rudolph.

The op.96 Sonata has one of Beethoven's most quietly arresting beginnings: a gentle unaccompanied violin phrase set in motion with a rustling trill. The phrase is immediately reiterated by the piano, before the theme's second half moves towards

---

[30] Spohr, *Selbstbiographie*, p.177.
[31] BGA no.614; LTB no.168.
[32] BGA no.615; Anderson no.402.

the subdominant, where the arching arpeggio figure of the fourth and fifth bars gives rise to a vast expansion which leaves the music unresolved, providing an early indication of both the breadth of its canvas, and its atmosphere of stillness. It is a moment not so much static, as quietly ecstatic.

Ex. 11.6. Beethoven. Violin Sonata in G, op.96 (i) bars 1–30.

The military-style dotted rhythm of the second group's opening subject is followed by a smoothly flowing idea in the flat submediant (B flat) which clearly recalls the first subject's thematic shape; and the resolution back into D major that is signalled in bar 62 is withheld, in favour of a second interrupted cadence, and an unfolding of the same material, now surmounted by a halo of trills.

Ex. 11.7. Beethoven. Violin Sonata in G, op.96 (i) bars 59–77.

The manner in which the exposition's tonal range is expanded through the use of the flat submediant recalls the similar scheme found in Beethoven's Violin Concerto and his Triple Concerto – where, however, far from creating an effect of enhanced serenity, the introduction of the new key functions as a dramatic surprise. (Beethoven is likely to have learned the idea from the interrupted cadences in the opening movement of Mozart's G major Piano Concerto K.453.) The op.96 Sonata is, indeed, relaxed enough to approach its interrupted cadence via a ritardando that minimises its shock value; but the parallel 'flat' key is insisted upon at some length in the recapitulation, where it provides the first appearance of what is to be the sonata's important secondary key of E flat major.

The closing subject again manifests a firm determination to maintain a sense of floating continuity through a deliberate elision of cadence points. The music here oscillates around the repeated interval of the minor second, almost akin to a broadened form of the sonata's initial trill, and the same idea continues into the development section, where the music is left suspended on the dominant of B flat minor. Beethoven's autograph score shows that at bar 101 he planned to insert an extended passage based on the sonata's opening subject, its initial phrase descending sequentially on the piano from the treble to the bass, before being answered by the violin.[33] This may have been deleted because it was both harmonically and rhythmically too well defined, and detracted from the music's feeling of timeless suspension. Instead, the idea was transferred to the coda (in another passage about which Beethoven had second thoughts), leaving the development section as it stands to be entirely based on the material of the exposition's closing stage – most of it in effect little more than a preparation for the return of the trill which, in a moment of remarkable stasis not so dissimilar to the parallel juncture in the 'Archduke' Trio, marks the start of the recapitulation. The moment is signalled by an anticipation of the return of the first subject, whose upbeat trill is passed back and forth between the two players in isolated repetition, with the piano's trills accompanied by left-hand pizzicatos on the open G string.

It is at least in part the uneventful nature of the development section that enables Beethoven to introduce a substantial and startling interpolation in the recapitulation after a mere eight bars. For Beethoven to move into a mediant key for the start of the recapitulation's second group, mirroring a similar event in the exposition, is, as we have seen, by no means unusual. Nor is it rare to find him seeking ways of expanding the recapitulation's tonal scope at a relatively early stage. But to include a lengthy and stable passage in the flat submediant so near the beginning of the recapitulation, and thereby seriously to undermine the newly re-established tonic key, is a highly unorthodox gesture; and the interpolation is the more remarkable given the fact that less than thirty bars later the second group is to return to E flat major, in echo of the exposition's similar tonal excursion at the parallel point. It is true that the 'Ghost' Trio's first movement had included a passage on the flat submediant within the opening group of its

---

[33] The passage may be interpreted with some degree of certainty as being in B flat major, and ending with the start of an answering pattern on the violin, on the dominant of that key.

recapitulation, and that Beethoven was to continue his experiments in the use of a similar key at an early stage of the recapitulation with the 'Hammerklavier' Sonata (where there is additionally a still more startling plunge into the flat supertonic minor, as a means of renewing the B flat major/B minor conflict that forms such an important element of the work's design); but what remains unique about the op.96 Sonata's recapitulation is the deliberately static nature of the E flat passage that unfolds so soon after the onset of this stage of the piece. The music here is harmonically even more non-eventful than the passage from the exposition which it echoes, since its arching arpeggios are so firmly anchored in the new key. The tonal emphasis at this point can be explained only in the context of the sonata's remaining movements, in all three of which E flat acts either as the tonic, or as an important secondary key.

Perhaps in view of his radical departure at the start of the recapitulation, Beethoven allows the remainder of the reprise to follow the pattern of the exposition closely. Only with the coda does he make a gesture towards resolving the gently undulating E flat arpeggios of bars 152–6. The coda begins with a series of diminished seventh arpeggios on the piano, beneath which the sonata's opening phrase, complete with its trill, appears in dialogue between the violin and piano, in a chromatically rising sequence that sees the phrase progressively foreshortened, until it forms the springboard for a cadenza-like passage in semiquavers. The figuration of this moment (bars 260–1) moves inexorably towards an apotheosis of the trill, and Beethoven's autograph shows the passage to have been largely an afterthought: the diminished seventh arpeggio of bar 247 was to have resolved onto a dominant seventh in the following bar, and thence to the tonic arpeggio of bar 259. Having eliminated a developmental passage based on the first subject from the movement's central section, Beethoven may have decided to insert it here as a means of drawing together the threads of a piece that is unusually contemplative in nature. Following the piano's quasi-cadenza, the music winds down once more, until the final bars at last resolve the subdominant arpeggios that had been so notably left in suspension near the beginning of the movement (bars 10–12), in a firm tonic cadence.

The slow movement is a fine example of Beethoven's ability to create and maintain an atmosphere of rapt intensity. Its distant cousin is the Adagio of the 'Pathétique' Sonata op.13, which similarly offers a serene melody unfolding above a smooth accompaniment in semiquavers; but that earlier piece contains nothing that can compare with the inspired manner in which the Adagio of op.96 prolongs the piano's dying phrase at the point where the violin enters, fusing it with a reiteration of the accompaniment's inner-voice rocking figure, until a moment of complete stasis is reached:

Ex. 11.8. Beethoven. Violin Sonata in G, op.96 (ii) bars 1–11.

In place of any restatement of the melody, the violin now launches on a floating new theme, while the piano, taking up both the syncopated rhythm and the falling major third of the new melody's upbeat phrase, accompanies with sighing, almost sobbing, phrases. Slowly, we are drawn towards the subdominant, and, once we are there, the piano quietly introduces a new murmuring accompaniment in demisemiquavers. Passing through the shadows of F minor and E flat minor, the music eventually settles on the dominant, where it remains in absolute repose for four very long bars, while the violin, in echo of its ornate earlier melody, has a series of increasingly elaborate phrases revolving around the keynote of the dominant, but striving ever further upwards, until the apex of a phrase is reached from which the music can pass seamlessly into a reprise of the opening theme.

The reprise reverses the roles of the two instruments, the violin taking over the opening theme before the piano responds with an ornamented version of the melody's continuation, its delicate tracery reflecting the lingering influence of the middle section. The theme, however, is cut short, and its sighing two-note phrases are transferred from violin to piano as the music passes into the coda. This last section unfolds throughout over a tonic pedal, and the music is spacious enough to allow it to go through the same extended harmonic sequence no fewer than four times: a dissonant flattened seventh (D flat) gravitating towards the subdominant minor. The reason for the stress on the flattened seventh becomes apparent in the closing bars: as the music subsides towards an ending formed out of a reiterated tonic chord, and a final *pianissimo* tremolando from the piano, the violin adds a postscript – the aural equivalent of the D flat that has run through the coda, now enharmonically notated as C sharp, so that it can form part of an augmented sixth chord in the scherzo's key of G minor. The dissonance in the final bar implies, of course, a continuation; but the ending of the movement has otherwise been so conclusive that it comes as a profound surprise. Not until the music of the succeeding generation of composers could a piece be allowed to end with such a question mark – though whether Schumann had Beethoven's example in mind in composing 'Warum?' from his *Kinderszenen*, and whether Chopin was similarly inspired to compose a similarly interrogative ending to the F major Prelude from his op.28 series is, of course, impossible to know.

The join between the inner movements of op.96 is made possible only by the expedient of writing the scherzo in the tonic minor. It is an idea of breathtaking simplicity and originality, with the resolution of the Adagio's inconclusive ending effected in the first bar of the subject presented at the start of the scherzo. The scherzo itself is of utmost symmetry and brevity: two eight-bar halves, each with a written-out repeat in which the theme passes from piano to violin. The music's jagged style and its continually displaced accents are counterbalanced by the smooth lyricism of the ländler-like trio, whose melodic similarity to the third movement of Mahler's 'Resurrection' Symphony has been noted.[34] The trio's second half takes the form of a simple three-part round, producing a result that is harmonically as static as the coda of the slow movement had been; and since the trio's key is also E flat major, the reprise of the scherzo brings with it what is in effect a renewal of the transition between slow movement and scherzo.[35] The scherzo also has a coda, in which Beethoven, as though tacitly acknowledging that his scherzo ought perhaps by rights to have been in the major, wittily transmutes its opening half into G major. At the same time, the coda, ending with a high-spirited trill from the violinist, provides a bridge to the finale.

Beethoven's earliest sketches for the theme of the sonata's variation finale lack the switch to the mediant in the melody's second half that lends the definitive version so much of its distinctive character. The theme's final harmonic shape is already fully formed in a fair copy housed at the Paris Bibliothèque nationale.[36] Here, however,

---

[34] See Osmond-Smith, *Playing On Words*, pp.41–2.

[35] Significantly, Beethoven's autograph score adds the direction that following the trio the reprise of the scherzo was to be written out in full. His instruction was carried out in Steiner's first edition.

[36] Collection Malherbe, MS 60. Reproduced in Obelkevich, 'The Growth of a Musical Idea', pp.98–9. Obelkevich's assertion that the theme's final four bars, written on a separate sheet, represent a less finished draft does not bear scrutiny. The bars in question are complete, even to the extent of including the dynamic markings – crescendo in bar 29, followed by *piano* in the final bar – that were carried over to Beethoven's definitive version.

the bass line, with its regular crotchet motion, is metronomic and stiff, and the melodic line of the theme's second half is unsatisfactory – not only as evinced in the ungainly shape of bars 19 and 21, but also the inelegant repetition of the ascending fourth, F sharp to B natural, in bars 17 and 18. The melodic A sharp at the start of bar 17 in the theme's definitive form provides a surprise of considerably greater effect.

Ex. 11.9. Beethoven. Violin Sonata in G, op.96 (iv), bars 1–32, sketch.

—(continued)

Ex. 11.9—*continued*

Beethoven also decided to 'verticalise' the violin accompaniment, perhaps because he felt that the pervasive semiquaver figure robbed the music of its essential poise at this early stage, and would have detracted from the effect of the murmuring semiquavers that run uninterruptedly through the third variation. Their elimination from the piano part during the theme's quasi-repeats posed the question of how the keyboard was to accompany the violin at these moments. Beethoven's solution was as simple as it was unconventional: the piano's repeats are literal as far as the right-hand part is concerned, and the melody is reinforced by the violin, which doubles it at the octave below. Finally, we may note how Beethoven substitutes a rising scale figure for the static minim of the preliminary version's eighth bar. The figure fills in the rising fourth which is the theme's most prominent melodic interval, and its reappearance on the violin in the last bar forms a natural link to the first variation.

Ex. 11.10. Beethoven. Violin Sonata in G, op.96 (iv) bars 1–32.

—(continued)

Ex. 11.10—*continued*

    The first two variations show a strikingly unvaried repetition of phrase lengths and rhythmic figuration. Variation 1, the only portion of the movement to feature literal repeats, places the emphasis consistently on the second beat of the bar through a relentless use of hairpin dynamics, while the second variation is no less persistent about reverting to a first-beat stress. The squared-off articulation of the first two variations meets its obverse side in variation 3. Not that the new variation is any less regular – it features a constant pattern of semiquavers in the piano's left-hand accompaniment – but the shadowy, syncopated melodic line running through it imparts an atmosphere of mystery that is rudely shattered by the almost comically abrupt chords thrown from one instrument to the other in variation 4.

    With the fifth variation we reach the movement's expressive heart: an ornate Adagio in 6/8 time, and a close relative of the similar piece found in both the 'Eroica' and the 'Diabelli' Variations. Since those independent variation sets are on a far larger scale, Beethoven can afford to be correspondingly more expansive in his treatment of the material at the parallel point. To have taken the repeats into consideration in the design of the Adagio variation of op.96's finale would have risked unbalancing the proportions of what is a much more compact piece. Beethoven, however, creates the illusion of having included the repeats, not only through the expansiveness of the music itself, but also by dividing the theme into segments of four bars, and giving the intricate melodic line to the players in turn. At the mid-point of each half of the variation Beethoven suspends the music's motion altogether through the insertion of a cadenza-like passage in which the outer limits of the piano's chromatic scales emphasise the sustained dominant seventh harmony that underpins them, as though seeking to exploit the instrument's overtones.

Ex. 11.11. Beethoven. Violin Sonata in G, op.96 (iv) bars 145–8.

The variation's coda, beginning at bar 159, is launched by the violin, whose initial notes, C and F sharp, mirror the range of the piano's final, expanded chromatic scale in the last bar of Ex.11.11 above. Pierre Rode's playing was known for its liberal use of portamento, and Beethoven's slurring of this widely spaced interval implies a slide between the two notes, played in sixth position on the A string, and first on the D string, respectively.[37] Beethoven's codetta concerns itself with moving, in strik-

---

[37] See Brown, 'Ferdinand David's editions of Beethoven', pp.132–3.

ingly similar fashion to the start of the first movement's recapitulation, via the tonic minor, towards the flat submediant, in which key there ensues a reprise of the start of the theme in all its original simplicity, and at its original tempo. This excursion into E flat major, short-lived as it is, sets the seal on the large-scale tonal plan of the sonata as a whole, in which this secondary key has exerted such a lasting influence.

The reprise of the theme breaks off on the dominant of E flat, whereupon Beethoven takes an oblique plunge onto the dominant of D, and thence to the home tonic for an Allegro variation with which he appears to be drawing proceedings to a close – the more so since he appends a coda that paves the way for a conclusive final cadence. However, the music is interrupted yet again, and Beethoven launches into a *pianissimo* fugato in the minor (bars 217ff.). The fugato subject itself represents what is surely one of the most remarkable thematic transformations in all Beethoven. It is one whose relationship to the original theme is easily discerned by the eye, but not so readily grasped by the ear. The subject's first three bars, albeit in the minor, trace the melodic outline of the corresponding bars of the Allegretto theme exactly (it was presumably for this reason that Beethoven did not write G sharp in the fugato's second bar to match the minor second of the successive entries, but instead maintained G natural), and there is even a nod towards the repeated Ds of the theme's second bar, in the shape of a tied note D; but the rhythmic change is so complete as to render the material all but unrecognisable.

Ex. 11.12. Beethoven. Violin Sonata in G, op.96 (iv) bars 1–4 and 217–21.

After so radical an intervention at this late point in the movement, Beethoven clearly needs to wind up the sonata by making a much closer return to his original material. At the same time, in order to lend greater excitement and rhythmic impetus to the reprise of the variation theme he now provides, he finds he can make use of the accompaniment in semiquavers which he had rejected from his early fair copy. But even at this stage the music's surprises are far from over. The final peroration takes the violin up to a cruelly exposed D^4, followed by a firm cadence into the tonic. Beethoven makes as though to repeat the procedure on the piano; but the cadence is wittily deflected onto the dominant of B major, and a mock-expressive version, played *Poco adagio*, of the theme's second half ensues. The cadence provides the clearest instance of the harmonic pun implicit in this portion of the theme, whereby the same chord can be notated in two different ways: as an augmented sixth chord in the key of B major, or as the dominant seventh of C major. (Compare bars 275–6 and 280–1 in Ex. 11.13 opposite.) The concluding eight bars in *Presto* tempo play on the repeated Ds of the theme's beginning, while at the same time recalling the rocking figure from the slow movement. The passage is one that may remind pianists of the dizzying conclusion to the F sharp major Piano Sonata op.78, though its key here makes it less awkward to play. On the other hand, the violin has a hard time of it in bars 268–71, and Beethoven's fingering – a relatively rare instance of his having proffered such advice in a passage for a stringed instrument – which has the fourth finger sliding up the fingerboard does nothing to make the moment easier to play.[38]

Ex. 11.13. Beethoven. Violin Sonata in G, op.96 (iv) bars 265–95.

—(continued)

[38] The violinist Max Rostal found Beethoven's fingering 'truly primitive, particularly since this passage is still today so risky and dangerous'. See his *Ludwig van Beethoven: Die Sonaten für Klavier und Violine*, p.172.

Ex. 11.13—continued

In their breadth and originality, the op.96 Sonata and the 'Archduke' Trio surpass all Beethoven's previous works in their respective genres. With them, he marked the end of an era in his creative output. His next chamber works, the two cello sonatas op.102, which followed after a gap of more than two years, were to find him on the threshold of his late style.

12

Works of 1815–16

At the end of the year 1812 Beethoven could look back on a remarkably productive decade that had seen him compose an array of large-scale masterpieces including the Third to Eighth Symphonies, the last two piano concertos, the Violin Concerto and the Triple Concerto, the string quartets opp.59, 74 and 95, two versions of the opera *Leonore*, and the Mass in C. In the two-and-a-half years that followed the completion of the Seventh and Eighth Symphonies, and the culmination of his serene manner marked by the 'Archduke' Trio and the op.96 Violin Sonata, Beethoven experienced a comparatively lean period in his output. Much of this time was taken up with the final revision of his opera, and with occasional pieces such as *Wellingtons Sieg* (the so-called 'Battle Symphony'), the cantata *Der glorreiche Augenblick*, the *Namensfeier* Overture, and the choral setting of Goethe's *Meeres Stille und glückliche Fahrt*. The only new work of real significance to emerge was the highly concentrated two-movement Piano Sonata op.90. It is possible that in the wake of the 'Immortal Beloved' letter of the summer of 1812 Beethoven experienced some form of mid-life crisis, as well as a prolonged period of depression. His state of mind is reflected in some of his diary entries from the end of 1812 and the early summer of 1813: 'You should not be a human being [*Mensch*], not for yourself, only for others; for you there is no longer any happiness except in yourself, in your art. O God! Give me strength to conquer myself, nothing at all must fetter me to life.'[1] For once we may be inclined to believe Schindler when he relates that 'according to information communicated to the author by [the piano maker] Andreas Streicher and his wife, who were especially close friends of our master at this time, Beethoven's state of mind was at a low ebb such as had not been witnessed since the difficult year of 1803'.[2]

Beethoven's fallow period between 1812 and 1815 is, however, also likely to have resulted from a process of re-evaluation, and a determination to push his style ever forwards in a new way, as though impelled by historical imperative. More than a decade later Beethoven remarked to Karl Holz of his late string quartets opp.127, 130 and 132, 'Art demands of us that we shall not stand still. You will find a new manner of voice treatment, and thank God there is less lack of imagination than ever before.'[3] Beethoven's re-emergence into the full flood of creativity was gradual – the years

---

[1] Solomon, *Beethovens Tagebuch*, pp.38–9. See also Solomon, 'Beethoven's Tagebuch of 1812–1818', pp.193–285.
[2] Schindler, vol.1, p.185.
[3] Lenz, *Beethoven, eine Kunststudie*, vol.5, p.217.

1815–17 saw him compose only the two cello sonatas op.102, the Piano Sonata op.101 and the song cycle *An die ferne Geliebte* – but it was marked by a reawakened interest in the Baroque discipline of the fugue, and in new approaches to cyclic form.

The first fruits of Beethoven's new manner were avowedly experimental, and the autograph score of the C major Cello Sonata op.102 no.1 describes the work as a 'free sonata'. The unorthodox design of both op.102 sonatas was a feature that perplexed the anonymous reviewer of the *Allgemeine musikalische Zeitung*, who complained: 'These two sonatas are quite certainly among the most unusual and strangest that have been written for piano for a long time, not only in this form, but altogether. Everything here is different, utterly different from what we have had even from this master himself. May he, however, not take it amiss if we add that not a little of it, as it stands here, and as it is ordered, laid out and organised, is shaped *so that* it will indeed appear unusual, very strange.'[4]

In view of the music's complexity, Simrock's first edition of the two op.102 sonatas published them in score – an unusual procedure for the time, particularly in Germany. These were not quite Beethoven's first works to appear in this form: as has already been mentioned, in 1816 the London publisher Robert Birchall issued the op.96 Violin Sonata in a similar format, with the violin part printed in a smaller size above that of the piano. It is possible that the new format for op.102 had been requested by Beethoven, though it was not followed in the Viennese edition published some two years later by Artaria.

The novel manner in which the op.102 sonatas were first issued was praised by the same *Allgemeine musikalische Zeitung*'s reviewer, who commented that 'the performance for both players would have been far harder if the perceptive publisher had not had the cello part placed throughout in small notes on special lines above the piano; as a result of which, comprehensibility and that unity of spirit are greatly simplified'.[5] Unlike the op.96 Sonata, op.102 was considered too esoteric for the English market. Charles Neate, who met Beethoven on several occasions in the summer of 1815 at his lodgings in Baden, was entrusted by the composer with the task of finding an English publisher for the sonatas, but he had to report back from London on 29 October of the following year: 'I have offered your Sonatas to a printer, but they say they are too difficult and would not be saleable, and consequently make offers, such as I cannot accept, but when I shall have played them to a few professors, their reputation will naturally be encreased by their merits, and I hope to have better offers.'[6]

The C major Sonata op.102 no.1 was by no means Beethoven's first work to explore notions of cyclic form – there had already been, for instance, the famous example of the Fifth Symphony, with its reprise of part of the scherzo during the course of the finale serving to underline the work's organic unity;[7] and the Sonata *quasi una*

---

4   AMZ, 45 (11 Nov. 1818), col.792.
5   Ibid., col.794.
6   BGA no.987; LTB no.234.
7   Haydn, who seems to have anticipated most of the nineteenth century's formal innovations, introduced a return of the minuet during the course of the finale in his B major symphony no.46.

fantasia op.27 no.1, in which a fragment from the slow movement returns shortly before the close of the finale. Those instances are nothing if not strikingly original, but they arise out of a design in which the relevant movements form a linked pair. The reappearance of the material of its very beginning at a much later stage of a work in discrete movements, as in the case of the C major cello sonata, creates an open-ended design on a broader scale.[8] At one stage, however, Beethoven had intended to have the sonata performed without a break: its first Allegro is followed in the autograph score by the direction 'Atacca' [*sic*], to which the words 'il seguente' were added in pencil. Beethoven clearly changed his mind about this, because he deleted the instruction from the engraver's score prepared by the copyist Wenzel Rampl. Rampl's copy bears ample corrections in Beethoven's hand, and must therefore be regarded as the primary source for op.102.[9] In the year following the op.102 sonatas, Beethoven wrote two further works in cyclic form: *An die ferne Geliebte*, which is circular enough for its first phrase also to be its last (as had also been the case in the C major Mass of 1807); and the Piano Sonata op.101, in which the return of the opening material occupies much the same position within the work's formal design as it does in the first of the two cello sonatas.[10] The influence of Beethoven's innovation, particularly as exemplified by the song cycle, on composers of the later nineteenth century can hardly be overestimated.

Of more lasting effect on the music of Beethoven's own final years was his new-found enthusiasm for the fugue. The fugal finale of the Sonata op.102 no.2 is the forerunner of the similar finales found in the 'Hammerklavier' Sonata and the Sonata op.110, as well as the String Quartet op.130 in its original form; and important fugal passages are to be found in the piano sonatas opp.101, 109 and 111. If we add to these the fugues of the 'Diabelli' Variations, the Ninth Symphony and the *Missa solemnis*, as well as the fact that the opening movement of the String Quartet op.131 is a fugue, and that the Ninth Symphony's scherzo is based on a subject Beethoven had earlier planned to elaborate in the form of a string quintet fugue in D minor, it is clear that the composer's reawakened interest in Baroque contrapuntal techniques around 1815 had an influence on his style that was as far-reaching as Mozart's discovery of Bach and Handel had been on his music more than three decades earlier. Although Beethoven's pieces are so clearly rooted in the past, the fugues of the Sonata op.102 no.2, the 'Hammerklavier' Sonata and the String Quartet op.130 are among the most uncompromisingly difficult and intractable pieces he ever composed.

---

[8] For a discussion of the question of recall in opp.101 and 102, see Sisman, 'Memory and Invention at the Threshold of Beethoven's Late Style', pp.51–87.

[9] See Del Mar, Critical Commentary to *Beethoven, Sonatas for Violoncello and Piano*, pp.51–6.

[10] Charles Rosen (*The Classical Style*, p.508) drew attention to parallels between op.102 no.1 and op.101. Both begin with a lyrical movement in 6/8, followed by a forceful march; and both have an elaborate slow movement leading to a reminiscence of the work's beginning, and finally to an exuberant finale. Despite such similarities in overall design, however, the cello sonata's hesitant, fragmentary opening section is very different in effect from the unending melody of op.101's self-contained first movement; and the two marches are strongly contrasted in both form and character.

The second of the op.102 sonatas was hardly the earliest work by a great composer to contain a finale in the form of a fugue. Three of Haydn's string quartets op.20 end with a fugue, as does his F sharp minor Quartet op.50 no.4. (Haydn's experiments in this direction may have been stimulated by the similar pieces found in many of the string quartets of the Viennese violinist and composer Carlo d'Ordoñez.) When, later in life, Haydn drew up his own catalogue of works, he placed the three quartets having a fugal finale at the head of the op.20 set, in ascending order of the number of subjects on which the fugue was based – a crescendo of contrapuntal ingenuity which assigns the finale of the C major Quartet op.20 no.2, with its quadruple fugue, a position as the culmination of the first half of the series. Unlike Haydn, Mozart did not regard a self-contained fugue as a viable component of large-scale symphonic form.[11] Mozart's greatest feats in absorbing contrapuntal textures into his symphonic style were the finales of the String Quartet K.387 and the 'Jupiter' Symphony K.551, both of which place passages of learned counterpoint alongside others of tongue-in-cheek simplicity, in a sublime juxtaposition carried out within the clear confines of a sonata form; but there is also the marginally less spectacular rondo from the Piano Concerto K.459. Beethoven was clearly inspired by the example of Mozart's string quartet when he came to write the finale of his C major 'Razumovsky' Quartet op.59 no.3.

Schindler's assertion that the finale of the Sonata op.102 no.2 was Beethoven's response to criticisms that he was incapable of writing a fugue can hardly be taken seriously.[12] It is true, however, that Beethoven had not produced a piece of the kind since the 'Eroica' Variations op.35 and the 'Cum Sancto spiritu' and 'Et vitam venturi' settings of the C major Mass op.86. In the 'Eroica' Variations, as in the later 'Diabelli' set op.120, the fugue forms the climax, but not the culmination of the work: both have an ending of deliberate understatement in which the music winds down – in the 'Eroica' Variations, to a transfigured *contredanse*; in the 'Diabelli', to a sublimated minuet. Beethoven's great achievement in his late fugal finales was to invest the form with a radically new style in which any sense of archaism was confined to the music's texture, and had little bearing on its substance. Of Beethoven's late fugue subjects, only those in the 'Gloria' of the *Missa solemnis*, and in the Piano Sonata op.110 and String Quartet op.131 may be said to invoke the manner of Bach. The remainder are wholly individual and forward-looking, and, in the cases of the Cello Sonata op.102 no.2 and the 'Diabelli' Variations, downright humorous in character.

Beethoven's sketches for various fugue subjects around the time of the two op.102 sonatas contain a marginal note indicating that one of the structural ideas underlying the pieces was to be the use of dynamic contrasts: 'Bei allen Fugen piano u. forte'.[13] The note may also show Beethoven's determination to produce a type of fugue very different from those found in the finales of Haydn's op.20 quartets. Until their concluding bars, those pieces are played *sotto voce* throughout – Haydn's method of ensuring that the players were able to hear each other in such complex

---

[11] Mozart's Violin Sonata K.402 consists of an Adagio in A major followed by an incomplete fugue in A minor, though whether the work was intended as an isolated prelude and fugue, or as the start of a projected sonata, is not known.

[12] Schindler, vol.1, p.245.

[13] See Nottebohm, *Zweite Beethoveniana*, p.319.

textures. In that respect, Haydn's fugal finales are as different as could be imagined from Beethoven's quartet fugue op.133, where the players shout at each other in an unrelieved *fortissimo* throughout the long opening stage of the piece. On the other hand, the finale of Beethoven's Cello Sonata op.102 no.2 is much more transparently scored, and its witty 'tripping' fugue subject is largely played in a delicate staccato.

Beethoven's preliminary plans for the op.102 cello sonatas show that it was not only the last movement of the second work in the pair that was initially conceived as a fugue. A sketch for the finale of the C major Sonata contained in the 'Mendelssohn 1' pocket book shows its main theme in the form of a fugue subject:[14]

Ex. 12.1. Beethoven. Cello Sonata in C, op.102 no.1, sketch.

It is possible, however, that Beethoven contemplated making use of his sketch not at the start of the movement, but for a fugal passage in its development section, in much the same way as he was to do in the finale of the Piano Sonata op.101. Another leaf of the same sketchbook contains plans for further fugues, one of which was clearly at the back of Beethoven's mind when he came to write the opening movement of the second of the op.102 sonatas.[15] (Compare last two bars of Ex. 12.2 with Ex. 12.6 on p.340.)

Ex. 12.2. Beethoven. Cello Sonata in D, op.102 no.2, sketch.

The typically Baroque figuration of the second half of that idea was to make its reappearance in the fugue subject of the 'Hammerklavier' Sonata's finale; and to have the figure sounded simultaneously with its own inversion is the easiest thing in the world, as Beethoven demonstrates not only at the lead-in to the recapitulation in the first movement of op.102 no.2, but also in the closing stages of the 'Hammerklavier' Sonata's fugue.

In its design consisting of two quick sonata-form movements each prefaced by a slow introduction, the C major Sonata op.102 no.1 is unique in Beethoven.[16] The function of the return of the sonata's initial material during the course of the second slow introduction is largely to reaffirm the home key after the radical

---

[14] *Ibid.*, p.316.

[15] *Ibid.*, p.319.

[16] Elaine Sisman ('Memory and Invention', p.59) questions whether the opening pages of op.102 no.1 constitute an introduction, or a first movement proper. However, the improvisatory nature of this slow beginning, together with the absence of any modulation, make it difficult to adhere to the latter interpretation of its function within the work as a whole.

departure of the first half of a work whose Allegro is not in the tonic, but its relative minor (A minor). Moreover, the absence of the sound of the work's home tonic in the first Allegro is assured by the rejection of the relative major key, C major, for its second group, which is located instead – as it is in the op.23 Violin Sonata and the 'Kreutzer' op.47 – in the dominant minor. Only during the opening bars of the development section does Beethoven momentarily present his first subject in C major, as though to acknowledge that this was the key in which the listener would have expected the movement as a whole to be written. As far as the choice of key for the exposition's second stage is concerned, Beethoven's later works in the minor tend in any case increasingly to avoid the relative major for their second subject, and to choose instead either the dominant minor (in addition to op.102 no.1 there is the case of the Piano Sonata op.90), or, as in the string quartets opp.95 and 132, the Piano Sonata op.111 and the Ninth Symphony, the submediant.

The drastic expedient of writing the main Allegro in a key other than the work's home tonality is one for which there can have been few, if any, precedents. According to Karl Holz, to whom the Beethoven played his ideas through on the piano, his tenth symphony was to have begun with a gentle Andante in E flat major, followed by a forceful Allegro in C minor,[17] but it was otherwise left to later nineteenth-century composers, among them Chopin and Schumann, to carry the exploration of 'progressive' tonal schemes of the kind manifested in the initial pair of movements of Beethoven's cello sonata a step further. The scheme of Beethoven's work is, however, mirrored in the C major Fantasy D.934 for violin and piano of Schubert, whose introduction is followed by a full-scale Allegretto in A minor. Moreover, like Beethoven, Schubert brings back the material of his introduction at a much later stage in the work.

The introduction to the first of the op.102 sonatas is of a curiously mosaic-like construction, and its contrapuntal intensity is symptomatic of the unusually compressed nature of the sonata as a whole. When the piano enters at the tail end of the cello's quiet unaccompanied beginning – an opening not dissimilar in both effect and actual material to that of the Piano Trio op.70 no.2 – it is with an inversion of the cello's initial phrase, after which the pianist proceeds to play the individual components of the cello's material in more or less reverse order. The latter half of the fifth bar expands the ascending leap of the opening bars' important motif in semiquavers, from a fifth to a minor seventh, thereby anticipating the prominent presence of the latter interval in bars 9–15. At the same time, the motif is stopped in its tracks by a fermata which robs it of its characteristic repeated-note rhythm, and transforms the concluding note of the bar into an upbeat to the return of the opening phrase:

---

[17] Cf. Thayer/Forbes, p.986; see also Cooper, *The Beethoven Compendium*, p.277.

Ex. 12.3. Beethoven. Cello Sonata in C, op.102 no.1 (i) bars 1–22.

—(continued)

Ex. 12.3—continued

Since his Allegro is to be in a foreign key, Beethoven is careful to centre the opening Andante entirely around the tonic, and the lack of any significant modulation combined with the absence of firm tonic cadences serves to underline the music's introductory function. Beethoven's means of intensifying the reprise of the opening material at bar 17 is to have it played against the background of a sustained trill. As the Andante sinks to a close with a series of C major arpeggios deep in the bass of the piano, the cello plays a rising fourth, G–C, answered in the following bar by a falling fifth an octave lower. The ascending fourth is taken over at the start of the Allegro, though that tenuous connection does little to lessen the shock of the advent of the new movement, with its tense, march-like theme played *fortissimo* in double octaves laced with *sforzando* accents. The contrast is overwhelming, and there is little to link the Allegro's first twelve bars with what has gone before. They are followed, however, by the only passage in this ferocious movement to invoke an *espressivo* marking (the same direction occurs at the parallel point in the recapitulation), and it is here, with the music moving towards the dominant minor for the second group, that Beethoven introduces an unmistakable recall of the introduction's material. Not only does the cello play the falling phrase from the latter half of the Andante's second bar, but the piano superimposes a descending four-note scale in echo of the sonata's initial phrase, so that the underlying unity of the two starkly opposed, but clearly linked, pieces is assured.

Ex. 12.4. Beethoven. Cello Sonata in C, op.102 no.1 (i) bars 25–43.

—(continued)

Ex. 12.4—*continued*

The Allegro's closing group offers further evidence of Beethoven's determination to bind together the sonata's seemingly heterogeneous elements. Here (bars 68ff.), the cello reiterates the ascending four-note scale from the Andante's first and second bars, but in the dactylic rhythm it will assume as the main subject of the finale.

The development section is as compressed as it is austere: barely more than twenty bars, the majority of them concerning themselves with exploring the first subject's staccato figure in sharply dotted rhythm, which is now heard in an ominously transparent, widely spaced texture. But that figure as it appears in the first subject has an unexpected pendant – a sudden drop in dynamic level from *fortissimo* to *piano*, as the players give out a mysterious rising minor third in sustained minims, and in bare octaves. It is this that gives rise to the hushed chorale-like passage in unadorned minims that acts as the springboard for the development section's closing moments (bars 90ff.). It is a characteristically Beethovenian gesture at this juncture, and the passage forcibly recalls the parallel point in the opening movement of the op.69 Sonata. It is followed by a crescendo over a full-blooded tremolo on the piano, while the cello intones the first subject's initial bars in the subdominant minor (D minor). This, in turn, serves to launch an intensified recapitulation (bars 98ff.) in which the subject's initial ascending phrase is played in canon, and the mysterious rising third is woven into the music's texture, the integration being achieved by means of a smooth descending line in the pianist's right hand.

The tremolos from the development section's closing moments make an electrifying return in the coda, confined this time to the pianist's left hand while the first subject's jagged staccato figure tumbles down from on high in the right hand. The coda's intensity and its extreme compression (it occupies a mere ten bars) lend the music a palpable sense of urgency, and a dramatic impact of considerable force.

Since the function of the sonata's second slow introduction is at least in part to act as a bridge between the two Allegros, its range in terms of tonal events and expressive intensity can afford to be wider than that of the opening Andante. In order to accommodate the more ornate nature of the music, the tempo during the first nine bars is slower, too – Adagio, as opposed to the previous Andante. Nevertheless, the opening bars clearly recall the sonata's beginning: the three-note phrase in broad dotted rhythm in the latter half of the first bar derives unmistakably from the Andante's beginning, and even the pitch at which the motif is heard is the same. The second bar inverts the texture, and in so doing emphasises the two main notes, G and A, around which these opening moments revolve. (The same two notes are heard in diminution at the start of the right hand's intricate flurries in the first two bars.) It is, too, these notes that Beethoven incorporates into the return of the Andante at bar 10, thereby managing at a stroke to fuse the material of the two slow introductions.

The Adagio's third bar introduces an angular motif which passes from the cello to the piano's accompaniment, and in so doing allows Beethoven to develop an altogether more sinister atmosphere, taking the music through the dominant of D minor, and eventually alighting in the seventh bar on the dominant of C minor. The angular figure gives the impression of being entirely new, but it has its source in the agitated fifth and sixth bars of the first Allegro's main subject, which are given out above a dominant pedal. (See Ex. 12.4 above.) The intensity of this passage, which at its climax has the cello itself playing in octaves, is remarkable; and so, too, is the music's re-emergence into the light of the major at bar 7, with a further variant of the sonata's beginning, marked *teneramente* – the same indication as is found over the cello part in the sonata's opening bar. The sweetly lyrical theme which unfolds here has much the same effect as the new melody introduced near the close of the slow movement in the second of the op.102 sonatas. Its concentration on the characteristic three-note figure from the latter half of the Adagio's opening bar is so great – it is heard no fewer than five times in bars 7–9 – that Beethoven omits the phrase altogether from the reprise of the sonata's opening Andante that follows, even though it had originally formed an integral part of that earlier portion of the work.

That the finale's subject grew out of the sonata's initial phrase for solo cello (or perhaps vice versa, since the sketch of the finale's theme in the guise of a fugue subject appears to predate Beethoven's conception of the remainder of the work) is indicated by the transition between the second slow introduction and the finale itself, where the two ideas appear in direct juxtaposition. The piano's entry in the *Allegro vivace* is simply an accelerated form of the cello's ascending phrase heard two bars earlier:

Ex. 12.5. Beethoven. Cello Sonata in C, op.102 no.1 (ii) bars 15–18.

The finale begins hesitantly, as though the players were reluctant to break the spell. The hesitation was at least in part a late addition: the Allegro's third and fourth bars are not found in Beethoven's autograph, and were added by him to Rampl's manuscript copy. The idea of setting the finale in motion in a halting manner like this is one that Beethoven was able to take up again, with more obviously humorous intent, in the second of the op.102 sonatas. In the C major work the pauses that separate the finale's initial phrases serve to isolate, and thus to throw into relief, this fragment of the main subject which so clearly derives from the germinal motif presented in the sonata's very first bar. Rather than cast his finale in the guise of a fugue, as he was to do in the second of the op.102 sonatas, Beethoven uses his subject as the basis of a sonata form with a contrapuntal development section. (He was to subject a similar theme to altogether Handelian treatment some seven years later, in the C major overture *Die Weihe des Hauses*, op.124.) Virtually the entire piece is governed by the subject's melodic shape, with its stepwise ascent through the interval of the perfect fourth, and its characteristic rhythm. The start of the second group (bars 47ff.) presents essentially the same subject in inversion and augmentation – while the exposition's closing moments (bars 70–3) revert to the original rhythm, at the same time maintaining the inverted melodic shape.

The start of the development section presents a gruffly humorous echo of the finale's faltering beginning. Three times, the cello plays a bare fifth (its pitch descends each time by a third, reflecting the internal construction of the first subject itself), while the piano interjects a tiny snatch of the same subject. The cello makes as though to join the piano in unison, but is too slow off the mark: its delayed entries lag behind those of the piano by half a beat, producing a grotesquely out-of-phase effect. Finally, on the third occasion, the cello sustains its fifth, while the piano calmly enters with a 'correct' contrapuntal version of the phrase. (At the start of the recapitulation the piano presents the same fragment of the first subject in a more tightly knit *stretto*, as though in mocking demonstration of how the cello could have made sense of the development's beginning.)

Beethoven goes through much the same procedure at the beginning of the coda, this time expanding the final appearance of the bare fifth on the notes D flat and A flat to vast proportions, to form a Neapolitan pedal underpinning the piano's *stretto* treatment of the subject. Its resolution onto the cello's two lowest open strings produces what may well be the most blatant pair of parallel fifths Beethoven ever wrote, though it sounds unerringly right in its context.

The sonata's closing bars abandon counterpoint altogether and have the subject quietly played in reassuring octaves, as though Beethoven were anxious to resolve the work's conflicts with a conclusion of childlike simplicity, while at the same renewing in startling fashion the juxtaposition of opposites that lies at the heart of its large-scale design. The final flurry of semiquavers, given out in octaves by both players, throws into relief the three-note figure from the sonata's second bar at its original pitch, on the notes G-F-D.

The D major Sonata op.102 no.2 is altogether more conventionally shaped than its companion, even going so far as to contain a full-scale slow movement – Beethoven's only such piece for piano and cello. Like the first Allegro of the C major Sonata, the opening movement is highly condensed, with an exposition scarcely exceeding fifty bars. Yet within that restricted framework Beethoven presents an almost bewildering proliferation of contrasting material: not only a first subject consisting of two strongly opposed ideas, but also an important subsidiary theme at the approach to the second group, moving from B minor (Beethoven's 'black key', as indicated in his sketches for the fugal finale) to the dominant of A. In addition, the second group (bars 29ff.) itself contains two subjects.

The first subject's initial bars, with their long-held accented note falling on the weak second beat of the common-time bar, generate a spring coil of tension that is released in the burst of semiquaver activity of the third bar, while the cello's entry with a rising phrase beginning *forte* and ending in an expressive *piano*, bridges the gap between the imperious opening bars and the calm lyrical idea that unfolds from the fifth bar onwards.[18] Altogether, this opening paragraph reflects the tension and release that lie at the heart of the Allegro, and whose elements Beethoven fuses into so richly satisfying a whole.

---

[18] The last quaver of the cello part in bar 7, familiar as a D from so many performances of the sonata, is unclear in Beethoven's autograph. Wenzel Rampl's copy read it as D, and his mistake was overlooked by Beethoven. Rampl's misreading was duly transferred to Simrock's first edition, and to the large majority of subsequent printings throughout the nineteenth and twentieth centuries. However, an additional set of manuscript parts copied by Rampl for Archduke Rudolph in 1816 (i.e. prior to the sonata's appearance in print) has C sharp here; and a copy of Simrock's edition with a few corrections in Beethoven's hand bears a marginal comment indicating that the note in question is C sharp, and that the mistake was 'ein Böcklein aus S[imrocks] Stall' (see Rosenthal, 'Ein Böcklein aus dem Stall', pp.229–38). The pun is untranslatable, though the meaning is 'a small blunder from Simrock's stable'. The C sharp reading, which perhaps allows the player greater expressive flexibility between bars 7 and 8, is to be found in one of Beethoven's sketches for the first subject, quoted in Nottebohm's *Zweite Beethoveniana* (p.325), and it was adopted in Artaria's second edition of January 1819.

Ex. 12.6. Beethoven. Cello Sonata in D, op.102 no.2 (i) bars 1–18.

Having presented so variegated a tapestry of material in the exposition, Beethoven concentrates in the latter portion of the development section largely on the subsidiary theme from the transition to the exposition's second group, making much out of its figure in minims, with their arpeggio-like grace notes (bars 25–8). Moving through the realms of C major and minor (bars 64ff.), the development reaches a moment of hushed intensity poised on the dominant of G minor, before Beethoven unleashes a torrent of semiquavers whose cumulative energy continues right through to the start of the recapitulation, where the first subject's long-held notes are now filled in, with the all-important octave leaps stressed through strategically placed accents. The music's momentum seems unstoppable, but Beethoven abruptly arrests the cascade of semiquavers by cutting to a reminiscence of the *dolce* phrase from the exposition's fifth bar. The recapitulation as a whole, indeed, leaves a curiously telescoped impression, each recall of ideas from the exposition appearing before the last has had time to run its course. Notably absent is the grace-note figure which had been so amply explored in the development section. In all, the recapitulation reduces the scope of the exposition by very nearly one third – a remarkable reversal of the corresponding proportions in the opening movement of the Piano Trio op.70 no.1 and the finale of op.70 no.2.

The condensed nature of the recapitulation throws increased weight on the coda (bars 126ff.), where for the only time in the movement the initial subject appears in *fortissimo* octaves, and on both instruments. This time the five-note rhythmic figure is hurled out not just twice, on tonic and supertonic, but three times: on tonic, subdominant and dominant. The last occurrence is reinforced by a full-blooded dominant seventh chord and a fermata, after which a calm statement of the second group's rising theme is followed by the movement's most prolonged moment of hushed stillness: a mysterious sequence of tremolos creating an atmosphere of a kind Beethoven more commonly reserved for the closing moments of a development section. The tremolos begin on the dominant of F sharp, and pass through the distant region of the flat supertonic, before a final cascade of the first subject's semiquavers generates a forceful ending.

The D minor *Adagio con molto sentimento d'affetto* is the last of Beethoven's four tragic slow movements in this dark key. Its companions also carry unusually evocative tempo markings indicating the intensity of their expression: *Largo e mesto* in the Piano Sonata op.10 no.3, *Adagio affettuoso ed appassionato* in the String Quartet op.18 no.1, and *Largo assai e espressivo* in the Piano Trio op.70 no.1. A review by Adolf Bernhard Marx in the Berlin *Allgemeine musikalische Zeitung* of an 1824 edition of the op.102 sonatas (in which the order of the two works was reversed) described the Adagio of the D major sonata as sustaining a 'gloomy feeling, almost of weariness and sickness, which is agreeably interrupted by an episode in D major which does not, however, bring as much comfort as its beginning would lead one to think'.[19] Certainly, it is a piece that shows a progressive increase in poignancy, from its dark,

---

[19] BAMZ, 48 (1 Dec. 1824), p.409. Robin Wallace (*Beethoven's Critics*) ascribes this and other reviews in the BAMZ to a colleague of Marx, on the grounds that they are signed with the initials 'v. d. O...r'. However, the abbreviation is likely to indicate 'von dem Oberredakteur' (by the editor-in-chief – i.e. Marx).

chorale-like opening theme (where the cello is heard above a piano accompaniment restricted to the instrument's low register throughout), through the warmly lyrical D major middle section, to the coda, in which the cello introduces a new bitter-sweet melody of infinite tenderness. The new melody bears a distant kinship with the start of the movement's middle section, whose initial ascending scale figure eventually reveals itself as an anticipation of the finale's fugue subject.

This is a piece which demonstrates Beethoven's ability to wring a remarkable degree of expressive contrast out of the simple change from minor to major. For Beethoven to write a work all of whose movements are in the same tonality is in itself not at all unusual; but on top of that, to eschew tonal contrast within one of those movements is a remarkable procedure. To Marx, the Adagio's lack of a secondary key-area proved a stumbling block: 'For four pages this Adagio moves in a strange way only through D minor and major. Is this perhaps the reason why, despite the fact that he finds individual moments infinitely beautiful, the piece as a whole has not endeared itself to the reviewer to the same degree as other movements by his celebrated and admired favourite composer?'[20]

Despite the lack of any change in tonality, the unstable nature of the slow movement's opening theme, coupled with a concentration on the dominant minor (A minor) during its continuation, makes the music's emergence into the light of D major for the middle section – *pace* Marx – an overwhelming experience. Each of the two-bar phrases that make up the brooding opening theme is separated from the next by a rest, as though the music were stifled with emotion – a feeling that is strengthened by the narrow compass of the melody itself. Furthermore, the theme gives the impression of beginning in midstream, with each of its short phrase modulating – the first of them coming to rest on the relative major, and the last on the dominant minor. Now, the piano begins an ornate, deeply tragic theme setting off in A minor. Its turn-like figuration, its overwhelming sense of weariness so aptly commented upon by Marx, and its concentration on diminished seventh harmony make it a close cousin of the Adagio introduction to the finale of the Piano Sonata op.101, which, although much briefer, carries a similar burden of expressive weight. The new theme is underpinned by a shuddering accompanimental figure, whose rhythm is subsequently taken over by the cello (bars 13ff.). The symmetry of the new theme, with its full counterstatement which finds the two players exchanging roles, serves in retrospect to increase the introductory feel of the movement's initial eight bars.

The harmonic stability of the D major middle section, coupled with the smoothness of its unbroken accompaniment in demisemiquavers, is enough to provide an air of serene consolation, and the expansiveness of the yearning new melody comes as a breath of fresh air following the constricted atmosphere of the opening section. The cello and the piano's bass line move largely in harmonious thirds, tracing in a form of murmuring pre-echo the outline of the melody that unfolds above them. The melody is a broad one, and it passes almost imperceptibly from one instrument to the other. As it sinks gently to a close, the veil suddenly falls again. Now the chords of the gloomy chorale are thickened and chromatically enriched, and the

---

[20] BAMZ, 48 (1 Dec. 1824), p.409.

feeling of oppression is still greater than before. Paradoxically, the increased tension is achieved by a diminishing of the dynamic level – *pianissimo*, as opposed to the *mezza voce* of the movement's beginning. The pauses between the two-bar phrases are now filled in by the cello, with a sharply dotted figure whose rhythmic animation makes each of the piano's successive entries seem heavier than the last, while the shuddering accompaniment of the theme's continuation is intensified, allowing it to absorb the newly introduced dotted rhythm.

With the onset of the coda (bars 67ff.), all rhythmic activity seems momentarily to cease. Here, in an atmosphere of mystery and anticipation, Beethoven at last moves further afield: first through B flat major, and then – once the music has come to rest on the dominant of D minor – by way of a remarkable side-stepping move, to the distant realm of C sharp minor. It is a moment in which time appears to stand still, until the piano gives out a reminiscence of the ascending scale figure from the opening bar of the middle section, leading once more to the dominant of D where the music at last comes to rest.

The calm of the slow movement is broken carefully, and with the most neutral material imaginable: an ascending cello scale passing through the range of an octave, and echoed, following a pause, by the piano. It is a remarkable transition, and one that Beethoven may distantly have remembered from the famous halting introduction, also based on an ascending scale, to the finale of his First Symphony. However, the moment in the sonata was a late inspiration, added by Beethoven to his autograph score, with the comment 'diese 4 Takte gelten' (these 4 bars hold good).

The wit with which Beethoven approached the serious business of writing a fugue was again something of which the Berlin *Allgemeine musikalische Zeitung* found it difficult to approve:

> If the reviewer is to give his frank opinion, he cannot call it beautiful even after having played it through as carefully as possible, despite the fact that it is skilfully written and highly original. Perhaps years of acquaintance with it will endear it to him ... The theme is too comical for such serious treatment, and for that reason, also, the contrast with the two preceding movements is too harsh. Instead of this fugue, how we would have preferred to hear another movement, a Beethovenian finale! It is therefore to be desired that Beethoven should not so wilfully take up the fugue, since his great genius is exalted in every form.[21]

Beethoven's finale is headed *Allegro fugato* – a disclaimer from strict contrapuntal procedure perhaps less explicit than those found in the fugue of the 'Hammerklavier' Sonata (*con alcune licenze*) and the op.133 String Quartet fugue (*tantôt libre, tantôt recherchée*), but similar in intent. The piano's answer to the initial statement of the fugue subject on the cello is a tonal one, in which the alteration to the subject's shape occurs between its first two notes. As a result Beethoven sacrifices the symmetry of the ascending scale, but manages to retain the distinctive shape of the subject's second and third bars:

---

[21] BAMZ, 48 (1 Dec. 1824), p.410.

Ex. 12.7. Beethoven. Cello Sonata in D, op.102 no.2 (iii) bars 1–15.

Some years later Beethoven appears to have had a change of heart about his tonal answer, and to have considered making the melodic alteration not in the subject's first bar, but in its second, so that the initial ascending scale would be preserved intact. A sketchbook largely taken up with material for the Ninth Symphony contains an amended version of the fugue's beginning, together with the remark, 'In den Violonschellsonaten zu verbessern' (To be corrected in the violoncello sonatas).[22] In this amended version the second full bar of the piano's answer in the passage quoted above would have read not E–F sharp, but D–F sharp. Beethoven did not, however, carry his plan through to the point of indicating how, or if, the change would have affected the countersubject in this and later passages.

The exposition of Beethoven's four-part fugue is followed by a lengthy, intricate development in which both subject and countersubject undergo a process of foreshortening, with the chain of *stretto* entries reaching at times bewildering proportions. Particularly intense from this point of view is the section following the *pianissimo* presentation of the fugue's inversion. Here, the music, with its chains of parallel sixths and its insistent off-beat accents, reveals a strong kinship with the fugue of the 'Hammerklavier' Sonata.

[22] Nottebohm, *Beethoveniana*, pp.33–4.

Ex. 12.8.
(a) Beethoven. Cello Sonata in D, op.102 no.2 (iii) bars 124–42.

Ex. 12.8.
(b) Beethoven. Piano Sonata in B flat, op.106 (iv) bars 96–105.

In both op.102 no.2 and the 'Hammerklavier' the energy and complexity of the fugue are momentarily suspended by the introduction of a calm new subject in long notes which is subsequently revealed to form a countersubject to the original fugue theme, in effect giving rise to a double fugue.[23] In the cello sonata the new subject retains the initial fugue theme's characteristic falling minor seventh, while its tiny countersubject clearly inverts the figure from the theme's latter half:

Ex. 12.9. Beethoven. Cello Sonata in D, op.102 no.2 (iii) bars 143–71.

[23] Marc D. Moskovitz and R. Larry Todd (*Beethoven's Cello*, p.166) point out the similarity of this angular second theme to the fugue in A minor from Book 2 of Bach's *Well-Tempered Clavier*.

Again in common with the finale of the 'Hammerklavier', the fugue ultimately dissolves in a chain of sustained trills – in op.102 the final left-hand trill stretches for fully twenty bars – and any semblance of counterpoint is abandoned in the closing bars, which instead present a fragment of the fugue subject in emphatic octaves. Even the illusory syncopation of the cello sonata's concluding cadences is mirrored in the later work.

Ex. 12.10.
(a) Beethoven. Cello Sonata in D, op.102 no.2 (iii) bars 235–44.

(b) Beethoven Piano Sonata in B flat, op.106 (iv) bars 389–400.

Like that of the 'Hammerklavier', the fugal finale of op.102 no.2 confronts the pianist with technical difficulties of an extreme nature, and it becomes increasingly complex and dissonant as it proceeds. Not surprisingly, it is a piece that seems to have found little favour either with Beethoven's contemporaries, or, indeed, with succeeding generations. One of the few outstanding late nineteenth-century musicians to have taken the op.102 sonatas into their repertoire was Hans von Bülow, who performed them together with the cellist Bernhard Cossmann in Munich, on 7 October 1874.[24] Reviewing their concert, the *Allgemeine musikalische Zeitung* again found fault with the second sonata's fugal finale:

> At the head [of their programme] stood Beethoven's op.102: the two sonatas for piano and violoncello in C major and D major which are very seldom programmed in public. It is true that the two works do not belong among those which one could call 'grateful' in the usual sense of the word: they do without brilliant and decorative passagework, and are at times less rounded in form and less comprehensible than at others; but in their intellectual musical content they nevertheless stand above rather than below the famous A major sonata with cello op.69 ... What appealed to us less in the second sonata, the concluding fugue, is – we do not shy away from saying so – the composer's responsibility. If Beethoven had heard the effect of so lively a fugue on two such very different instruments as the piano and cello, he would himself probably not have found it entirely appropriate.[25]

The first edition of the op.102 sonatas bore no dedication, but Artaria's 1819 second edition was inscribed to Countess Erdödy. It seems, however, that Beethoven may at one stage have intended to dedicate the pieces to Charles Neate, who arrived in Vienna in May 1815 with the hope of being able to study with the great composer. At any rate, Neate's own copy of op.102 bore a dedication in Beethoven's hand, "à son ami Mr. Charles Neate". However, Beethoven was willing only to look through some of Neate's compositions, while entrusting manuscript copies of several of his own works to him in the hope that he would find English publishers for them. Neate purchased the overtures to *Die Ruinen von Athen* op.113, *König Stephan* op.117 and *Namensfeuer* op.115 on the spot, on behalf of the Philharmonic Society of London. A letter to him of 18 May 1816, written in English by another hand, but signed by Beethoven, instructed him: 'As for the Quatuor in F minor [op.95] you may sell it without delay to a printer, and signify me the day of its publication, as I am intentioned to sit it abroad here at the very day. The same you be pleased to do with the two Sonatas for Violoncello; yet with these last it needs no haste.'[26] In the collection of Beethoven's letters to Neate and to Ferdinand Ries published as one of the supplements to his English edition of Schindler's biography, Ignaz Moscheles appended a footnote apropos the op.102 sonatas, indicating that 'these were dedicated by the author to Mr. Neate'.[27] Moreover, in signing off a letter to Countess Erdödy five

---

[24] For a discussion of the critical reception of the two op.102 sonatas during the course of the nineteenth century, see Moskovitz and Todd, *Beethoven's Cello*, pp.175–92.
[25] AMZ, 13 (1 April 1874), cols.201–2.
[26] BGA no.937; Anderson no.636.
[27] Schindler, *The Life of Beethoven*, vol.2, p.237.

days before he wrote to Neate, Beethoven told her: 'there will be an alteration in the dedication of the cello sonatas, which, however, will not alter you and me.'[28]

Following the op.102 sonatas, Beethoven began formulating ideas for a piano trio in F minor – a project that was never carried through to fruition. In quoting two fragments from the composer's sketches,[29] Gustav Nottebohm was firmly of the opinion that this was the piece Beethoven had in mind when, on 1 October 1816, he offered two new works to Robert Birchall in London: 'A Grand Sonata for the pianoforte alone £40. A Trio for the piano with accomp^t. of violin and violoncello for £50.'[30] The piano sonata was clearly op.101. However, a marginal note among the sketches which reads 'Variationen aus meinem Jünglingsalter' (Variations from my younger days) may indicate that Beethoven abandoned his work on the F minor trio in order to take up the threads of a much earlier piece for piano trio.[31] In the same letter of 13 May 1816 in which he informed Countess Erdödy that he intended to dedicate his cello sonatas to someone else, Beethoven told her, 'I embrace your children and I am expressing this in a trio.' Perhaps it is more likely that the composer would have given voice to his tender feelings towards the Countess's children in a good-humoured work based on a popular tune than in a trio in F minor – a key he normally reserved for some of his darkest and most dramatic utterances; and it is by no means impossible that the trio in question was the 'Kakadu' Variations op.121a. However, the terminology Beethoven used in his letter to describe the new piece to the Countess – 'Terzett', rather than 'Trio' – also leaves open the possibility that he had a vocal piece in mind.

Beethoven's drafts for the F minor trio occupy nearly twenty pages of the 'Scheide' sketchbook of 1815–16,[32] where they follow on from ideas for the second movement of the op.101 Piano Sonata. Further material for the trio, in the shape of a fragmentary draft for its first movement in full score, is held at the Berlin State Library,[33] and there are additional leaves in the British Library (Add. MS 29997), as well as at the *Gesellschaft der Musikfreunde* in Vienna. All this material was examined in detail in articles by Nicholas Marston and William Kinderman, both coincidentally published in 2006.[34]

The surviving fragment of the F minor trio's opening movement reveals a slow introduction of 52 bars, followed by the exposition and the start of the development section of an Allegro. The introduction begins with rumblings deep in the bass of

---

[28] Letter of 13 May 1816. BGA no.934; Anderson no.633.
[29] Nottebohm, *Zweite Beethoveniana*, p.345.
[30] BGA no.982; Anderson no.662.
[31] See Tyson, 'Beethoven's "Kakadu" Variations and their English History', p.108.
[32] Princeton, New Jersey, M. 130.
[33] MS Grasnick 29.
[34] Kinderman, 'Beethoven's Unfinished Piano Trio in F minor from 1816'; and Marston, 'In the "Twilight Zone": Beethoven's Unfinished Piano Trio in F minor'. Both writers provide a complete transcription of the Berlin sketches; Marston's article additionally transcribes the relevant British Library leaves

the piano, leaving open the question as to whether the music is to be in minor or major. Above these, from the third bar onwards, the violin and cello give out a broad triadic motif in octaves which bears some kinship with the subject of Bach's *The Art of the Fugue*. Eventually, a new four-note motif in dotted rhythm is introduced by the piano, and it is this that forms the ensuing Allegro's main subject. The subject clearly holds potential as the basis for some fugal writing – a fact which renders the fragment still more tantalising in the context of the composer's preoccupation with such procedures at the time. Like that of the F minor String Quartet op.95, the piano trio's second group was to have been in D flat.

Beethoven began drafting ideas for the F minor trio's finale before he turned his attention to the first movement. Its chromatic subject was to be played in octaves, and was heralded by a brief prefatory flourish. The piece was to have been in 6/8 metre, but would also have incorporated a German dance in 3/4 time: Beethoven's sketch for the latter section bears the inscription, 'als Deutscher vom letztem Stück' (for the German dance from the last movement).[35]

In the year before his sketches for the F minor piano trio, Beethoven began work on a piano concerto in D major, composing a substantial portion of its opening movement in full score before he abandoned the project. It is always tempting when works by a major artist remain incomplete to seek an explanation in external circumstances, and in Beethoven's case illness in the latter half of the year 1816 may have played a part. On top of that, his perpetual concern for the welfare of his nephew Karl can only have increased when, following the death of his brother Karl Kaspar in November 1815, he assumed guardianship of the then nine-year-old boy. Certainly, as late as October 1816 Beethoven was still intending to finish the F minor trio: a scribbled entry of that time in the diary he maintained sporadically between 1812 and 1818 reads, 'Ar-a vorschießen kann die Sonate und Trio endigen bey Karl Medizin' (Ar[tari]a can pay in advance finish the sonata and the trio medicine at Karl's).[36] There is a mention of a piano trio in the previous diary entry, too: 'Beeilung mit dem Trio an Seine K.H. wegen 400 fl alles eiligst – im Nothfall schießt er auch vor' (Make haste with the trio for His Imperial Highness; everything most urgent regarding the 400 florins; if necessary he will pay in advance). This, however, must refer to the 'Archduke' Trio, which was about to appear in print. In the end, Beethoven may simply have felt that the material he had drafted for the F minor trio was insufficiently promising, and decided instead to press ahead with the op.101 Piano Sonata, which continued the exploration of cyclic forms already so strongly in evidence in *An die ferne Geliebte* and the first of the cello sonatas op.102.

The dating of the Variations on 'Ich bin der Schneider Kakadu' op.121a has been the subject of much debate. The only unambiguous reference to the work in Beethoven's correspondence is found in a letter to Gottfried Christoph Härtel of 19 July 1816, offering him, in addition to the sonata op.101 and various other

---

[35] See Kinderman, 'Beethoven's Unfinished Piano Trio', pp.10–11.
[36] Solomon, 'Beethoven's Tagebuch of 1812–1818', p.275. The mention of 'medicine at Karl's' is likely to refer to a minor operation the boy underwent on 18 September 1816.

works, 'Variations with an introduction and appendix [*Einleitung und Anhang*] for pianoforte, violin and violoncello on a well-known theme by Müller. They belong to my earlier compositions, yet they are not among those to be discarded.'[37] As things turned out, the variations did not see the light of day for a further eight years, when Steiner issued them as 'Adagio, Variations and Rondo' [*sic*] op.121.[38]

How much earlier than the op.101 Sonata the 'Kakadu' Variations are is impossible to establish with any certainty, though it has sometimes been assumed they belong to Beethoven's early years in Vienna, on the grounds that the Singspiel *Die Schwestern von Prag* from which their theme is taken was first produced there on 11 March 1794. It became one of the greatest successes of its two authors, the playwright and actor Joachim Perinet and the composer Wenzel Müller.[39] In the 1790s Beethoven wrote several sets of variations on tunes from popular Singspiels and operas of the day, including two for solo piano on themes from Paisiello's *La Molinara* (WoO 69 and 70), and others based on themes by Grétry (WoO 72) and Wranitzky (WoO 71). Alan Tyson suggested that the 'Kakadu' Variations, too, may have originated as a work for solo piano, and were perhaps recast for piano trio at a later date.[40] However, the piece shows similarities to the variation finale of the Clarinet Trio op.11, with its theme by Joseph Weigl: both sets are based on a Viennese song that had already achieved widespread popularity, and both exploit the various instrumental duos afforded by the ensemble involved. In each case the first variation is a piano solo, and there is a subsequent variation in the form of a duet for violin – or clarinet – and cello. (The prolongation of that duet into the succeeding variation in the 'Kakadu' set, allowing for a surprise piano entry in the variation's fourth bar, is an inspiration that has no parallel in the op.11 Trio.) The 'Kakadu' Variations carry the process to its logical conclusion, and follow the initial piano solo with duos for violin and piano, and cello and piano, respectively.

The chronology of the 'Kakadu' Variations is complicated by the existence of a letter of 27 August 1803 from Beethoven's brother Karl to Breitkopf & Härtel, offering them a set of 'variations for piano, violin and violoncello with introduction and large final piece' (*mit Introduzzion und grosem letzem* [*sic*] *Stück*).[41] This has sometimes been taken to refer to the Variations op.44, which were published the following January by Hoffmeister & Kühnel;[42] but while it is true that op.44 contains

---

[37] BGA no.950; Anderson no.642.

[38] The eventual opus number of 121a is explained by the fact that the *Opferlied* for soprano, chorus and orchestra, published in 1825 by Schott & Sons, was also assigned the opus number of 121. To add to the confusion, the early arietta *Der Kuss* appeared as op.121, too, in the spring of the same year. The *Opferlied* ultimately became known as op.121b, and *Der Kuss* as op.128.

[39] See Edelmann: 'Wenzel Müller's Lied vom "Schneider Wetz" und Beethovens Trio-Variationen op.121a', pp.76–102.

[40] Tyson, 'Beethoven's "Kakadu" Variations', p.108.

[41] BGA no.153; LTB no.66.

[42] See Schmidt-Görg, *Ludwig van Beethoven*, p.130.

a substantial coda, Karl van Beethoven's reference to an introduction cannot be reconciled with that work. His specific mention of the introduction and large-scale coda ties in much more closely with the composer's letter of July 1816 regarding the 'Kakadu' Variations, despite the different wording. The same two sections are specifically mentioned again at the head of Beethoven's autograph score of the work, and the heading was adopted on the title page of Steiner's original edition of 1824 (though not on that of the English edition which was published around the same time by Chappell & Co., where the piece was described simply as a 'Trio for Piano Forte, Violin and Violoncello').

In the absence of any reliable documentary evidence, it is tempting on purely musical grounds to ascribe the central portion of the 'Kakadu' Variations to a date around 1803, and at least the final versions of their introduction and coda to a considerably later period. It is in any case unlikely that Beethoven would have offered the work for publication in 1816, albeit unsuccessfully, without at the very least carrying out revisions. His autograph score is undated, but the type of paper on which it is written has been identified as being the same as found on the manuscripts of *An die ferne Geliebte* and the song 'Der Mann von Wort' op.99, both of which are known to have been composed in the spring of 1816.[43] The autograph of the 'Kakadu' Variations clearly represents a clean copy, but it is perhaps significant that the one section that shows evidence of substantial revision is the coda. A particularly noteworthy change concerns the piano figuration of the fugato section at bars 372–6, which was first written in quavers. The more brilliant passagework in semiquavers which represents the composer's final thoughts is given on a hand-drawn stave in the bottom margin of the page.

One aspect of the coda that rules out an origin – or at least a definitive version – as early as 1803 is the range of its keyboard part. The penultimate bar of variation 8 takes the piano up to D^4, and the coda contains two moments (bars 323–5 and 430) which continue the ascent by a further whole tone, the former of them by way of a trill on the D. The compass is wider than anything Beethoven wrote for piano before the Trio op.70 no.2, of 1808. Furthermore, the sonority of the closing pages of op.121a, with the piano ascending in rapidly moving arpeggios while the two stringed instruments give out a broad descending phrase derived from the theme itself, contains echoes of the final variation from the slow movement of the 'Archduke' Trio:

---

[43] See Schmidt-Görg, 'Die Wasserzeichen in Beethovens Notenpapieren', p.183.

Ex. 12.11.
(a) Beethoven. Variations on 'Ich bin der Schneider Kakadu', op.121a, bars 426–32.

(b) Beethoven. Piano Trio in B flat, op.97 (iii) bars 136–40.

Further stylistic evidence in support of a late date for the outer sections of op.121a is provided by the slow introduction. It is surely among the most beautiful examples of Beethoven's piano trio writing, and much of it is based on a sinuous phrase which is like a version in slow motion of the 'Archduke' Trio's famous opening theme. The introduction actually respects the keyboard compass Beethoven used up to and including the violin sonatas op.30 and the piano sonatas op.31, of 1801–2, though the absence of higher pitches does not in itself, of course, provide any evidence that Beethoven would have wanted to use the additional notes even had they been available to him. The notion of prefacing a set of variations with a substantial introduction is, in any case, so unusual for its time that it is tempting to think of the opening pages as a form of commentary on a pre-existing work. For all their air of tragedy, they transform the work as a whole into a comic masterpiece, one that deserves a place of honour alongside the 'Diabelli' Variations op.120, even if the individual variations of its central portion cannot be said to match the visionary quality and range of inventiveness of those of the late piano work.

The Singspiel *Die Schwestern von Prag* was an adaptation of a play by the Viennese comic writer Philipp Hafner entitled *Der von dreyen Schwiegersöhnen geplagte Odoardo, oder Hannswurst und Crispin, die lächerliche Schwestern von Prag* (Odoardo plagued with three sons-in-law, or Hannswurst and Crispin, the ridiculous sisters from Prague). The risqué plot involves the three suitors of young Mitzerl, and the attempts of her stepfather, Odoardo (described in the *dramatis personae* as 'a capitalist'), to prevent them from gaining access to her bedchamber. To add to the complications, Odoardo's wife, Kunegunde, is herself attracted to one of the suitors, whom she desires as her own *cicisbeo*, while Odoardo has designs on Mitzerl's chambermaid, Lorchen. In a rowdy first-act finale, Mitzerl is serenaded simultaneously, and in distinctly amateur fashion, by most of the male members of the cast in what is described as a 'horrendous sextet'. In the end, order is restored with the entrance of the nightwatchman proclaiming the midnight hour, and we may well wonder if Wagner was acquainted with this scene when he composed the second-act finale of *Die Meistersinger von Nürnberg*.

In Act Two, Odoardo declares that he won't allow Mitzerl to marry until his sister comes from Prague to decide when and how the event should take place. However, since he hasn't seen her for twenty years and is unlikely to recognise her, the tailor Krispin and the Marquis von Kletzenbrod's servant both take advantage of the situation to disguise themselves *en travesti* as the absent sister. In addition, the Marquis himself assumes the role of a doctor, supposedly in order to heal the lovesick Mitzerl, of whom he is secretly enamoured, and she is able to claim him as her bridegroom after all.

The song theme Beethoven used for his 'Kakadu' Variations is sung by Krispin, in a simple *Eintrittsarie*, of a kind more famously exemplified by Papageno's 'Der Vogelfänger bin ich ja' (Ex. 12.12: 'I am Tailor Whet and Whet, have journeyed half way round the world. From my hat to my trimmings I'm a flat-iron hero. I've just come from Eipeldau,[44] went to the toll-gate just to take a look. There they examined me minutely, as though I'd caught the plague').

---

[44] The reference to the ongoing *Briefe eines Eipeldauers* by the satirical journalist Joseph Richter would not have been lost on the public of Perinet's and Müller's day.

Following the first performances of *Die Schwestern von Prag*, Perinet's libretto went through many changes, including alterations in the names of the characters involved that saw the transmutation of the tailor Krispin into the parrot-like figure of Kakadu. The 'Wetz und Wetz' of his opening song suggests both sharpness and speed (the verb 'wetzen' means to dash), but also something rather different. In Viennese dialect, a 'Wetz' (or 'Watz') refers to an uncastrated pig,[45] and the sexual undertones of Perinet's words would not have gone unappreciated by his audience. That Müller's song was, however, still widely known with its original text is indicated by a review of Beethoven's variations which appeared as late as 1830, in the Vienna *Allgemeiner musikalischer Anzeiger*:

> The old song of the tailor Crispinus, alias 'Wetz, Wetz, Wetz', varied in a manner and style, with such spirit and daring imagination as only a master can vary. The task is certainly not easy; nor is it supposed to be, for it is in no way meant for idle dallying. Just as the principal has to be up to his task, so the two adjutants [i.e. the string players] need their man. If each of them successfully brings out and masters everything demanded of him by the genius of the composer, who always follows his own path, and never ages or repeats himself, then the triple-alliance can mutually wish itself luck. In any case, it is more than conventional *façon de parler*.[46]

Ex. 12.12. Müller. Aria, 'Ich bin der Schneider Wetz und Wetz' (*Die Schwestern von Prag*).

—(*continued*)

---

[45] See Edelmann, 'Wenzel Müller's Lied vom "Schneider Wetz" und Beethovens Trio-Variationen op.121a', p.79.

[46] *Allgemeiner musikalischer Anzeiger*, no.12 (20 March 1830), pp.47–8.

Ex. 12.12—*continued*

The four strophes of Müller's song are themselves arranged as a miniature set of variations, and in the penultimate strophe the words are no longer punctuated by a jaunty fanfare-like figure, as in Ex.12.12 above, but by an eight-note figure descending stepwise in triads through an octave whose smoothness provides a contrast to the crisp articulation of the remainder of the setting ('The needle is his be-all and end-all, and so I go on busily sewing').

Ex. 12.13. Müller. Aria, 'Ich bin der Schneider Wetz und Wetz' (*Die Schwestern von Prag*).

As we shall see, Beethoven seizes on this innocuous-sounding punctuation-mark in order to generate some altogether visionary moments in the later progress of his variations. He also transposes Müller's tune into the brighter key of G major, though not before he has presented his solemn slow introduction in the minor. The use of a substantial tragic slow introduction to herald what is no more than a simple street-song is of course an elaborate and delicious joke – one that was repeated in the twentieth century by Ernö Dohnányi, in his 'Variations on a Nursery Song'; and by Franz Schmidt, in his 'Variations on a Theme of Beethoven', again for piano and orchestra (where, however, the solo part is for the left hand only, and the theme is the less simplistic scherzo of the 'Spring' Sonata op.24). But Beethoven's introduction far transcends the spirit of parody with which it sets out, and in its genuinely tragic atmosphere it leaves any notion of mere mockery far behind.

In addition to its sinuous opening phrase, the introduction makes use of the repeated-note opening bars of Müller's tune, imbuing them with a portentous tread and an air of drama whose wit can only be appreciated in retrospect, once the cat has been let out of the bag with the theme itself. Beethoven develops this fragment from the tune into a symphonic argument of considerable breadth; and as Müller's actual theme draws nearer he intensifies it still further, with a plethora of off-beat accents, piling on the agony still more in bar 41 with a bathetic false relation between the violin's C sharp and the piano's C natural. (The effect is recalled in the last bar of the only G minor piece among the variations themselves, the *Adagio espressivo* ninth variation.)

Ex. 12.14. Beethoven. Variations on 'Ich bin der Schneider Kakadu', op.121a, bars 38–46.

Seldom can an atmosphere of gloom and foreboding have been built up to similar proportions, only to be deflated with such devastating humour. Of the variations themselves, the most comical is the sixth, which has the pianist's virtuoso flurry of broken octaves accompanied only by sarcastic, chirping acciaccaturas from the two string players. Beethoven returns to G minor not only in the penultimate variation, where the rising shape of the theme's initial phrase is transmogrified into a poignant series of harmonic suspensions between violin and cello, but also in the Presto coda. Here, the theme undergoes a rhythmic change, to 6/8 time, and the same phrase gives rise to an extended fugato. It is a powerful piece of writing in all conscience, and its function is at least in part to renew the joke perpetrated on the listener in the introduction. The harmonic outline of the Presto's final twelve bars seems deliberately to recall that of the introduction's closing moments, though Beethoven clearly has not allowed himself comparable space in which to build up a feeling of exaggerated grandeur and suspense. As a result, and in order to enable him to administer a final twist of the knife, he is constrained to bring back the original theme in a form of even greater tongue-in-cheek simplicity.[47] However, between the string players' straightforward melodic phrases in the theme's latter half, the pianist interjects a transfigured version of Beethoven's own descending scale figure, now hovering between the keys of B major and B minor, and lending the music a visionary quality of which Wenzel Müller can scarcely have dreamed. The concentration on this descending motif counterbalances the lengthy development of the theme's initial rising phrase that had been presented in the introduction.

---

[47] Beethoven omitted to indicate any change in tempo at the point where the 6/8 Presto gives way to the return of the 2/4 metre of Müller's theme. In both the autograph score and Steiner's first edition the moment bears only the indication *semplice*. On practical grounds, a tempo quicker than the Allegretto of the theme cannot have been intended; and both the intricacy of the keyboard figuration during the closing pages, and the music's inherently expressive character, suggest if anything a speed more relaxed than that of the theme itself.

Ex. 12.15. Beethoven. Variations on 'Ich bin der Schneider Kakadu', op.121a, bars 398–423.

Beethoven's final pages expand the same descending phrase into a splendid apotheosis which has the strings sweeping repeatedly down the scale in a broad arch, the flattened sixth lending the music a tinge of minor-mode melancholy, while the piano climbs ever upwards in a spiral of demisemiquavers. (See Ex. 12.11(a) on p.354.) But even the grandeur of this moment gives way to a last return of Müller's tune, now played with graceful sarcasm by the pizzicato strings, before a final crescendo dismisses it with an imperious gesture. The sonority of the closing bars is rich, with sweeping arpeggios covering a keyboard range of five octaves, and Beethoven's pedal marking (apart from the last, *pianissimo*, chord of the introduction, his only such indication in the score) adding weight to the sound.[48]

If, as seems likely, the 'Kakadu' Variations is a hybrid work, it is one in which late Beethoven looks fondly back to the music of a bygone era. The latter aspect, at least, was one that elicited an unconcealed sigh of relief from the reviewer of the first English edition of the variations in *The Harmonicon* of June 1824:

> Nearly all the new compositions of Beethoven which it has been our lot to notice, in this part of our work [i.e. as a reviewer], have been of so elaborate and difficult a kind, so full of harsh and unaccountable combinations, and strange modulation, that we have found it an arduous task to escape from mentioning them in terms of downright censure, and have struggled hard with duty, out of respect and gratitude to a genius of the first magnitude, whose former productions have afforded, and must always afford, us so much pleasure. But in reviewing the present trio we have nothing of so painful a kind to contend with; it is in a style quite different from those alluded to, and is, for Beethoven, so familiar in its manner, that some determined admirers of whatever is far-fetched and obscure, will, very likely, despise it for its comparative simplicity. In fact it might pass as Haydn's; the subject, as will presently appear, cannot fail

---

[48] As was his custom at the end of a work, Beethoven's autograph shows no release sign for the pedal in the final bar, though such a sign was included in Steiner's first edition.

to recal [sic] him to the performer's memory, it has all his clearness of melody and distinctness of rhythm …

We are much pleased by this Trio, and recommend it to all who do not insist upon liking compositions that are overcharged with musical learning, and repulsive from excessive difficulty.[49]

---

[49] *The Harmonicon*, no.18, June 1824, pp.112–13.

13
Postlude: Beethoven and George Thomson

Beethoven's last chamber works with piano are intimately bound up with the nearly two hundred arrangements of folk songs he made in the decade between 1810 and 1820, the large majority of them for the Scottish philanthropist and folksong enthusiast George Thomson. Thomson's mission was to publish as comprehensive as possible a collection of Scottish folk melodies (and later, songs from Wales and Ireland), in settings with preludes, postludes and accompaniments for piano trio made by some of the leading composers of central Europe. To this end, he turned first to Haydn's pupil Ignaz Pleyel, then to the Bohemian composer Leopold Kozeluch (described at one point by the exasperated Beethoven in his voluminous correspondence with Thomson as a *miserabilis*); and eventually to Haydn himself, who had already provided two folksong collections for the Scottish publisher William Napier. But by 1803 it was clear that Haydn was becoming too frail to continue with this work for much longer, and it was in that year that Thomson made an initial approach to Beethoven.

Thomson's first letter to Beethoven, dated 20 July 1803, has not survived, but in his reply of 5 October the composer agreed to write six sonatas based on Scottish national airs for a fee of 300 ducats.[1] This, however, was too high for Thomson, who was prepared to pay only half the requested amount; and, perhaps not surprisingly, negotiations at this stage came to nothing. All the same, Beethoven appears to have begun work on the project, and to have jotted down a few brief piano sketches of Scottish tunes in the summer of 1804.[2]

Nearly three years later, in another letter that has been lost, Thomson put a proposal of a rather different kind, asking the composer to provide him with new trios and quintets for performance by amateurs. In the postscript to his reply, Beethoven clearly refers back to their earlier correspondence:

> Je veux encore satisfaire à votre souhait d'harmoniser des petits airs écossais, et j'attends la dessus une proposition plus précise, sachant bien qu'on a donné à Mr Haydn un £ argent de la grande Bretagne pour chaque air.[3]

(I still want to satisfy your wish to harmonise some short Scottish airs, and I await a more precise proposal on this matter, knowing full well that Mr. Haydn was given one £ of British money for each air.)

---

[1] BGA no.161; Anderson no.83.
[2] Staatsbibliothek zu Berlin, aut. 19e, f.35v. See Cooper, *Beethoven's Folksong Settings*, p.11.
[3] Letter dated 9 November 1806. BGA no.259; Anderson no.136.

Of greater interest in the light of his future dealings with Thomson, and in particular in connection with the variations for piano and flute opp.105 and 107, are two other points raised in Beethoven's letter:

> Je m'éfforcerai de rendre les compositions faciles et agréables autant que je pourrai, et autant que cela peut s'accorder avec cette Elévation et cette originalité du Style, qui selon votre propre aveu caracterisent mes ouvrages asses [sic] avantageusement, et dont je ne m'abaisserai jamais.
>
> Je ne peux pas me resoudre de travailler pour la flute, cet instrument étant trop borné et imparfait.
>
> (I shall endeavour to render the compositions easy and agreeable inasmuch as I can, and inasmuch as that may accord with the loftiness and originality of style which as you yourself confess characterises my works very much to their advantage, and from which I shall never lower myself.
>
> I cannot bring myself to work for the flute, that instrument being too limited and imperfect.)

In response, Thomson sent Beethoven twenty-one melodies to be harmonised. Beethoven, however, was busy with the completion of his rapidly composed 'Razumovsky' string quartets op.59; and it was not until towards the end of 1809 that he was able to embark on his folksong settings for Thomson. By that time he also had behind him – in addition to other, smaller, works – the Mass in C, the Fifth and Sixth Symphonies, the Cello Sonata op.69 and the two piano trios op.70. As for the sonatas and chamber works Thomson had requested, the two men again failed to reach a financial agreement, Thomson being willing to offer no more than half the £120 or 240 ducats Beethoven was now demanding for three quintets and three sonatas.

On 15 October 1814 Thomson wrote to Beethoven, asking for an overture for piano – 'in a style as gay or *scherzando* as you like', and no shorter than Mozart's overtures to *Don Giovanni* and *Die Zauberflöte* – for which he would pay 12 ducats, or 18 if it included parts for violin, flute, viola and cello.[4] Such a naïve proposal was unlikely to have been of interest to Beethoven, and in the end it was not Thomson but the London publisher Robert Birchall who first suggested a project that perhaps appealed to him rather more. In the autumn of 1815 Birchall entered into negotiations with Beethoven for the English rights to some of his latest works – the Violin Sonata op.96 and the Piano Trio op.97, as well as piano arrangements of *Wellingtons Sieg*, which had been rejected the previous year by Thomson, and the Seventh Symphony. On 14 August 1816 Birchall's associate Christopher Lonsdale wrote to the composer:

> When you write again, Mr Birchall will be glad to know your sentiments respecting writing Variations to the most favorite English, Scotch or Irish airs for the Pianoforte with an Accompaniment either for the Violin or Violoncello – as you find best, about the same length as Mozart's Airs '*La dove prende*' and '*Colomba o tortorella*'[5] and Handel's *See the conquering Hero comes* with your Variations, be

---

[4] BGA no.752; LTB no.190.

[5] In other words, the variations on 'Bei Männern' op.66 and 'Ein Mädchen oder Weibchen' WoO 46.

so good when you oblige him with your terms &c. to say whether the Airs need be sent you, if you have many perhaps mentioning the names will be sufficient – In fixing the price Mr Birchall wishes you to mention a Sum that will include Copying and Postages.[6]

Once more, however, Beethoven's asking price was too high, and the matter was dropped. The field was now left open for Thomson to seize the initiative again. On 25 June 1817, after a complaint that the composer's fee for the overtures was out of the question, and another that some of the folksong settings he had received from him were "certainement recherchés, trop bizarres", Thomson suggested that the composer should select a dozen airs of different nationalities:

> ceux qui vous paroitront le mieux adaptés pour être variés: et si vous composez des Variations (non plus que huit) à chaque Air, pour le Piano Forte d'un style agréable, et pas trop difficile, je vous payerai 72 ducats. Il vous sera un travail très leger de faire quelques Variations pour 12 Themes deja composés. Je voudrois que la derniere Variation, ou une Coda de chaque Air, ou de quelques uns des Airs, fût dans le style d'une Valse.
>
> Si vous n'agréez pas cette proposition, il ne me reste que de vous temoigner mes regrets pour l'avoir faite; car se seroit une imprudence de depenser sur ces Airs étrangers plus que ce que j'ai proposé. J'aurois mieux fait de ne pas m'y être mêlé. Les Airs du Tyrol sont vraiment beaux et pleins de vivacité: Je les admire beaucoup.[7]
>
> (those that seem to you best suited to be varied, and if you compose some variations (no more than eight) on each air, for pianoforte in a style that is pleasant and not too difficult, I will pay you 72 ducats. It will be a very small task for you to make a few variations for 12 themes that are already composed. I should like the last variation, or a coda to each air, or to some of the airs, to be in the style of a waltz.
>
> If you do not agree to this proposition, all that remains is for me to convey to you my regrets for having made it; for it would be unwise to spend more on these foreign airs than I have proposed. I should have done better not to have become involved with it. The Tyrolean airs are really beautiful and full of life: I admire them a great deal.)

Beethoven responded the following February, offering to compose twelve overtures for 140 ducats, and twelve themes with variations for 100 ducats – or, if Thomson wanted to take all 24 works, he would accept a total of 224 ducats.[8] On 22

---

[6] BGA no.958; LTB no.229. Also quoted in Thayer/Forbes, pp.649–50. The German translation of this letter by Johann Baptist von Häring, who assisted Beethoven in his various dealings with English publishers, contains a significant interpolation following the request that the variations should be of similar length to those Beethoven had already composed for piano and cello: 'Sie können mit oder ohne accompagnement seyn wie Sie es am besten finden. Zum hiesigen Verkaufe würde die Begleitung einer Flöte – Violin oder Violoncell am nützlichsten seyn, doch wird H^r· van Beethoven darinn ganz seiner Willkühr folgen' (They can be with or without accompaniment, as you find best. For sale here the accompaniment of a flute, violin or violoncello would be the most useful, but in this Herr van Beethoven will absolutely follow his own desire).

[7] BGA no.1133; LTB no.240.

[8] BGA no.1244; Anderson no.892.

June 1818 Thomson confirmed that he would meet Beethoven's fee for the variations, the majority of them to be based on Scottish songs the composer had already harmonised. Once again he expressed his admiration for Beethoven's talent, which did not, however, prevent him from addressing the composer as 'My good man': 'Mais helas! Mon bon Monsr. tout le monde dans ce pays-ci trouvent que vos ouvrages sont beaucoup trop difficiles.' Not only did Thomson specify an accompaniment for flute *ad libitum* (he had earlier informed Beethoven that in Britain good flute players were more common than good violinists), he also stressed that the variations should be written 'd'un style *familier* et *facile* et un peu *brillant*; afin que les [sic] plus grand nombre de nos Demoiselles puissent les executer et les goûter' (in a style that is *familiar* and *easy* and slightly *brilliant*, so that the majority of our young ladies can play them and enjoy them).[9]

Beethoven clearly composed the variations at great speed, because he dispatched all twelve sets to Thomson before the year was out – and that at a time when he was also working on the last two movements of the 'Hammerklavier' Sonata, and was beginning to formulate ideas for the opening movement of the Ninth Symphony. Thomson acknowledged receipt of the variations in a letter dated 28 December 1818, and added:

> Je trouve la plupart des Variations pleines de beauté et de genie, – et toutafait digne de votre talent. J'en eu [sic] entendu jouer Six avec grand plaisir: – je regrette de dire qu'il y en a deux autres qui ne reusseraient pas ici, je veux parler de celles-ci. ... [Thomson quotes the opening bars of op.107 nos.8 and 10.]
>
> Je n'ai pas encore entendre [sic] le quatre derniers des 12.
>
> Afin que j'aye le nombre entier des 12, d'un style qui plaira au public, permettez moi de vous prier de me faire la grâce de composer deux autres, au lieu de ceux dont je viens de parler. Et je vous prie de les faire d'un style agrèable et *cantabile*, brillants pour la main droite, autant qu'il vous plaira, mais *faciles* à executer.[10]

> (I find the majority of the variations full of beauty and genius, and altogether worthy of your talent. I have heard six of them played with great pleasure; I regret to say that there are two others which will not go down well here – I mean these [Thomson quotes the opening bars of op.107 nos.8 and 10].
>
> I have not heard the last four of the 12.
>
> In order for me to have the complete number of 12, in a style which will please the public, allow me to ask you to have the courtesy to compose two others in place of those of which I have just spoken. And I would ask you to do them in a pleasant and *cantabile* style – as brilliant as you like for the right hand, but *easy* to play.)

Less than a fortnight later Thomson wrote to Beethoven again. He had now heard the remaining four sets, and had found another (op.107 no.1) that was not suitable for the young ladies of his country. The piece was, he said, 'beaucoup trop difficile pour les personnes qui s'amuse avec des Thêmes variés; – et je vous assure qu'il me serait tout-a-fait inutile de le publier' (much too difficult for those who enjoy varied themes; and I assure you it would be completely useless to publish it). He invited Beethoven to select another air, and to compose variations that would be

---

[9] BGA no.1262; LTB no.249.
[10] BGA no.1275; LTB no.253.

brilliant but not too difficult, 'car il s'en faut beaucoup que les dames de l'Ecosse ne soient aussi fortes que celles de votre Pays ou la musique èst si cultiviée' (For Scottish women are by no means as skilled as those of your country where music is so cultivated). At the same time, Thomson informed the composer that he found the minor-mode variation of op.107 no.4 'trop maigre', and the set as a whole too short.[11] Beethoven must have taken these last criticisms to heart, because he furnished a substitute for the variation in the minor (his original has not survived, though what were presumably its initial two bars are quoted in Thomson's letter), and inserted a new one immediately following it. He also complied with Thomson's request for three sets of variations to replace those which were deemed unsuitable for the British market. (The new pieces were op.105 no.3, and op.107 nos.6 and 7.)

Thomson was enchanted by the new variations, which gave him more pleasure than he could express. He invited Beethoven to choose another 'foreign' theme to vary.

> Permettez moi seulement de vous prier de le faire aussi agréable, chantant, et brillant que le Thème Autrichien [op.105 no.3], et aussi facile. Et j'espere que vous le ferez aussi longue que le Thème Russe [op.107 no.7], avec un petite [*sic*] Adagio Cantabile.[12]

(Allow me just to ask you to make it as pleasant, melodious and brilliant as the Austrian theme, and just as easy. And I hope you will make it as long as the Russian theme, with a little Adagio cantabile.)

Once again Beethoven complied, with the 'Air de la petite Russie' op.107 no.3. But in the same letter Thomson was forced to confess that he was unable to publish the two variation sets based on Tyrolean themes, op.107 nos.1 and 5. A friend of his, one of the best lady pianists in Edinburgh, had tried to play them and had been forced after much effort to give up in despair, having found them 'trop recherchès, chromatiques, et terriblement difficiles':

> Elle èst convainçue que nos amateurs ne pourrait ni les executer, ni les goûter. Le derniere Air j'aime particulierement [i.e. op.107 no.5], mais probablement il seroit inutile de vous demander d'en faire les Variations plus simples et faciles, afin de les rendre au gout de la Public ici. – Je crains que cette peine ne vous serait pas agrèable, et dans cette cas qu'il me sera inutile de la publier; c'est grand dommage.

(She is convinced that our amateurs will neither be able to play them, nor to enjoy them. I am particularly fond of the last air, but it would probably be useless to ask you to make the variations on it simpler and easier, in order to render them to the taste of the public here. – I fear that this trouble would not be agreeable to you, and in that case that it would be useless for me to publish it. It is a great pity.)

In view of the extreme difficulty of the third variation in op.107 no.5 – the trills are if anything technically even more awkward than the examples found in the variations of the piano sonatas opp.109 and 111 – it is hard not to feel a touch of sympathy for the hapless Thomson. His philistinism was, however, more than Beethoven could stomach. 'Vous ecrivés toujours facile très facile,' he told Thomson:

---

[11] BGA no.1283; LTB no.255.
[12] Letter of 5 April 1819. BGA no.1297; LTB no.258.

je m'accomode tout mon possible, mais – mais – mais – l'honorare pourroit pourtant être plus *difficile*, ou plutôt pesant!!!!!¹³ ... L'honorare pour un Thème avec Variations j'ai fixé, dans ma dernière lettre à vous par Messieurs le Friesz, a moien dix ducats en or, c'est, je vous jure, malgre cela seulement par complaisance pour vous, puisque je n'ai pas besoin, de me mêler avec de telles petites choses, mais il faut toujours pourtant perdre du temps avec de telles bagatelles, et l'honneur ne permet pas, de dire à quelqu'un, ce qu'on en gagne – je vous souhaite toujours bon gout pour la vrai Musique et si vous cries facile – je crieroi *difficile pour facile*!!!!¹⁴

(You always write easy very easy – I do everything to adapt myself, but – but – but – the fee could nevertheless be more *difficult*, or rather, heavier!!!! In my last letter to you via Messrs. Fries I fixed the fee for a theme with variations at ten gold ducats; it is, I assure you, only out of kindness towards you, since I do not need to involve myself with such small things, but one always has to waste time with such bagatelles, and honour does not allow one to tell anyone how much one earns from it, – I wish you all the same good taste for real music, and if you cry easy – I shall cry *difficult for easy*!!!!)

Nothing daunted, Thomson had further criticisms to make six months later. The additional variations he had requested the previous April (op.107 no.3) were unsuitable for England. This, he complained, was the fifth variation set he had been forced to discard as being too esoteric (*recherché*) and difficult for the ladies of his country. 'Quel dommage', he told Beethoven, with admirable *sang-froid*, 'que votre gènie admirable ne peut pas dans ces morceaux s'accomoder à l'habilitè de ceux pour qui ils sont composès. J'en souffre beaucoup' (What a pity your admirable genius cannot adapt itself in these pieces to the skill of those for whom they are composed. It pains me greatly).¹⁵ Thomson also informed the composer that he had had eleven of the variation sets engraved, of which he had published nine, but they were not selling well. He nevertheless wanted to keep faith with the number of varied themes announced on the title page of that published volume; and to make up the twelfth he proposed after all to include one of the sets he had rejected. His choice fell on 'Mary, at thy Window be' (op.107 no.8), as being the simplest. However, it seemed to him excessively short, containing, as it did, only two variations. He hoped, therefore, that the composer would add some further variations to it, 'chantans et brillants, mais non pas difficiles'. Beethoven seems to have fallen in with this suggestion, since the published version of op.107 no.8 contains five variations.

As things turned out, Thomson never issued a follow-up to the collection of nine variation sets he had published in April 1819. (That collection contained op.105 nos.3, 4, 1, 6, 2 and 5, together with op.107 nos.7, 6 and 2.) Six numbers from Thomson's publication were taken over by Domenico Artaria in September 1819, when they appeared as op.105. Since, as Thomson had already advised Beethoven, there were more competent amateur violinists on the Continent than in Britain, Artaria's edition of September 1819 was issued with a separate alternative part for violin, complete with double-stops and

---

[13] Beethoven is punning on the two meanings of the German word 'schwer': 'difficult' and 'heavy'.

[14] Letter of 25 May 1819. BGA no.1303; Anderson no.945.

[15] Letter of 23 November 1819. BGA no.1357; LTB no.766

pizzicatos. The additional part is unlikely to have originated with Beethoven: there is no mention of a stringed instrument in his correspondence regarding these pieces, and the fussy use of pizzicato in several of the variations, as well as passages such as the unidiomatic high-lying octaves in the third variation of op.105 no.3, suggest that the composer had no hand in the violin writing. Artaria's title page disingenuously promised a collection of *Thèmes variés bien facile à éxécuter pour le Piano-Forte seul ou avec accompagnement d'une flûte ou d'un violon ad libitum*. It is true that in his correspondence with Simrock concerning the op.107 series Beethoven described the variations as being for piano with a flute *ad libitum*,[16] and that in his two surviving autograph scores (nos.6 and 7) the flute part appears beneath the piano staves, almost as though it were an afterthought; but although the piano clearly has the lion's share of the music, the flute's contribution is indispensable. Such moments as the start of the last variation on the Russian folk song op.107 no.3, where the wind instrument superimposes fragments of the melody above the piano's long-held chords, or the *Andante comodo* of the concluding 'Schöne Minka' variations op.107 no.7, where it again has the melody to itself, would sound conspicuously bare without the presence of the flute. Significantly, Simrock's first edition of op.107, which appeared in the autumn of 1820, bore a title page on which the words 'ad libitum' were buried in tiny print within an elaborately curlicued design.

The story of Thomson's efforts to dispose of the remaining variation sets he had in his possession – and for which he had paid – was pieced together in a valuable article by Cecil B. Oldman.[17] On 25 October 1819 Thomson wrote to Breitkopf & Härtel, who had already expressed an interest in his publications, informing them that he had three as yet unissued sets of variations which might be of particular interest to them since they were based on 'foreign' themes, and offering to sell them at cost price (i.e. 25 gold ducats). These negotiations, however, came to nothing, perhaps because, as Breitkopf must have been aware, Thomson did not actually own the continental rights to the pieces in question. When Simrock issued the remaining ten variation sets the European market was effectively closed to Thomson, and he had to seek an English buyer. On 8 June 1821 he wrote to Boosey & Sons, setting out full details of the material in his possession. He had, he told Boosey, printed 200 copies of nine themes with variations, of which 100 were still in his hands. Moreover, a tenth theme had been engraved, and 100 copies printed, but it had never been put on sale. Thomson offered all ten at the price he had paid for them plus the cost of having them engraved, taking care to stress that Beethoven's fee had been considerably lower than usual since he (Thomson) had negotiated a global sum to include straightforward folksong arrangements. Thomson's dealings with Boosey were, however, unsuccessful. Nor did he have more luck the following year, when he attempted to sell twelve sets of variations, with the plates, to Goulding & D'Almaine of Soho Square for £80. They had, he informed them, cost him £94. 4^s. 0^d.

It was not until 1823 that Thomson at last managed – albeit by default – to find a home for his unpublished material. In the summer of that year he discovered that the firm of Paine & Hopkins had issued unauthorised editions of some of the themes and variations. Thomson now saw the opportunity of housing not only the three additional variation sets

---

[16] Letter of 9 March 1820. BGA no.1370; Anderson no.1011.
[17] Oldman, 'Beethoven's Variations on National Themes', pp.45–51.

he had offered to Goulding, but also the remaining four which he had always regarded as unfit for publication. He demanded that either Paine & Hopkins surrender all the plates and copies of their pirated editions, or that they purchase outright the copyright to all 16 themes and variations for £80. The tenth of the themes (op.107 no.9), he assured them, 'is engraved, and 100 copies taken, but it is not publish'd. 'Tis so pretty that I was thinking of publishing it singly.' Paine & Hopkins responded by offering £50 for the 16 themes with variations and for Beethoven's arrangements of 24 foreign melodies. Reluctantly, Thomson found himself having to accept.

Beethoven's variations for piano and flute belong among the least-known compositions of his late years, and they have scarcely merited more than a footnote in the Beethoven literature.[18] It is true that they show all the signs of having been written in great haste, and that the composer's impatience to draw the final double-bar line and to return to projects closer to his heart is at times tangible; yet quite apart from the intrinsic beauty of much of the music itself, these pieces date from an important turning-point in Beethoven's creative life, and seem to have provided him with a veritable experimenting-ground for ideas he was to explore in greater depth in his larger works to come. Moreover, it appears that Beethoven's late-found interest in variation form, as evinced in the piano sonatas opp.109 and 111, the 'Diabelli' Variations op.120 and the string quartets opp.127, 131, 132 and 135, may well have been sparked off by this comparatively minor project for George Thomson.

The majority of Thomson's variation sets were written, as we have seen, during the latter half of 1818, at a time when Beethoven was busy with the last two movements of the 'Hammerklavier' Sonata. The harmonic structure of much of the sonata is governed by chains of descending thirds[19] – as, for instance, in the opening bars of the slow introduction to the finale.

Ex. 13.1. Beethoven. Piano Sonata in B flat, op.106 (iv) bars 1–2.

[18] Exceptions are the more detailed treatment of these pieces in Jürgen Uhde's *Beethovens Klaviermusik*, vol.1, pp.426–503, and Barry Cooper's *Beethoven's Folksong Settings*.

[19] This aspect of the sonata is perceptively discussed by Charles Rosen in *The Classical Style*, pp.404–34.

At the end of the variations on 'The Last Rose of Summer' op.105 no.4, the music falls through a similar, but more extended, sequence, leaving it poised on the key of C flat, before the final two bars make a return to the home key. The effect of this conclusion, following the unexpected harmonic activity of the preceding bars, is of entrancing nostalgia. In its context the entire moment is so startling that it is difficult not to feel that it was directly linked to Beethoven's work on the op.106 Sonata – though which of the two came first is impossible to determine.

Ex. 13.2. Beethoven. Variations on 'The Last Rose of Summer', op.105 no.4, bars 64–72.

—(continued)

Ex. 13.2—continued

Besides their large-scale use of descending thirds, the first two movements of the 'Hammerklavier' exploit the secondary key of B minor as an important source of harmonic conflict. A striking instance of the intrusion of B minor is provided by the beginning of the first movement's recapitulation, where the music is disrupted by a dramatic explosion in that key, heralded by a mysterious empty fifth on its dominant, F sharp.

Ex. 13.3. Beethoven. Piano Sonata in B flat, op.106 (i) bars 262–8.

The variations on 'I bin a Tyroler Bue' op.107 no.1 contain a similar enharmonic excursion into the flat supertonic minor. It is rather less well prepared, but the curious isolated *pianissimo* flute note at the start of the new variation establishes the key-change in a sort of punctuation-mark. This time, in contradistinction to the 'Hammerklavier', it is the return to the home key, and not the departure from it, that is effected via an unceremoniously sounded empty fifth.

Ex. 13.4. Beethoven. Variations on 'I bin a Tiroler Bua', op.107 no.1, bars 77–117.

—(continued)

Ex. 13.4—*continued*

Var. IV
Maggiore
Allegro

It might have been thought that Beethoven's highly unorthodox E minor variation was motivated by uncharacteristic anxiety lest the amateur pianists of Scotland take fright at the sight of the key signature of E flat minor, were it not for the fact that op.107 no.9, based on the Scottish song 'O thou art the Lad of my Heart', does not fight shy of an E flat minor variation. The E minor variation of op.107 no.1, with the flute gradually providing a skeletal harmonisation of the piano's austere line before shadowing it in freely canonic imitation, provides further proof, if such were needed, that the accompanying instrument, far from being dispensable, is an essential part of the musical discourse.

The straightforward 'yodelling' theme of 'A Madel, ja a Madel' op.107 no.5 is one with which Beethoven appears to have as much fun as he was soon to do with Diabelli's little waltz-tune. The chromatic, rhythmically eccentric first variation is followed by another which transforms the tonic-dominant harmony of the theme beyond all recognition, alternating powerful passages in broken octaves, and shadowy tremolandos surmounted by piquant harmonic suspensions. But this is as nothing compared with what follows, where Beethoven seizes on the innocent-sounding trill which separates the two halves of the original theme, and expands it to fill an entire variation. Beethoven clearly remembered the passage when he came to write not only the variation movement of the sonatas opp.109 and 111, but also the C major Bagatelle op.119 no.7. The trill of the folksong variation is of extreme difficulty, and nor does the flute have an easy time of it: its part may be skeletal, but the player is required to sustain a single tied note over a span of very nearly thirteen bars.

Ex. 13.5.
(a) Beethoven. Variations on 'A Madel, ja a Madel' op.107 no.5, bars 137–52.

—(continued)

Ex. 13.5a—*continued*

Ex. 13.5.
(b) Beethoven. Bagatelle in C, op.119 no.7, bars 15–27.

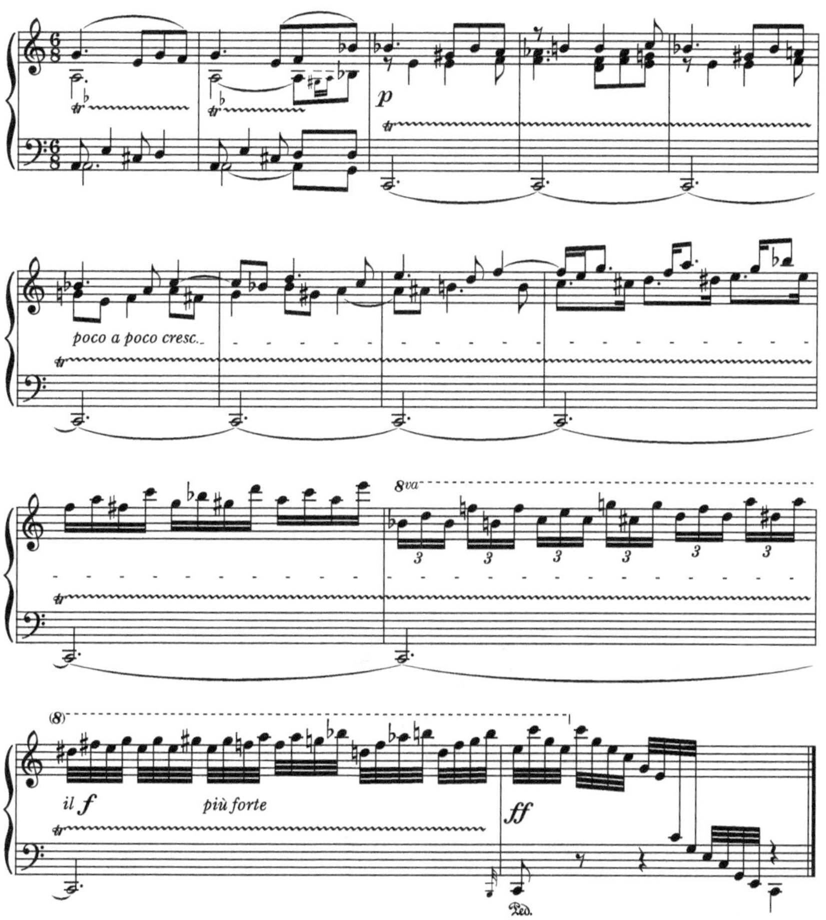

The variation is followed by a brief *Maestoso* interpolation based on the theme's initial four bars. Both its tempo indication and its dramatic, double-dotted rhythm seem to offer a distant foretaste of the opening page of the Sonata op.111.

Ex. 13.6.
(a) Beethoven. Piano Sonata in C minor, op.111 (i) bars 1–2.

Ex. 13.6
(b) Beethoven. Variations on 'A Madel, ja a Madel' op.107 no.5, bars 153–6.

More strikingly close to the world of Beethoven's late piano sonatas is the fourth variation of the stylistically much simpler set based on the Ukrainian tune 'Schöne Minka', op.107 no.7.[20] Here, unmistakably, is the model for the second variation in the finale of the E major Piano Sonata op.109.

Ex. 13.7.
(a) Beethoven. Variations on 'Schöne Minka', op.107 no.7, bars 65–80.

[20] Beethoven's vocal setting of the melody (WoO 158 no.16) is labelled 'Air cosaque'. The tune appeared in 1809 in W.G. Becker's *Taschenbuch zum geselligen Vergnügen* under the title of 'Schöne Minka, ich muß scheiden', with words by Christoph August Tiedge. Cf. the Critical Commentary by Armin Raab to *Beethoven Werke*, series 5, vol.4, p.155.

Ex. 13.7.
(b) Beethoven. Piano Sonata in E, op.109 (iii) bars 33–40.

In a generally sympathetic notice of the op.107 series, the reviewer of the *Allgemeine musikalische Zeitung* expressed surprise that from time to time the variations were even simpler than the themes themselves.[21] That feature clearly ran counter to the tradition of salon variations, which invariably showed a progressive increase in brilliance, but it had also been true of Beethoven's op.105 set. A case in point is the fifth variation from the remarkably attractive set based on 'A Schüsserl und a Reinderl', op.105 no.3. The theme itself is not strictly speaking a folk melody: it first appeared in 1796, in a comic Singspiel called *Die Kaufmannsbude* (The Merchant's Booth), attributed to the Austrian composer Johann Baptist Henneberg.[22]

Ex. 13.8. Beethoven. Variations on 'A Schüsserl und a Reinderl', op.105 no.3, bars 1–16.

The first four of Beethoven's variations respect the theme's simple harmony, while at the same time presenting a progressive increase in animation. The conventional plan is one that serves only to enhance the profound stillness of the chromatic minor-mode fifth variation, in which the C minor triad of its initial bar is followed

[21] AMZ, 33 (15 Aug. 1821), cols.567–9.
[22] See Raab, Critical Commentary, p.156.

by a series of dominant chords whose resolution at the start of the fourth bar is presented as a bare octave. The result is to increase the surprise of the C minor chord of bar 8, the first minor harmony since the downbeat of the first bar. In addition, the rising melodic shape of bars 5–8 falls across the bar line, in such a way as to create the illusion of an alternation between duple and triple metres. The switch to the relative major (E flat) of bar 8 resolves four bars later onto the initial note of the theme's ascending phrase, and Beethoven again varies the pattern of repeated notes: following the expanded form of three beats each in which the first two melody notes of G and A are heard, the B natural is curtailed, cadencing onto the final C two beats earlier than expected.

Ex. 13.9. Beethoven. Variations on 'A Schüsserl und a Reinderl', op.105 no.3, Var5.

The progressive shift in register of this variation, with each successive phrase placed an octave higher than the last, paves the way for the luminous sonority of the final variation – much of it located in the keyboard's highest octave. In its intricacy and sonority, indeed, this last variation foreshadows the radiant ecstasy of the concluding variations from the Sonata op.111. As for the C minor variation, it seems to offer a foretaste of the mysteriously skeletal variation 20 from the 'Diabelli' set:

Ex. 13.10. Beethoven. 33 Variations on a Waltz by Diabelli, op.120, Var.20, bars 1–16.

Another anticipation of the 'Diabelli' Variations is found in the final variation of op.107 no.4 ('The Pulse of an Irishman'[23]) where, following a variation that transforms the theme's gently lilting 6/8 rhythm into a 2/4 Vivace, Beethoven brings the set to a close with what to all intents and purposes is an elegant minuet, similar in character to the concluding minuet of the later work. But perhaps of greater significance to Beethoven's variation procedure in the 'Diabelli' set are the variations on a Ukrainian theme op.107 no.3. (In a letter to Simrock of 23 April 1820, Beethoven was clearly confused about the theme's nationality, quoting the melody and describing it as 'Ecossais u. nicht italienne wie es [in] dem Manuscript steht' [Scottish and not Italian as it is stated in the manuscript].[24] Ferdinand Ries was among other composers who wrote variations on the same melody.) Once again, the theme itself is of utmost simplicity, its colour subtly varied in Beethoven's setting by the intermittent participation of the flute:

Ex. 13.11. Beethoven. Variations on a Ukrainian Folksong, op.107 no.3, bars 1–16.

[23] Simrock's first edition gives the title of these variations as 'St. Patrick's Day'.
[24] BGA no.1384; Anderson no.1019.

In Beethoven's variations the theme's harmony – especially at the approach to the concluding cadence of each of its halves – is altered on every occasion, in a manner that was to be explored with such inventiveness in the 'Diabelli' set. In the solo piano second variation, following a first half obstinately restricted to tonic and dominant harmony, the theme's second half suddenly makes a move towards the relative minor (E minor).

Ex. 13.12. Beethoven. Variations on a Ukrainian Folksong, op.107 no.3, bars 33–48.

The fifth variation reduces the theme to a shadowy outline of its former self, and the pace of its harmonic change is ironed out: in order to fit the proportions of the original melody's harmonic scheme, the duration of the variation's first and fifth bars would have to be doubled, and that of each intervening pair of bars halved.

Ex. 13.13. Beethoven. Variations on a Ukrainian Folksong, op.107 no.3, bars 89–104.

The following variation is an Adagio whose second half takes up the E minor colouring of variation 2, developing it into an elaborate aria whose expressive character once again looks forward to the piano music of Beethoven's final years.[25] Nor, excepting the 'Eroica' Variations op.35, is there likely to be another instance in Beethoven of the procedure followed in the final variation, whereby the theme's bass line is elevated to a thematic status. Here, the bass of the theme as shown in Ex. 13.11 above generates a fugato whose harmonic peregrinations, including an enharmonic change taking the music from B flat minor into B minor within the space of five bars, enlarge the music's terms of reference to a remarkable degree.

Ex. 13.14. Beethoven. Variations on a Ukrainian Folksong, op.107 no.3, bars 144–74.

[25] Jürgen Uhde (*Beethovens Klaviermusik*, pp.469–70) sees an affinity between the start of the second half in this variation and the parallel point in the theme of the 'Arietta' from the Sonata op.111.

Altogether, Beethoven's folksong variations, while undeniably occasional pieces, deserve deeper study than they have hitherto received. If they are of uneven quality (not surprisingly, the themes of central European origin seem to have struck a more sympathetic chord in the composer than those emanating from the British Isles), they contain much that is of striking beauty. It is not without irony that Beethoven's career as a composer of chamber music with piano should have drawn to a close with these pieces in the anachronistic form of accompanied keyboard music, but it did so in a manner that unmistakably bears the stamp of his genius.

Bibliography

Albrecht, Theodore (trans. and ed.), *Letters to Beethoven & Other Correspondence* (Lincoln, Neb., 1996).

Baillot, Pierre, Pierre Rode and Rodolphe Kreutzer, *Méthode de violon* (Paris, 1803).

Beethoven, Ludwig van, *Ein Notierungsbuch aus dem Besitze der Preussischen Staatsbibliothek zu Berlin* ('Landsberg 7'), ed. Karl Lothar Mikulicz (Leipzig, 1927).

——, *Ein Skizzenbuch zur Pastoralsymphonie op.68 und zu den Trios op.70, 1 und 2*, ed. Dagmar Weise (Bonn, 1961).

——, *Supplemente zur Gesamtausgabe*, vol.9, ed. Willy Hess (Wiesbaden, 1965).

——, *Autograph Miscellany from circa 1786 to 1799. British Museum Additional Manuscript 29801 (the 'Kafka Sketchbook')*, ed. Joseph Kerman (London, 1970).

——, *Keßlersches Skizzenbuch*, ed. Sieghard Brandenburg (Bonn, 1978).

——, *Briefwechsel. Gesamtausgabe*, ed. Sieghard Brandenburg (Munich, 1996).

Bente, Martin (ed.), *Musik, Edition, Interpretation: Gedenkschrift Günter Henle* (Munich, 1980).

Berlioz, Hector, *Voyage musical en Allemagne et Italie* (Paris, 1844).

Blindow, Martin, *Bernhard Romberg (1767–1841), Leben und Wirken des großen Violoncello-Virtuosen* (Munich/Salzburg, 2013).

Bockholdt, Rudolf and Petra Weber-Bockholdt (eds.), *Beethovens Klaviertrios. Symposion München 1990* (Munich, 1992).

Bockhold, Rudolf, 'Zum Andante cantabile des Trios op.97 und seiner Stellung im Werkganzen', in *Beethovens Klaviertrios* (Munich, 1992), pp.185–96.

Bone, Philip J., *The Guitar and Mandolin: Biographies of Celebrated Players and Composers* (London, 1954).

Brandenburg, Sieghard, 'Bemerkungen zu Beethovens op.96', in *Beethoven-Jahrbuch 9*, ed. Hans Schmidt and Martin Staehelin (Bonn, 1977).

——, 'Über die Bedeutung der Änderungen von Taktschriften in einigen Werken Beethovens', in *Beethoven-Kolloquium 1977*, ed. Rudolf Klein (Kassel, 1978).

——, 'Zur Textgeschichte von Beethovens Violin-Sonate op.47', in *Musik, Edition, Interpretation: Gedenkschrift Günter Henle*, ed. M. Bente (Munich, 1980).

——, 'Beethoven's Opus 12 Violin Sonatas: On the Path to His Personal Style', in *The Beethoven Violin Sonatas*, ed. Lewis Lockwood and Mark Kroll (Urbana and Chicago, 2004).

——, 'Die Skizzen zu Beethovens Cellosonate op.69', in *Beethovens Werke für Klavier und Violoncello*, ed. Sieghard Brandenburg, Ingeborg Maass and Wolfgang Osthoff (Bonn, 2004).

Braubach, Max and Michael Landburger (eds.), *Die Stammbücher Beethovens und der Babette Koch* (Bonn, 1970).

Breuning, Gerhard von, *Aus dem Schwarzspanierhaus. Erinnerungen an L. van Beethoven aus meiner Jugendzeit* (Vienna, 1874).
Broughton, Mrs Vernon Delves, *Court and Private Life in the Time of Queen Charlotte: Being the Journals of Mrs Papendieck, Assistant Keeper of the Wardrobe and Reader to Her Majesty* (London, 1887).
Brown, Clive, 'Ferdinand David's Editions of Beethoven', in *Performing Beethoven*, ed. Robin Stowell (Cambridge, 1994).
Brown, Malcolm Hamrick and Roland John Wiley, *Slavonic and Western Music: Essays for Gerald Abraham* (Ann Arbor and Oxford, c.1985).
Brubaker, Bruce and Jane Gottlieb (eds.), *Pianist, Scholar, Connoisseur: Essays in Honor of Jacob Lateiner* (Stuyvesant, NY, 2000).
Brummer, E., *Beethoven im Spiegel der zeitgenössischen Presse* (Würzburg, 1932).
Buchner, Alexander, 'Beethovens Kompositionen für Mandoline', in *Beethoven Jahrbuch* 3 (1957–8), ed. Paul Mies and Joseph Schmidt-Görg (Bonn, 1959), pp.38–50.
Cahn, Peter, 'Zu Beethovens Klaviertrio in Es-Dur op.70 Nr.2', in *Beethovens Klaviertrios*, ed. Rudolf Bockholdt (Munich, 1992).
——, 'Formprobleme in Beethovens "Freyer Sonate" op.102 Nr.1', in *Beethovens Werke für Klavier und Violoncello*, ed. Sieghard Brandenburg, Ingeborg Maass and Wolfgang Osthoff (Bonn, 2004).
Chitz, Arthur, 'Beethovens Kompositionen für Mandoline', *Der Merker*, no.12 (June 1912), pp.446–50.
——, 'Une Oeuvre inconnue de Beethoven pour mandoline et piano', *S.I.M. Revue musicale*, 8, no.12 (Dec. 1912).
Clive, Peter, *Beethoven and His World: A Biographical History* (Oxford, 2001).
Cooper, Barry, *Beethoven and the Creative Process* (Oxford, 1990).
—— (ed.), *The Beethoven Compendium* (London, 1991).
——, *Beethoven's Folksong Settings: Chronology, Sources, Style* (Oxford, 1994).
Czerny, Carl, 'Anekdoten und Notizen über Beethoven', in *Über den richtigen Vortrag der sämtlichen Beethoven'schen Klavierwerke*, ed. P. Badura-Skoda (Vienna, 1963).
——, *Erinnerungen aus meinem Leben*, ed. Walter Kolneder. Sammlung Musikwissenschaftlicher Abhandlungen, vol.46 (1968).
Dalhaus, Carl, '"Von zwei Kulturen der Musik"'. Die Schlußfuge aus Beethovens Cellosonate opus 102,2', *Die Musikforschung*, 31 (Oct./Dec. 1978), pp.397–405.
——, *Ludwig van Beethoven: Approaches to His Music* (Oxford, 1991).
Del Mar, Jonathan, *Beethoven, Sonatas for Violoncello and Piano*, Critical Commentary (Kassel, 2004).
——, 'Once Again: Reflections on Beethoven's Tied-Note Notation', *Early Music*, 32 (Feb. 2004).
——, *Beethoven, Trios op.1*, Critical Commentary (Kassel, 2023), pp.134–54.
Deutsch, Otto Erich, *Franz Schubert: Die Erinnerungen seiner Freunde* (Leipzig, 1957).
——, *Mozart. Die Dokumente seines Lebens* (Kassel, 1961).
Donat, Misha, Introduction to *Beethoven. Sonata for Pianoforte and Horn or Violoncello op.17*, ed. Jonathan Del Mar (Kassel, 2020).

———, Introductions to Beethoven's Piano Trios opp.1, 70 and 97, ed. Jonathan Del Mar (Kassel, 2023, 2024 and 2022).
Dorfmüller, Kurt, ed., *Beiträge zur Beethoven-Bibliographie* (Munich, 1978).
Dorfmüller, Kurt, Norbert Gertsch and Julia Ronge (eds.), *Ludwig van Beethoven. Thematisch-bibliographisches Werkverzeichnis* (Munich, 2014).
Drabkin, William, 'The "Kreutzer" Sonata: A Perspective', in *The Beethoven Violin Sonatas*, ed. Lewis Lockwood and Mark Kroll (Urbana and Chicago, 2004).
Dufner, Jens, *Ludwig van Beethoven. Sonata for Violoncello and Piano op.69. 1 Movement*. Facsimile edition, commentary (Bonn, 2015).
Duport, Jean-Louis, *Essai sur le Doigté du Violoncelle et sur la Conduite de l'Archet* (Paris, 1806).
Edelmann, Bernd, 'Wenzel Müller's Lied vom "Schneider Wetz" und Beethovens Trio-Variationen op.121a', in *Beethovens Klaviertrios, Symposion München 1990*, ed. Rudolf Bockholdt and Petra Weber-Bockholdt (Munich, 1992).
Edwards, F.G., 'George P. Bridgetower and the Kreutzer Sonata, *The Musical Times*, 49, no.783 (1 May 1908), pp.302–8.
Gerber, Ernst Ludwig, *Neues historisch-biographisches Lexikon der Tonkünstler* (Leipzig, 1812).
Grove, George, *A Dictionary of Music and Musicians* (London, 1879–89).
Haberl, Dieter, 'Beethovens erste Reise nach Wien 1786/87', in *Beethoven. Die Bonner Jahre*, ed. Norbert Schloßmacher (Bonn, 2020).
Halm, August, *Von zwei Kulturen der Musik* (Munich, 1920).
Jahn, Otto, *W.A. Mozart* (Leipzig, 1856–9).
Heartz, Daniel, *Mozart's Operas* (Berkeley and Los Angeles, 1990).
Hassel, G. and W. Müller (eds.), *Allgemeine Encyklopädie der Wissenschaften und Künste* (Leipzig, 1834), section 2, vol.10, p.7.
Hess, Willy, *Verzeichnis der nicht in der Gesamtausgabe veröffentlichte Werke Ludwig van Beethovens* (Wiesbaden, 1957).
Hoffmann, E.T.A., Review of Beethoven's two Piano Trios op.70, in *Allgemeine musikalische Zeitung* no.9, 3 March 1813, cols. 141–54
Johnson, Douglas, *Beethoven's Early Sketches in the 'Fischhof Miscellany'*, Berlin autograph 28 (Ann Arbor, 1980).
———, 'Music for Prague and Berlin: Beethoven's Concert Tour of 1796', in *Beethoven, Performers, and Critics*, ed. Robert Winter and Bruce Carr (Detroit, 1980).
———, '1794–1795: Decisive Years in Beethoven's Early Development', in *Beethoven Studies 3*, ed. Alan Tyson (Cambridge, 1982).
Johnson, Douglas, Alan Tyson and Robert Winter, *The Beethoven Sketchbooks: History, Reconstruction, Inventory* (Berkeley, 1985).
Kagan, Susan, *Archduke Rudolph, Beethoven's Patron, Pupil, and Friend* (New York, 1988).
Kerman, Joseph, 'Tändelnde Lazzi', in *Slavonic and Western Music: Essays for Gerald Abraham*, ed. Malcolm Hamrick Brown and Roland John Wiley (Ann Arbor and Oxford, c.1985).
Kinderman, William, 'Beethoven's Unfinished Piano Trio in F minor from 1816: A Study of Its Genesis and Significance', *Journal of Musicological Research*, 25, no.1 (2006), pp.42–76.

——, *Beethoven* (Oxford, 2009).
Kinsky, Georg, *Das Werk Beethovens. Thematisch-Bibliographisches Verzeichnis seiner sämtlichen vollendeten Kompositionen*, completed and edited by Hans Halm (Munich, 1955).
Klein, Rudolf (ed.), *Dokumentation und Aufführungspraxis: Beethoven-Kolloquium 1977* (Kassel, 1978).
Komlós, Katalin, 'The Viennese Keyboard Trio in the 1780s: Sociological Background and Contemporary Reception', *Music & Letters*, 68, no.3 (July 1987), pp.222–34.
Kramer, Lawrence, 'Saving the Ordinary: Beethoven's "Ghost" Trio and the Wheel of History', in *Beethoven Forum*, 12, no.1 (Urbana-Champaign, 2005), pp.50–81.
Kunze, Stefan, 'Beethovens "Besonnenheit" und das Poetische', in *Beethovens Klaviertrios, Symposion München 1990*, ed. Rudolf Bockholdt and Petra Weber-Bockholdt (Munich, 1992).
—— (ed.), *Ludwig van Beethoven. Die Werke im Spiegel seiner Zeit* (Laaber, 1996).
Ladenburger, Michael, *Beethoven auf Reisen* (Bonn, 2016).
Landon, H.C. Robbins, *Haydn in England, 1791–1795* (London, 1976).
——, *Haydn: The Years of 'The Creation'* (London, 1977).
Leitzmann, Albert, *Ludwig van Beethoven. Berichte der Zeitgenossen, Briefe und persönliche Aufzeichnungen* (Leipzig, 1921).
Lenz, Wilhelm von, *Beethoven et ses trois styles* (St Petersburg, 1852).
——, *Beethoven, eine Kunststudie* (Hamburg, 1860).
Lockwood, Lewis, 'The Autograph of the First Movement of Beethoven's Sonata for Violoncello and Pianoforte, Opus 69', in *The Music Forum*, 2, ed. William J. Mitchell and Felix Salzer (New York and London, 1970), pp.1–109.
——, 'The Beethoven Sketchbook in the Scheide Library', *The Princeton University Library Chronicle*, 37, no.2 (Winter 1976).
——, 'Beethoven's Early Works for Violoncello and Contemporary Violoncello Technique', in *Beethoven-Kolloquium 1977*, ed. Rudolf Klein (Kassel, 1978), pp.174–82.
—— and Phyllis Benjamin (eds.), *Beethoven Essays: Studies in Honor of Elliot Forbes* (Cambridge, Mass., 1984).
——, 'Beethoven and the Problem of Closure: Some Examples from the Middle-Period Chamber Music', in *Beiträge zu Beethovens Kammermusik*, ed. Sieghard Brandenburg and Helmut Loos (Munich, 1987), pp.254–72.
——, *Beethoven: Studies in the Creative Process* (Cambridge, Mass., and London, 1992).
——, 'Beethoven before 1800: The Mozart Legacy', in *Beethoven Forum*, 3, ed. Glenn Stanley (Lincoln, Neb., and London, 1994), pp.39–52.
——, 'Beethoven's Emergence from Crisis: The Cello Sonatas of op.102 (1815)', *The Journal of Musicology*, 16, no.3 (Summer 1998), pp.301–22.
——, 'Beethoven's "Kakadu" Variations, op.121a: A Study in Paradox', in *Pianist, Scholar, Connoisseur: Essays in Honor of Jacob Lateiner*, ed. Bruce Brubaker and Jane Gottlieb (Stuyvesant, NY, 2000).

——, 'Beethoven's Op.69 Revisited: The Place of the Sonata in Beethoven's Chamber Music', in *Beethovens Werke für Klavier und Violoncello*, ed. S. Brandenburg, Ingeborg Maass and Wolfgang Osthoff (Bonn, 2004), pp.145–72.
——, *Ludwig van Beethoven. Sonata for Violoncello and Piano op.69. 1 Movement*. Facsimile edition, commentary (Bonn, 2015).
Lockwood, Lewis and Mark Kroll (eds.), *The Beethoven Violin Sonatas: History, Criticism, Performance* (Urbana and Chicago, 2004).
MacArdle, Donald W., 'Beethoven and the Archduke Rudolph', in *Beethoven-Jahrbuch 1959/60*, ed. Paul Mies and Joseph Schmidt-Görg (Bonn, 1962), pp.36–58.
Marston, Nicholas, 'In the "Twilight Zone": Beethoven's Unfinished Piano Trio in F minor', *The Journal of the Royal Musical Association*, 131, no.2 (2006), pp.227–86.
Marx, Adolf Bernhard, *Ludwig van Beethoven* (Berlin, 1875).
Matthews, Betty, 'George Augustus Polgreen Bridgtower', *The Music Review*, 29 (Feb. 1968), pp.22–6.
May, Jürgen, 'Beethoven and Prince Karl Lichnowsky', in *Beethoven Forum*, 3, ed. Christopher Reynolds (Lincoln, Neb., and London, 1994).
Mentzos, Georgios, *Beethovens Klaviertrios op.70 und ihre Skizzen* (Regensburg, 2019).
Mies, Paul, *Beethoven's Sketches: An Analysis of his Style Based on a Study of his Sketchbooks* (Oxford, 1929).
Miller, Malcolm and William Kinderman (eds.), *Beethoven the European* (Brepols, 2022).
Misch, Ludwig, 'Beethovens "Variierte Theme" op.105 und op.107', in *Beethoven Jahrbuch 1959/60*, ed. Paul Mies and Joseph Schmidt-Görg (Bonn, 1962), pp.102–42.
Morley-Pegge, Reginald, *The French Horn: Some Notes on the Evolution of the Instrument and of Its Technique* (London, 1960).
Moscheles, Charlotte, *Aus Moscheles' Leben. Nach Briefen und Tagebüchern herausgegeben von seiner Frau* (Leipzig, 1872).
Moskovitz, Marc D. and R. Larry Todd, *Beethoven's Cello: Five Revolutionary Sonatas and Their World* (Woodbridge, 2017).
Mozart, Wolfgang Amadé, *Briefe und Aufzeichnungen*, ed. Wilhelm A. Bauer and Otto Erich Deutsch (Kassel, 1962–75).
Müller-Blattau, Josef, 'Beethoven und die Variation', in *Neues Beethoven-Jahrbuch* 5 (Augsburg, 1933).
Münch, Ernst (ed.), *Julius Schnellers Lebensumriß und vertraute Briefe* (Leipzig, 1834).
Nissen, Georg Nikolaus, *Biographie W.A. Mozart's* (Leipzig, 1828).
Nohl, Ludwig, *Beethoven. Nach den Schilderungen seiner Zeitgenossen* (Stuttgart, 1877).
Nottebohm, Gustav, *Ein Skizzenbuch von Beethoven* (Leipzig, 1865).
——, *Beethoveniana. Aufsätze und Mittheilungen* (Leipzig and Winterthur, 1872).
——, *Zweite Beethoveniana* (Leipzig, 1887).
Obelkevich, Mary Rowen, 'The Growth of a Musical Idea – Beethoven's Opus 96', *Current Musicology* 11 (1971).

Oldman, Cecil B., 'Beethoven's Variations on National Themes: Their Composition and First Publication', *The Music Review* 12, no.1 (Feb. 1951).

Ong, Seow-Chin, 'Beethoven's "Archduke"-Trio. The Sketches for the Scherzo', in *Bonner Beethoven-Studien*, vol.3, ed. Sieghard Brandenburg and Ernst Herttrich (Bonn, 2003).

Osmond-Smith, David, *Playing on Words: A Guide to Luciano Berio's 'Sinfonia'* (London, 1985).

Pare, Arabella, 'Beethoven as a Transnational Composer: *Straßenmusik*, Verbunkos and the Trio op.11 "Gassenhauer"', in *Beethoven the European*, ed. Malcolm Miller and William Kinderman (Brepols, 2022).

Raab, Armin, Critical Commentary to *Beethoven Werke*, series 5, vol.4 (Munich, 1993).

——, 'Beethovens op.17 – Hornsonate oder Cellosonate?', in *Neues Musikwissenschaftliches Jahrbuch* 3, ed. Franz Krautwurst (Augsburg, 1994).

Rees, Abraham (ed.), *The Cyclopædia; or, Universal Dictionary of Arts, Sciences and Literature* (London, 1819).

Reichardt, Johann Friedrich, *Vertraute Briefe geschrieben auf eine Reise nach Wien und den österreichischen Staaten zu Ende 1808 und zu Anfang 1809* (Amsterdam, 1810).

Reynolds, Christopher, 'Ends and Means in the Second Finale to Beethoven's op.30 no.1', in *Beethoven Essays: Studies in Honor of Elliot Forbes*, ed. Lewis Lockwood and Phyllis Benjamin (Cambridge, Mass., 1984).

Ronge, Julia, *Beethovens Lehrzeit. Kompositionsstudien bei Joseph Haydn, Johann Georg Albrechtsberger und Antonio Salieri* (Bonn, 2011).

—— (ed.), *Beethoven. Kompositionsstudien bei Joseph Haydn, Johann Georg Albrechtsberger und Antonio Salieri*, Beethoven Werke XIII, vols.1–3 (Munich, 2014).

Rosen, Charles, *The Classical Style* (London, 2005).

Rosenthal, Albi, 'Ein Böcklein aus dem Stall', in *Beethovens Werke für Klavier und Violoncello*, ed. Sieghard Brandenburg, Ingeborg Maas and Wolfgang Osthoff (Bonn, 2004).

Rostal, Max, *Ludwig van Beethoven: Die Sonaten für Klavier und Violine* (Munich, 1981).

Schachter, Carl, 'The Sketches for the Sonata for Piano and Violin op.24', in *Beethoven Forum*, 3, ed. Glenn Stanley (Lincoln, Neb., and London, 1994).

Schenk, Johann Baptist, 'Autobiographische Skizze', *Studien zur Musikwissenschaft* 11 (1924).

Schenker, Heinrich, *Der freie Satz* (Vienna, 1935).

Schering, Arnold, *Beethoven und die Dichtung* (Berlin, 1936).

Schiedermair, Ludwig, *Der junge Beethoven* (Leipzig, 1939).

Schindler, Anton Felix, *The Life of Beethoven*, ed. Ignace Moscheles (London, 1841).

——, *Biographie von Ludwig van Beethoven* (Münster, 1860).

Schmid, Ernst Fritz, *Carl Philipp Emanuel Bach und seine Kammermusik* (Kassel, 1931).

Schmidt-Görg, Joseph, *Beethoven. Die Geschichte seiner Familie* (Bonn, 1964).

——, *Ludwig van Beethoven* (Bonn, 1969).

——, 'Die Wasserzeichen in Beethovens Notenpapieren', in *Beiträge zur Beethoven-Bibliographie*, ed. Kurt Dorfmüller (Munich, 1978).
Schwager, Myron, 'A Fresh Look at Beethoven's Arrangements', *Music & Letters*, 54, no.2 (1973).
Schwarz, Boris, 'Beethoven and the French Violin School', *The Musical Quarterly*, 44 (1958), pp.431–77.
Seyfried, Ignaz von, *Ludwig van Beethoven's Studien im Generalbass, Contrapunkt und in der Compositions-Lehre* (Vienna, 1832).
Shedlock, J.S., 'Beethoven's Sketch Books. Chamber Music, &c.', *The Musical Times*, 33, no.597 (1 Nov. 1892).
Sisman, Elaine, 'Memory and Invention at the Threshold of Beethoven's Late Style', in *Beethoven and His World*, ed. Scott Burnham and Michael P. Steinberg (Princeton, 2000).
——, '"The Spirit of Mozart from Haydn's Hands": Beethoven's Musical Inheritance', in *The Cambridge Companion to Beethoven*, ed. Glenn Stanley (Cambridge, 2000).
Solomon, Maynard, 'Beethovens Tagebuch of 1812–1818', in *Beethoven Studies*, ed. A. Tyson (Oxford, 1982).
——, *Beethoven Essays* (Cambridge, Mass., 1988).
——, *Beethovens Tagebuch*, ed. Sieghard Brandenburg (Mainz, 1990).
Spohr, Louis, *Selbstbiographie* (Kassel and Göttingen, 1860–1).
Stanley, Glenn, ed., *The Cambridge Companion to Beethoven* (Cambridge, 2000).
Steblin, Rita, *Beethoven in the Diaries of Johann Nepomuk Chotek* (Bonn, 2013).
Stein, Erwin (ed.), *Arnold Schoenberg Letters*, trans. Eithne Wilkins and Ernst Kaiser (London, 1964).
Stowell, Robin (ed.), *Performing Beethoven* (Cambridge, 1994).
Sutcliffe, William Dean, 'Haydn's Piano Trio Textures', *Music Analysis*, 6, no.3 (1987).
——, 'The Haydn Piano Trio: Textual Facts and Textural Principles', in *Haydn Studies* (Cambridge, 1998).
Szigeti, Joseph, *The Ten Beethoven Sonatas for Piano and Violin* (Urbana, Ill., 1965).
Tellenbach, Marie-Elisabeth, *Beethoven und seine 'unsterbliche Geliebte' Josephine Brunswick* (Zurich, 1983).
Thayer, Alexander Wheelock, *Chronologisches Verzeichnis der Werke Ludwig van Beethoven's* (Berlin, 1865).
——, *Ludwig van Beethovens Leben*, ed. and completed by Hermann Deiters and Hugo Riemann (Leipzig, 1917–23)
——, *Thayer's Life of Beethoven*, rev. and ed. Elliot Forbes (Princeton, 1977).
Tovey, Donald Francis, *Beethoven Sonatas for Pianoforte*, ed. Harold Craxton. Commentaries and Notes (London, 1931).
——, *Beethoven* (Oxford, 1944).
Truscott, Harold, 'The Piano Music I', in *The Beethoven Companion*, ed. Denis Arnold and Nigel Fortune (London, 1971).
Tusa, Michael C., 'Beethoven's "C-Minor Mood": Some Thoughts on the Structural Implications of Key Choice', in *Beethoven Forum*, 2 (Lincoln, Neb., and London, 1993).

Tyler, James and Paul Sparks, *The Early Mandolin* (Oxford, 1988).
Tyson, Alan, *The Authentic English Editions of Beethoven* (London, 1963).
——, 'Beethoven's "Kakadu" Variations and Their English History', *The Musical Times*, 104 (Feb. 1963), pp.108–10.
——, 'Stages in the Composition of Beethoven's Piano Trio op.70, no.1', *Proceedings of the Royal Musical Association*, 97 (1970–1).
——, 'The Authors of the op.104 String Quintet', in *Beethoven Studies*, ed. A. Tyson (Oxford, 1974).
——, Introduction to *Ludwig van Beethoven. Violin Sonata in G major, op.30 no.3*. Facsimile of the autograph in the British Library Add. MS 37767 (London, 1980).
—— (ed.), *Beethoven Studies 3* (Cambridge, 1982).
Uhde, Jürgen, *Beethovens Klaviermusik* (Stuttgart, 1968).
Wallace, Robin, *Beethoven's Critics* (Cambridge, 1986).
Watkin, David, 'Beethoven's Sonatas for Piano and Cello: Aspects of Technique and Performance', in *Performing Beethoven*, ed. R. Stowell (Cambridge, 1994).
Weber-Bockholdt, Petra, 'Beethovens Opus 44', in *Beethovens Klaviertrios. Symposion München 1990*, ed. Rudolf Bockholdt and Petra Weber-Bockholdt (Munich, 1992).
——, '"Eliminating Potentiality": Beethoven's Work on the First Movement of the Cello Sonata in G minor, Op.5, No.2', in *Beethoven Forum*, 10, ed. José Bowen and Richard Will (Urbana-Champaign, n.d.).
Webster, James, 'The Falling-Out between Haydn and Beethoven: The Evidence of the Sources', in *Beethoven Essays: Studies in Honor of Elliot Forbes*, ed. Lewis Lockwood and Phyllis Benjamin (Cambridge, Mass., 1984).
Wegeler, Franz and Ferdinand Ries, *Biographische Notizen über Ludwig van Beethoven* (Koblenz, 1838).
Weston, Pamela, 'Beethoven's Clarinettists', *The Musical Times*, 61 (1970), pp.1212–13.
——, *Clarinet Virtuosi of the Past* (London, 1971).
Wright, Josephine R.B., 'George Polgreen Bridgetower: An African Prodigy in England 1789–99', *The Musical Quarterly*, 66, no.1 (Jan. 1980), pp.65–82.

Classified index of works by Beethoven

Main references are indicated in bold; music examples in italics

Stage Music

Die Geschöpfe des Prometheus op.43   80
Fidelio/Leonore op.72   190, 224n.45, 295, 327
Egmont (Goethe), incidental music
  op.84   295

Choral Music

Oratorio, *Christus am Ölberge* op.85   222
Meeres Stille und Glückliche Fahrt (Goethe)
  op.112   327
Opferlied (Matthisson) op.121b for soprano,
  chorus and orchestra   352n.38
Fantasia for piano, chorus and orchestra
  op.80 ('Choral Fantasy')   291, 310
Mass in C op.86   254, 327, 329, 330, 366
Mass in D ('Missa solemnis') op.123   20, 175,
  175, 295, 329, 330
Cantata, *Der glorreiche Augenblick*
  op.136   327
Cantata *Auf den Tod Josephs des Zweiten*
  WoO 87   39n.20
Cantata *Auf die Erhebung Leopolds des Zweiten
  zur Kaiserwürde* WoO 88   39n.20
'Gesang der Mönche' (Schiller)
  WoO 104   130
Canon, 'Glück zum neuen Jahr'
  WoO 176   254

Concert Arias

'Ah! Perfido' (Metastasio) op.65   91, 131
Scene and aria, 'No, non turbati'
  (Metastasio) WoO 92a   155

Songs

'Adelaide' op.46 (Matthisson)   19n.15
Six Songs op.48 (Gellert)   129
Eight Songs op.52
  No.2 'Feuerfarb' (Mereau)   77
Six Songs op.75
  No.1 'Kennst du das Land?'
    (Goethe)   310
Song cycle 'An die ferne Geliebte' op.98
  (Jeitteles)   294, 328, 329, 351
'Der Mann von Wort' (Kleinschmid)
  op.99   353
'Der Kuss' (Weisse) op.128   352n.38
'Sehnsucht' (Goethe) WoO 134   114
29 National airs for voices and piano trio
  WoO 158
  No.16 'Air cosaque'   380n.20

Orchestral Music

Overtures:
Coriolan op.62   265
Die Ruinen von Athen op.113   349
Zur Namensfeier op.115   327, 349
König Stephan op.117   349
Die Weihe des Hauses op.124   125, 338

Symphonies:
Symphony No.1 in C op.21   206, 277, 343
Symphony No.3 in E flat ('Eroica') op.55   82,
  117n.22, 196, 227, 235, 259, 327
Symphony No.4 in B flat op.60   204, 247,
  253, 327
Symphony No.5 in C minor op.67   68, 90,
  209, 211, 231, 237, 254, 255, 327, 328, 366
Symphony No.6 in F ('Pastoral') op.68   90,
  179, 237, 247, 250, 254, 255, 296, 327,
  366
Symphony No.7 in A op.92   128, 247, 279,
  294, 327, 366
Symphony No.8 in F op.93   203, 206, 207,
  258–9, 277, 279, 285, 286, 294, 327
Symphony No.9 in D minor ('Choral')
  op.125   20, 203, 206, 207, 269, 329,
  332, 344, 368

Concertos:
Piano Concerto No.1 in C op.15   49, 71, 74,
  83, 140, 154
Piano Concerto No.2 in B flat op.19   40, 49,
  51, 154, 161n.10
Piano Concerto No.3 in C minor op.37   65,
  66, 68, 71, 83, 168, 200n.11, 209, 222
Piano Concerto No.4 in G op.58   71, 179,
  192, 196, 253, 294, 300, 327

Piano Concerto No.5 in E flat ('Emperor')
op.73   84n.7, 152, 192, 196, 231, 291,
295, 327
Violin Concerto in D op.61   71, 152, 196, 296,
315, 327
Transcription for piano and
orchestra   152, 253
Triple Concerto in C op.56   71, 99, 192, 315,
327

Miscellaneous Orchestral Pieces:
Wellingtons Sieg ('Battle Symphony')
op.91   294, 327, 366

Chamber Music for Strings

String Trio in E flat op.3   46 n.13
Serenade in D for string trio op.8   98–9, *98*,
200
String Trios op.9   129, 155
   No.1 in G   49, 65
   No.3 in C minor   48, 58, 68
String Quartets op.18
   No.1 in F   71, 107, 180, 265, 341,
   No.3 in D   49, 77
   No.4 in C minor   68, 74n.36, 209
   No.5 in A   173n.17
   No.6 in B flat   74n.36, 173
String Quartets ('Razumovsky') op.59   155,
196, 224, 253, 327, 366
   No.1 in F   107, 173n.17, 203, 206, 231, 250,
   303
   No.2 in E minor   49, 120, 173n.17, 191–2,
   247
   No.3 in C   107, 330
String Quartet in E flat ('Harp') op.74   255,
302, 305, 327
String Quartet in F minor ('Serioso')
op.95   294, 327, 332, 349, 351
String Quartet in E flat op.127   235, 282n.58,
327, 372
String Quartet in B flat op.130   50, 274, 327,
329
String Quartet in C sharp minor op.131   120n.23,
274, 305n.22, 330, 372
String Quartet in A minor op.132   50, 171,
235, 274, 327, 329, 332
String Quartet in B flat op.133 (Grand
Fugue)   331, 343
String Quartet in F op.135   173n.17, 372
String Quintet in C op.29   49–50, 128, 171,
196, 285
String Quintet in E flat op.4 (after the Wind
Octet op.103)   44
String Quintet in C minor op.104 (after the
Piano Trio op.1 No.3), 71–2, 74

Chamber Music with Piano

Piano Trios op.1   19, 40, **41–77**, 77, 90, 155, 183
   No.1 in E flat   44, 51, **52–60**, 53–4, *55*, *56*,
   57, *58*, *59–60*, 77
   No.2 in G   43, 44–5, *45*, 48, 49, 58, **61–8**,
   61, *62–3*, *64*, *65*, 150
   No.3 in C minor   44, 46–8, 47, 52, 60,
   68–77, *69*, *70*, *73*, *75–6*, *133*, 160, 207,
   209, 214
Piano Trios op.70   10, 18, 237, **254–92**, 295,
366
   No.1 in D ('Ghost')   19–20, 155, 158n.9,
   173n.17, **255–76**, *256*, *257–8*, *259–60*,
   261–3, *266–8*, *270–1*, *272*, *273–4*, *275*,
   300, *302*, 315–16, 341
   No.2 in E flat   35, 40, 49, 50, 247, 264,
   276–92, *278*, *281*, *284*, *287–9*, *289–91*,
   332
Piano Trio in B flat ('Archduke') op.97   18,
19, 20, 49, 50, 179, 200n.11, 224, 247,
285, **293–307**, *297–9*, *301*, *307*, 315, 327,
351, 354–5, *356*, 366
Piano Trio in E flat WoO 38   **32–5**, *33–5*,
65, 278
Allegretto in B flat for piano trio
WoO 39   37, 308–9
Variations for piano trio ('Kakadu')
op.121a   30, 77n.42, 114, 144, 145,
200n.10   294, 350, **351–64**, *354*, *360–1*,
362–3
Variations in E flat for piano trio
op.44   77–80, *79*, 200, 352–3
Clarinet Trio in B flat op.11   59, 65, 83, 85,
140–50, *141–3*, *146*, *147–8*, *149*, 200, 352
Trio for piano, flute and bassoon
WoO 37   17, **29–32**, *30–1*, *33*, 102, 152
Violin Sonatas op.12   152, **154–71**, 186
   No.1 in D   60, 152, *153*, **155–61**, *156–8*,
   159–60, *163*
   No.2 in A   152, **161–7**, *162*, *163*, *164*, *165*,
   166–7, *174*
   No.3 in E flat   49, 108, 152, **168–71**, *169*
Violin Sonata in A minor op.23   117n.22, 128,
154, 162, **171–7**, *172*, *174*, *175*, *176*, 186–7,
219, 227n.51, 255, 332
Violin Sonata in F ('Spring') op.24   17, 128,
151, 152, 154, 171, 174, **177–87**, *178*, *179*,
180, *181–2*, *183*, *184*, *185*, *186*, 192, 227n.51,
255, 302, 360
Violin Sonatas op.30   17, 155, **196–220**, 356
   No.1 in A   151, 152, **197–206**, *198*, *199*,
   202–3, *204*, *205*, 222, 232
   No.2 in C minor   68, 71, 124, 151, 168–71,
   197, 203, **206–14**, *208*, *209*, *210*, *212–13*

No.3 in G   49, **214–20**, *215, 216, 217, 218*
Violin Sonata in A ('Kreutzer')   18, 71, 138, 151, 160, *171, 172, 173,* 197, 199, **220–36**, *228, 229, 230, 232–3, 234, 235–6, 283,* 332
Violin Sonata in G op.96   18, 49, 151, 160, 179, 227, 246, 294, 295, 296, 305, 306, **309–26**, *310, 311, 313, 314, 317, 319–20, 321–2, 323, 324, 325–6,* 327, 328, 366
Variations for violin and piano on 'Se vuol ballare' (Mozart) WoO 40   **35–7**, 80
Rondo in G for violin and piano WoO 41   37–8, *38*
Six Contredanses for violin and piano WoO 42   138–9
Notturno for viola and piano op.42 (after the Serenade for string trio op.8)   98–9, *99*
Cello Sonatas op.5   17, 90, 91, **94–124**, *99*, 152
  No.1 in F   67 n.32, *99*, **103–14**, *103–4, 105, 107, 108, 109–11, 112, 113–14,* 130, 170
  No.2 in G minor   33, 48 n.16, 65, 94, 95, *96,* 100–1, 102, **114–24**, *115, 116–17, 118, 119, 120, 122, 123,* 173n.17
Cello Sonata in A op.69   17, 18, 90, 91, 95, *99,* 124, 227, **237–54**, *238–9, 241, 242, 243, 244, 245, 251–2,* 310, 336, 366
Cello Sonatas op.102   17–18, 20, 90, 91, 254, **328–50**
  No.1 in C   102, 173n.16, 227, 279, 328–9, **331–9**, *331, 333–4, 335–6, 338*
  No.2 in D   155, 207, 255, 256, 257–8, 265, 329, 330, *331,* 338, **339–50**, *340, 344, 345, 346–7, 348*
Variations for cello and piano on 'See, the Conqu'ring Hero Comes' (Handel) WoO 45   **124–7**, 129, 200
Variations for cello and piano on 'Bei Männern' (Mozart) WoO 46   35, 114, **128–30**, *129,* 366
Variations for cello and piano on 'Ein Mädchen oder Weibchen' (Mozart) op.66   35, 36–7, **127–8**, *129,* 366
Horn Sonata in F op.17   83, 85, **188–95**, *191, 193–4*
  Transcription for cello and piano   192–4, *193–4*
Sonatina in C minor for mandolin and piano WoO 43a   130, 133, *133,* 134
Adagio in E flat for mandolin and piano   WoO 43b   130, 132, 134, 135, *135–7*
Sonatina in C major for mandolin and piano WoO 44a   130, 132, 137, 138n.52
Andante con variazioni for mandolin and piano WoO 44b   130, 138

Six national airs with variations for piano and flute op.105   20, **365–87**
  No.1 'The Cottage Maid'   200n.10, 370
  No.2 'Air Ecossais' ('Of Noble Race was Shinkin')   370
  No.3 'A Schüsserl und a Reindl'   369, 370, 371, 382–3, *382, 383*
  No.4 'The Last Rose of Summer'   370, 373, *373–4*
  No.5 'Chiling O'Guiry'   370
  No.6 'Paddy Whack'   370
Ten national airs with variations for piano and flute op.107   20, 200, **365–87**
  No.1 'I bin a Tiroler Bua'   368, 369, 374, *375–7,* 377
  No.2 'Bonny Laddie, Highland Laddie'   370
  No.3 'Air de la Petite Russie'   369, 371, 384–6, *384, 385, 386*
  No.4 'St. Patrick's Day' ('The Pulse of an Irishman')   369, 384
  No.5 'A Madel, ja a Madel'   369, 377, *377–8,* 379, *380*
  No.6 'Peggy's Daughter'   369, 370
  No.7 'Schöne Minka'   369, 370, 371, *380*
  No.8 'O Mary, at thy Window be'   368, 370
  No.9 'O thou art the Lad of my Heart'   372, 377
  No.10 'The Highland Watch'   368
Piano Quartets WoO 36   17, **21–9**, 22, 27, 88–9, 152
  No.1 in E flat   22, **23–7**, *23–6,* 29, 102, 114
  No.2 in D   **27–8**, 29
  No.3 in C   **22–3**, 22, 28, 29
Quintet for piano and wind op.16   17, 43, 65, **82–9**, *84, 86, 87, 88,* 103, 140, 248
  Transcription for piano quartet   17, 23, **85–9**, *86, 87, 89*

Chamber Works with Wind

Octet for wind in E flat op.103   44
Septet in E flat op.20   77, 140
Serenade in D for flute, viola and cello op.25   98
Sextet for wind in E flat op.71   140

Works for Piano Solo & Piano Duet

Sonatas:
Sonatas op.2   26 n.8, 29, 40, 42 n.5, 51, 52, 155
  No.1 in F minor   27, 29, 33, 49, 74, 173n.17
  No.2 in A   170
  No.3 in C   29, 47, 49, 58, 65, 103
Sonata in E flat op.7   49, 51, 117n.22, 170

Sonatas op.10 155
   No.1 in C minor 48, 74, 211
   No.2 in F 162, 173n.17, 246
   No.3 in D 49, 168, 255, 265, 341
Sonata in C minor ('Pathétique') op.13 83, 211, 316
Sonatas op.14 83, 190
   No.1 in E 133, 134, 161–2, 191, 291n.64
   No. 2 in G 246
Sonata in B flat op.22 83, 129, 135, *135*, 171
Sonata in A flat op.26 161
Sonatas op.27 83
   No.1 in E flat 84, 222, 328–9
   No.2 in C sharp minor ('Moonlight') 83–4, 224n.44
Sonata in D ('Pastoral') op.28 49, 83, 247–8
Sonatas op.31 155, 356
   No.1 in G 33, 34, 49–50, 205–6, 214, 247n.16, 285
   No.2 in D minor ('Tempest') 83, 196, 206, 219, 265
   No.3 in E flat 197, 214, 232, 279, 281–2, 283
Sonatas op.49
   No.2 in G 149, 150
Sonata in C ('Waldstein') op.53 37, 50, 74, 83, 192, 224, 285, 291
Sonata in F op.54 102, 107, 219
Sonata in F minor ('Appassionata') op.57 68, 71, 173n.17, 206, 209, 219, 231, 286
Sonata in F sharp op.78 102, 173n.17, 325
Sonata in G op.79 173n.17
Sonata in E flat ('Les Adieux') op.81a 192, 281–2, 294–5
Sonata in E minor op.90 102, 206, 327, 332
Sonata in A op.101 253, 294, 328, 329, 342, 350, 351, 352
Sonata in B flat ('Hammerklavier') op.106 28, 184n.26, 247, 285, 295, 316, 329, 331, 343, 344, 346, *346*, 348, 349, 368, 372–3, *372*, 374, *374*
Sonata in E op.109 37, 74, 246, 304, 305, 308, 329, 369, 372, 377, 380, *381*
Sonata in A flat op.110 246, 247, 308, 329, 330
Sonata in C minor op.111 37, 102, 120n.23, 204, 282, 295, 308, 329, 332, 369, 372, 377, 379, 383

Variations:
Variations in F op.34 196–7, 200
Variations in E flat ('Eroica') op.35 80, 129, 196–7, 322, 330, 386
33 Variations on a Waltz by Diabelli op.120 20, 144, 308, 322, 329, 330, 356, 372, 377, 383, *384*, 384
Variations for piano on 'Venni Amore' (Righini) WoO 65 13
Variations on 'Es war einmal ein alter Mann' (Dittersdorf) WoO 66 80
Variations on 'Quant' è più bello' (Paisiello) WoO 69 352
Variations on 'Nel cuor non più mi sento' (Paisiello) WoO 70 352
Variations on 'Das Waldmärchen' (Wranitzky) WoO 71 200, 352
Variations on 'Une fièvre brulante' (Grétry) WoO 72 128, 352
Variations on 'La stessa, la stessima' (Salieri) WoO 73 155, 200
Variations on 'Rule, Britannia' (Arne) WoO 99 144
Variations for piano duet on 'Ich denke dein' WoO 74 77
Grand Fugue for piano duet op.134 (after the String Quartet op.133) 295

Miscellaneous Piano Pieces:
Fantasia op.77 114n.21
Polonaise in C op.89 220
Eleven Bagatelles op.119 20, 195
   No.1 in G minor 114n.21
   No.2 in C 72
   No.7 in C 377, 379
Six Bagatelles op.126 20
   No.2 in G minor 114n.21
Bagatelle in A minor ('Für Elise') WoO 59 224

Unfinished and Projected Works:
Romance for piano, flute, bassoon & orchestra (Hess Catalogue no.13) 29
Piano Concerto in D (Hess Catalogue no.15) 351
Opera, *Macbeth* 265
Symphony in C minor 26–7, 27
Symphony no.10 in E flat 332
Piano Trio in F minor 350–1

Index of Beethoven's works by opus number

Main references are indicated in bold; music examples in italics

Opus

1 Piano Trios   19, 40, **41–77**, 90, 155, 183
   No.1 in E flat   44, 51, **52–60**, *53–4*, *55*, *56*, *57*, *58*, *59–60*, 77
   No.2 in G   43, 44–5, *45*, 48, 49, 51, 58, **61–8**, *61*, *62–3*, *64*, *65*, 150
   No.3 in C minor   44, 46–8, 47, 52, 60, **68–77**, *69*, *70*, *73*, *75–6*, 133, 160, 207, 209, 214
2 Piano Sonatas   26 n.8, 29, 40, 42 n.5, 51, 52, 155
   No.1 in F minor   27, 29, 33, 49, 74, 173n.17
   No.2 in A   170
   No.3 in C   29, 47, 49, 58, 65, 103
3 String Trio in E flat   46 n.13
4 String Quintet in E flat (after the Wind Octet op.103)   44
5 Cello Sonatas   17, 90, 91, **94–124**, 99, 152,
   No.1 in F   67 n.32, 99, **103–14**, *103–4*, *105*, *107*, *108*, *109–11*, *112*, *113–14*   130, 170
   No.2 in G minor   33, 48 n.16, 65, 94, 95, 96, 100–1, 102, **114–24**, *115*, *116–17*, *118*, *119*, *120*, *122*, *123*, 173n.17
7 Piano Sonata in E flat   49, 51, 117n.22, 170
8 Serenade in D for string trio   98–9, *98*, 200
9 String Trios   129, 155
   No.1 in G   49, 65
   No.3 in C minor   48, 58, 68
10 Piano Sonatas   155
   No.1 in C minor   48, 74, 211
   No.2 in F   162, 173n.17, 246
   No.3 in D   49, 168, 255, 265, 341
11 Clarinet Trio in B flat   59, 65, 83, 85, **140–50**, *141–3*, *146*, *147–8*, *149*, 200, 352
12 Violin Sonatas   152, **154–71**, 186
   No.1 in D   60, 152, 153, **155–61**, *156–8*, *159–60*, *163*
   No.2 in A   152, **161–7**, *162*, *163*, *164*, *165*, *166–7*, *174*
   No.3 in E flat   49, 108, 152, **168–71**, *169*

13 Piano Sonata in C minor ('Pathétique')   83, 211, 316
14 Piano Sonatas   83, 190
   No.1 in E   133, 134, 161–2, 191, 291n.64
   No. 2 in G   246
15 Piano Concerto No.1 in C   49, 71, 74, 83, 140, 154
16 Quintet for piano and wind   17, 43, 65, **82–9**, *84*, *86*, *87*, *88*, 103, 140, 248
   Transcription for piano quartet   17, 23, **85–9**, *86*, *87*, *89*
17 Horn Sonata in F   83, 85, **188–95**, *191*, *193–4*
   Transcription for cello and piano   192–4, *193–4*
18 String Quartets
   No.1 in F   71, 107, 180, 265, 341,
   No.3 in D   49, 77
   No.4 in C minor   68, 74n.36, 209
   No.5 in A   173n.17
   No.6 in B flat   74n.36, 173
19 Piano Concerto No.2 in B flat   40, 49, 51, 154, 161211.10
20 Septet in E flat   77, 140
21 Symphony No.1 in C   206, 277, 343
22 Piano Sonata in B flat   83, 129, 135, *135*, 171
23 Violin Sonata in A minor   117n.22, 128, 154, 162, **171–7**, *172*, 174, 175, 176, 186–7, 219, 227n.51, 255, 332
24 Violin Sonata in F ('Spring')   17, 128, 151, 152, 154, 171, 174, **177–87**, *178*, 179, 180, 181–2, 183, 184, 185, 186, 192, 227n.51, 255, 302, 360
25 Serenade in D for flute, viola and cello   98
26 Piano Sonata in A flat   161
27 Piano Sonatas   83
   No.1 in E flat   84, 222, 328–9
   No.2 in C sharp minor ('Moonlight')   83–4, 224n.44
28 Piano Sonata in D ('Pastoral')   49, 83, 247–8
29 String Quintet in C   49–50, 128, 171, 196, 285

30 Violin Sonatas   17, 155, **196–220**, 356
     No.1 in A   151, 152, **197–206**, *198*, *199*,
        202–3, *204*, *205*, *222*, *232*
     No.2 in C minor   68, 71, 124, 151, 197,
        203, **206–14**, *208*, *209*, *210*, *212–13*
     No.3 in G   49, **214–20**, *215*, *216*, *217*, *218*
31 Piano Sonatas   155, 356
     No.1 in G   33, 34, 49–50, 205–6, 214,
        247n.16, 285
     No.2 in D minor ('Tempest')   83, 196,
        206, 219, 265
     No.3 in E flat   197, 214, 232, 279, 281–2,
        283
34 Variations in F for piano   196–7, 200
35 Variations in E flat for piano
     ('Eroica')   80, 129, 196–7, 322, 330, 386
37 Piano Concerto No.3 in C minor   65, 66,
     68, 71, 83, 168, 200n.11, 209, 222
42 Notturno for viola and piano (after the
     Serenade for string trio op.8)   98–9, 99
43 *Die Geschöpfe des Prometheus*   80
44 Variations in E flat for piano trio   **77–80**,
     79, 200, 352–3
46 'Adelaide' (Matthisson)   19n.15
47 Violin Sonata in A ('Kreutzer')   18,
     71, 138, 151, 160, 171, 172, 173, 197, 199,
     220–36, *228*, *229*, *230*, *232–3*, *234*, *235–6*,
     283, *332*
48 Six Songs (Gellert)   129
49 Piano Sonatas
     No.2 in G   149, 150
52 Eight Songs
     No.2, 'Feuerfarb' (Mereau)   77
53 Piano Sonata in C ('Waldstein')   37, 50,
     74, 83, 192, 224, 285, 291
54 Piano Sonata in F   102, 107, 219
55 Symphony No.3 in E flat ('Eroica')   82,
     117n.22, 196, 227, 235, 259, 327
56 Triple Concerto in C   71, 99, 192, 315, 327
57 Piano Sonata in F minor ('Appassionata')
     68, 71, 173n.17, 206, 209, 219, 231, 286
58 Piano Concerto No.4 in G   71, 179, 192,
     196, 253, 294, 300, 327
59 String Quartets ('Razumovsky')   155,
     196, 224, 253, 327, 366
     No.1 in F   107, 173n.17, 203, 206, 231,
        250, 303
     No.2 in E minor   49, 120, 173n.17,
        191–2, 247
     No.3 in C   107, 330
60 Symphony No.4 in B flat   204, 247, 253, 327
61 Violin Concerto in D   71, 152, 196, 296,
     315, 327
     Transcription for piano and
        orchestra   152, 253

62 Overture, *Coriolan*   265
65 Concert aria 'Ah! Perfido'
     (Metastasio)   91, 131
66 Variations on 'Ein Mädchen oder
     Weibchen' (Mozart)   35, 36–7,
     127–8, *129*, 366
67 Symphony No.5 in C minor   68, 90, 209,
     211, 231, 237, 254, 255, 327, 328, 366
68 Symphony No.6 in F ('Pastoral')   90, 179,
     237, 247, 250, 254, 255, 296, 327, 366
69 Cello Sonata in A   17, 18, 90, 91, 95, 99,
     124, 227, **237–54**, *238–9*, *241*, *242*, *243*,
     244, *245*, *251–2*, *310*, *336*, 366
70 Piano Trios   10, 18, 237, **254–92**, 295, 366
     No.1 in D ('Ghost')   19–20, 155, 158n.9,
        173n.17, **255–76**, *256*, *257–8*,
        259–60, *261–3*, *266–8*, *270–1*, *272*,
        273–4, *275*, 300, 302, 315–6, 341
     No.2 in E flat   35, 40, 49, 50, 247, 264,
        276–92, *278*, *281*, *284*, *287–9*,
        289–91, *332*
71 Sextet for wind in E flat   140
72 *Fidelio*/*Leonore*   190, 224n.45, 295, 327
73 Piano Concerto No.5 in E flat
     ('Emperor')   84n.7, 152, 192, 196, 231,
     291, 295, 327
74 String Quartet in E flat ('Harp')   255,
     302, 305, 327
75 Six Songs
     No.1 'Kennst du das Land?'
        (Goethe)   310
77 Fantasia for piano   114n.21
78 Piano Sonata in F sharp   102, 173n.17, 325
79 Piano Sonata in G   173n.17
80 Fantasia for piano, chorus and orchestra
     ('Choral Fantasy')   291, 310
81a Piano Sonata in E flat ('Les
     Adieux')   192, 281–2, 294–5
84 *Egmont* (Goethe), incidental music   295
85 Oratorio, *Christus am Ölberge*   222
86 Mass in C   254, 327, 329, 330, 366
89 Polonaise in C for piano   220
90 Piano Sonata in E minor   102, 206, 327, 332
91 *Wellingtons Sieg* ('Battle
     Symphony')   294, 327, 366
92 Symphony No.7 in A   128, 247, 279, 294,
     327, 366
93 Symphony No.8 in F   203, 206, 207,
     258–9, 277, 279, 285, 286, 294, 327
95 String Quartet in F minor
     ('Serioso')   294, 327, 332, 349, 351
96 Violin Sonata in G   18, 49, 151, 160,
     179, 227, 246, 294, 295, 296, 305, 306,
     309–26, *310*, *311*, *313*, *314*, *317*, *319–20*,
     321–2, *323*, *324*, *325–6*, *327*, *328*, 366

97 Piano Trio in B flat ('Archduke')   18, 19, 20, 49, 50, 179, 200n.11, 224, 247, 285, **293–307**, 297–9, 301, 307, 315, 327, 351, 354–5, 356, 366
98 Song cycle *An die ferne Geliebte* (Jeitteles)   294, 328, 329, 351
99 'Der Mann von Wort' (Kleinschmid)   353
101 Piano Sonata in A   253, 294, 328, 329, 342, 350, 351, 352
102 Cello Sonatas   17–18, 20, 90, 91, 254, **328–50**
   No.1 in C   102, 173n.16, 227, 279, 328–9, 331, **331–9**, 333–4, 335–6, 338
   No.2 in D   155, 207, 255, 256, 257–8, 265, 329, 330, 331, 338, **339–50**, 340, 344, 345, 346–7, 348
103 Octet for wind in E flat   44
104 String Quintet in C minor (after the Piano Trio Op.1 No.3)   71–2, 74
105 Six national airs with variations for piano and flute   20, **365–87**
   No.1 'The Cottage Maid'   200n.10, 370
   No.2 'Air Ecossais' ('Of Noble Race was Shinkin')   370
   No.3 'A Schüsserl und a Reindl'   369, 370, 371, 382–3, 382, 383
   No.4 'The Last Rose of Summer'   370, 373, 373–4
   No.5 'Chiling O'Guiry'   370
   No.6 'Paddy Whack'   370
106 Piano Sonata in B flat ('Hammerklavier')   28, 184n.26, 247, 285, 295, 316, 329, 331, 343, 344, 346, 346, 348, 349, 368, 372–3, 372, 374, 374
107 Ten national airs with variations for piano and flute   20, 200, **365–87**
   No.1 'I bin a Tiroler Bua'   368, 369, 374, 375–7, 377
   No.2 'Bonny Laddie, Highland Laddie'   370
   No.3 'Air de la Petite Russie'   369, 371, 384–6, 384, 385, 386
   No.4 'St. Patrick's Day' ('The Pulse of an Irishman')   369, 384
   No.5 'A Madel, ja a Madel'   369, 377, 377–8, 379, 380
   No.6 'Peggy's Daughter'   369, 370
   No.7 'Schöne Minka'   369, 370, 371, 380
   No.8 'O Mary, at thy Window be'   368, 370
   No.9 'O thou art the Lad of my Heart'   372, 377

   No.10 'The Highland Watch'   368
109 Piano Sonata in E   37, 74, 246, 304, 305, 308, 329, 369, 372, 377, 380, *381*
110 Piano Sonata in A flat   246, 247, 308, 329, 330
111 Piano Sonata in C minor   37, 102, 120n.23, 204, 282, 295, 308, 329, 332, 369, 372, 377, 379, 383
112 *Meeres Stille und Glückliche Fahrt* (Goethe)   327
113 *Die Ruinen von Athen*, overture   349
115 *Zur Namensfeier*, overture   327, 349
117 *König Stephan*, overture   349
119 Eleven Bagatelles for piano   20, 195
   No.1 in G minor   114n.21
   No.2 in C   72
   No.7 in C   377, 379
120 33 Variations on a Waltz by Diabelli   20, 144, 308, 322, 329, 330, 356, 372, 377, 383, *384*, 384
121a Variations for piano trio ('Kakadu')   30, 77n.42, 114, 144, 145, 200n.10, 294, 350, **351–64**, 354, 360–1, 362–3
121b *Opferlied* (Matthisson) for soprano, chorus and orchestra   352n.38
123 Mass in D ('Missa solemnis')   20, 175, 175, 295, 329, 330
124 Overture, *Die Weihe des Hauses*   125, 338
125 Symphony No.9 in D minor ('Choral')   20, 203, 206, 207, 269, 329, 332, 344, 368
126 Six Bagatelles for piano   20
   No.2 in G minor   114n.21
127 String Quartet in E flat   235, 282n.58, 327, 372
128 *Der Kuss* (Weisse)   352n.38
130 String Quartet in B flat   50, 274, 327, 329
131 String Quartet in C sharp minor   120n.23, 274, 305n.22, 330, 372
132 String Quartet in A minor   50, 171, 235, 274, 327, 329, 332
133 Grand Fugue for string quartet   331, 343
134 Grand Fugue for piano duet   295
135 String Quartet in F   173n.17, 372
136 Cantata, *Der glorreiche Augenblick*   327

WoO

36 Piano Quartets   17, **21–9**, 88–9, 152
   No.1 in E flat   22, **23–7**, 23–6, 29, 102, 114
   No.2 in D   **27–8**, 29
   No.3 in C   22, **22–3**, 28, 29
37 Trio for piano, flute and bassoon   17, **29–32**, 30–1, 33, 102, 152

38 Piano Trio in E flat **32–5**, *33*–5, 65, 278
39 Allegretto in B flat for piano trio 37, **308–9**
40 Variations for violin and piano on 'Se vuol ballare' (Mozart) **35–7**, 80
41 Rondo in G for violin and piano 37–8, *38*
42 Six Contredanses for violin and piano 138–9
43a Sonatina in C minor for mandolin and piano 130, 133, *133*, *134*
43b Adagio in E flat for mandolin and piano 130, *132*, *134*, 135, *135–7*
44a Sonatina in C major for mandolin and piano 130, *132*, 137, 138n.52
44b Andante con variazioni for mandolin and piano 130, 138
45 Variations for piano and cello on 'See, the Conqu'ring Hero Comes' (Handel) **124–7**, 129, 200
46 Variations for piano and cello on 'Bei Männern' (Mozart) 35, 114, **128–30**, 129, 366
59 Bagatelle in A minor ('Für Elise') 224
65 Variations for piano on 'Venni Amore' (Righini) 13
66 Variations for piano on 'Es war einmal ein alter Mann' (Dittersdorf) 80
69 Variations for piano on 'Quant' è più bello' (Paisiello) 352
70 Variations for piano on 'Nel cuor non più mi sento' (Paisiello) 352
71 Variations for piano on 'Das Waldmärchen' (Wranitzky) 200, 352
72 Variations for piano on 'Une fièvre brulante' (Grétry) 128, 352
73 Variations for piano on 'La stessa, la stessima' (Salieri) 155, 200
74 Variations for piano duet on 'Ich denke dein' 77
79 Variations for piano on 'Rule, Britannia' 144
87 Cantata Auf den Tod Josephs des Zweiten 39n.20
88 Cantata Auf die Erhebung Leopolds des Zweiten zur Kaiserwürde 39n.20
92a Scene and aria, 'No, non turbati' (Metastasio) 155
104 'Gesang der Mönche' (Schiller) 130
134 'Sehnsucht' (Goethe) 114
158 29 National airs for voices and piano trio No.16 'Air cosaque' 380n.20
176 Canon, 'Glück zum neuen Jahr' 254

Unfinished and Projected Works

Romance for piano, flute, bassoon and orchestra (Hess Catalogue no.13) 29
Piano Concerto in D (Hess Catalogue no.15) 351
Opera, *Macbeth* 265
Symphony in C minor 26–7, *27*
Symphony No.10 in E flat 332
Piano Trio in F minor 350–1

General Index

Music examples are indicated in italics

Albrechtsberger, Johann Georg 41, 151
Alexander I, Tsar of Russia 220
Appelby, Samuel 124
Apponyi, Count Anton 43
Arne, Thomas 144
Arnold, Samuel 125
Artaria & Comp. 21–2, 32, 36, 52, 155, 162, 171
Artaria, Domenico 141, 370–1

Bach, Carl Philipp Emanuel 1–2, 3
   Quartets for piano, flute, viola and bass
      Wq.93–5 2
   Sonata in C minor for two violins and
      continuo Wq.161.1 2
   Sonata in G for flute and continuo
      Wq.133 1–2
   Sonatas for keyboard with violin and cello
      Wq.89 3
Bach, Johann Christian 2–3
   Six sonatas for keyboard and violin
      op.2 2–3
      No.1 in F 3
   Six sonatas for keyboard and violin
      op.10 3
      No.2 in C 3
Bach, Johann Christoph Friedrich 90n.1
Bach, Johann Sebastian 1
   The Art of the Fugue BWV 1080 351
   Chromatic Fantasia and Fugue
      BWV 903 303
   A Musical Offering BWV 1079 1, 20
   Sonatas for violin and keyboard
      BWV 1014–19 1
      No.2 in A, 96
      No.3 in E 1
      No.4 in C minor 1
   Sonatas for viola da gamba and keyboard
      BWV 1027–9 1
      No.1 in G, BWV 1027, 1
   Sonata for 2 flutes and continuo
      BWV 1039 1
   St. John Passion BWV 245 245
   Trio Sonatas for organ BWV 525–30 1

Bähr, Joseph 140
Baillot, Pierre 226
Barthélémon, François-Hippolyte 221
Bartók, Bela 276
   Sonata for Two Piano and
      Percussion 276
Baumeister, Ignaz von 227n.51
Beethoven, Kaspar Karl (brother) 197, 351, 352–3
Beethoven, Karl (nephew) 225, 351
Berlioz, Hector 224–5
Boccherini, Luigi 90, 92
Bertolini, Andreas 220
Birchall, Robert 328, 350, 366–7
Bochsa, Nicholas 141
Bolla, Maria 40
Bonaparte, Jérôme 295
Boosey & Sons 371
Brahms, Johannes 18, 255, 275–6, 283n.60
   Clarinet Trio in A minor op.114 150n.7
   Piano Quartet in G minor op.25 18
   Piano Trio in B op.8 283
   Rhapsody for piano in E flat op.119
      no.4 283
   Symphony no.1 in C minor 48n.16
   Symphony no.2 in D 275–6
   Violin Sonata in D minor op.108 276
Braun, Baroness Josephine 190
Braun, Baron Peter Anton 190
Breitkopf & Härtel 130, 134, 154, 171, 222, 248–9, 254, 279, 289, 293–4, 371
Bremner, Robert 3
Brentano, Antonie 308
Brentano, Maximiliane 308
Breuning, Eleonore 36, 37
Breuning, Gerhard 125
Bridgetower, George Augustus
   Polgreen 220–3, 226n.48
Browne, Count Johann Georg von 128–9
Bülow, Hans von 349
Burney, Charles 190

Cappi, Giovanni 36

Cartellieri, Antonio 188
Catherina Amalia Christina, Princess of Baden 293
Chappell & Co. 353
Cherubini, Luigi 225
Chitz, Arthur 132, 134, 137
Chopin, Frédéric 245, 284, 318, 332
    Ballade no.2 op.38 283n.60
    Prelude in F op.28 no.23 318
Chotek, Count Johann Nepomuk 253
Clam-Gallas, Count Christian von 130, 138
Clary-Aldringen, Countess Josephine 130, 131, 134
Clementi, Muzio 52, 177, 182, 253, 308
    Piano Sonata in A op.25 no.4 177, 177
Collin, Heinrich 265
Corelli, Arcangelo 1
Cossmann, Bernhard 349
Czerny, Carl 32, 82–3, 103n.18, 140, 141, 192, 223, 225–6, 234, 247–9, 265, 275, 282, 294

Deiters, Hermann 22, 48, 138
Del Mar, Jonathan 237n.1, 247, 303
Diabelli, Anton 32, 182
Dietrichstein, Count Moritz von 21
Dittersdorf, Carl Ditters von 77–80, 78 (Illustration 1)
Dohnányi, Ernö 360
Domanovecz, Zmeskall von 253
Dragonetti, Domenico 124
Dufner, Jens 238n.2
Duport, Jean-Louis 90–1, 93–7, 126
    Sonata for two cellos in D op.4 no.6 96, 97 (Illustration 2)
    Essai sur le Doigté du Violoncelle 95, 100–2
Duport, Jean-Pierre 90–3, 126
    Sonata for two cellos in C op.3 no.2 94
    Sonata for two cellos in D op.4 no.6 92
    Sonata for two cellos in E minor op.4 no.2, 94–5, 95
Duschek, Josepha 131

Elisabeth Alexievna, Tsarina of Russia 220
Elisabeth Maria, Electress Palatine 102
Erdödy, Count Joseph 43
Erdödy, Countess Anna Maria 254, 289, 349, 350
Ertmann, Baroness Dorothea 253–4
Esterházy, Prince Nicolaus I 221
Esterházy, Prince Nicolaus II 4n.3, 43, 221, 222
Esterházy, Countess Josephine 43
Esterházy, Princess Marie Hermenegild 102

Frank-Gerhardi, Christine 189

Friederiecke, Princess of Prussia 92
Friedrich II ('Frederick the Great'), King of Prussia 92
Friedrich Wilhelm II, King of Prussia 91, 93
Fries, Count Moritz 128, 144, 171
Fries, Countess Maria Theresia 128–9
Fröhlich, Franz Joseph 188
Fuchs, Aloys 77

Gallenberg, Count Wenzel Robert von 224n.44
Gamerra, Giovanni de 140
Gavaux, Pierre 224n.45
Gelinek, Joseph 127n.31, 141
Gellert, Christian Fürchtegott 129
George III, King of England 220
Gerber, Ernst Ludwig 93
Giornovichi, Giovanni 220
Gleichenstein, Ignaz von 245–6, 253
Goulding & D'Almaine 371–2
Gräffer, Anton 32
Grétry, André-Ernest-Modeste 352
Guicciardi, Giulietta 224n.44

Habeneck, François-Antoine 224n.43
Hafner, Philipp 356
Halm, Hans 134, 245
Hampel, Anton Joseph 188, 190
Handel, George Frederic 124–6
    Acis and Galatea 126
    Alexander's Feast 126
    Messiah 126
Häring, Johann Baptist von 367n.6
Härtel, Gottfried Christoph 351–2
Haslinger, Tobias 124, 294
Haydn, Joseph 2, 3, 39–40, 42–4, 48–9, 51, 70–1, 171, 188, 189, 221, 276, 328n.7, 365
    Andante con Variazioni in F minor for piano H.XVII.6 190
    The Creation 43, 52n.25, 276
    Fantasia in C for piano H.XVII.4 74
    Piano Concerto in D H.XVIII.11 44
    Piano Sonatas H.XVI.40–42 102
    Piano Sonata in C H.XIV.50 83, 291
    Piano Sonata in D H.XVI.51 102
    Piano Trio in A H.XV.9 6, 6–7, 8–10, 9–10
    Piano Trio in A flat H.XV.12 4
    Piano Trio in A flat H.XV.14 48–9n.19
    Piano Trio in B flat H.XV. 20 4–5, 49
    Piano Trio in E flat H.XV.22 49, 51
    Piano Trio in G H.XV.25 ('Gipsy Rondo'), 44
    Piano Trio in F sharp minor H.XV.26 28n.10

Piano Trio in C H.XV.27   51, 74
Piano Trio in E H.XV.28   2, 5, 5
Piano Trio in E flat H.XV.29   3–4, 4
Piano Trio in E flat minor H.XV. 31   4n.3
The Seasons   43
The Seven Last Words   140
String Quartet in C minor op.17
   no.4   47n.14, 120
String Quartets op.20   8, 330–1
   No.2 in E flat   46
   No.3 in G minor   3   46, 46
   No.4 in D   44
String Quartets op.33   51
   No.1 in B minor   120
   No.3 in C ('Bird')   51
   No.4 in B flat   51
String Quartet in B flat op.50 no.1   120
String Quartet in F sharp minor op.50
   no.4   28n.10, 330
String Quartet in F op.50 no.5   56–7
String Quartet in D op.50 no.6
   ('Frog')   121, *121*
String Quartet in B minor op.64 no.2   120
String Quartet in D op.64 no.5
   ('Lark')   80
String Quartets opp.71 and 74   43, 44, 52
String Quartet in C op.74 no.1   49
String Quartet in F op.74 no.2   105–6, *106*
String Quartet in G minor op.74 no.3
   ('Rider')   49
String Quartet in G op.76 no.1   51
String Quartet in D op.76 no.5   206
String Quartet in E flat op.76 no.6   51, 303
String Quartets op.77   51
   No.2 in F   71
Symphony no.45 in F sharp minor
   ('Farewell')   28n.10
Symphony no.46 in B   328n.7
Symphony no.90 in C   45, 52n.25, 120
Symphony no.92 in G ('Oxford')   221
Symphony no.94 in G
   ('Surprise')   52n.25, 112, *112*, 206–7
Symphony no.95 in C minor   48, 71, 76
Symphony no.97 in C   45, 277
Symphony no.98 in B flat   45
Symphony no.99 in E flat   44, 49
Symphony no.103 in E flat ('Drum
   Roll')   40, 276–7
Henneberg, Johann Baptist   382
Hiller, Johann Adam   309
Himmel, Friedrich   93
Hoffmann, Ernst Theodor Amadeus   18–19, 264, 265, 277, 280
Hoffmeister, Franz Anton   16–17

Hoffmeister & Kühnel   352
Holz, Karl   255, 327, 332
Huber, Franz Xaver   222
Hummel, Johann Julius   3
Hummel, Johann Nepomuk   131, 277
   Sonata for mandolin and piano in C minor
     op.10a   131

Jahn, Otto   21, 77
Johnson, Douglas   61, 66, 76n.38

Kalkenbrenner, Frédéric   18, 141
Kerman, Joseph   269n.44, 274n.45, 275–6
Kinderman, William   350
Kinsky, Georg   134
Kinsky, Prince Ferdinand Johann
   Nepomuk   295
Kleinheiz, Franz Xaver   98
Klumpar, Joseph   237n.1
Kozeluch, Leopold   365
Kraft, Anton   43, 99, 253
Kraft, Nikolaus   99, 253
Kramer, Lawrence   264–5n.38
Kreisler, Fritz   37
Kreuzer, Rodolphe   177, 222–5, 226
   Violin Concerto no.2 in A   177
Krumpholz, Wenzel   130, 132, 134, 151, 196
Kuchař, Jan Křitel   131
Kuhlau, Friedrich   182

Lamotte, Franz   221
Lenz, Wilhelm von   196, 277
Leopold II, Holy Roman Emperor   294
Leutgeb, Joseph   190
Liechtenstein, Prince Alois I   140
Liechtenstein, Princess Josephine   222
Lichnowsky, Prince Karl   41, 91, 221–2
Linke, Joseph   82, 83n.4, 248
Liszt, Franz   18
Lobkowitz, Prince Franz Joseph   43, 222, 295
Lockwood, Lewis   269n.43, 237n.2, 244
Lonsdale, Christopher   366–7
Louis Ferdinand, Prince   295–6

Mahler, Gustav   318
Maisch, Ludwig   138
Mandyczewski, Eusebius   132, 134
Maria Elisabeth, Archduchess
Marie Antoinette, Queen of France   93
Marston, Nicholas   350
Marx, Adolf Bernhard   277, 341–2
Maximilian Franz, Archduke   42–3
Méhul, Etienne-Nicolas   188

Mendelssohn, Felix
    Symphony no.3 in A minor
        ('Scottish')   48n.16
    Piano Quartets opp.1–3   28
Mollo, Tranquillo   36, 83, 85–6, 128–9,
        141n.4, 171, 192
Mondonville, Jean-Joseph Cassanéa de   2
    Pièces de clavecin en sonates op.3   2
    Pièces de clavecin avec voix ou violon
        op.5   2
Moreau, Eugénie   4n.3
Moreau, Jean Victor   4n.3
Moscheles, Ignaz   19, 295, 349
Mozart, Konstanze   16
Mozart, Wolfgang Amadeus   2, 21, 40, 48–9,
        91, 92, 126, 131, 152, 171, 188–9, 201, 240,
        306, 329
    Adagio and Fugue for violin and piano
        K.402   2
    'Ah, lo previdi' K.272   131
    Andante for piano and cello K.Anh.46
        (fragment)   90n.1
    'Bella mia fiamma' K.528   131
    Die Zauberflöte K.620   84–5, 85, 127, 128
    'Die Zufriedenheit' K.349   130–1
    Divertimento in E flat for string trio
        K.563   46n.13
    Don Giovanni K.527   47n.15, 131
    Fantasia for piano in D minor
        K.397   47n.15
    Horn Concerto in E flat K.447   190
    Idomeneo K.366   130–1
    'Komm, liebe Zither, komm' K.351   130–1
    La Clemenza di Tito K.621   52
    Le Nozze di Figaro K.492   131
    Piano Concerto in B flat K.39   15
    Piano Concerto in E flat K.449   306
    Piano Concerto in G K.453   315
    Piano Concerto in F K.459   330
    Piano Concerto in E flat K.482   190
    Piano Concerto in A K.488   28, 53
    Piano Concerto in B flat K.450   81
    Piano Concerto in D K.451   81
    Piano Concerto in E flat K.482   81, 190
    Piano Concerto in C minor K.491   26,
        47, 68, 71, 200n.11
    Piano Concerto in B flat K.595   181
    Piano Quartet in G minor K.478   16–17, 22
    Piano Quartet in E flat K.493   17, 53, 54
    Piano Sonata in C K.330   173
    Piano Sonata in A K.331   49n.20
    Piano Sonata in A minor K.310   52n.25
    Piano Sonata in F K.332   53
    Piano Sonata in C minor K.457   27, 47
    Piano Trio (Divertimento) in B flat
        K.254   10
    Piano Trio in G K.496   10–12, 11, 173
    Piano Trio in E K.542   12, 12–13
    Piano Trio in G K.564   37, 38, 309
    Quintet in E flat for piano and wind
        K.452   17, 81, 85
    Requiem in D minor K.626   47n.15
    Rondo for piano in A minor K.511   36
    Serenade in E flat for wind K.375   49n.20,
        206n.15
    Serenade in C minor for wind
        K.388   47n.15, 89
    Sinfonia concertante in E flat
        K.297b   49n.20
    Sonata in D for two pianos K.448   173,
        291n.64
    String Quartet in D minor K.173   47n.15
    String Quartet in G K.387   58, 330
    String Quartet in D minor K.421   47n.15
    String Quartet in E flat K.428   240–1, 240
    String Quartet in D K.575   53, 92–3
    String Quartet in B flat K.589   92–3
    String Quartet in F K.590   92–3
    String Quintet in D K.593   276
    Symphony no.25 in G minor K.183   24
    Symphony no.31 in D K.297 ('Paris')   207
    Symphony no.33 in B flat K.319   207
    Symphony no.34 in C K.338, 207
    Symphony no.35 in D K.385
        ('Haffner')   206, 207
    Symphony no.38 in D K.504
        ('Prague')   207
    Symphony no.39 in E flat K.543   277
    Symphony no.40 in G minor K.550   74,
        181
    Symphony no.41 in C K.551
        ('Jupiter')   58, 330
    Trio in E flat for clarinet, viola and piano
        K.498 ('Kegelstatt')   58, 206
    Variations for piano on a Theme of Duport
        K.573   92
    Violin Sonatas K.6–9   3
    Violin Sonatas K.10–15   3
    Violin Sonata in C K.296, 22, 22
    Violin Sonatas K.301–6   102
        Sonata in G K.301   152
        Sonata in E flat K.302   152, 155, 155
        Sonata in C K.303   152
        Sonata in A K.305   152–3, 153
        Sonata in D K.306   111
    Violin Sonatas K.376–80   22
        Sonata in F K.376   160
        Sonata in F K.377   160–1
        Sonata in B flat K.378   160
        Sonata in G K.379   22, 23–5, 23, 24, 25

27, 29–30, *30*, 102, 114, 22
    Sonata in E flat K.380   27–8, 31, 85
    Violin Sonata in B flat K.454   18, 152n.4
    Violin Sonata in F K.547   49n.20
    Violin Sonata in A K.526   17, 18, 181–2, *181*
    Zaide K.344   24
Müller, Wenzel   352, 356n.44, 357–9, 361
Münch, Ernst   246

Napier, William   365
Neate, Charles   328, 349–50
Neefe, Christian Gottlob   43
Nissen, Georg Nikolaus   16
Nohl, Ludwig   195
Nottebohm, Gustav   41, 48, 77, 138, 149, 215n.21, 244–5, 265, 309, 339n.18, 350

Oldman, Cecil B.   371
Ordoñez, Carlo d'   330
Oliva, Franz   293–4
Öttingen-Wallerstein, Prince Kraft Ernst   140

Paer, Ferdinando   188
Paganini, Nicolò   141
Paine & Hopkins   371–2
Paisiello, Giovanni   352
Panerai, Vincenzo   131
Papendieck, Charlotte   221
Perinet, Joachim   352, 356n.44, 357
Plankenstern, Wetzlar von   141, 222
Pleyel, Ignaz Josef   52, 365
Ployer, Barbara von   190n.10
Potter, Cipriani   141, 247
Punto, Giovanni   85, 188–91

Ramm, Friedrich   82
Rampl, Wenzel   329, 338, 339n.18
Rauzzini, Venanzio   221n.26
Razumovsky, Count Andrei Kyrillovich   222
Reichardt, Johann Friedrich   93, 253–4, 283, 295–6
Reynolds, Christopher   199
Riccardi, Francesca   188
Richter, Joseph   356n.44
Riemann, Hugo   80
Ries, Ferdinand   21, 32, 39, 41, 42, 43, 48, 82, 91, 144, 150n.7, 151–2, 189–90, 197, 222–3, 227n.51, 232, 308, 349, 384
Ries, Franz Anton   151
Rode, Pierre   226, 309, 310–12, 323
    Air varié op.10   310, *311*
Romberg, Andreas   99
Romberg, Bernhard   29, 127, 253
Ronge, Julia   39

Rosen, Charles   329n.10, 372n.19
Rosenbaum, Joseph Carl   221
Rosenthal, Albi   339n.18
Rostal, Max   325n.38
Rovantini, Franz Georg   151
Rudolph, Archduke   18, 150n.7, 254, 289, 294–6, 308, 309, 312, 339n.18
Salieri, Antonio   155, 276
Salomon, Johann Peter   39, 221
Schenk, Johann Baptist   39, 44
Schenker, Heinrich   241, 247n.16
Schikaneder, Emanuel   128
Schindler, Anton Felix   21, 32, 33, 41–2, 125, 265, 327, 330
Schlemmer, Wenzel   293, 303
Schlesinger, Maurice   308
Schmidt, Franz   360
Schneller, Julius   246
Schobert, Johann   3, 15–16
    Piano Trio in B flat, op.16 no.1, 15–16, *16*
    Sonata for keyboard and violin op.17 no.2   15
    Sonata in A for keyboard and violin op.14 no.5   16
    Sonates en quatuor op.7   16
Schoenberg, Arnold   18
    Transcription of Brahms's Piano Quartet op.25   18
Schubert, Franz   232, 277
    Fantasia in C for violin and piano D.934   332
    'Im Frühling' D.882   27n.9
    Impromptu D.899 no.2   283
    Moment musical D.780 no.6   283
    Piano Sonata in C minor D.958   232
    Piano Sonata in B flat D.960   302–3
    Piano Trio in E flat D.929   285
    String Quartet in D minor D.810 ('Death and the Maiden')   232
    String Quartet in G D.887   232
    Symphony no.4 in C minor ('Tragic')   48n.16
Schultz, J.R.   124–5
Schumann, Robert   318, 332
    Symphony no.4 in D minor   48n.16
    'Warum?' (*Kinderszenen* op.15)   318
Schuppanzigh, Ignaz   19, 82, 99, 140, 151, 253
Schwarz, Boris   177
Shakespeare, William   265
Sedlaczek, Johann   225
Seidler, Ferdinand August   296
Seyfried, Ignaz von   124
Simrock, Nikolaus   223–4, 328, 339n.18, 371, 384
Sisman, Elaine   46n.13, 277n.49, 331n.16

Spaun, Joseph von 295
Spohr, Louis 19–20, 312
Starke, Friedrich 194–5
Steibelt, Daniel 144
Steiner, Sigmund Anton 294, 303, 312, 352
Sterkel, Johann Franz 13–15,
    Piano Trio in B flat, op.30 no.3 14, *14–15*
Streicher, Andreas 253–4, 327
Strinasacchi, Regina 152n.4
Stumpff, Johann Andreas 125
Süssmayr, Franz Xaver 52
Swieten, Gottfried van 43, 125

Tellenbach, Marie-Elisabeth 245n.11
Teyber, Anton 295
Thalberg, Sigismond 18
Thayer, Alexander Wheelock 41, 48, 77, 80, 124, 125–6, 246
Thomson, George 365–72
Thun, Count Franz Joseph Anton 188
Tomášek, Václav 138

Tourte, Louis and François 18
Tovey, Donald Francis 103, 247–8, 269, 277, 280
Traeg, Johann 127
Tyson, Alan 255, 352

Viotti, Giovanni Battista 93, 221

Wagner, Richard 356
Waldstein, Count Ferdinand 39
Wallace, Robin 341n.19
Webster, James 39
Wegeler, Franz Gerhard 36, 43
Weigl, Joseph 140–1, 144–5, 150, 352
Westerholt, Maria Anna Wilhelmine 29, 32
Witt, Friedrich 140
Wölfl, Joseph 140–1
Wranitzky, Paul 352

Zemlinsky, Alexander 150n.7